Mental Health Communication for Underserved Populations

Mental Health Communication for Underserved Populations

Edited by

Do Kyun David Kim & Jin-Ae Kang

BLOOMSBURY ACADEMIC
NEW YORK • LONDON • OXFORD • NEW DELHI • SYDNEY

BLOOMSBURY ACADEMIC
Bloomsbury Publishing Inc
Bloomsbury Publishing Inc, 1359 Broadway, New York, NY 10018, USA
Bloomsbury Publishing Plc, 50 Bedford Square, London, WC1B 3DP, UK
Bloomsbury Publishing Ireland, 29 Earlsfort Terrace, Dublin 2, D02 AY28, Ireland

BLOOMSBURY, BLOOMSBURY ACADEMIC and the Diana logo are trademarks of Bloomsbury Publishing Plc

First published in the United States of America 2026

A catalog record for this book is available from the Library of Congress

ISBN: HB: 978-1-6669-5099-1
ePDF: 979-8-7651-6504-1
eBook: 979-8-7651-5388-8

Typeset by Deanta Global Publishing Services, Chennai, India

For product safety related questions contact productsafety@bloomsbury.com.

To find out more about our authors and books visit www.bloomsbury.com and sign up for our newsletters.

Contents

About the Editors and Contributors

Dr. Do Kyun David Kim is the Richard D'Aquin/BORSF-Endowed Professor of Strategic Communication at the University of Louisiana at Lafayette, USA. As an internationally renowned interdisciplinary scholar and practitioner, he has collaborated with professionals, researchers, and governmental agencies on diverse communication projects related to public health promotion, environmental risk and crisis preparedness, human–robot communication, organizational and social change, community engagement, and advancing technologies for a desirable future. Scholarly, he is a renowned scholar in dissemination and implementation science, social marketing, and diffusion of information and innovations. Dr. Kim has led or participated in numerous domestic and international strategic communication projects for over twenty years. He has published his research, practice, opinions, and insights through various books, academic journals, and other publication outlets and presented at numerous conferences, educational institutions, governmental agencies, and professional organizations. For more information about Dr. Kim, visit DiffusionExpert.com.

Dr. Jin-Ae Kang is Professor of Communication at East Carolina University. Her research lies in the areas of public relations ethics, communication technology, and health communication, navigating the impact of emerging media on PR strategies, health-related crisis/risk communication, and community building. Her research areas also include the role of strategic storytelling in various communication contexts. She is recently exploring the positive impact of social media on individuals' well-being and mental health. Dr. Kang has published in *PR Review, Journal of Communication Management, Journal of Consumer Behavior, and Journalism & Mass Communication Educator* among others.

* * *

Dr. Walid A. Afifi is Professor in the Communication Department and Associate Dean in the Division of Social Sciences at the University of California, Santa Barbara. He is both a Fellow of the International

Communication Association and a Distinguished Scholar of the National Communication Association (NCA), where he has also served as President. His research developed and refined the Theory of Motivated Information Management. He has also been a leading critic of the centering of US college-educated, Caucasian populations in the discipline's knowledge production practices, and has published calls to center indigenous and liberatory frames for understanding Palestinian mental health.

Regina Ogechi Alabere is a doctoral candidate at the University of Memphis studying Health Communication. Her research interest includes cancer communication in the interpersonal and family context, developing ehealth literacy interventions for health organizations and tackling issues of health disparities. Her past research has explored developing health literacy interventions for medical providers in Aga Khan, Kenya, and Central Texas Medical Center and spearheading equity and anti-racist practice training for UofM School of Public Health. She is a two-time PEO international peace scholar and holds a master's in communication studies from Texas State University.

Anne Amegbeha Amissah is a PhD candidate in Health Communication at the University of Kentucky. With a research focus on mental health communication, she explores strategies to enhance mental well-being among graduate student parents. Anne has authored multiple publications and presented her findings at national conferences. Her work aims to address mental health disparities and promote effective health communication. Anne's dedication to academic excellence and community engagement underscores her commitment to advancing public health and fostering inclusive, supportive environments for diverse populations.

Dr. Theodore A. Avtgis is Assistant Professor in the Communication Department at Utah Tech University. He specializes in health communication, organizational communication processes and communication predispositions in general business and healthcare organizations. Dr. Avtgis has authored sixteen books and more than sixty-five peer-reviewed articles and book chapters. His work has appeared in journals such as *Management Communication Quarterly*, *Journal of Trauma: Injury, Infection, and Critical Care*, *Communication Education*, and *Communication Research Reports*, among many others.

Dr. Tharwa Bilbeisi is a communication and health researcher specializing in addressing health inequities and empowering underserved communities. Her doctoral research at the University of Memphis examined socioenvironmental influences on health beliefs, using ethnographic methods like photovoice and narrative storytelling to highlight the voices of individuals experiencing homelessness in Memphis. Currently, she is Clinical Research Scientist in the Department of Global Pediatric Medicine at St. Jude Children's Research Hospital, where she applies her expertise in qualitative methodologies to advance global pediatric cancer care. Dr. Bilbeisi is passionate about storytelling, collaboration, and fostering health equity worldwide.

Dr. Surin Chung is Assistant Professor at Sogang University in South Korea. His research interests include crisis, risk, & disaster communications, international public relations, and digital media. Surin Chung was Assistant Professor in the E. W. Scripps School of Journalism at Ohio University. Also, he is a former public relations professional in South Korea. His work has been featured in many journals such as *Journal of Health Communication, Journal of Communication Management, Public Relations Review, Communication Quarterly*, etc.

Dr. Karlene Cunningham is Associate Professor in the Department of Psychiatry and Behavioral Medicine at East Carolina University's Brody School of Medicine. She directs the Sexual Health and Reproductive Equity Engagement (SHaRE2) lab. Her passion lies in using a reproductive justice lens to address gaps in perinatal mental health research and improve systems of care for birthing people, especially those in marginalized and rural communities. Her clinical work focuses on hospital-based consultation liaison, with a special interest in reproductive psychology.

Dr. Amnee K. Elkhalid is Assistant Professor of Communication at the University of Arkansas. Dr. Elkhalid researches diversity and adversity with a specific interest in how messages influence identity, relationships, and well-being. Her recent work includes intergenerational and parent–child communication, narrative sense-making, stigma, as well as immigrant, refugee, and interfaith family experiences. Dr. Elkhalid has been published in journals such as *Communication Monographs, Journal of Family Communication, and Journal of Social and Personal Relationships.* She also has experience working alongside and providing services to non profit organizations that relate to education and/or refugee family services.

Dr. Sarah A. Geegan is Assistant Professor in the Department of Integrated Strategic Communication in the College of Communication and Information at the University of Kentucky. Her scholarship focuses on persuasion and social influence with an applied focus on public relations and health. Her work has been featured in book chapters, such as *Handbook of Applied Communication Research* and in journals such as *Journal of Social Marketing, Hispanic Journal of Behavioral Sciences, Journal of Communication and Media Studies, Western Journal of Communication, and Communication Quarterly.* Dr. Geegan has more than ten years of experience working in the PR industry.

Dr. Joy V. Goldsmith conducts research about health communication science in the contexts of healthcare provider training and serious and chronic illness. Her numerous books and articles in clinical as well as communication journals address health literacy, communication pedagogy, simulation training, oncology nurse communication, interprofessional communication, and family caregiver communication. CommunicateComfort.com, a long-time initiative of Dr. Goldsmith, serves to house and disseminate a range of research interventions and education/training curriculum for healthcare providers. Storyboard creation and development, e-learning module formation, and mhealth design and navigation are dimensions of Goldsmith's applied research linking media, theater, and film across her body of work.

Dr. Kyung Jung Han is Associate Professor of Communications, directing public relations concentration at California State University, Bakersfield. Her research areas are on eHealth communication intervention content and modality development in strategic health communication. Her work can be read in *Journal of Prevention, Journal of Health Communication, and Health Informatics.* She uses multi-method with either/both quantitative or/and qualitative approach. Her interdisciplinary research projects are with public health, nursing, family medicine, and social work. Within the relevant discipline, her grant experiences are with Kern Health System, Adobe Creative Suite Digital Literacy Fund, and Agency for Healthcare Research and Quality (AHRQ).

Dr. Lindsey Jo Hand is a contractor with the Federal government, where she works with an education and training team. In this role, she applies her expertise as a health communication scholar and practitioner to develop educational resources on science and health topics. Her scholarship focuses on stigmatized health issues and marginalized populations. Much of her work has focused on rural populations and mental health stigma. Her work has been featured in publications such as the *International Encyclopedia of Health Communication, Telemedicine and eHealth, Health Education Research,* and *Risk Analysis.*

Dr. Leandra Hernández (she/her/ella) is Associate Professor and Director of Graduate Studies in the Department of Communication at the University of Utah. Her teaching and research interests lie at the intersections of critical health communication and critical journalism/media studies. She has co-authored and co-edited seven books on these topics, in addition to other topics such as Latino communication studies, military communication studies, and critical communication pedagogy. Her research is published in *Women's Studies in Communication, Frontiers in Communication, Health Communication,* and *QED: A Journal in GLBTQ Worldmaking,* among others. She is a former co-director of the Salt Lake Area Queer Climbers organization and recently was awarded the 2023 Access Fund DEI Stewardship Award, the NCA 2023 Activism and Social Justice Division Community Engagement Award, and the NCA 2023 LGBTQ+ Caucus Lambda Award for her community outreach and activism.

Diana R. Humble is a doctoral candidate and instructor at the University of Memphis in the Department of Communication and Film. As an applied communication scholar, her primary research interest rests with identity—specifically, self-selected identity. She's particularly intrigued by identities that result in isolation from the status quo and revulsion from mainstream media. Her work seeks to bridge the knowledge gap that stigma and fear perpetuate and emphasize how it affects individual mental and physical health.

Dr. Jaehyun Kim is Assistant Professor in the Department of Recreation Sciences and Sport Management at East Carolina University. As Certified Therapeutic Recreation Specialist, Dr. Kim has examined the impact of leisure engagement on mental health, life satisfaction, happiness, and quality of life among diverse and often disadvantaged groups, including individuals with disabilities, immigrants, cancer patients, and older adults with psychological issues. Recently, he has investigated the effectiveness of technology-based interventions, such as mindfulness-based virtual reality programs, in enhancing mental health for older adults with dementia and those with physical disabilities.

Ma. Angelica Mercado is a master's student specializing in digital media at Sogang University in South Korea. Her research interests include the role of new media in Philippine society and politics as well as its psychological impacts on the users. Angelica is dedicated to exploring how digital platforms shape political engagement and public discourse. Passionate about the interaction between digital media and personal well-being, she seeks to provide insights that may contribute to a broader understanding of media's societal and psychological roles. Angelica is committed to developing strategies that harness the positive potential of media while addressing its challenges.

Dr. Adrienne F. Muldrow is Associate Professor at East Carolina University. Her interdisciplinary research explores how communication assists decision-making, well-being, or human behavior. She studies how communicated representations—written and visual—help promote or hinder subsequent behaviors. She explores content from real people to social media. She often employs a lens with an intersectional perception of gender, nationality, and race with a strong focus on Black women. Her research covers the topic of inclusion in realms spanning from advertising to health communication. Her research has been published in the *Journal of Health Communication, Health Communication, and Qualitative Health Research.*

Dr. Veronica Nuzzolo is an experienced independently licensed psychotherapist who serves the communities of Maine, Massachusetts, and New Hampshire. Dr. Nuzzolo has experience treating severe mental health, substance use, and co-occurring disorders. Her area of expertise is in treating alcohol, opioid, and stimulant use disorders. She has been practicing for more than fifteen years, serving in inpatient/outpatient detox programs, clinical stabilization services, medication assisted treatment programs, and structured outpatient addictions programs.

Dr. Kimberly A. Parker is a former Fulbright Scholar. She studies strategic communication, social marketing, and social influence. Her scholarship focuses on strategic message design and promoting positive social change. Her work has appeared in numerous presentations (five top paper awards), book chapters, and journal publications, such as *Communication Monographs, Journal of Communication, Human Communication Research, Journal of Public Relations*

Research, Communication Quarterly, Communication Research Reports, and Health Communication, among other journals. Dr. Parker also has twenty-five years of experience working with nonprofits on social marketing campaigns.

Dr. John Parrish-Sprowl is the Director of the Global Health Communication Center of the Indiana University School of Liberal Arts and is Professor and former Chair of the Department of Communication. In addition, he is a member of the One Health Action Collaborative of the National Academy of Science, Engineering, and Medicine. An award-winning educator and consultant, Dr. Parrish-Sprowl has worked extensively in community engagement activity. He has served as Fulbright Senior Specialist, been a visiting faculty member, lectured and conducted research and consultancies with universities, businesses, and NGOs in a number of countries.

Natalia Peraza is a doctoral student in the Department of Psychology at the University of Southern California. Her research interests include investigating the relationship between substance use and psychological vulnerabilities to better understand and reduce affect-driven substance use among underserved and vulnerable populations. She is also interested in understanding the abuse potential and therapeutic effects of drugs to inform public health policy. She has co-authored several manuscripts examining populations that may be at greater risk for maladaptive substance use and mental health outcomes. She is an active member of USC's *Committee on Leadership In Multicultural Advancement & Training for Everyone* and currently serves as a producer and audio editor for USC's *PsychOverflow* podcast, which explores diversity, equity, and inclusion (DEI) themes within the field of psychology.

Dr. Rikki A. Roscoe is Assistant Professor in the Department of Communication Studies at the University of Kansas. Rikki is a critical-interpretive scholar who investigates stigma, identity, and inequity as they impact health communication and organizing. She is particularly interested in how stigma, when understood as an inherently power-laden communication process, impacts health and creates health inequities in a variety of contexts, including mental health and sexual and reproductive health. Through this work, Rikki hopes to improve health outcomes for underserved communities.

Jorge Seifert is a doctoral student whose work focuses on communication and mental health. He has presented at multiple conferences on this topic and participated in a community engagement program to promote mental health through a Communication for Whole Health approach.

Dr. Sachiko Terui is Assistant Professor in the Department of Communication Studies at the University of Georgia. Her research addresses communicative challenges pertaining to linguistic and cultural aspects of health and health management, communication interventions, health literacy, and health disparities experienced among marginalized and underserved populations. Her recent projects center on interdisciplinary collaborations, including communities and healthcare organizations.

Jacob Watson is a doctoral student in the Dept. of Communication at Indiana University, Indianapolis. Specialized in health communication, his work explores community engagement, action research, and community health via the Communication for Whole Health approach under the Communication Complex meta-perspective.

Introduction

Reaching the Unreached: Enhancing the Mental Health of Underserved Populations through Effective Communication Strategies

Do Kyun David Kim and Jin-Ae Kang

Health communication plays a crucial role in promoting mental health, particularly among underserved and marginalized populations. These groups face unique barriers to accessing mental health care, including economic challenges, cultural barriers, and systemic inequalities. Effective health communication campaigns and interventions can address these challenges by providing essential information, fostering supportive environments, and empowering individuals to seek and receive appropriate care (Kreps & Sparks, 2008). Especially, the COVID-19 pandemic has further highlighted the need for robust health communication strategies, as marginalized communities have been disproportionately affected by its impact on mental health (Liu et al., 2023). This book explores the significance of health communication in promoting mental health and offers effective health communication strategies to enhance mental health among underserved populations, drawing on recent academic literature, governmental resources, and expert insights.

The Role of Health Communication

Health communication involves the use of communication strategies to inform the public with accurate health information and influence health decisions at the individual, family, community, and policy levels. It encompasses various communicative methods, including media campaigns, health education, interpersonal interactions, and digital platforms. For marginalized populations, health communication must be culturally sensitive, accessible, and tailored to meet their specific needs (Rimal & Lapinski, 2009).

In terms of specific roles of health communication, health communication is primarily to disseminate accurate and timely information about mental health conditions, treatment options, and resources to target populations. Effective information dissemination helps individuals understand mental health issues, which improves health literacy and significantly impacts individuals' ability to manage mental health conditions and navigate the healthcare system (Hu, 2015). Tailoring information to specific audiences, considering literacy levels and cultural contexts, enhances the effectiveness of health communication efforts (Noar & Harrington, 2012).

Health communication ultimately aims to promote behavioral change by encouraging healthy behaviors and coping strategies. This can be achieved through persuasive communication and behavior change techniques that motivate individuals to adopt healthier lifestyles. For instance, motivational messages and adoptable action plans can greatly contribute to promoting behavioral change (Witte et al., 2001).

Empowering individuals with sufficient knowledge and necessary skills is a crucial role of health communication. By providing education on mental health issues, available resources, and coping strategies, health communication helps individuals make informed decisions and advocate for their mental health needs. This empowerment is particularly vital for marginalized populations who may face unique barriers to accessing information and support (Kreps & Sparks, 2008). Recent studies emphasize the importance of tailored health communication strategies to effectively reach and support these populations (Atkinson, 2007).

Reducing the stigma associated with mental health issues is a vital function of health communication. Stigma can deter individuals from seeking help and lead to discrimination and social exclusion, which can create a double burden to marginalized populations who already experience discrimination and inequity due to their social identities and demographic characteristics, such as race, religion, and gender identities. Responding to such challenges, effective public awareness campaigns and personalized interventions are urgently needed to normalize mental health issues and promote empathy (Corrigan et al., 2012; Mascayano et al., 2015).

Health communication is also crucial for creating supportive social and policy environments that enhance access to mental health care. This involves advocating for policies that improve mental health services, increase funding, and address systemic barriers. Engaging policymakers and community leaders can drive significant changes, improving access and quality of health care among underserved populations (Quinn & Kumar, 2014).

Health Communication in Promoting Mental Health among Underserved and Marginalized Populations

Health communication is particularly crucial for promoting mental health among underserved and marginalized populations due to their unique challenges. The following factors are key considerations identified in numerous studies and practices, affecting mental health communication for underserved populations.

Enhancing Health Literacy

Health literacy is a critical component of health communication that impacts mental health outcomes. Health literacy involves individuals' ability to access, understand, and use health information effectively. Scholars and practitioners in mental healthcare emphasize the importance of health literacy for individuals to manage their mental health conditions and access appropriate care (Hu, 2015). Individuals with higher health literacy are better equipped to comprehend mental health information, adhere to treatment plans, and navigate healthcare systems.

Effective health communication strategies enhance health literacy by providing clear, accessible, and culturally appropriate information. In order to achieve this goal, Levin-Zamir (2020) emphasized building an integrated and user-friendly health system, a familiar and compatible technology, transparency regarding health information, culturally appropriate messages in digital and offline media, acknowledging diverse health literacy needs, and role-modeling by political/religious opinion leaders. These strategies help demystify mental health issues, reduce misconceptions, and empower individuals to make informed decisions about their care.

Addressing health literacy remains challenging, particularly in marginalized communities. Barriers include low educational levels, language differences, and limited access to reliable information sources (Tulane University, 2024).

Health communication strategies must overcome these barriers by providing information in multiple languages, using visual aids, and leveraging community health workers to facilitate people's understanding and access.

Reducing Mental Health Stigma

The stigma associated with mental health issues can be particularly intensified in marginalized communities, preventing individuals from seeking help and resulting in social exclusion. Responding to this individual and social misperception, scholars and practitioners have emphasized the role of health communication in challenging and changing stigma-related attitudes while also providing appropriate stigma-reduction strategies.

Effective stigma-reduction strategies include media campaigns, storytelling, community engagement, and message dissemination through social media. In particular, Corrigan and Watson (2012) highlight that anti-stigma campaigns featuring personal narratives and positive portrayals of mental health can shift public perceptions and reduce stigma. It is also important that mental health communication campaigns include partnerships with individuals who have lived experiences of mental illness, providing authentic and relatable perspectives that challenge negative stereotypes.

Ultimately, reducing stigma through health communication should impact help-seeking behaviors. When stigma is reduced, individuals are more likely to seek professional help and adhere to treatment recommendations. Related to this, DeLuca et al. (2021) found that stigma-reduction interventions, including educational workshops and media campaigns, lead to increased mental health service utilization and improved treatment outcomes.

Promoting Behavioral Change through Communicative Interventions

Health communication strategies are instrumental in promoting behavioral change related to mental health. Behavioral change theories, such as the Health Belief Model, Social Cognitive Theory, and many others, provide frameworks for designing interventions that encourage healthy behaviors and coping strategies (Rosenstock et al., 1988). Practically, health communication scholars, mental health service providers, and public health officials emphasize the effectiveness of tailored interventions in promoting mental health-related behaviors. As an example, Philippe et al. (2022) found that, due to the prevalence of using mobile communication tools and devices, digital health interventions, such as mobile health apps and online therapy programs, can significantly improve mental health outcomes by providing accessible and engaging tools for behavior change. Such interventions using digital communication technology often feature goal-setting, progress tracking, and personalized feedback, which enhance motivation and adherence to mental health coping strategies.

Despite the potential of behavioral change interventions, there are some notable challenges that include ensuring accessibility, maintaining user engagement, and addressing diverse needs. In order to overcome these challenges, Philippe and colleagues (2022) suggest that health communication strategies should incorporate user-centered design principles, provide ongoing support, and address barriers such as digital literacy and access to technology.

Diffusion of Information

Health communication also plays a crucial role in disseminating information about mental health resources, navigating the healthcare system, and overcoming barriers to care. Atkin and Rice (2009) emphasize that targeted information campaigns, including online directories and community outreach, improve awareness of mental health services and facilitate access for underserved populations. While disseminating information, mental health communication campaigns should highlight available resources, explain eligibility criteria, and provide guidance on how to access care.

Navigating the healthcare system can be challenging for individuals with limited information, resources, or knowledge. Therefore, health communication strategies should offer clear guidance on accessing services, understanding insurance coverage, and managing appointments, which can help individuals overcome barriers to mental health wellness (Liu et al., 2023). Practical tools such as service navigation guides and helplines can also provide essential support and assistance.

Leveraging Technology and Digital Platforms

As mentioned above, the use of technology and digital platforms has become increasingly important in health communication. Its importance became more crystallized during the COVID-19 pandemic when face-to-face interactions were drastically limited. Digital tools offer innovative ways to reach and engage individuals, providing new opportunities for enhancing mental health support. Empirically, digital health interventions, such as telehealth services, mobile apps, and online support groups, have proven effective in providing mental health care and support.

While digital platforms offer significant benefits, challenges include ensuring equitable access, addressing privacy concerns, and maintaining user engagement. Hence, mental health communication professionals should carefully consider effective strategies to address critical challenges, such as providing digital literacy training, ensuring data security, and designing engaging and user-friendly platforms.

Impact of the COVID-19 Pandemic on Mental Health

The COVID-19 pandemic has significantly impacted mental health globally, with marginalized populations experiencing heightened effects due to increased vulnerabilities and exacerbated stressors that negatively affected their mental health (Gómez et al, 2021). First of all, the economic impact of the pandemic has been severe for many low-income individuals and families, leading to increased financial stress and anxiety (Witteveen & Velthorst, 2020). Job losses, reduced income, and economic instability have heightened mental health challenges for many individuals struggling to meet basic needs while facing additional mental health stressors.

In addition, social isolation due to lockdowns and physical distancing measures has further exacerbated mental health issues, particularly for individuals with limited social support networks. Marginalized populations, including those with lower socioeconomic status and limited access to social services, have been disproportionately affected by isolation and loneliness (Xiong et al., 2020).

The pandemic has evidently disrupted accessibility to mental health services as well, with many individuals experiencing delays or interruptions in care. This disruption has had a particularly severe impact on marginalized populations, who may already face barriers to accessing mental health services (Nazemi et al., 2023). Consequently, health communication strategies have evolved to adopt and develop online/mobile methods, ensuring continued access to care through digital platforms. This trend has persisted even in the post-pandemic period.

As many medical scientists expect more frequent health crises in the future, the experiences from the COVID-19 pandemic in health communication will serve as strong cornerstones for future mental health promotion efforts.

Challenges and Overall Recommendations

Despite the success of various health communication strategies, challenges remain in more rapidly reaching and effectively engaging underserved populations. Addressing the challenges requires sustained efforts and innovative approaches. First, sustainable funding is essential to maintain momentum and build long-term capacity for health communication initiatives. Continuous funding should support ongoing projects, ensure continuity, and allow for the development of effective strategies as needed (Rimal & Lapinski, 2009). Public-private partnerships and community-based funding models can help address financial constraints and support comprehensive and diverse health communication efforts.

Capacity-building that involves training community members and health workers in effective communication techniques and mental health literacy is also necessary. Capacity-building initiatives should focus on enhancing skills in delivering culturally sensitive messages, utilizing digital tools, and engaging with diverse audiences (Noar & Harrington, 2012). Training programs should be designed to address the specific needs of marginalized populations and equip individuals with the tools to advocate for mental health care.

Next, ongoing evaluation and research are needed to assess the effectiveness of communication strategies and develop new strategies as needed. Evaluation should focus on measuring the impact of mental health communication efforts, identifying areas for further improvement, and determining best practices (Glik, 2007). Based on careful evaluation of past and current mental health communication campaigns and interventions, more research should explore innovative and effective mental health communication strategies and technologies to enhance outreach and engagement with underserved populations.

At the organizational and social systems level, policy advocacy is crucial for systemic improvement, supporting mental healthcare access, and addressing systemic barriers. Specifically, health communication efforts should include advocacy components that promote policy changes, increase funding for mental health services, and address inequities within healthcare systems (Quinn & Kumar, 2014). Engaging policymakers and community leaders in advocacy efforts can help drive meaningful change and improve mental health care for underserved populations.

Bridging Gaps through Effective Health Communication

This book is for anyone interested in understanding how health communication plays a vital role in promoting mental health among underserved and marginalized populations in the post-COVID-19 pandemic era. By providing culturally sensitive information, reducing stigma, and empowering individuals, effective communication strategies can bridge gaps in mental healthcare access and support. During challenging times, such as the COVID-19 pandemic, the importance of adaptive and inclusive health communication approaches becomes even more evident. Moving forward, sustained efforts and innovative communication strategies are needed to ensure that all individuals, regardless of their background or circumstances, have the opportunity to achieve optimal mental health.

References

Atkin, C. K., & Rice, R. E. (2009). Theory and principles of public communication campaigns. In R. E. Rice & C. K. Atkin (Eds.), *Public communication campaigns* (4th ed., pp. 3–19). SAGE Publications.

Atkinson, J. M. (2007). Protecting or Empowering the Vulnerable? Mental Illness, Communication and the Research Process. *Research Ethics*, 3(4), 134-138. https://doi.org/10.1177/174701610700300410.

Corrigan, P. W., Morris, S. B., Michaels, P. J., Rafacz, J. D., & Rüsch, N. (2012). Challenging the public stigma of mental illness: a meta-analysis of outcome studies. *Psychiatric services (Washington, D.C.)*, 63(10), 963–973. https://doi.org/10.1176/appi.ps.201100529.

DeLuca, J. S., Tang, J., Zoubaa, S., Dial, B., & Yanos, P. T. (2021). Reducing stigma in high school students: A cluster randomized controlled trial of the National Alliance on Mental Illness' Ending the Silence intervention. *Stigma and Health*, 6(2), 228–242. https://doi.org/10.1037/sah0000235.

Glik, D. C. (2007). Risk communication for public health emergencies. *Annual Review of Public Health*, *28*, 33–54.

Gómez, J. M., Gobin, R. L., & Barnes, M. L. (2021). Discrimination, Violence, & Healing within Marginalized Communities. *Journal of Trauma & Dissociation*, 22(2), 135–140.

Hu, Y. (2015). Health communication research in the digital age: A systematic review. *Journal of Communication in Healthcare*, *8*(4), 260–288.

Kreps, G. L., & Sparks, L. (2008). Meeting the health literacy needs of immigrant populations. *Patient education and counseling*, 71(3), 328–332. https://doi.org/10.1016/j.pec.2008.03.001.

Levin-Zamir, D. (2020). Communication, health literacy and a systems approach for mitigating the COVID-19 pandemic: The case for massive vaccine roll-out in Israel. *Journal of Health Communication*, *25*(10), 816–818.

Liu, P. L., Ao, S. H., Zhao, X., & Zhang, L. (2023). Associations between COVID-19 information acquisition and vaccination intention: The roles of anticipated regret and collective responsibility. *Health Communication*, *38*(10), 2198–2209.

Mascayano, F., Armijo, J. E., & Yang, L. H. (2015). Addressing stigma relating to mental illness in low- and middle-income countries. *Frontiers in Psychiatry*, 6, 38.

Nazemi, M., Kiani, S., & Zakerabasali, S. (2023). Tele-mental health during the COVID-19 pandemic: A systematic review of the literature focused on technical aspects and challenges. *Health science reports*, 6(10), e1637. https://doi.org/10.1002/hsr2.1637.

Noar, S. M., & Harrington, N. G. (2012). *eHealth applications: Promising strategies for behavior change*. Routledge.

Philippe, T. J., Sikder, N., Jackson, A., Koblanski, M. E., Liow, E., Pilarinos, A., & Vasarhelyi, K. (2022). Digital Health Interventions for Delivery of Mental Health Care: Systematic and Comprehensive Meta-Review. *JMIR mental health*, 9(5), e35159. https://doi.org/10.2196/35159.

Quinn, S. C., & Kumar, S. (2014). Health inequalities and infectious disease epidemics: a challenge for global health security. *Biosecurity and bioterrorism : biodefense strategy, practice, and science*, 12(5), 263–273. https://doi.org/10.1089/bsp.2014.0032.

Rimal, R. N., & Lapinski, M. K. (2009). Why health communication is important in public health. *Bulletin of the World Health Organization*, 87(4), 247–247a. https://doi.org/10.2471/blt.08.056713.

Rosenstock, I. M., Strecher, V. J., & Becker, M. H. (1988). Social learning theory and the Health Belief Model. *Health education quarterly*, 15(2), 175–183. https://doi.org/10.1177/109019818801500203.

Tulane University School of Public Health and Tropical Medicine. (2024, April 13). *Mental Health Literacy: Definition, Importance, and Impact*. https://publichealth.tulane.edu/blog/mental-health-literacy/.

Witte, K., Meyer, G., & Martell, D. (2001). *Effective health risk messages: A step-by-step guide*. SAGE Publications.

Witteveen, D., & Velthorst, E. (2020). *Economic hardship and mental health complaints during COVID-19.* Proceedings of the National Academy of Sciences of the United States of America, 117(44), 27277–27284. https://doi.org/10.1073/pnas.2009609117.

Xiong, J., Lipsitz, O., Nasri, F., Lui, L. M. W., Gill, H., Phan, L., Chen-Li, D., Iacobucci, M., Ho, R., Majeed, A., & McIntyre, R. S. (2020). Impact of COVID-19 pandemic on mental health in the general population: *A systematic review. Journal of affective disorders*, 277, 55–64. https://doi.org/10.1016/j.jad.2020.08.001.

1

The Use of Storytelling as a Form of Liberatory Agency

Palestinian Refugees in the United States

Amnee K. Elkhalid and Walid A. Afifi

There are over nine million Palestinians worldwide who are considered forcibly displaced persons, including the largest and most protracted population of refugees. Refugees are people who "owing to a well-founded fear of persecution for reasons of race, religion, nationality, membership of a particular social group or political opinions, are outside the country of [their] nationality and [are] unable or, owing to such fear, [are] unwilling to avail [themselves] of the protection of that country" (Douglas et al., 2019, p. 2). Palestinian refugees include those who were forced to flee Palestine during the Nakba of 1948, during the 1967 War, or during several other moments of forced displacement by the Israeli government. It is a category that also applies to their descendants because of Israel's ongoing refusal to grant the right of return (Khalidi, 1992). The best estimates are that there are approximately 160,000[1] Palestinian refugees in the United States, although that number may be much larger, given that many may identify themselves as members of other Arab countries (to which they originally fled).

This population experiences many of the same challenges faced by all refugee communities but also carries particular burdens tied to the long history within the United States of unquestioning political support for Israel, the vilification of Palestinians, and efforts to falsely conflate Palestinian desires for freedom with antisemitism.[2] When combined with existence within a US population that generally lacks accurate knowledge about the history of the Palestinian struggle for liberation and even does poorly on knowledge indices related to Israel's highly discussed current genocidal attacks on Gaza (Silver et al., 2024), this refugee population faces unique struggles that make them especially susceptible to mental health deficits and related sequelae.

Communicated narrative sense-making (CNSM) theory (Koenig Kellas, 2022) proposes that humans create and tell stories of their lived and inherited experiences in order to make sense of, and cope with, difficult experiences. Stories told in families, specifically, affect and reflect family members' understandings of themselves, their family, and their culture. This chapter applies this theory, together with data collected from interviews with Palestinian refugees in the United States, to argue that storytelling is an essential response to help shape intergenerational identity and mitigate multifaceted experiences of felt harm for this population. To our knowledge, this is the first study that systematically examines the mental health of Palestinian refugees in the United States and proposes narratives as a form of healing through liberatory agency.

The Context of Palestine and Palestinian Refugees in the United States

Palestinians are tasked with making sense of their own experiences and/or of their ethnic roots while living within the relative comfort of the United States. They also exist within the ongoing realities of contemporary and historical displacement and discrimination and are never far from regular reports from friends and family of systemic violence against Palestinians living within Israel or in the Palestinian territories it occupies. The Hamas attack on Israel on October 7th, 2023, and the months of indiscriminate attacks on Gaza, primarily, and the West Bank, secondarily, that have followed situate the Palestinian experience for many people as "starting" a few months ago. Of course, that is deeply ahistorical and inaccurate. It overlooks the ethnic cleansing of the Indigenous Palestinian population starting in 1947 and the decades of settler colonial violence since (Seikaly, 2020). Just in the last 20 years, Israel (a) began a land, air, and sea blockade on Gaza (in 2006), closing the 141 square mile (25-mile long and between 3.7 and 7.5 mile wide) territory for human entry–exit and to most products and suffocating its population, (b) initiated several military assaults on Gaza,[3] killing approximately 1,400 Palestinians in 21 days in 2008, 200 Palestinians in 8 days in 2012, 2,100 Palestinians in 46 days in 2014, 260 Palestinians in 11 days in 2021, 30 Palestinians in 3 days in 2022, prior to the more than 60,000

Palestinians that Israel has killed in Gaza since October 7th, 2023, (c) killed over 150 Palestinians and injured over 10,000 (mostly shooting them in the knees) who were peacefully protesting weekly at the Gaza–Israel border across nearly two years between 2018 and 2019,[4] (d) greatly expanded illegal settlements (the number of illegal settlers in the West Bank has more than doubled since 2004[5]), (e) continued a policy of forced evictions and ethnic cleansing throughout East Jerusalem and other areas it occupies,[6] (f) dramatically increased the frequency of child detention rates, with Palestinian child detainees reporting frequent sexual violence, physical violence, and denial of food and basic rights,[7] among other ways in which the state continues the ongoing Nakba. The prior fifty years were also witness to various forms of extreme settler colonial violence.

The thousands of Palestinian refugees in the United States carry these histories of trauma with them and, most recently, absorb the daily reports of unfathomable death and destruction, all while their government funds[8] the ongoing Israeli genocide[9] and representatives accuse Palestinians and allies of antisemitism for speaking against the violence in Gaza.[10] Any credible analysis of the well-being of this population can only be done within a framework that recognizes the structural and historical violence they carry.

Mental Health and Healthcare Utilization

While data on mental health among Palestinian refugees in the United States seems to be unavailable, recent studies have shown that Arab immigrants, broadly, in the US experience low levels of mental health. For example, Bulut and Brewster (2021), using data from over 265,000 respondents who took part in the U.S. National Health Interview Survey, found that immigrants from the Middle East reported greater psychological distress than either the US-born White population or immigrants from Africa, Asia, Europe, or South/Central America. Almutairi et al. (2022) completed a scoping review of twenty-four studies published between 2000 and 2021 that examined the mental health of Arab female immigrants living in the United States. The results suggested a "high prevalence of mental health disorders" (p. 3079), with individuals typically struggling with multiple such challenges simultaneously. Their analysis also showed that rates of PTSD were as high as 84 percent for those in this population who came from conflict zones (in their case, studies with US immigrants from

Syria and Iraq). Similarly, Elshahat and Moffat (2022) reviewed 49 studies examining mental health determinants among Arabic-speaking immigrants in North America. Their analyses also revealed elevated levels of mental distress in this community and found several factors that worsened those experiences, including stigmatization, the pre-immigration experience of trauma and/or violence, and their status as refugees (vs. immigrants), among others. It is worth noting that none of the reviewed studies focused on the Palestinian refugee experience in the United States—a population already identified as especially likely to experience both historical and ongoing trauma and discrimination.

This pattern is especially problematic when we account for the finding that Arab immigrants are also especially likely to underutilize available mental health resources. Shaimaa and Bialous' (2024) review of underutilization among Arab refugees in the United States led to the identification of "(1) a lack of trust between clients and health care workers; (2) language and cultural hurdles; (3) treatment and custody issues for racial and ethnic minorities; (4) a greater frequency of diagnoses of anxiety or depression in Arabs; (5) an absence of health insurance coverage; and (6) clinical prejudice among nonminority facility contributors" as common factors (p. 377). Consistent with their findings, Armstrong-Mensa et al.'s (2023) analysis of underutilization of mental health resources by Syrian immigrants in the United States found similar causal explanations, but added stigma as a significant factor.

The particular susceptibility of Palestinian refugees in the United States to mental distress and the factors that lead to under utilization of mental health services demands an approach to mental health that is both centered in a broader liberatory understanding of the population's needs and recognizes the role of the family as providers of tools that buffer experiences leading to mental health deficits. A commitment to these two elements shapes the remainder of our analysis.

Liberatory Frameworks

The vast majority of research and "knowledge" about health and well-being adopts a Western, individually focused, and often colonial approach (see Giacaman, 2018; Veronese et al., in press; Veronese et al., 2023 for related critique). The resulting analysis is one that focuses on the individual as primarily responsible for the condition of their health, a medicalization of health, which promotes drugs as the primary solution to improvement, and a value of individualism at the foundation of all therapeutic interventions. To understand the conditions that shape the lives of Palestinians, both within the occupied territories and those in the diasporic community, it is essential that we replace these "traditional" framings of well-being with ones that begin with a recognition of the violent historical and structural conditions that shape the Palestinian experience, that honor the fact that health will never be attained without liberation, and that recognize agency at the heart of liberatory projects. Indeed, Garcini et al. (2025) describes the liberatory approach as being "centered on fostering agency to encourage communities to create change rather than perpetuate their capacity to tolerate misfortune" (p. 11).

Martín-Baró (1994), the pioneer of Liberatory psychology, described the impact of Western, colonial approaches on communities this way:

> [Marginalized or oppressed people] learn to be resigned and submissive, not so much as the result of the transmission of values through a closed subculture as through the everyday demonstration of how impossible and useless it is to strive to change their situation, when that environment itself forms part of an overall oppressive social system. (p. 210)

It is precisely through this system that Palestinians become fatalistic about their own well-being, resigned to the seeming impossibility of emergence from the structural violence in which they exist. To add to their resignation, they are then typically diagnosed by health professionals as having a mental disorder (e.g., "post-traumatic stress disorder") that is best treated through drugs that increase serotonin in the brain, neurologically improving mood, while neither changing the underlying structural conditions that are causing the mental health deficit nor creating increased agency for them to do so. In contrast, a liberatory approach creates "opportunities for communities to believe that they can alter conditions of oppression and hardship . . . vital for liberation" (Garcini et al., 2025, p. 11). One of the strategies for such vital beliefs is the transmission of legacies of empowerment (Garcini et al., 2025).

In congruence, and specifically related to the Palestinian mental health experience, Atallah (2017) showed that Palestinians expelled from their homes use shared narratives of defiance within their families as a method of intergenerational empowerment and disruption of trauma. Ramos (2014) examined the "Freedom Theatre" in the West Bank (in the occupied Palestinian territories) as a space in which theatrical storytelling creates individual and communal agency. Ramos describes how the Freedom Theatre makes it so that "tellers are re- humanized" which "allows the recognition and representation of alternative ways to subvert the occupation." As such, the plays narrate Palestinian experiences that challenge the resignation that comes from violent occupation. Most recently, Buheji and Khunji (2023) take a liberatory approach to their analysis of well-being in the context of Israel's genocidal assault on Gaza. Noting that "giving someone life and dreams to the cause of liberation has been and will continue to be one of the main sources of 'collective hardiness'" (p. 12), the authors examine storytelling as a central communication strategy for rehabilitation, especially for displaced Palestinians. Their analysis argues that sharing narratives is cathartic, assists in the processing of trauma, builds community, contributes to a sense that "they are still participating in resistance" (p. 15), is empowering, and "lead(s) to increased support and sustenance of resistance till freedom is achieved" (p. 15), among other functions (see also Buheji, 2022).

In a welcome recent intervention to the scholarly and public health discussion of under utilization of mental health services among Arab immigrants in the United States, Shaimaa and Bialous' (2024) demanded that solutions center the lived experience of this population and, seriously consider the factors that shape the decisions of many in that community regarding the use of these services. High among those is the place of family, which Elshahat and Moffat (2022) describe as "being important over self and representing the principal social unit in the Arabic culture" (p. 490). Consistent with these calls, we propose Communicated Narrative Sense-Making Theory as uniquely suited to help explain the impact of family storytelling on mental health among Palestinian refugees in the United States. Essential to that impact is the role of family in the Palestinian community and the effect of storytelling in the development of agency—both central to liberatory possibilities (see also Montero & Sonn, 2009, for review).

Communicated Narrative Sense-Making (CNSM) Theory

CNSM theory anchors itself in the connection between narrative sense-making and health outcomes (Koenig Kellas, 2022). Each of CNSM's three heuristics uniquely links storytelling with individual and relational well-being. First, with a focus on storytelling content, retrospective storytelling captures the meaning-making, values, and beliefs inherited through storytelling (proposition one) and how the framing of stories will influence health outcomes (proposition two). Second, interactional storytelling focuses on the storytelling process by taking a deeper look into the interactional sense-making process and its relation to narrative sense-making (proposition three), health (proposition four), as well as the relationship between communicated perspective-taking and well-being (proposition five). Third, translational storytelling focuses on how narrative reflections and sense-making interventions (proposition six) and interventions focused on storytelling framing or degree of interactional sense-making (proposition seven) can improve well-being.

In all, CNSM provides a promising lens to better understand the coping and healing that storytelling can provide. For example, with a focus on storytelling and mental health, Flood-Grady and Koenig Kellas (2019) demonstrated how family storytelling communicated lessons and expectations surrounding mental illness. In another study, Willer and Kellas (2019) examined narrative interventions with adolescent girls experiencing social aggression. Findings revealed how narrative interventions, through stories that included expressive writing and drawings, as well as reframing practices and externalization, improved participants' well-being and ability to cope.

Through the three heuristics, CSNM speaks to how story content and the storytelling process influence who we are, our relationships, and our views of the world (Koenig Kellas, 2022). CNSM also addresses how storytelling can connect people, create identity, and help cope with difficulty (Koenig Kellas, 2022). In doing so, storytelling can aid in our greater understanding and meaning-making as it relates to our self, relationships, families, and our larger identities (e.g., race). Although a large amount of research using CNSM encompasses a White, Western point of view, emerging work has started to expand the scope of CNSM through its population under study. For example, Denson (2022) examined intergenerational storytelling about love within Black families and Horstman et al. (2023) analyzed parent–child storytelling as it related to the South African apartheid. By further globally expanding CNSM research, CNSM not only has the opportunity to theoretically grow and strengthen through testing and examining its assumptions across different social groups but has the potential to practically aid in improving narrative interventions (improving mental health and general well-being) for historically marginalized, minoritized, and non-Western populations.

In line with the context of this chapter, for Palestinians in the United States, the government and mainstream media's unwavering support of Israel places Palestinians in a precarious position. This silencing of the Palestinian narrative, paired with ongoing devastation, land theft, and killing of the Palestinian people, US tax dollars supporting Israel's military, the consistent conflation of criticism of the Israeli government with antisemitism, and the stigmatization of Arabs and Palestinians, make Palestinians in the United States especially vulnerable.

To date, two studies have examined Palestinians in the United States through a CNSM framework. Using the retrospective framework, Elkhalid and colleagues (2025a) found that intergenerational storytelling in Palestinian families was not only infused with traumatic experiences but had an emotional and behavioral impact on younger generations. Secondly, utilizing narrative and resilience theorizing, Elkhalid et al. (2025b) examined how Palestinians in the United States conceptualized and enacted a particular form of resilience. Findings specifically revealed different layers and elements of sumud, an Indigenous Palestinian concept. Growing this body of literature would gain greater insight into how Palestinians in the United States "story" their lives and history. This work would not only continue to expand CNSM but would, in turn, practically inform mental health practitioners and providers, and ideally empower individuals and family members who are left making sense of historic and present-day trauma.

Intergenerational Trauma and Mental Health

Trauma can be passed down through family stories, and it is crucial to recognize how stories that are embedded in hardships (such as famine or genocide) are communicated, as they can either perpetrate or deter intergenerational trauma (Cardwell et al., 2023). Furthermore, as noted by Duran and colleagues (1998), the generational passing down of trauma can occur through conscious memory. When considering mental health and colonized populations, such as Native Americans, the term "soul wounds" speaks to the pain and traumatic experiences of the past that influence the present (Duran et al., 1998). Palestinians are unique, in that their ethnic/racial and colonial trauma is not only in the past but it has remained continuous.

The intergenerational transmission of trauma generally refers to the passing down of traumatic experiences, and its consequences can reverberate for generations. This transmission can be biological, psychological, or behavioral (Bowers & Yehuda, 2016). Children may learn and mimic stress response behaviors from their parents (as social learning theory would indicate; Bandura, 1977). Moreover, the consequences of trauma can alter one's genetic makeup, which would inherently and biologically pass down trauma (Bowers & Yehuda, 2016). For instance, research has suggested that Holocaust survivors' offspring are increasingly susceptible to mental and physical health concerns and diagnoses (Baider et al., 2000; Yehuda et al., 1998). Although Indigenous population research is limited, similar findings have been found within this group. For example, Matheson et al. (2022) examined Canada's colonial genocide of the Indigenous people, highlighting the ongoing system neglect that has resulted in consequences such as, but not limited to, generational physical and mental health implications, poor housing, and food scarcity. Matheson et al. (2022) also argued that a significant number of the Indigenous people did not trust healthcare professionals—understandably given the colonial disruption and harm.

Similarly, Palestinians are placed in systems that are not equipped to support and treat the population (Barron & Abdallah, 2015; Jabr & Berger, 2023; Veronese & Cavazzoni, 2020). Although narrative interventions designed for the population have been proven beneficial, researchers have still stressed that many standard trauma intervention programs and practices are limiting and lacking social context (Veronese & Cavazzoni, 2020). For example, Veronese and Cavazzoni (2020) conducted a narrative analysis where 122 Palestinian children residing in refugee camps in Palestine were asked to write and draw a story that centers around their self-characterization. Findings revealed that when the children's work was interpreted through a diagnosis-focused perspective, children displayed signs of mental distress, with drawings indicating complex trauma in need of intervention (i.e., "the pathological child"). Yet, when the children's work was analyzed through a thematic content analysis, findings suggested signs of personal growth, psychological well-being, social-relational domain, and contextual domain (i.e., "the competent child"). These findings highlight how (a) individual meaning-making, agency, and coping are important and contextual, and (b) researchers and practitioners should question the role of efficacy and degree of effectiveness in intervention practices.

Another example, while studying intergenerational trauma in Palestinian children within the occupied territories, Barron and Abdallah (2015) stated that, "despite an increasing awareness of the context and nature and extent of symptoms, trauma recovery programs have failed to incorporate an understanding of the dynamics of intergenerational trauma into program design and evaluation" (p. 107). Barron and Abdallah (2015) argued how trauma interventions have often been designed for "post" traumatic stress disorder (PTSD), but this approach is limiting for Palestinians, particularly given the cultural, complex, and ongoing trauma. Indeed, recently Atallah and Abu-Jamei (2025) reflected on Palestinian healing during genocide, identifying the unique experience of trauma that shapes Palestinian lives. Essential to healing and mental health, in their articulation, is intergenerational listening and storytelling. These traumatic experiences are not limited to wars, bombings, shootings, checkpoint requirements, loss of their homes, or mass detentions. Indeed, "traumatic violence has formed the core of the Palestinian experience since the Nakba or catastrophe of 1948" (Jabr & Berger, 2023, p. 154). Although communicating about traumatic experiences could be cathartic, communication surrounding these traumatic experiences could also be vulnerably exposing, personally and collectively triggering, as well as humiliating for a Palestinian.

One of the ways that trauma can be passed down to younger generations is through storytelling, and when younger generations hear such messages, they are left making sense of the traumatic experiences (Cardwell et al., 2023). "Listening to trauma is not easy, and listening to the trauma of humiliation may be even more painful than reports of physical violence" (Jabr & Berger, 2023, p. 156). With regard to mental health, these stories and conversations may cause people to either relive their experiences or vicariously live through their family's history or present-day realities. Although these stories may serve to teach the younger generation about their identity, as well as their place within the larger system (see Elkhalid et al., 2025a; Elkhalid et al., 2025b), these younger generations may also feel tasked with supporting their parents' or grandparents' unresolved trauma. For a plethora of reasons, examining and implementing strategies to manage and cope with trauma is essential for mental health, especially given its cost is consequential for individuals in the present day and their future offspring.

Interviews with Palestinian Refugees in the United States

In order to explore the fit of our analysis with the experience of Palestinian refugees in the United States, we analyzed the transcripts of interviews conducted with a sample from that population. The data were collected for another study (see

Elkhalid et al., 2025a; Elkhalid et al., 2025b). As a result, the interview questions were not developed to query the liberatory and agentic potential of storytelling.

However, since they *were* developed to explore narratives more broadly, we wondered whether qualities that reflect the liberatory and agentic potential of storytelling would be referenced naturally. This data set included semi-structured interviews with twenty-five Palestinians living in the United States (fourteen females, 10 males and one unidentified). Of note, interviews took place between Fall 2022 and Summer 2022. Participants were between eighteen and eighty-two years old ($M = 44$) and either immigrated to ($n = 12$) or were born ($n = 13$) in the United States. The majority of the participants earned at least a bachelor's degree ($n = 18$), and 12 of the twenty-three participants said their annual household income was at least $100,000.

Participants were recruited after IRB approval. Sixteen interviews were conducted over the phone, seven over Zoom, and two were in person. Interview questions focused on family stories, intergenerational communication, resilience, and lived experience as a Palestinian in the United States. After the interviews, each participant was offered a $50 gift card to compensate for their time and participation. Interviews were audio-recorded with participant consent, and three undergraduate students assisted with transcriptions and data cleaning. The data set totaled about 775 pages of transcripts. Pseudonyms were created for anonymity.[11]

A thorough coding of the transcripts revealed several themes related to the functions that stories served for participants. Specifically, stories were identified as the space where (a) recognition of cultural bonds was reinforced, and a sense of inheritance occurred, (b) where histories of trauma were transmitted, and (c) where a sense of personal agency in the struggle toward Palestinian liberation was developed. Earlier, we enforced the essentiality of situating the mental health of Palestinian refugees in the United States within the particular experiences of that community and within the broader scholarly knowledge of mental health deficits among Arab immigrants in the United States and the related under utilization of mental health services by that population. We argue that storytelling plays an essential role therein. The emergence of these themes lends credence to that position. Next, we briefly elaborate on each theme and situate them within the broader project of understanding mental health among Palestinian refugees in the United States.

Reinforcement of Cultural Bonds

Participants shared the stories that they were told were largely where they developed connections to their Palestinian identities and inherited cultural bonds (see also Elkhalid et al., 2025a). In that way, Palestinian history became inextricably tied to their own identity and served as a lens through which to understand themselves, as well as present-day violence against Palestinians. For example, Amal, a 38-year-old female, noted how she "inherited Palestine through [my mom's stories]," and Hamza, a 60-year-old male, discussed the fact that his Palestinian grandparents "wanted to preserve the culture more so than anyone else," continuing by reflecting that "they did it in a very fun way, [through] the stories they told us." Hamza continued by noting "that's their way of teaching us how to really stick to our roots and stay true to [our Palestinian identity]." Another interviewee, Rahaf, a 27-year-old female, recounted the importance of narrative expression this way: "It's up to the next generations to make sure that the world knows this perspective that's been silenced for too long." Finally, another participant, Farah, a 26-year-old female, elaborated on this transmission of culture more thoroughly:

> I remember being younger and my dad [saying] "you know, you're Palestinian." This is where it is. This is what it looks like. Look, this is where you're from. This is where our family originated and grew up. . . . This was what happened to the land. This is the history of land. This is what's happening now. I mean, those kinds of things were what my dad would share with me and that shaped my identity a lot.

The voices of these Palestinian refugees speak unambiguously about the role of storytelling in shaping that identification and laying the foundation of knowledge of related oppression. While this connection and cultural reinforcement are educational and collectively sustaining, it may also influence family members' mental health.

Transmission of Trauma

Another (often unintended) function of storytelling was the intergenerational transmission of trauma through narrative. Although intergenerational storytelling has been associated with positive psychosocial identity (Weststrate et al., 2023), trauma also may be embedded in intergenerational storytelling (Elkhalid et al., 2025a; Elkhalid et al., 2025b). Thus, through communication, one may learn and reinforce their cultural connection while simultaneously being susceptible to family and cultural trauma.

Several participants spoke of the ways in which their family's experience of trauma, either directly through the retelling of their own experience or indirectly through the history of Palestine, was communicated through stories. One interviewee, Amal, described it this way:

> I think with that trauma those stories were very deep. They weren't going to come up, naturally. They would have to be kind of provoked into talking about certain things, because otherwise, they were just moving ahead. Like, they weren't looking back, they were just moving forward. And I think probably, especially after 1967, like, suddenly, it goes from, "We're leaving" to like, "We can't go back" and they already had a complicated relationship to home because of the trauma.

Other participants speak about caution in soliciting stories from those who lived through the Nakba because of their awareness of the retraumatization that it produces—an experience that in itself reminds them of the historical trauma that is embedded in any Palestinian narrative. For instance, Dania, a 26-year-old, grappled with that issue this way:

> Yeah, [um] I sort of, because he's my dad, I could sort of tell by his facial expressions or his tone. So you know, if I notice the conversation is, is getting too much, and I'll just stop it and change subjects, or, you know. I, again, that's because he's my dad. So I'm able to pick up on those cues. But it's, I mean, anything can be a retraumazing. That's sort of the tricky part, you know. Like, I could ask him about, "Oh, you know, what, what kind of food did you eat in the camp?" It seems like an innocent question, it's just about food. But then that could trigger [uh] memories of people fighting over food, people [not] eating for days. You know, like that kind of thing. So you never really know what your question is going to trigger.

Dania continued to share how her mom was protective of her father and often discouraged communication about their past traumas. Dania elaborated:

> She's really protective of him. It's not that she doesn't want it to be known. Oh, although she does say there are certain things that shouldn't be said. So I'm wondering, "My God, what happened in those camps that you don't want us to know about?" He has opened up. You know, things that he's witnessed.

Agency and Liberation

Finally, consistent with the analysis of this chapter but without intentional querying in the interview process, participants spontaneously voiced the function of stories as agentic and liberatory. For example, Farah described her father's storytelling itself as a form of resistance that empowered others to continue the fight. Jana, a forty-year-old female, argued that some people believe that "it's never going to change" and "have become numb" to Palestinian disenfranchisement, but that she shares her stories because "[they are] something that I really want people to keep." Similarly, Abdullah (42-year-old male), noted his hope that, partly through the power of sharing stories, "the next generation will do something about Palestine."

Another way in which storytelling functions as agentic is by providing younger generations with a model for how to create change, as Aya, a 32-year-old female, said (in talking about her mother):

> And she also lived in Chicago. So she's always had, like, those stories about Chicago organizing [around] Palestine, and all of the things that [our family and my uncle] have been a part of. And so it's always been a huge thing. And I feel like she passed that down to us.

In that same vein, one participant discussed using stories to give family members a roadmap for organizing focused on Palestinian liberation. She discussed the content of some of these stories this way:

> So the Palestinians have gathered together many, many times on different occasions. But they were faced with lots of resistance, with lots of fighting, with lots of pushback. But nowadays, for example, here in the United States the Palestinians try to get together. Whether it is in the form of a demonstration or a lecture or this or that. But not as much as they can. They need to be doing more in this country here. To get together, to discuss these events, to formalize a plan. To formalize a path to bring their cause more to the surface. To talk more to other people, to explain to other people.

The consistent theme in all of these quotes is an awareness of the ways that stories function to provide agency to their listeners, an essential element of mental health when understood from a liberatory framework.

Recommendations for Mental Health Practitioners

Our point of departure for recommendations to mental health practitioners working with Palestinian refugees in the United States is Diab et al's (2020) essential call for a decolonization of the practice of therapy, with particular attention to its violence against Palestinians. Indeed, these authors appropriately question whether "psychology's silence and inaction in the face of social injustice is an ideological strategy to ensure its relevance by helping individuals adapt to an unjust social and political context" (p. 185). As a counter, they argue that liberated pedagogy and therapy requires theory and practice that facilitates Indigenous and self-determined approaches to healthcare, which are centered on the creation of agency in the ultimate pursuit of liberation. Moreover, they state that "rather than being passive recipients of Israeli military aggression, both clinicians and clients [must be] active agents capable of harnessing psychological knowledge and processes to effect individual change, which in turn provides a platform for political resistance" (p. 189). When applied to the context of storytelling, this approach demands that practitioners drop the deeply embedded Western frameworks of understanding and medicalization around mental health, and commit to treating patients with culturally informed, trauma-based, and liberatory-centered practices that focus on the development of agency.

Results from our analyses provide preliminary evidence in support of CNSM as a framework that can shed light on the transmission of trauma, its effect on family members' mental health, and the power of families to communicatively shape generational sense-making (as noted in proposition one; Koenig Kellas, 2022). In a similar fashion, Cardwell et al. (2023) discussed the transmission of trauma (socially and biologically), the role of family storytelling, the sociopolitical influence, and the limitations Western perspectives have in adequately treating marginalized groups, and argued that through CNSM's translational heuristic, interventions may be created to support marginalized and minoritized family members. This is an important consideration, especially given the knowledge that immigrants, broadly, and Palestinian refugees specifically, are not adequately supported within existing systems. In other words, through CNSM-informed intervention, there is hope that marginalized groups can regain power by placing it back into their control through the voices of the individual, family, and community, and ultimately this approach to creating interventions can improve current practices.

In addition to the reframing of narratives and each family defining what "positive" means, a focus on narrative agency and counter-narratives may serve as a tool to mitigate intergenerational trauma and simultaneously empower Palestinians (Cardwell et al., 2023). Bishop (2018b) defined narrative agency as "the experiential, partial, public, oppositional, and incondensable stories that marginalized individuals use to assert their right to speak and reframe audience understanding" (as cited in Bishop, 2018a, p. 160). For example, Bishop (2018a) examined how undocumented immigrants can use narrative agency to reclaim what it means to be an immigrant and advocate for immigrants through their own lived experience. In doing so, undocumented immigrants can take power back into their own hands and push against the mainstream media and political rhetoric that communicates on their behalf (Bishop, 2018a). As Lindemann (2001) said, "how we identify ourselves establishes our own view of what we can do" (p. xi). The relationship we have with our own identity consequently relates to how we act or what we feel is within our control. This redefining of self is especially important for social identities that are defined and misunderstood within the power system.

Counter-narratives oppose a master narrative (being the collective or predominantly understood discourse) and the counter-narrative typically comes from the oppressed identity with personal experience (Bamberg & Wipff, 2020). These types of narratives are designed to redefine, resist, and combat the narrative given by the harmful power system (Lindemann, 2001). Individuals can counter the master narrative or mainstream discourse with their own truth, which in turn can foster agency and enable identity redefining (i.e., self-perception). An example of counter-narrative research that integrates liberation psychology was the examination of women's rights within the Movimiento Autónomo de Mujeres in Nicaragua (Grabe & Dutt, 2020). Through this qualitative analysis, findings demonstrated how deepening one's connection to their own identity can help a person understand their own oppression within the larger system while also strengthening their commitment to fight the injustice. Moreover, they stress how engaging in counter narratives, as a collective, empowered the group to mobilize, which led them to act on the injustice and challenge the discourses surrounding their rights.

Throughout these examples, individual, relational, and community meaning-making was instrumental. Moreover, these studies demonstrated the power of personal testimonies. Identity (re)construction develops through storytelling, and testimonies can collectively challenge the status quo (Bishop, 2018a; Cardwell et al., 2023; Grabe & Dutt, 2020; Lindemann, 2001). In line, Kellas et al.'s (2020) *narrative connection* intervention may be beneficial as it brings a small group together to share their experiences and collaboratively engage in sense-making. This type of intervention was demonstrated through a parenting study, and findings suggested benefits such as feelings of solidarity, support, and reassurance. Exploring different translational storytelling interventions, such as *narrative connection*, may be especially helpful to marginalized people as it centers the intervention around lived experiences and the voices of the population (Kellas et al., 2020). To those ends, these personal narratives put together to create a collective counter-narrative could lead to positive mental health outcomes (e.g., intergenerational healing, empowerment, and action).

Conclusion

In this chapter, we began with a brief articulation of the unique historical and ongoing trauma and discrimination within which Palestinian refugees in the United States exist. We then summarized existing knowledge about mental health deficits among Arab immigrants in the United States, and factors that impact their underutilization of mental health services, including status as refugees. That was followed by a reminder of some of the reasons why the Palestinian community, within the broader Arab immigrant population, was particularly susceptible to those trends, and a review of recent calls for mental health understandings and interventions that centered on the particular experiences of communities. An understanding of the role of family within Palestinian communities, the essentiality of shifting from Western approaches to mental health to liberatory ones, and an appreciation for the role of storytelling as a place for identity articulation and agency, among other functions, led us to examine CNSM Theory as a productive framework to help shape a response to underutilization of mental health services and to guide mental health practitioners working with Palestinian refugee communities in the United States.

An additional, broad takeaway is that meaning-making, agency, and counter-narratives aid in healing (Cardwell et al., 2023), but we can also imagine how storytelling could go beyond fostering agency and coping and speak to liberation. Or, reflexively, contribute to liberation *through* the agentic force of narratives. Perhaps healing and liberation stem not from the systems that confine and constrain a population but from within the community. Indeed, it is essential that researchers and practitioners take a decolonial, non-Western, liberatory approach to understanding mental health. How healthcare providers approach mental health and, relatedly, the ways in which members of the community communicate about trauma are consequential to individual and collective well-being. It is crucial to recognize ways individuals and communities can imagine liberated futures and, ultimately, contribute to the development of agency that leads to liberatory potentials and realities. The failures of mental health services to reach immigrants broadly and Palestinian refugees specifically cannot continue. It is past time to demand that governments and practitioners take community-centered approaches to mental health work and prioritize liberation therein. In such systems, storytelling plays an essential role.

Notes

1 Shoichet, C. E. (2023, October 30). *Who are Palestinian refugees? The Gaza war brings attention to a decades-old question.* CNN. https://www.cnn.com/2023/10/30/us/palestinian-refugees-gaza-war-cec/index.html

2 Palestine Legal. (n.d.). *The Distorted Definition: Redefining antisemitism to silence advocacy for Palestinian rights.* https://palestinelegal.org/distorted-definition

3 Al Jazeera. (2022, August 7). *Timeline: Israel's attacks on Gaza since 2005.* https://www.aljazeera.com/news/2022/8/7/timeline-israels-attacks-on-gaza-since-2005

4 Amnesty International. (2018, October 19). Six Months On: *Gaza's Great March of Return.* https://www.amnesty.org/en/latest/campaigns/2018/10/gaza-great-march-of-return/

5 Peace Now. (n.d.). *Settlements population data.* https://peacenow.org.il/en/settlements-watch/settlements-data/population

6 Amnesty International. (2023, July 28). *Israel/OPT: 500 Palestinians facing forcible eviction, displacement, and segregation.* https://www.amnesty.org/en/latest/news/2023/07/israel-opt-500-palestinians-facing-forcible-eviction-displacement-and-segregation/

7 Save the Children. (2023). *Injustice: Palestinian children's experience of the Israeli military detention system.* https://resourcecentre.savethechildren.net/document/injusticepalestinian-childrens-experience-of-the-israeli-military-detention-system/

8 Williams, A. & Lebowitz, M. (2023, December 29). *Biden Administration Sidesteps Congress Again for Emergency Arms Sale to Israel.* NBC News. https://www.nbcnews.com/politics/white-house/biden-administration-sidesteps-congress-arms-sale-israel-rcna131661

9 International Court of Justice. (2023, December 28). *Application of the Convention on the Prevention and Punishment of the Crime of Genocide in the Gaza Strip (South Africa v. Israel).* https://www.icj-cij.org/sites/default/files/case-related/192/192-20231228-app-01-00-en.pdf

10 Cochran, L. (2023, November 16). *Students for Justice in Palestine Becomes Flashpoint in College Antisemitism, Free Speech Debate.* The Hill. https://thehill.com/homenews/education/4311746-students-justice-palestine-antisemitism-free-speech-hamas-israel/

11 Pseudonyms were chosen in honor of the children who were killed in Gaza following October 7, 2023.

Recommended Readings/Resources

Diab, M., Veronese, G., Jamei, Y. A., & Kagee, A. (2020). The interplay of paradigms: Decolonizing a psychology curriculum in the context of the siege of Gaza. *Nordic Psychology, 72*(3), 183–198. https://doi.org/10.1080/19012276.2019.1675087

Jabr, S., & Berger, E. (2023). Community mental health, psychoanalysis, and freedom: The case of Palestine. *International Journal of Applied Psychoanalytic Studies, 20*(2), 285–301. https://doi.org/10.1002/aps.1801

Jewish Voice for Peace. (2024, February 1). *About.* https://www.jvphealth.org/

Palestine-Global Mental Health Network. (2024, February 1). *Who are we?* https://www.pgmhn.org/about-us

Palestine Remember. (2024, February 1). *Nakba"s oral history interviews listing.* https://www.palestineremembered.com/OralHistory/Interviews-Listing/Story1151.html

Veronese, G., & Cavazzoni, F. (2020). "I hope I will be able to go back to my home city": Narratives of suffering and survival of children in Palestine. *Psychological Studies, 65*(1), 51–63. https://doi.org/10.1007/s12646-019-00502-5

References

Almutairi, W., Seven, M., Poudel-Tandukar, K., & VanKim, N. (2022). Mental health disorders among Middle Eastern immigrant women living in the United States: A scoping review. *Perspectives in Psychiatric Care, 58*(4), 3079–3102.

Armstrong-Mensah, E., Mitha, N.,& McNair, A. (2023). The mental health of Syrian refugees in the United States: Examining critical risk factors and major barriers to mental health care access. *International Journal of Translational Medical Research and Public Health, 7*(1), 1–8. https://doi.org/10.21106/ijtmrph.e431

Atallah, D. G. (2017). A community-based qualitative study of intergenerational resilience with Palestinian refugee families facing structural violence and historical trauma. *Transcultural Psychiatry, 54*(3), 357–383. https://doi.org/10.1177/1363461517706287.

Atallah, D. G., & Abu-Jamei, Y. M. (2025). Rethinking Trauma Against a Genocidal World: Palestinian Healing Is a Sound of Our Victory. *Journal of Palestine Studies, 54*(1), 51–61. https://doi.org/10.1080/0377919X.2025.2481819

Baider, L., Peretz, T., Hadani, P. E., Perry, S., Avramov, R., & De-Nour, A. K. (2000). Transmission of response to trauma? Second-generation Holocaust survivors' reaction to cancer. *American Journal of Psychiatry, 157*(6), 904–910. https://pubmed.ncbi.nlm.nih.gov/10831469/

Bamberg, M., & Wipff, Z. (2020). Reconsidering counter-narratives. In *Routledge handbook of counter-narratives* (pp. 70–82). Routledge.

Bandura, A., & Walters, R. H. (1977). *Social learning theory* (Vol. 1). Prentice Hall.

Barron, I. G., & Abdallah, G. (2015). Intergenerational trauma in the occupied Palestinian territories: Effect on children and promotion of healing. *Journal of Child & Adolescent Trauma, 8*, 103–110. https://doi.org/10.1007/s40653-015-0046-z

Bishop, S. C. (2018a). "Nobody can take our story": Competing representational narratives of immigrants without legal status. *Communication & Society, 3*(3), 159–173. https://doi.org/10.15581/003.31.3.159-173

Bishop, S. C. (2018b). *Undocumented storytellers: Narrating the immigrant rights movement.* Oxford University Press.

Bowers, M. E., & Yehuda, R. (2016). Intergenerational transmission of stress in humans. *Neuropsychopharmacology, 41*(1), 232–244. https://doi.org/10.1038/npp.2015.247

Buheji, M. (2022). Storytelling during pandemics– a focused review. *Information Sciences Letters, 11*(1), 161–165. http://dx.doi.org/10.18576/isl/110117

Buheji, M., & Khunji, A. (2023). Rehabilitating Gaza's wellbeing through storytelling (during & after war 2023). *International Journal of Advanced Research in Social Sciences and Humanities (IJARSSH), 7*(1), 2023. https://doi.org/10.17605/OSF.IO/QH38D

Bulut, E., & Brewster, K. L. (2021). Psychological distress in Middle Eastern immigrants to the United States: A challenge to the healthy migrant model? *Social Science & Medicine, 274*, 113765. https://doi.org/10.1016/j.socscimed.2021.113765

Cardwell, M., Soliz, J., & Koenig Kellas, J. (2023). Intergenerational transmission of trauma: Understanding histories and narratives. In R. C. Diggs & T. J. Socha (Eds.), *Family communication and cultural transformation: (Re)Awakening legacies of equality, social justice, freedom, and hope* (pp. 110–124). Routledge.

Denson, S. (2022). *Retrospective storytelling, meaning-making, and generativity (the passing down of wisdom): black intergenerational stories about love* (Doctoral dissertation, University of Maryland).

Diab, M., Veronese, G., Jamei, Y. A., & Kagee, A. (2020). The interplay of paradigms: Decolonizing a psychology curriculum in the context of the siege of Gaza. *Nordic Psychology, 72*(3), 183–198. https://doi.org/10.1080/19012276.2019.1675087

Douglas, P., Cetron, M., & Spiegel, P. (2019). Definitions matter: migrants, immigrants, asylum seekers and refugees. *Journal of Travel Medicine, 26*(2), 1–3. https://doi.org/10.1093/jtm/taz005

Duran, B., Duran, E., & Brave Heart, M. Y. H. (1998). Native Americans and the trauma of history. In R Thornton (Ed.), *Studying Native America: Problems and prospects in Native American studies* (pp. 60–78). University of Wisconsin Press.

Elkhalid, A. K., Horstman, H. K., Afifi, W. A., & Afifi, T. D. (2025). "Baba, you're not gonna live forever....we need these stories": Intergenerational storytelling in Palestinian families connecting history, identity, and (the loss of) place. *Communication Monographs*, 92(2), 239-261. https://doi.org/10.1080/03637751.2024.2415611.

Elkhalid, A. K., Afifi, T. D.,Afifi, W. A., & Tchamdjoci, M. D. (2025b). "Carrying Your History is a Form of Resilience": Reconceptualizing Resilience from an Indigenous Perspective Through Family Storytelling Among Palestinians Residing in the United States. *Journal of Family Communication*, 1–18. https://doi.org/10.1080/15267431.2025.2550729

Elshahat, S., & Moffat, T. (2022). Mental health triggers and protective factors Among Arabic- speaking immigrants and refugees in North America: A scoping review. *Journal of Immigrant Minority Health, 24*, 489–505. https://doi.org/10.1007/s10903-021-01215-6

Flood-Grady, E., & Koenig Kellas, J. (2019). Sense-making, socialization, and stigma: Exploring narratives told in families about mental illness. *Health Communication, 34*(6), 607–617. https://doi.org/10.1080/10410236.2018.1431016

Garcini, L. M., Barrita, A., Cadenas, G. A., Domenech Rodríguez, M. M., Galvan, T., Mercado, A., Moreno, O., Paris, M., Rojas Perez, O. F., Silva, M., & Venta, A. (2025). A decolonial and liberation lens to social justice research: Upholding promises for diverse, inclusive, and equitable psychological science. *American Psychologist*, 80(1), 1–14. https://doi.org/10.1037/amp0001255.

Giacaman, R. (2018). Reframing public health in wartime: From the biomedical model to the "wounds inside". *Journal of Palestine Studies, 47*(2), 9–27. https://doi.org/10.1525/jps.2018.47.2.9

Grabe, S., & Dutt, A. (2020). Community intervention in the societal inequity of women's political participation: The development of efficacy and citizen participation in rural Nicaragua. *Journal of Prevention & Intervention in the Community, 48*(4), 329–347. https://doi.org/10.1080/10852352.2019.1627080

Horstman, H. K., Pedro, A., Goldschmidt, T., Watson, O., & Butauski, M. (2023). Exploring resilience and communicated narrative sense-making in South Africans' stories of apartheid. *International Journal of Communication, 17*, 19.

Jabr, S., & Berger, E. (2023). Community mental health, psychoanalysis, and freedom: The case of Palestine. *International Journal of Applied Psychoanalytic Studies, 80*(2), 285–301. https://doi.org/10.1002/aps.1801

Kellas, J. K., Morgan, T., Taladay, C., Minton, M., Forte, J., & Husmann, E. (2020). Narrative connection: Applying CNSM theory's translational storytelling heuristic.

Journal of Family Communication, 20(4), 360–376. https://doi.org/10.1080/15267431.2020.1826485

Khalidi, R. I. (1992). Observations on the right of return. *Journal of Palestine Studies, 21*(2), 29–40. https://doi.org/10.2307/2537217

Koenig Kellas, J. (2022). Communicated narrative sense-making theory: Bridging storytelling, relationships and well-being. In D. O. Braithwaite & P. Schrodt (Eds.), *Engaging theories in interpersonal communication* (3 ed., pp. 117–129). Routledge.

Lindemann, H. (2001). *Damaged identities, narrative repair.* Cornell University Press.

Martín-Baró, I. (1994). *Writings for a liberation psychology* (A. Aron & S. Corne, Eds.). Harvard University Press.

Matheson, K., Seymour, A., Landry, J., Ventura, K., Arsenault, E., & Anisman, H. (2022). Canada's colonial genocide of indigenous peoples: A review of the psychosocial and neurobiological processes linking trauma and intergenerational outcomes. *International Journal of Environmental Research and Public Health, 19*(11), 6455. https://doi.org/10.3390/ijerph19116455

Montero, M., & Sonn, C. C. (2009). About liberation and psychology: An introduction. In M. Montero & C. C. Sonn (Eds.), *Psychology of liberation: Theory and applications* (pp. 1–11). Springer.

Ramos, I. F. (2014). Storytelling, agency and community-building through playback theatre in Palestine. *SOAS Journal of Postgraduate Research, 7*, 14–25.

Seikaly, S. (2020). The history of Israel/Palestine. In O. El Shakry (Ed.), *Understanding and teaching the modern middle east* (pp. 101–116). University of Wisconsin Press.

Shaimaa, E., & Bialous, S. (2024). Mental health care access among Arab immigrants in the United States: Application of Public Arena Model. *Community Mental Health Journal, 60*, 376–384. https://doi.org/10.1007/s10597-023-01182-2

Silver, L., Alper, B. A., Reeter, S., Lippert, J., & Mohamed, B. (2024). Majority in the U.S. say Israel has valid reasons for fighting, fewer say the same about Hamas (Section 4: Emotions, news and knowledge about the Israel-Hamas War). Pew Research Center, Washington, D.C. (March 21, 2024) https://www.pewresearch.org/2024/03/21/emotions-news-and-knowledge-about-the-israel-hamas-war

Veronese, G., Afifi, W. A., & Giacaman, R. (in press). Mental health in the occupied Palestinian territories. In P. Crawford & P. Kadetz (Eds.), *Encyclopedia of health humanities*. Palgrave.

Veronese, G., & Cavazzoni, F. (2020). "I hope I will be able to go back to my home city": Narratives of suffering and survival of children in Palestine. *Psychological Studies, 65*(1), 51–63. https://doi.org/10.1007/s12646-019-00502-5

Veronese, G., Mahamid, F., & Bdier, D. (2023). Transgenerational trauma and collective resilience: A qualitative analysis of the experiences of settler-colonial violence among three generations of Palestinian refugees. *International Journal of Social Psychiatry, 69*(7), 1814–1824. https://doi.org/10.1177/00207640231175787

Weststrate, N. M., Turner, K., & McLean, K. C. (2023). Intergenerational storytelling as a developmental resource in LGBTQ+ communities. *Journal of Homosexuality, 71*(7), 1626–1651. https://doi.org/10.1080/00918369.2023.2202295

Willer, E. K., & Kellas, J. K. (2019). Testing a social aggression and translational storytelling intervention: The impact of communicated narrative sense-making on adolescent girls' mental health. In L. R. Lippert, R. D. Hall, A. E. Miller-Ott, & D. C. Davis (Eds.), *Communicating mental health: History, contexts, and perspectives* (pp. 101–122). Lexington Books/Rowman & Littlefield.

Yehuda, R., Schmeidler, J., Wainberg, M., Binder-Brynes, K., & Duvdevani, T. (1998). Vulnerability to posttraumatic stress disorder in adult offspring of Holocaust survivors. *American Journal of Psychiatry, 155*(9), 1163–1171. https://doi.org/10.1176/ajp.155.9.1163

2

Mental Health and LGBTQ+ Populations

Communicative Solutions for LGBTQ+ Well-Being

Leandra Hinojosa Hernández and Natalia Peraza

Attacks on LGBTQ+ populations are on the rise across the United States. According to Liou (2023), 75 anti-LGBTQ+ bills became law in 2023 across twenty-three states, ranging from restrictions on drag bans to bathroom use, gender-affirming care, and the inclusion of LGBTQ+ youth in sports. In Utah, for example, state legislators passed House Bill 527, which sets restrictions on transgender individuals' ability to use bathrooms in various institutions. Such legislation has dramatic impacts on LGBTQ+ communities' mental health and well-being. The Substance Abuse and Mental Health Services Administration (SAMHSA, 2023) notes that LGBTQ+ patient populations are more likely than straight adults to use substances, experience mental health conditions including major depressive episodes, and experience serious thoughts of suicide. These health outcomes are influenced by harassment, stigma, and discrimination (Pachankis et al., 2021; SAMHSA, 2023). Furthermore, LGBTQ+ youth are at higher risk of mental health deterioration, depression, and ideation. According to the Trevor Project (2024), 45 percent of LGBTQ+ youth seriously considered attempting suicide in 2021, 60 percent of LGBTQ+ youth who wanted mental health care in 2021 were not able to get access to it, and those who live in affirming communities are significantly less likely to attempt suicide than those who do not. Ultimately, research highlights the detrimental and dire state of LGBTQ+ mental health in the United States, particularly for LGBTQ+ youth.

Uniquely poised to, through a social justice and ethics lens, utilize tools to address the barriers and stigmas that LGBTQ+ communities face, this chapter traces representative mental health issues among LGBTQ+ populations and interrogates how cultural, legislative, political, and religious factors shape and contribute to such mental health concerns through a critical and queer health communication lens. Furthermore, this chapter provides communication-based solutions and a review of LGBTQ+ community-based interventions to offer a snapshot of programs that address and improve LGBTQ+ mental health, well-being, and inclusion through the goal of queer surviving and thriving.

LGBTQ+ Mental Health: Trends and Perspectives

Definitions and Terms: Gender, Sex, and Sexuality

The LGBTQ+ acronym, encompassing Lesbian, Gay, Bisexual, Transgender, Queer, and other identities across diverse spectrums of sexual orientation and gender identity, consists of individuals who identify beyond heteronormative and cisnormative standards (American Psychological Association, 2022; Garofalo, 2011). Differences in sexual orientation (e.g., sexual behavior and attraction) as well as variances in gender (e.g., identity and expression) are integral components of human diversity.

It is crucial to acknowledge the intricacies involved in defining the full scope of the LGBTQ+ community, as this understanding is essential for promoting inclusivity and addressing the diverse needs and experiences within the community. Sexual orientation pertains to an individual's attraction to others and their selection of sexual partners. Gender identity encompasses the inner gender with which a person identifies, typically reflected in their chosen pronouns (American Psychological Association, 2022; Garofalo, 2011). Meanwhile, gender expression involves the outward presentation of one's gender identity through attire, appearance, and conduct. Gender also manifests in everyday life through gender roles and gender norms that dictate socially acceptable behaviors. Gender norms are defined as social rules and expectations that individuals face at societal, cultural, and interpersonal levels. In other words, gender can best be conceptualized as a "social system that apportions resources, roles, power, and entitlements according to whether a person or practice is perceived as male or female, masculine or feminine" (Cislaghi & Heise, 2020, p. 410). It is crucial to distinguish between "gender" and "sex" as they are frequently interchanged. Notably, a person's gender identity may or may not align with the sex they were assigned at birth (American Psychological Association, 2022; Garofalo, 2011).

The percentage of Americans identifying as LGBTQ+ has increased over the years (Jones, 2022). Current estimates indicate that approximately 7 percent of individuals identify as LGB, while the Transgender/Nonbinary community makes up approximately 1.6 percent of the total US population (Brown, 2023; Jones, 2022). Despite these seemingly modest percentages, the LGBTQ+ community comprises approximately 20 million Americans (Powell, 2021). Importantly, due to the pervasive stigma, discrimination, and violence faced by LGBTQ+ individuals, statistics regarding LGBTQ+ populations often underestimate the actual number of individuals who identify as LGBTQ+ or those who exist beyond cisnormative or heteronormative expressions of gender identity and sexual orientation (Bochicchio et al., 2022).

LGBTQ+ Mental Health Trends

LGBTQ+ mental health trends and statistics have demonstrated both changes and persistent challenges over time. In 1952, when the Diagnostic Statistical Manual (DSM) was first developed in the United States, identifying as LGBTQ+ was pathologized as a mental disorder (Drescher, 2015). These early categorizations of homosexuality as a disorder were primarily influenced by politically and socioculturally contingent concepts of deviance, rather than scientific validation. After nearly 20 years, this was finally removed from the DSM in 1973, reflecting a shift in societal attitudes and understanding of sexual orientation (Drescher, 2015; Kawa & Giordano, 2012). Since then, there has been increased recognition and visibility of LGBTQ+ mental health issues (Russell & Fish, 2016), with statistics highlighting disparities in mental health outcomes for LGBTQ+ individuals (Garofalo, 2011). Various factors play significant roles in shaping these mental health trends and disparities.

Positive factors, such as changes in societal attitudes (Movement Advancement Project, 2018; Poushter & Kent, 2020), the legalization of same-sex marriage (Perone, 2015), the implementation of antidiscrimination laws in certain states (Movement Advancement Project, 2018), and access to affirming healthcare services in certain states (US Department of Health and Human Services, 2022) have contributed to improved mental health outcomes for some LGBTQ+ individuals. However, ongoing stigma, discrimination, and marginalization within society and healthcare systems continue to pose significant barriers to LGBTQ+ mental health (Substance Abuse and Mental Health Services Administration, 2023). Seventy percent of the LGBTQ+ community reports experiencing pervasive discrimination in their everyday lives, often occurring within family dynamics, workplaces, social media platforms, public spaces, and interactions with individuals at their children's schools. Thirty-six percent of LGB individuals, as well as 54 percent of transgender and nonbinary individuals, report diminished feelings of safety in various everyday settings (e.g., walking in their own neighborhood or shopping at a store; GLAAD, 2022). These concerning statistics underscore the significant barriers faced by the LGBTQ+ community, with profound implications for their mental health and well-being.

Mental health outcomes of the LGBTQ+ population are often worse than those of heterosexual and cisgender individuals, with research indicating that LGB adults are twice as likely and transgender adults are four times as likely to suffer from a mental health condition compared to heterosexual or cisgender adults (National Alliance on Mental Illness, 2023). Based on US Census Data of LGBTQ+ individuals between the ages of 18 and 29, 61 percent experienced anxiety symptoms and 50 percent experienced depressive symptoms (Marlay, 2022). Among older adult LGBTQ+ individuals, 31 percent reported experiencing depressive symptoms (American Psychiatric Association, 2017), and 26 percent experiencing anxiety symptoms (Marlay, 2022). Additionally, research suggests that LGBTQ+ youth may also be particularly vulnerable to mental health challenges, experiencing higher rates of depression, anxiety, and suicidal ideation compared to their heterosexual and cisgender peers (National Alliance on Mental Illness, 2023).

Moreover, for individuals who belong to both the LGBTQ+ and ethnically minoritized groups, the convergence of these identities brings unique challenges and stressors that can significantly impact their mental health. For example, numerous global meta-analyses and systematic reviews have reported that individuals identifying as LGBTQ+ and ethnically minoritized face an increased risk of experiencing mental disorders in comparison to heterosexual individuals and ethnically privileged individuals (Ross et al., 2018; Tarricone et al., 2012). Thus, it is also critical to recognize the intricate interplay of intersecting identities, as it sheds light on the distinct mental health challenges faced by these populations and underscores the need for tailored and culturally competent mental health services for individuals with intersecting identities. Addressing these disparities requires comprehensive communicative approaches that address both individual-level and systemic factors influencing LGBTQ+ mental health.

Factors Related to LGBTQ+ Mental Health

LGBTQ+ mental health is multifaceted and influenced by a range of political, cultural, and social factors. Political actions, such as the passage of anti-LGBTQ+ legislation and policies, can have detrimental effects on mental health outcomes within LGBTQ+ communities. For example, no federal law exists that explicitly and comprehensively prohibits discrimination in public accommodations based on sexual orientation or gender identity (Movement Advancement Project, 2018). Additionally, growing efforts to limit and undermine nondiscrimination protections for LGBTQ+ people have been proposed in state legislatures in the United States, with over 520 bills targeting the LGBTQ+ community broadly and 220 bills specifically targeting the transgender and nonbinary community (Peele, 2023). Many of these bills are designed to restrict gender-affirming health care, bathroom access, teaching of LGBTQ+ educational content in K-12 schools, legal definitions of sex/gender, as well as allowing for misgendering or deadnaming of transgender individuals, and generally promoting discriminatory actions toward the LGBTQ+ community in various states (Peele, 2023). These measures contribute to a climate and culture of fear, discrimination, and exclusion, exacerbating mental health disparities among the LGBTQ+ community.

Stigma remains a pervasive and damaging force in the lives of LGBTQ+ individuals, exerting its influence across various facets of society. Whether in familial, educational, workplace, or societal settings, LGBTQ+ individuals often encounter prejudice, discrimination, and marginalization due to their sexual orientation or gender identity. This stigma can manifest in overt forms, such as hate speech and violence, as well as more subtle expressions like microaggressions and exclusionary practices (Bochicchio et al., 2022; Substance Abuse and Mental Health Services Administration, 2023; Terrace, 2011). These experiences of stigma not only undermine the mental health and well-being of LGBTQ+ individuals but also contribute to disparities in access to healthcare, education, employment opportunities, and social support networks (White, Sepúlveda, & Patterson, 2021). Addressing stigma against LGBTQ+ individuals requires comprehensive efforts to challenge discriminatory attitudes and policies, promote LGBTQ+ visibility and acceptance, and create inclusive environments that affirm the dignity and rights of all individuals, regardless of sexual orientation or gender identity.

Given the aforementioned problems—stigma, lack of inclusion and belonging, bullying, and anti-queer political legislation, to name a few—the question remains as to how communication theorists, practitioners, and interventions can make significant, positive impacts on LGBTQ+ individuals' health experiences. A cursory search of LGBTQ+ mental health on Google News, for example, reveals several articles that highlight the disproportionately high suicide rates that LGBTQ+ individuals face, particularly those who are LGBTQ+ adolescents. One case that generated many headlines in late 2023 was that of Pranshu, a queer 16-year-old makeup artist from Divine City, Ujjain, who died by suicide after an onslaught of relentless cyberbullying. Pranshu was an aspiring makeup artist and received over 4,000 comments on an Instagram reel, many of which were homophobic with problematic slurs. Pranshu's death has prompted many to critique problematic structures that do not hold individuals and organizations accountable for such deaths.

According to the Trevor Project (2024), suicide is the second leading cause of death among young people aged 10–14, and the third leading cause of death among 15–24-year-olds. Furthermore, LGBTQ+ teens are at a higher risk of suicide, as they are more than four times as likely to attempt suicide than their heterosexual or cisgender peers (Johns et al., 2019, 2020). According to the Trevor Project (2024), "more than 1.8 million LGBTQ+ young people (ages 13–24) seriously consider suicide each year in the US, and at least one attempts suicide every 45 seconds." LGBTQ+ adults are also more likely to attempt suicide than their cisgender and heterosexual peers, further highlighting the disparity and urgency shaping LGBTQ+ mental health (Ramchand et al., 2022).

Relevant Concepts and Theories to LGBTQ+ Mental Health Communication

Several concepts and theories emerge that can assist communication scholars in creating support and interventions aimed at addressing LGBTQ+ mental health concerns, such as cisheteronormativity, queer theory, intersectionality, minority stress theory, the Disclosure Decision-Making Model, the Theory of Resilience and Relational Load, and Relational Turbulence Theory. Such approaches represent a constellation of concepts, models, and theories that address various parts of the LGBTQ+ mental health spectrum. Cisheteronormativity helps us understand the structures that contribute to stigma for LGBTQ+ populations. Queer theory, minority stress theory, and intersectionality provide foundations for addressing the multiplicity of queer experiences, as well as a more complex and complete understanding of the various oppressions queer individuals face in multiple contexts. The Disclosure Decision-making Model, Theory of Resilience and Relational Load, and Relational Turbulence Theory provide theoretical insights into how queer individuals discuss their identities and experiences with family members, healthcare providers, and others in their social networks. Taken together, such concepts, theories, and models provide multifaceted approaches to exploring both the trends shaping LGBTQ+ mental health and the communicative health outcomes of interventions meant to address LGBTQ+ mental health. Thus, this section provides an overview of the concepts and theories before transitioning to an overview of interventions that utilize such approaches with improved health outcomes.

First, heteronormativity is defined as a "separate but overlapping relationship between heterosexual and cisgendered privilege stemming from patriarchal forces; having prejudice against non-hetero-sexuality and gender deviance" (Marchia & Sommer, 2019, p. 282). Discourses of heteronormativity pervade both contemporary society and medical contexts. Given the prioritization of biomedical discourses in the evolution of American medicine, cisgender masculinity has served as the cornerstone of medical research. Cisheteronormativity then foregrounds the impact of discourses of cissexism in their relationship to heteronormativity that position LGBTQ+ individuals as falling outside of the traditional bounds of biomedical bodies, science, and care (Franco-Rocha et al., 2023). In other words, cisheteronormativity positions cisgender, heterosexual individuals as the medical default and medical norm. As Franco-Rocha and colleagues (2023) note, cisheteronormativity can create discrimination-related and disparity-related challenges for queer individuals in healthcare systems. Furthermore, it can function as a social determinant of health because of the anxieties, tensions, and struggles it causes for LGBTQ+ individuals.

Second, queer theory provides a fruitful point of origin for considering how queer epistemologies can be utilized to enhance health communication research. In a forum article about queer theory and communication studies, Stephanie Young states:

> Queer theory is about possibilities. And queering communication research means challenging taken-for-granted aspects of communication scholarship through queerness and queer theory. Queer theory is about interrogating discourses of the deviant, the perverse, the stigmatized, the taboo, the grotesque, the non-normative, the sexual other. It's about ambiguity, contradiction, hybridity, fluidity, and sitting in uncertainty. It's about radically shifting our understandings. (Manning et al., 2020, p. 415)

Young elaborates further by noting:

> Although essential to queer scholarship and activism, queer means going beyond the inclusion and highlighting of gay, lesbian, bisexual, and transgender voices and experiences. Queer theory is about disrupting various regimes of normal, problematizing heteronormativity and critically examining sexual and gender binaries (see Warner, 1993). It's about using the sensual and sexual to reexamine the taken-for-granted epistemologies, ontologies, and ideologies that repress us. How do we understand the queer in queer research? We open ourselves up to possibilities. (Manning et al., 2020, p. 416)

In a forum piece entitled *Queering Communication Studies*, several queer communication studies scholars gathered to discuss considerations such as what it means to *do* queer communication studies research, *how* to do queer communication studies research, and how to work within and disrupt pre-existing paradigms to create new perspectives. Several important considerations emerged from this forum piece: (1) research on queer communities is not inherently queer, and queer theory can apply to communities that are not queer; (2) there is not one static definition for queer or one static approach for queer theory or queer communication research; (3) queering communication research provides space for possibility and transformation; and (4) it is activism oriented with the hopes of inspiring and creating change (Manning et al., 2020).

Third, minority stress theory and intersectionality explain the interrelated oppressions and barriers that queer individuals face. Minority stress theory articulates how prejudice, stigma, and discrimination collide to create a stressful, hostile social environment that can potentially lead to worsened mental health and general health outcomes (Meyer, 2003). Minority stress theory also positions minoritized individuals in a complicated societal space because it illustrates how minoritized communities face multiple societal, environmental, personal, and political stressors (Cyrus, 2017). As Cyrus's (2017) research illustrates, when utilized in LGBTQ+ mental health contexts, minority stress theory illuminates the excess stressors that LGBTQ+ individuals of color face because of their multiple oppressed identities. Similarly, intersectionality emerges as both an analytic and a guiding framework that could and should be utilized in studies and interventions targeting LGBTQ+ mental health. Intersectionality is defined as "the interconnected nature of social categorizations such as race, class, and gender as they apply to a given individual or group, regarded as creating overlapping and interdependent systems of discrimination or disadvantage" (Intersectionality, 2017). First coined and popularized by critical race and legal theorist Kimberle Crenshaw, intersectionality has significantly impacted a diverse number of fields and scholarly approaches:

> Intersectionality was introduced in the late 1980s as a heuristic term to focus attention on the vexed dynamics of difference and the solidarities of sameness in the context of antidiscrimination and social movement politics. It exposed how single-axis thinking undermines legal thinking, disciplinary knowledge production, and struggles for social justice. (Cho et al., 2013, p. 787)

In studies of LGBTQ+ communities of color and mental health, Cyrus (2017) asserts that "uncoupling identities and exploring ways in which intersectionality of not only gender, sexual orientation, and race, but also other identities (such as disability status), would provide greater insight into the heterogeneity that exists within each of these groups," adding greater insight into the unique experiences that queer individuals of color have across the spectrum of lived experiences (p. 200).

Fourth, the Disclosure Decision-Making Model, Relational Turbulence Theory, and Theory of Resilience and Relational Load provide a small network of approaches across communication subfields that illuminate communicative dynamics and tensions LGBTQ+ individuals face when communicating with family members, loved ones, and healthcare providers. The Disclosure Decision-Making Model (Greene, 2009) explores how individuals determine whether to disclose certain types of information to certain communicative and interactive participants. For LGBTQ+ individuals, the Disclosure Decision-Making Model illustrates the sense-making approaches that underlie whether an individual discloses their identities, preferences, their needs, and mental health concerns to those in their networks. As Friley and Venetis (2022) explain, the Disclosure Decision-Making Model positions information assessment as a driving disclosure force, meaning it reflects how individuals evaluate the content and reception of their disclosure. In this model, information assessment includes five factors: stigma, symptoms, relevance, prognosis, and preparation (Friley & Venetis, 2022).

Similarly, Relational Turbulence Theory holds promise for investigating LGBTQ+ experiences in family and mental health contexts (Lannutti et al., 2021). Relational Turbulence Theory, according to Solomon and colleagues (2016), expands the relationships among relational uncertainty and dependence, emotional, cognitive, and communicative experiences of specific episodes within relationships, and the effects and outcomes of relational turbulence. As Lannutti and colleagues (2021) illustrate, this theory can be utilized to explore significant transitions in family relationships, particularly LGBTQ+ relationships and transitions. Furthermore, this theory can be a fruitful framework for exploring LGBTQ+ individuals' mental health struggles amid relational conflict and transitions, as well. Lastly, the Theory of Resilience and Relational Load (Afifi, 2018) helps scholars understand how routine maintenance behaviors enact both resilience and thriving in relationships, particularly during stressful encounters or moments. The theory can also provide a useful lens through which to analyze how LGBTQ+ family relationships can assist queer individuals with mental health resilience, thriving, and relational satisfaction.

Taken together, concepts such as cisheteronormativity and intersectionality, when coupled with theories such as minority stress theory, the Disclosure Decision-Making Model, Relational Turbulence Theory, and the Theory of Resilience and Relational Load, provide a constellation of frameworks that can help scholars, researchers, and communicators further understand the communicative dynamics that shape LGBTQ+ relationships, as well as solutions for LGBTQ+ well-being. The next section provides an overview of various studies and interventions that have utilized diverse combinations of such concepts and theories to create programs for improved LGBTQ+ mental health and resilience.

Communicative Interventions: Strategies to Enhance LGBTQ+ Well-Being and Mental Health

In recent years, several studies have explored how to improve health outcomes and mental health outcomes for LGBTQ+ individuals at various stages in their lives and in various communicative contexts: as adolescents/young individuals, as college students, and when interacting with healthcare providers, to name a few. Thus, this section provides a snapshot of studies in this context that utilized a combination of the aforementioned concepts and theories to create better mental health spaces for LGBTQ+ individuals.

First, several studies have explored the impacts of family relationships, social friendships, and patient-provider relationships on LGBTQ+ individuals' mental health, experiences with stigma, and general discrimination in health communication contexts. In community contexts for LGBTQ+ youth, research has shown that narrative- and culture-based digital storytelling programs can meaningfully support health promotion efforts for queer youth. As Fiddian-Green, Gubrium, and Peterson (2017) found, their program entitled "Let's Talk About Sex: Digital Storytelling for Puerto Rican Latina Youth" helped Latina teens discuss their sexual values, practices, and experiences. Utilizing guiding frameworks of stigma, discrimination, sexuality, digital storytelling, and the culture-centered approach, their program highlighted the coming out experiences of Latina youth and the health implications of their queer experiences in cultural contexts. Fiddian-Green et al. (2017) concluded that when blended together, the culture-centered approach and digital storytelling methods break down barriers of heteronormativity, deconstruct dominant discourses of sexuality in Latino contexts, bring light to the stigma and fear that queer youth face, and present a mode of empowerment for queer youth to tell their stories in a supportive context with the goal of better health outcomes and experiences.

Second, research has also interrogated queer mental health experiences in patient-provider contexts. Due to prevailing discourses of healthism and cisheteronormativity, LGBTQ+ individuals rarely experience compassion in healthcare contexts (Joy et al., 2022). In a study of sexual disclosures with predominantly White, queer communities, Hudak and Carmack (2018) found that several factors impact LGB patients' communicative disclosure willingness and experiences, such as fear of gossip and connection, positive and negative relationships with family members, and varying levels of trust with providers. Hudak and Bates (2019) also found that queer patients are often concerned about how disclosing their gender identity or sexuality could negatively impact them, particularly if they suspected that their providers were not queer-friendly. Similarly, Burdick and Nicholus (2022) found that Latinx LGB patients faced fears and experiences when considering providing disclosures of their sexuality, namely fears of gossip and discrimination and fears about whether they could open pathways of disclosure with healthcare providers and trust them.

One strategy that can improve LGBTQ+ patients' mental health in patient-provider contexts is addressing medical student gaps in LGBTQ+ health education. As Fadus (2019) asserts, medical students must become familiar with core aspects of mental health considerations for LGBTQ+ patients, such as stigma, discrimination, body image issues, experiences associated with identity disclosures (or the coming out process), and substance use disorders. Furthermore, as Fadus (2019) explains, medical students should also receive formal training on the communicative dynamics of having such conversations, given the lack of educational and clinical opportunities provided to medical students during their curriculum. Another strategy that can improve LGBTQ+ patients' mental health in patient-provider contexts is physician heteronormativity awareness training, which sensitizes healthcare providers' knowledge of LGBTQ+ terms and identities and seeks to reduce further stigmatization and discrimination of LGBTQ+ patients (Burdick & Nicholus, 2022; Utamsingh et al., 2016). Culture-centered approaches to improving patient-provider communication with transgender individuals could also result in better health outcomes for transgender patients (Friley & Venetis, 2022; Ross & Bell, 2017).

Third, interventions have explored how school-based programs, peer counseling programs, and camp programs can result in better mental health experiences and relationships for LGBTQ+ individuals. Through the lens of minority stress theory, Goldbach et al. (2023) created an intervention promoting LGBTQ+ adolescent mental health. Their program entitled "Proud & Empowered" was designed to help LGBTQ+ adolescents cope with minority stress experiences. The program connected LGBTQ+ adolescents with other individuals who served as facilitators, and the adolescents learned about stressors, coping mechanisms, relationships, resilience, social justice, and community building. LGBTQ+ adolescents discussed in the intervention the impacts of structural stressors, particularly in school contexts, and the intervention later partnered with school-based training facilitators to ensure that such an intervention could be provided in schools.

Another program explored by Gillig and Bighash (2023) analyzed self-esteem, depressive symptoms, and anxiety in 238 LGBTQ+ adolescents who participated in a summer camp intervention. The nonprofit organization Brave Trails, founded in Los Angeles, hosts an annual summer camp for LGBTQ+ youth ages 12–18, and this program served as the basis of Gillig and Bighash's study. The program is designed to inclusively affirm LGBTQ+ identity and includes components focusing on workshops, drag classes, traditional camp programming, and activism training. Gillig and Bighash (2023) found that the Brave Trails camp programming affirmed LGBTQ+ adolescents' identities and was associated with increased self-esteem, decreased depressive symptoms, and decreased anxiety.

Lastly, Eger et al. (2024) analyzed the impacts of a US university student health communication outreach program referred to as SHARE-Pride (Sexual Health Assessment and Risk Education). In the SHARE-Pride program, college students served as mentors who communicate about health, gender, and sexuality with their peers. Through the lens of intersectionality and identity affirmation, Eger et al. (2024) explored the impacts of a SHARE-Pride program approach with LGBTQ+ college students and found that it (1) empowered undergraduate students as experts with peers by connecting them with critical organizations on campus and other students; (2) supported the call for more culturally relevant programming for LGBTQ+ students; (3) highlighted the need for more LGBTQ+ inclusive health communication programming and research; and (4) illustrated the complexity of how intersectionality, stigma, and oppression shape LGBTQ+ experiences and programming, particularly in health contexts.

Conclusion

LGBTQ+ populations experience disproportionately negative health and mental health outcomes resulting from cisheteronormativity, discrimination, and stigma, among other causes. As illustrated in this chapter, concepts such as intersectionality and identity affirmation and theories such as minority stress theory can work together to create better mental health outcomes in family relationship, social relationship, and patient-provider relationship contexts. Culturally competent programming and interventions have great potential and promise to encourage better mental health outcomes for LGBTQ+ communities, and further research should continue to explore effective strategic approaches to improve LGBTQ+ mental health.

Recommended Readings/Resources

Garofalo, R. (2011). *The health of lesbian, gay, bisexual, and transgender people: Building a foundation for better understanding*. The National Academies Press.

Manning, J., Asante, G., Huerta Moreno, L., Johnson, R., LeMaster, B., Li, Y., ... & Young, S. (2020). Queering communication studies: a Journal of Applied Communication Research forum. *Journal of Applied Communication Research, 48*(4), 413–437.

Marlay, M., F. Thom, & Scherer, Z. (2022). Mental health struggles higher among LGBT adults than non-LGBT adults in all age groups. Retrieved from https://www.census.gov/library/stories/2022/12/lgbt-adults-report-anxiety-depression-at-all-ages.html

Trevor Project. (2022). 2022 *National survey on LGBTQ youth mental health.* Retrieved from https://www.thetrevorproject.org/survey-2022/

References

Afifi, T. D. (2018). Individual/relational resilience. *Journal of Applied Communication Research, 46*(1), 5–9.

American Psychiatric Association, A. P. A. (2017). Mental health disparities: LGBTQ.

American Psychological Association, A. P. A. (2022). A guide to sexual orientation and gender diversity terms. Retrieved from https://www.apa.org/ed/precollege/psychology-teacher-network/introductorypsychology/diversity-terms

Bochicchio, L., Reeder, K., Ivanoff, A., Pope, H., & Stefancic, A. (2022). Psychotherapeutic interventions for LGBTQ+ youth: A systematic review. *Journal of LGBT youth, 19*(2), 152–179.

Brown, A. (2023). 5 key findings about LGBTQ+ Americans. Retrieved from https://www.pewresearch.org/short-reads/2023/06/23/5-key-findings-about-lgbtq-americans/

Burdick, S., & Nicholus, S. (2022). A pilot study of Latinx lesbian, gay, and bisexual adolescent patients' goal prioritizations in patient-provider sexual orientation and health disclosures. *Health Communication, 37*(9), 1215–1228.

Cho, S., Crenshaw, K. W., & McCall, L. (2013). Toward a field of intersectionality studies: Theory, applications, and praxis. *Signs: Journal of Women in Culture and Society, 38*(4), 785–810.

Cislaghi, B., & Heise, L. (2020). Gender norms and social norms: Differences, similarities and why they matter in prevention science. *Sociology of Health & Illness, 42*(2), 407–422.

Cyrus, K. (2017). Multiple minorities as multiply marginalized: Applying the minority stress theory to LGBTQ people of color. *Journal of Gay & Lesbian Mental Health, 21*(3), 194–202.

Drescher, J. (2015). Out of DSM: Depathologizing homosexuality. *Behavioral Sciences, 5*(4), 565–575.

Eger, E. K., Villagran, M. M., & Burney, M. (2024). LGBTQ+ peer advocates' health communication praxis for college student health outreach and intersectional needs. *Health Communication, 39*(13), 3084–3096.

Fadus, M. (2019). Mental health disparities and medical student education: Teaching in psychiatry for LGBTQ care, communication, and advocacy. *Academic Psychiatry, 43*(3), 306–310.

Fiddian-Green, A., Gubrium, A. C., & Peterson, J. C. (2017). Puerto Rican Latina youth coming out to talk about sexuality and identity. *Health Communication, 32*(9), 1093–1103.

Franco-Rocha, O. Y., Wheldon, C. W., Osier, N., Lett, E., Kesler, S. R., Henneghan, A. M., & Suárez-Baquero, D. F. M. (2023). Cisheteronormativity and its influence on the psychosocial experience of LGBTQ+ people with cancer: A qualitative systematic review. *Psycho-Oncology, 32*(6), 834–845.

Friley, L. B., & Venetis, M. K. (2022). Decision-making criteria when contemplating disclosure of transgender identity to medical providers. *Health Communication, 37*(8), 1031–1040.

Garofalo, R. (2011). *The health of lesbian, gay, bisexual, and transgender people: Building a foundation for better understanding*. The National Academies Press.

Gillig, T. K., & Bighash, L. (2023). Network and proximity effects on LGBTQ youth's psychological outcomes during a camp intervention. *Health Communication, 38*(4), 641–647.

GLAAD. (2022). *Unsafe in American: Annual GLAAD accelerating acceptance study finds sharp increase in LGBTQ Americans experiencing discrimination*. https://glaad.org/releases/unsafe-america-annual-glaad-accelerating-acceptance-study-finds-sharp-increase-lgbtq/

Goldbach, J. T., Rhoades, H., Rusow, J., & Karys, P. (2023). The Development of Proud & Empowered: An Intervention for Promoting LGBTQ Adolescent Mental Health. *Child Psychiatry and Human Development*, 54(2), 481–492. https://doi.org/10.1007/s10578-021-01250-2.

Greene, K. (2009). An integrated model of health disclosure decision-making. In T. D. Afifi & W. A. Afifi (Eds.), *Uncertainty and information regulation in interpersonal contexts: Theories and applications* (pp. 226–253). Routledge.

Hudak, N., & Bates, B. R. (2019). In pursuit of "queer-friendly" healthcare: An interview study of how queer individuals select care providers. *Health Communication, 34*(8), 818–824.

Hudak, N. C., & Carmack, H. J. (2018). Waiting for the doctor to ask: Influencers of lesbian, gay, and bisexual identity disclosure for health-care providers. *Qualitative Research in Medicine and Healthcare, 2*(20), 20–29.

Johns, M. M., Lowry, R., Andrzejewski, J., Barrios, L. C., Zewditu, D., McManus, T., et al. (2019). Transgender identity and experiences of violence victimization, substance use, suicide risk, and sexual risk behaviors among high school student–19 states and large urban school districts, 2017. *Morbidity and Mortality Weekly Report, 68*(3), 65–71.

Johns, M. M., Lowry, R., Haderxhanaj, L. T., et al. (2020). Trends in violence victimization and suicide risk by sexual identity among high school students — Youth Risk Behavior Survey, United States, 2015–2019. *Morbidity and Mortality Weekly Report*, *69* (Suppl- 1), 19–27.

Jones, J. M. (2022). LGBT identification in US ticks up to 7.1%. Retrieved from https://news.gallup.com/poll/389792/lgbt-identification-ticks-up.aspx

Joy, P., Thomas, A., & Aston, M. (2022). Compassionate discourses: A qualitative study exploring how compassion can transform healthcare for 2SLGBTQ+ people. *Qualitative Health Research*, *32*(10), 1514–1526.

Kawa, S., & Giordano, J. (2012). A brief historicity of the Diagnostic and Statistical Manual of Mental Disorders: Issues and implications for the future of psychiatric canon and practice. *Philosophy, Ethics, and Humanities in Medicine*, 7, 1–9.

Oxford University Press. (2017). *Intersectionality.* In Oxford English dictionary online. Retrieved from https://en.oxforddictionaries.com/definition/intersectionality

Lannutti, P. J., Butauski, M., Rubinsky, V., & Hudak, N. (2021). Setting the agenda: LGBTQ+ and SGM family communication. *Journal of Family Communication*, *21*(2), 138–143.

Liou, D. (2023). From drag bans to sports restrictions, 75 anti-LGBTQ bills have become law in 2023. *NBC News*. Retrieved from https://www.nbcnews.com/nbc-out/out-politics-and-policy/75-anti-lgbtq-bills-become-law-2023-rcna124250

Manning, J., Asante, G., Huerta Moreno, L., Johnson, R., LeMaster, B., Li, Y., & Young, S. (2020). Queering communication studies: A journal of applied communication research forum. *Journal of Applied Communication Research*, *48*(4), 413–437.

Marchia, J., & Sommer, J. M. (2019). (Re)defining heteronormativity. *Sexualities*, *22*(3), 267–295.

Marlay, M., F. Thom, & Scherer, Z. (2022). Mental health struggles higher among LGBT adults than non-LGBT adults in all age groups. Retrieved from https://www.census.gov/library/stories/2022/12/lgbt-adults-report-anxiety-depression-at-all-ages.html

Meyer, I. H. (2003). Prejudice, social stress, and mental health in lesbian, gay, and bisexual populations: Conceptual issues and research evidence. *Psychological Bulletin*, *129*(5), 674–697.

Movement Advancement Project, M. A. P. (2018). LGBT policy spotlight: Public accommodations nondiscrimination laws. Retrieved from https://www.lgbtmap.org/policy-and-issue-analysis/policy-spotlight-public-accommodations

National Alliance on Mental Illness, N. A. o. M. I. (2023). LGBTQ+. Retrieved from https://www.nami.org/Your-Journey/Identity-and-Cultural-Dimensions/LGBTQ

Pachankis, J. E., Clark, K. A., Jackson, S. D., Pereira, K., & Levine, D. (2021). Current capacity and future implementation of mental health services in US LGBTQ community centers. *Psychiatric Services*, *72*(6), 669–676.

Patterson, C. J., Sepúlveda, M.-J., & White, J. (2021). *Understanding the well-being of LGBTQI+ populations*. The National Academies Press.

Peele, C. (2023). Roundup of anti-LGBTQ+ legislation advancing in states across the country. *Human Rights Campaign*, 2023–2009.

Perone, A. K. (2015). Health implications of the Supreme Court's Obergefell vs. Hodges marriage equality decision. *LGBT Health*, *2*(3), 196–199.

Poushter, J., & Kent, N. (2020). The global divide on homosexuality persists. *Pew Research Center*, *25*.

Powell, L. (2021). We are here: LGBTQ+ adult population in United States reaches at least 20 million, according to Human Rights Campaign Foundation report. *Human Rights Campaign*. https://www.hrc.org/press-releases/we-are-here-lgbtq-adult-population-in-united-states-reaches-at-least-20-million-according-to-human-rights-campaign-foundation-report

Ramchand, R., Schuler, M. S., Schoenbaum, M., Colpe, L., & Ayer, L. (2022). Suicidality among sexual minority adults: gender, age, and race/ethnicity differences. *American Journal of Preventive Medicine*, *62*(2), 193–202.

Ross, K. A., & Castle Bell, G. (2017). A culture-centered approach to improving healthy trans-patient–practitioner communication: Recommendations for practitioners communicating with trans individuals. *Health Communication*, *32*(6), 730–740.

Ross, L. E., Salway, T., Tarasoff, L. A., MacKay, J. M., Hawkins, B. W., & Fehr, C. P. (2018). Prevalence of depression and anxiety among bisexual people compared to gay, lesbian, and heterosexual individuals: A systematic review and meta-analysis. *The Journal of Sex Research*, *55*(4–5), 435–456.

Russell, S. T., & Fish, J. N. (2016). Mental health in lesbian, gay, bisexual, and transgender (LGBT) youth. *Annual Review of Clinical Psychology*, *12*, 465–487.

SAMHSA. (2023). SAMHSA releases new data on lesbian, gay and bisexual behavioral health. Retrieved from https://www.samhsa.gov/newsroom/press-announcements/20230613/samhsa-releases-new-data-lesbian-gay-bisexual-behavioral-health

Solomon, D. H., Knobloch, L. K., Theiss, J. A., & McLaren, R. M. (2016). Relational turbulence theory: Explaining variation in subjective experiences and communication within romantic relationships. *Human Communication Research*, *42*(4), 507–532.

Substance Abuse and Mental Health Services Administration, S. (2023). *Moving beyond change efforts: Evidence and action to support and affirm LGBTQI+ youth*. Retrieved from https://store.samhsa.gov/product/moving-beyond-change-efforts-evidence-and-action-support-and-affirm-lgbtqi-youth/pep22-03-12-001

Tarricone, I., Stivanello, E., Poggi, F., Castorini, V., Marseglia, M. V., Fantini, M. P., & Berardi, D. (2012). Ethnic variation in the prevalence of depression and anxiety in primary care: A systematic review and meta-analysis. *Psychiatry Research*, *195*(3), 91–106.

Terrace, O. (2011). *Advancing effective communication, cultural competence, and patient- and family-centered care for the lesbian, gay, bisexual, and transgender (LGBT) community: A field guide*. Joint Commission.

Trevor Project. (2024). 2022 National survey on LGBTQ youth mental health. Retrieved from https://www.thetrevorproject.org/survey-2022/.

U.S. Department of Health and Human Services, U. S. D. o. H. a. H. S. (2022). *HHS notice and guidance on gender affirming care civil rights and patient privacy.* Retrieved from https://www.hhs.gov/sites/default/files/hhs-ocr-notice-and-guidance-gender-affirming-care.pdf

Utamsingh, P. D., Richman, L. S., Martín, J. L., Lattanner, M. R., & Chaikind, J. R. (2016). Heteronormativity and practitioner-patient interaction. *Health Communication, 31*(5), 566–574.

Warner, M. (Ed.). (1993). Fear of a queer planet: Queer politics and social theory. University of Minnesota Press.

3

An Examination of the Multifaceted Mental Health Stigma Surrounding US Military Veterans

Rikki A. Roscoe

Military Stigma

> *Being a man, trying to be a leader of people who are being asked to kill other human beings, it takes a certain level of mental focus, of mental strength, and when you start to lose that edge, and you start to not be able to do your job because of those things . . . there's a stigma behind it. Mental health . . . there's no such thing. You suck it up and drive on. I truly believed that while I was leading soldiers all the way up to the point where I was having a bunch of mental health problems. I was a 25-year-old kid in charge of forty guys in Bagdad—all of them with more experience than me. I had to keep it together. There could be no chinks in my armor. I had no choice but to be strong. I totally believed that—suck it up and drive on—but after a while, that stuff starts to weigh on you, and, you know, it's like a bottle of champagne. You just keep shaking it up until you pop the cork, and it's everywhere. You don't really know how to get it back in the bottle.*
>
> —Matthew, Research Participant, US Military Veteran of Operations Post-9/11

Here, Matthew is explaining the impact of *military stigma*, which is described as "the military enculturation that seeking mental health services would be discrediting or embarrassing, cause harm to career progression, or cause peers or supervisors to have decreased confidence in members' ability to perform assigned duties" (Hernandez et al., 2016, p. 191). The United States (US) military organization has historically promoted "stoicism, self-reliance, and prioritizing the needs of the unit over the needs of the individual" (True et al., 2014, p. 4).

Indeed, resilience is instilled in military personnel from basic training onward, as is the importance of being psychologically and physically healthy in order to contribute to the success of the mission (Britt & Klinefelter, 2022). Thus, service members are expected to "maintain a high level of mental, technical, and physical preparedness so that they can perform duties when called upon" (Hernandez et al., 2016, p. 190).

Within the military organization, mental illness is likely to be regarded as a sign of weakness (Roscoe, 2023a) that poses a threat not only to the success of a mission but also to service members' careers (Mittal et al., 2013). A study by the National Academies of Sciences (2018) stated that veterans were severely chastised and discouraged from reporting any medical issues that showed weakness. Furthermore, veterans expressed that they had a hard time believing they could share their concerns regarding mental health without receiving backlash, even after leaving active duty (National Academies of Sciences, 2018). When service members do leave active duty, they face a new form of stigma as they reintegrate into civilian life: public stigma.

Public Stigma

> *When it comes to the news, it's only the negative stories that are ever put out there. You know what I mean? Everyone has heard news stories on how someone who may have had PTSD killed themselves in a parking lot or stole a car and ran some people over on a highway. If a marine beat up his wife and he had PTSD, that's all they're going to say. He was a marine with PTSD that beat his wife to death. That's going to be the story. The guy who went crazy and killed his whole family or something in a drunken rage. There's not going to be any context as to what was happening.*
>
> —Austin, Research Participant, US Military Veteran of Operations Post-9/11

This vignette comes from just one of many US military veterans who voiced their frustration at the media during in-depth interviews regarding the stigma surrounding veterans experiencing post-traumatic stress[1] (PTS). Specifically, these veterans, who had experienced PTS firsthand, argued that the media poorly portrayed veterans with PTS as "crazy," "psycho," or "murderers," and ultimately perpetuated stigma about them (Roscoe, 2023a, p. 459). These comments demonstrate the *public stigma*, a term used to describe a set of stigmatizing attitudes and beliefs held by members of society (Corrigan, 2004).

Research has shown that veterans are less likely to participate in mental health treatment if they perceive more significant levels of public stigma (Kulesza et al., 2015). Furthermore, military veterans may internalize the public's stigmatizing perceptions, which can lead to self-stigma.

Self-Stigma

"I didn't go to be seen for probably several years, and then I was medically diagnosed with PTSD. I didn't go in looking for PTSD. I went in for other issues I was having, and that came up while I was there." When asked why he waited to go seek help, Andrew, a research participant, responded, *"Because I am an old-timer, and to me, it's kind of a weakness . . . I don't hold others to the same standard that I hold myself, though. That's a little wrong, but that's the way it is."* After the diagnosis, Andrew felt *"angry"* and described working *"harder and harder to address the situation because [his] ultimate goal is to get rid of the diagnosis."*

These comments from Andrew demonstrate how military veterans internalize mental health stigma or self-stigmatize. Corrigan and Rao (2012) describe self-stigma as the endorsement of negative stereotypes and prejudice that result in self-discrimination. Self-stigma has "often been equated with perceived stigma, a person's recognition that the public holds prejudice and will discriminate against them because of their mental illness" (Corrigan & Rao, 2012, p. 2). Thus, a veteran experiencing PTS may engage in self-stigma when they internalize the public or military stigma about their social group (e.g., that they are weak). Self-stigma is concerning, considering it can lead to low self-esteem and poor self-efficacy, which can then lead to self-isolation, decreased healthcare service use, poor health outcomes, and poor quality of life (Corrigan & Rao, 2012).

The Problem of Mental Illness Stigma among Military Veterans

Thus far, we have established how military veterans with PTS experience stigma within the military (i.e., military stigma) and from members of society (i.e., public stigma). Veterans may then internalize this stigma, endorsing the negative perceptions of themselves (i.e., self-stigma). Ultimately, the effects of stigmatizing messages among people diagnosed with mental illness can be devastating. Previous research demonstrates that, due to mental health stigma, military veterans experiencing PTS often attempt to cope without seeking professional treatment (Hernandez et al., 2016; Roscoe, 2021). This is troubling because the veterans who forego needed psychiatric treatment are at greater risk of isolation and reduced self-esteem (West et al., 2011), as well as substance abuse, severe depression, and suicide (Hoge et al., 2006). In 2020, an average of 17 US veterans died by suicide each day (Veterans Affairs, 2021). Furthermore, while just over 7,000 US service members died in post-9/11 war operations, it is estimated that 30,177 died by suicide (Suitt, 2021).

It is vital to understand the multifaceted stigma that deters many veterans from seeking help, as well as how veterans manage the stigma. Thus, the next sections will use the model of stigma communication (MSC; Smith, 2007) to outline how stigma is communicated about military veterans experiencing PTS and stigma management communication theory (SMC; Meisenbach, 2010) to outline how veterans communicatively manage and cope with mental health stigma. A better understanding of the role of mental health stigma is necessary in order to develop interventions that can reduce the prevalence of stigma and thereby facilitate treatment-seeking among military veterans.

Understanding and Assessing Mental Health Stigma Through the Model of Stigma Communication

Stigma is understood as a deeply discrediting attribute that diminishes individuals from whole and usual to tainted and discounted (Goffman, 1963). Stigma relies heavily on communication, considering messages must be shared between group members. Stigma communication, then, is described as "the messages spread through communities to teach their members to recognize the disgraced and react accordingly" (Smith, 2007, p. 464).

MSC (Smith, 2007) was developed to better understand the role of communication in stigmatizing individuals and groups. According to Smith (2007), stigmatizing messages must include content that rapidly gains attention, encourages stereotyping, validates emotional reactions in response to a stigmatized individual, and creates a separation between stigmatized groups and the rest of society. MSC outlines four message content cues that achieve this purpose, including *marks* (nonverbal content used to identify members of a stigmatized group), *labels* (terms created and used by stigmatizers to refer to the stigmatized group), *etiology* (cues that imply responsibility or blame for attaining or maintaining the stigma), and *social peril* (cues that link the group to physical and social peril). Ultimately, these four content cues evoke emotional reactions (e.g., fear, anger, disgust) that result in stigma-related outcomes (e.g., discrimination), including the spread of the message, which facilitates diffusion (Zhu & Smith, 2021). MSC is useful in helping assess how stigma is communicated about military veterans experiencing PTS in a variety of contexts. Thus, we will walk through each content cue.

Marks

First, marking a stigmatized individual or group involves using nonverbal content to identify members of a stigmatized group (Zhu & Smith, 2021). Marks may include symbols (e.g., tattoos), attributes (e.g., sores on the skin), or stereotypes (e.g., laziness), and can be visible or invisible (Zhu & Smith, 2021). Marks may evoke quick recognition and instinctive responses (Smith, 2007), but recognition depends on the stigma's visibility or awareness. For example, Smith (2007) explained that marks that cannot be easily concealed provide a greater opportunity to be recognized. However, some stigmatized groups, such as veterans experiencing PTS, are unique in having an invisible stigma attribute that can be concealed. Although not categorized as marks, previous research by Mittal et al. (2013) suggested that veterans perceived being stereotyped as "nonsocial," "numb," and "cold-hearted"—among other things. Again, these are not physical nor visible attributes that would evoke quick recognition but represent stigmatizing stereotypes about veterans experiencing PTS.

The largely invisible nature of mental illness may lead society members to blanket veterans with stigma (Roscoe, 2023a). Since members of society cannot see a physical mark on a veteran experiencing PTS, they are left to assume whether a veteran has the condition. In this case, the veteran identity alone is enough to evoke a stigmatizing or speculative reaction. Therefore, all veterans may be at risk of facing communicative mental health stigma, whether they experience symptoms of mental illness or not (Roscoe, 2023a).

One mark of significant importance is weakness. Previous research has demonstrated that the majority of veterans returning home from Iraq and Afghanistan who reported symptoms of mental illness thought they would be perceived as weak if they sought help (Hoge et al., 2004). More recently, during a one-on-one research interview, a military veteran reinforced that mental illness was a weakness by arguing that other veterans "need to stop being such Jell-O" and instead "be tougher people" (quoted from Roscoe, 2023a, p. 454). Instead of seeking help, this veteran concealed his mental illness "in order to portray or be viewed as a legitimate stone" despite "freaking out because [he] thinks about picking up [his] battle buddies' brains off the floor every day" (quoted from Roscoe, 2021, pp. 453–454). In this revelation, we see a subscription to military cultural norms of stoicism and self-reliance (True et al., 2014) and how it may lead to a lack of help-seeking overall.

Weakness as a stigmatizing mark may be more prominent within the military context. Roscoe and Anderson (2019) examined differences between veterans' and civilians' perceptions of veterans experiencing PTS and found that 40 percent of veterans associated weakness with veterans who experience PTS. In contrast, only 16.3 percent of civilians made the same association. A similar finding was found when interviewing military veterans with PTS. Specifically, weakness was frequently discussed when participants described military stigma, but was not mentioned when describing public stigma (Roscoe, 2023a). These differences may exist because the discourse about veterans experiencing PTS is different in the military than it is throughout society.

Group Labels

Second, stigmatizers may develop and use group labels to refer to stigmatized individuals or groups (Smith, 2007). For example, stigmatizers may use the term *schizophrenic* to refer to individuals diagnosed with schizophrenia (Zhu & Smith, 2021). Group labels often bring attention to the stigma and suggest that they are a separate and different social entity from those who are considered normal (Smith, 2007). Several labels have been assigned to military veterans experiencing PTS, including "blackouts," "psychos," and "damaged goods" (Roscoe, 2023a, p. 455).

Although not explicitly stated as such, previous research demonstrates that stigmatizing labels often represent metaphors that compare military veterans experiencing PTS to animals, monsters, and machines (Mittal et al., 2013; Roscoe, 2023a). For instance, veterans perceived being viewed as "diseased animals," "beasts," and "monsters" by members of society (Roscoe, 2023a, p. 455). One veteran argued that veterans with PTS are considered "cold-blooded killers." In terms of machine labels, one veteran used the term "robots" (p. 455), and another self-labeled, sharing, "I went from being a civilian to being a freaking machine" (p. 453). Ultimately, these metaphorical labels depict veterans as dangerous, unpredictable, and different from what is considered a normal human being.

Mental illness is essentially invisible, and therefore, military veterans are afforded the ability to choose whether to disclose their condition or not. Awareness of group labels such as *malingerer* can impact veterans' willingness to disclose. Specifically, the invisibility of PTS, according to some veterans, may allow veterans to fake the illness to get out of work, get medically discharged, or receive disability benefits (Roscoe, 2023a). Veterans described experiences where they felt another military service member might be faking their symptoms but described difficulty addressing the issue. Roscoe (2023a) pointed out that veterans experiencing PTS sometimes engaged in prototype matching, which is when people "have a prototypic model of an illness and must determine if the symptoms experienced are consistent with that prototype" (Spoont et al., 2009, p. 1460). Specifically, veterans compared other service members to what they believed was consistent with PTS. In one case, the prototype was a veteran with PTS who had lost his life to suicide (Roscoe, 2023a).

Not only did veterans have difficulty distinguishing whether their peers were genuine about having PTS, but they feared others would stigmatize them for faking the diagnosis. Roscoe (2023a) explained that this form of stigma, which is unique to those who have invisible illnesses, may decrease help-seeking. This may especially be the case for veterans who feel they may not match the prototypical individual with PTS.

Etiology

Third, stigmatizing messages may frame people as personally responsible for choosing their stigmatized condition or eliminating the stigma (Smith, 2007). More recently, this content cue has been described in relation to etiology, which frames how people become associated with a stigmatized group (Zhu & Smith, 2021). Etiology content focuses on stigmatized individuals' agentic, voluntary, and controllable decisions rather than recognizing health conditions as a product of multiple and complex forces—such as one's environment (Zhu & Smith, 2021).

Personal responsibility was an emerging theme in the study conducted by Mittal et al. (2013), where participants expressed that society held them accountable for their mental illness because "they volunteered for military service, and therefore, knowingly put themselves at risk" (p. 89). Another study found that 51 percent of combat veterans returning from Operation Iraqi Freedom (OIF) and Operation Enduring Freedom (OEF) felt they would be blamed for their illness if they sought help (Hoge et al., 2004).

In contrast, a study of 164 veterans and non-veterans conducted by Roscoe and Anderson (2019) showed that participants rarely held veterans personally responsible for developing or overcoming PTSD. Interestingly, personal responsibility content often converged with marking. Specifically, Roscoe (2023a) pointed out that those who were unwilling to take on the responsibility of seeking help and instead chose to take their own lives were marked as weak. For example, one military veteran shared, "I do think there is a touch, even my friends who kill themselves, I do see a touch of weakness there because they couldn't ask for help. They couldn't try to figure out how to get help" (quoted from Roscoe, 2023a, p. 454). Similarly, another veteran claimed:

> If you've got a problem . . . you're going to get help before you take your own life. The way I look at it, if you're not going to go get help, it means you're weak. . . . If you need help, go get it.

Earlier, we saw that veterans were stigmatized as weak when they acknowledged or sought help for mental illness. Here, veterans with PTS are being held personally responsible for not seeking help and are considered weak for dying by suicide, or as one veteran described, "eating the muzzle" (Roscoe, 2023a, p. 454).

Social Peril

Fourth, stigmatizers may frame individuals or groups as morally or physically perilous by highlighting the danger or threat they pose (Smith, 2007). Stigmatizing messages that highlight peril imply that people must take action to avoid the stigmatized person. Thus, perilous messages resemble product warning labels that signal hazards and negative consequences (Zhu & Smith, 2021). The threat posed by veterans experiencing PTS is largely dependent on the context (e.g., within the military or among the general public).

Within the military context, active service members with PTS may be perceived as a threat to group functioning and the success of operations. As previously described, military stigma is the discrediting and devaluation of a military service member due to seeking mental health services, which can lead to decreased confidence in members' ability to perform assigned duties (Hernandez et al., 2016). Indeed, mental stability and toughness are "unwritten requirements for surviving in the military environment" (Simmons & Yoder, 2013, p. 18). As a result of military stigma, service members may feel pressure to conceal their mental health issues. For example, previous research by Hoge et al. (2004) demonstrated that returning OIF/OEF combat veterans felt that if they sought help, their unit members would have less confidence in them (59%), felt that they would be treated differently by others (63%), and felt that it would harm their careers (50%). Furthermore, another study of US Marines found that 48.9 percent of participants feared that their commands would lose trust in them if they sought mental health services (Momen et al., 2012).

Outside of the military, veterans experiencing PTS may be viewed as unstable and physically dangerous by members of society. Indeed, many of the previously described stigmatizing labels and marks communicate perilous messages about military veterans experiencing PTS. Specifically, veterans held the perception that civilians viewed them as *violent*, *crazy*, and *untrustworthy* (Mittal et al., 2013; Roscoe, 2023a). One veteran argued that civilians think they "have to watch" veterans or "be careful of them" because they "don't know what they're going to do" (quoted from Roscoe, 2023a, p. 456). Once again, stigmatizing messages suggest that veterans are unstable and dangerous and, therefore, should be feared and avoided.

As aforementioned, veterans argue that the media is partially to blame for perpetuating stigmatizing, particularly perilous perceptions of veterans experiencing PTS (Parrott, 2023; Roscoe & Anderson, 2019; Roscoe, 2023a). While veterans in previous research discussed news representations (Parrott, 2023; Roscoe et al., 2024), mental health stigma is also perpetuated in entertainment media. Specifically, Armstrong and Olatunji (2009) described that since the US invasion of Iraq, news and entertainment media have increasingly showcased veterans in a stigmatizing light, with fictional characters embodying stigmatizing stereotypes associated with PTS.

Overall, MSC is a helpful tool in analyzing how stigma is communicated about stigmatized groups. All four stigma communication content cues (marks, labels, etiology, and peril) are used to communicate stigma about military veterans experiencing PTS. The interrogation of the communication surrounding PTS is vital in destigmatizing mental health and developing interventions. However, it is also essential to consider how military veterans experiencing PTS manage and cope with mental health stigma.

Stigma Management Communication

SMC theory includes three axioms, several propositions, and a strategy typology that can "improve understanding of and can suggest paths for stigma management for many individuals suffering from moments and consequences of stigmatization" (Meisenbach, 2010, p. 270). SMC organizes stigma management strategies according to the stigmatized individual's acceptance or denial of (a) public perceptions of a stigma's existence and (b) the stigma's applicability to them individually, generating four overarching categories of strategies (Meisenbach, 2010). Derived from the four categories are six major management strategies: acceptance, avoidance, evading responsibility, reducing offensiveness, denial, and ignoring/displaying. These six strategies are then broken down into twenty-four sub-strategies. Ultimately, SMC helps address how military veterans communicatively manage and cope with mental health stigma as well as the implications of specific approaches (e.g., lack of help-seeking). Thus, strategies for each of the six major categories will be discussed alongside examples from previous research.

Acceptance

First, a stigmatized individual may engage in *acceptance* when they accept societal expectations of the stigma and its applicability to the self (Meisenbach, 2010). Acceptance sub-strategies include passive acceptance, displaying and disclosing stigma, apologizing, using humor, blaming stigma for adverse outcomes, isolating, and bonding with stigmatized individuals—all of which have been engaged by military veterans (see Roscoe, 2021). For example, veterans experiencing PTS made jokes to reduce tension when they were exuding symptoms of mental illness and blamed mental health stigma for adverse outcomes, such as not being hired because employers are afraid of how they will act when the "switch is triggered" and "the animal is let out of the cage" (cited from Roscoe, 2021, p. 1381).

Previous research also demonstrated the value of *bonding* among veterans, a stigma management strategy in which stigmatized individuals socialize with other stigmatized individuals (Meisenbach, 2010). In this case, veterans described it as more meaningful to talk to other veterans who had the same experience and could relate, especially in comparison to civilians who do not understand (Roscoe, 2021). Ultimately, bonding may represent a positive coping mechanism among military veterans, considering they are opening up and talking about their condition and receiving peer mentorship and support (Lebel, 2008) instead of concealing their condition.

Avoidance

Second, an individual engages in *avoidance* when they accept the existence of the stigma on a societal level but challenge that the stigma applies to the self (Meisenbach, 2010). Avoidance strategies include hiding the stigma attribute, avoiding stigma situations, ceasing the stigma behavior, distancing oneself from the stigma, and making favorable social comparisons. While all of these avoidance strategies have been used among military veterans (Roscoe, 2021), two common strategies with notable adverse consequences are hiding the stigma attribute and making social comparisons.

Hiding the stigma attribute, or passing (Goffman, 1963), is one of the most common ways in which military veterans manage mental health stigma. Military veterans have been shown to hide mental illness both while actively serving and after leaving the service and reintegrating into civilian life (Roscoe, 2021). In the opening vignette of the current chapter, a military veteran felt pressure to conceal symptoms of mental illness because he did not want others to think he had lost his edge as a leader of forty soldiers. While veterans of all ranks and occupations are likely to conceal PTS, higher ranked military personnel holding leadership positions may feel added pressure to hide symptoms of mental illness (Roscoe, 2021).

Upon retirement and reintegration into civilian life, veterans continue to hide their mental illness rather than seek help. For example, one veteran admitted to never talking about his PTS symptoms after returning home from war when he was "traveling down the eternally black abyss" (quoted from Roscoe, 2021, p. 1382). He continued to explain that he did not want anyone to know he was "suffering" due to his ego and the stigma attached to having PTS. As previously described, another veteran refrained from seeking help so that he would be perceived as a stone, which supports the argument that military culture promotes stoicism and self-reliance (Hernandez et al., 2016; Mittal et al., 2013; National Academies of Sciences, 2018). Ultimately, hiding the stigma attribute is problematic because it translates to veterans not seeking the professional mental health treatment they need, which can have detrimental health outcomes (Hoge et al., 2006).

Another important way in which veterans may manage the stigma of PTS is by *making favorable comparisons* between themselves and others (Meisenbach, 2010). In one study, veterans managed stigma for PTS by making favorable comparisons to those experiencing schizophrenia. Specifically, treatment-seeking veterans reported they would rather be diagnosed with PTS than schizophrenia because PTS "doesn't sound as bad as schizophrenia" and "PTSD is the lesser of two evils" (Mittal et al., 2013, p. 90).

Interestingly, in another study, participants' favorable comparisons justified their lack of help-seeking. For instance, one veteran explained that he did not think his symptoms were bad enough to "waste time with a doctor" when the mental health professionals "could go help someone who has it worse" (quoted from Roscoe, 2021, p. 1383). Another veteran in the study justified that "so-and-so did way more than you'll ever do, so you shouldn't try to claim PTSD because you haven't done any of that" and "you don't have a right to talk about [PTSD] because you didn't get blown up." This suggests that veterans with PTSD make favorable comparisons with others to determine whether their problems are severe or legitimate enough to seek help.

Evading Responsibility

Third, an individual *evades responsibility* when acknowledging that the stigma applies to the self but seeks to deviate control and/or responsibility away from the self (Meisenbach, 2010). Sub-strategies of evading responsibility include provocation, defeasibility, and unintentionality. Ultimately, these strategies help individuals distance themselves from the stigma. Although less prominent in the literature, military veterans have been shown to evade responsibility for PTS by assigning responsibility for the stigma to something beyond their control. In one case, a veteran reasoned that people need to consider what veterans with PTS went through during their deployment that led to their mental illness (Roscoe, 2021). Indeed, combat experiences can be severely traumatizing and may involve seeing others get wounded or killed or even wounding or killing another person (Veterans Affairs, 2022).

That being said, veterans need not be involved in combat to experience mental health problems. Simply knowing you are at risk for death or injury and spending long periods away from home and work can cause significant stress (Veterans Affairs, 2022). With this in mind, military caregivers—all of whom were romantic partners—of veterans experiencing PTS worked to evade responsibility in conversation with military veterans when attempting to persuade them to seek help for their mental illness (Roscoe, 2023b). In this case, the military caregiver managed stigma on behalf of the veteran in an attempt to validate the presence of the condition. Specifically, military caregivers would point to challenging experiences that the veteran had during deployment that were out of their control (e.g., *unintentionality*; Meisenbach, 2010), including making split-second decisions that could have dire consequences (e.g., death) and constantly being vigilant about possible danger (e.g., bombs, the enemy). Again, we see how a strategy may help to manage stigma but simultaneously justifies not seeking professional treatment.

Reducing Offensiveness

Fourth, an individual *reduces the offensiveness* of a stigma when they accept the stigma's applicability to the self but attempts to change how others perceive the stigma (Meisenbach, 2010). Sub-strategies for reducing offensiveness include bolstering/refocusing, minimizing, and transcending/reframing. Research has demonstrated the use of minimization strategies, where veterans highlight how the stigma attribute (mental illness) does not inconvenience or harm others (Roscoe, 2021). In these instances, veterans point out being a good parent, coaching children's sports teams, owning a business, graduating from college, safely working with firearms, and more. On a larger scale, these examples work to demonstrate that veterans with PTS can live what might be considered "normal" and prosperous lives—having jobs, success in school, and/or a family—rather than being an inconvenience to others and causing harm to those around them as stigmatizing messages might suggest.

Denying

Fifth, an individual engages in *denial* when they deny or ignore the existence of the stigma at the societal level and the applicability of the stigma to the self (Meisenbach, 2010). Denial sub-strategies include simple denials and logical denials (i.e., discrediting the discreditors, providing evidence or information, and highlighting logical fallacies). The strategy of *discrediting the discreditors* was a frequently engaged strategy among military veterans experiencing PTS. In this case, military veterans pointed out that a stigmatizer (i.e., a civilian) who has never experienced the condition does not understand it and, therefore, is not credible to speak on the topic. For example, one veteran claimed that civilians "don't have any real understanding of veterans and what they have gone through," as well as what it is like to have PTS (quoted from Roscoe, 2021, p. 1383). Furthermore, in response to veterans with PTS being stigmatized as crazy, a veteran retorted:

> If you knew what [veterans] went through, you would shut the hell up. If you want to know what they went through, why don't you join the army and come back and see what life's like? Walk in our shoes.

Research has long demonstrated a divide between military veterans and civilians. As one veteran described, "There's always going to be a certain line between civilian and veterans that do not mix, like oil and vinegar." Howe and Bisel (2023) assessed how military veterans experience contempt (e.g., cool disregard and feelings of superiority) toward civilians' communication habits. While contempt toward civilians can disrupt veterans' healthy reintegration into society (Howe & Bisel, 2023), it is possible that this contempt also impacts the management of mental illness and associated stigma. Due to civilians' inability to understand military-related PTS, veterans may be less willing to open up and talk about their condition. This may especially be the case in civilians who have provided unhelpful social support regarding military-related PTS. Furthermore, veterans may be uninterested in seeking help from a mental health professional who has no military background.

Ignoring and Displaying

Sixth, an individual ignores and displays the stigma when they purposefully ignore moments of stigma communication and continue to display the stigma characteristic openly (Meisenbach, 2010). According to Meisenbach (2010), ignoring and displaying may appear similar to the passive acceptance strategy, but it stems from a desire to challenge rather than passively accept public stigma perceptions. To demonstrate this strategy, one veteran described ignoring mental health stigma because he does not need to prove himself to anyone else, as he knows who he is (Roscoe, 2021). He explained:

> These people who are making these negative comments, they don't know me. There's nothing that they are going to be able to say to take that away from me. I

guess I ignore it. I don't think about it. There's not much to what they are saying. (p. 1383)

Ultimately, despite experiencing PTS, the veteran actively ignores the stigma and chooses to remain true to himself.

Insights for Interventions

Communication-based stigma theories can help to understand the stigma surrounding military-related PTS, as well as how military veterans manage mental health stigma. For example, the MSC helps provide more context behind the stigmatizing language about military veterans experiencing mental illness. Furthermore, SMC helps to illuminate what strategies are used by veterans experiencing PTS and how certain strategies justify not seeking professional mental health treatment. The remainder of this section outlines several insights and recommendations related to health campaigns and interventions. Broadly, interventions can target a variety of stigmatizing beliefs about and among veterans experiencing mental illness, as well as work to destigmatize PTS and encourage veterans to seek help.

Addressing the Cultural Norms of the Weakness Paradox

First, interventions must address the weakness paradox. As outlined in the chapter, veterans are viewed as weak when they *do* seek professional help for mental illness, and they are viewed as weak when they *do not* seek help and instead die by suicide. As a result, veterans may be stigmatized as weak regardless of how they manage mental illness. Scholars should work toward developing destigmatizing campaigns that push back on veterans' perception that mental illness is a weakness. Specifically, campaigns might frame help-seeking behavior as a strength rather than a weakness.

The perception that mental illness is a weakness is likely the result of military cultural norms of stoicism and self-reliance (Hernandez et al., 2016). Indeed, weakness was frequently discussed within the military context but was not mentioned when describing public stigma (Roscoe, 2023a). This aligns with previous research that demonstrated veterans associate weakness with veterans experiencing PTS significantly more than civilians (Roscoe & Anderson, 2019).

In fact, civilians in the previous study did not find that weakness was an accurate perception of veterans experiencing PTS. This supports the argument that perceptions of weakness stem from military cultural norms.

The military organization should work to address beliefs associated with military stigma—such that military members should remain stoic and self-reliant, that experiencing mental illness is discrediting or embarrassing, or that the needs of the unit must be prioritized over the needs of the individual (Hernandez et al., 2016; True et al., 2014). That being said, changing military norms is easier said than done. Howe and Bisel (2023) point out that military socialization is intense for a good reason, such as ensuring its members' safe, reliable, and effective performance to achieve national security. Even so, there may be ways to train and develop effective teams without perpetuating hyper-masculine norms that inform stigmatizing beliefs about mental illness and deter help-seeking. Instead of expecting military members to set problems aside and get their work done (National Academies of Sciences, 2018; Roscoe, 2021), they might set a new ideal wherein looking after the team cannot be achieved without first looking after the self. Research should continue to explore ways the military can minimize mental health stigma within the organizational culture.

Transforming Social Normative Beliefs

Beyond the weakness paradox, interventions and campaigns could work to target social normative beliefs among military veterans. Indeed, much of the stigma communication outlined in the current chapter is the perception of military veterans, and not all of these perceptions may be accurate (Roscoe, 2023a). Still, these perceptions reflect the veterans' understanding of mental health stigma and become the basis for not seeking professional help. Thus, these perceptions can inform interventions that correct social normative beliefs about the prevalence of social stigma and help combat what might be veterans' inaccurate perceptions of stigma (e.g., when they perceive that society stigmatizes them, but it does not). Indeed, one stigma-reduction strategy used by the National Veterans Homeless Support Organization involves the promotion of accurate information about mental health conditions in order to dispel harmful myths and misconceptions (McElhinny, 2023).

Previous research demonstrates that although stigmatizing labels remain *associated* with veterans experiencing PTS, it does not necessarily indicate that they are perceived as *accurate* descriptors of the group (Roscoe & Anderson, 2019).

Specifically, Roscoe and Anderson (2019) observed that both civilians and veterans considered most stigmatizing labels about veterans with PTS to be *inaccurate,* including the descriptor "dangerous." These types of findings can inform interventions, such as the End Self-Stigma (ESS) program, which aims to mitigate the effects of both public and self-stigma through personalized strategies that embody cognitive behavioral therapy (Reger et al., 2020; Veterans Affairs, 2019). Indeed, according to the ESS program, some effective tactics for reducing stigma include "reminding yourself consciously and repeatedly that stigmatizing messages and assumptions are not true" and "delegitimizing stigmatizing messages as untrue, ignorant, and harmful" (Veterans Affairs, 2019, para. 6). Ultimately, more research should target normative beliefs (theory of social normative behavior, Rimal & Real, 2005) among military veterans as a means to interrogate harmful inaccurate perceptions.

Malingerers, Prototype Matching, and Social Comparison

Interventions might also address veterans' use of prototype matching and social comparison, which operate to invalidate a veteran's mental illness and discourage them from seeking the professional treatment they need. As a reminder, prototype matching involves comparing illness experiences to a prototypical model of an illness to determine if symptoms are consistent with the prototype (Spoont et al., 2009). In previous research, veterans feared that they would be stigmatized as someone faking the illness (e.g., malingerer) and would compare their own and others' experiences and symptoms to what they believed was consistent with PTS (Roscoe, 2023a).

Developing a campaign that corrects misconceptions about the prototypical veteran who experiences PTS may be helpful. Veterans may hold the misconception that mental illness is only valid when it is the result of severely traumatizing combat experiences, such as seeing others get wounded or killed or even wounding or killing another person (Veterans Affairs, 2022). Indeed, veterans made comparisons to veterans who got "blown up" or "did way more" in some capacity to determine whether their problems were severe or legitimate enough to seek help (Roscoe, 2021).

However, as previously described, veterans need not be involved in combat to experience mental health problems. Simply knowing you are at risk for death or injury and spending long periods away from home and work can cause stress (Veterans Affairs, 2022). In several cases, veterans may experience sexual assault, the death of a fellow service member, non-combat-related accidents, constant vigilance, and survivor guilt—all of which can contribute to poor mental health. Thus, campaigns could develop and emphasize a new prototype wherein a veteran experiences PTS—despite not engaging in combat—and seeks professional treatment. Similar to the "Make the Connection" campaign, which provides veterans with a platform to share their stories and talk about their experiences, challenges, and recovery to inspire hope among others (Make the Connection, n.d.), veterans who were willing could share their stories about attaining PTS despite not experiencing combat. Ultimately, this could work to discourage social comparison and validate that military veterans experience mental illness even when they do not experience combat, injury, or death. Researchers should continue to examine prototype matching as it relates to mental illness and help-seeking.

Addressing Public Stigma

While it may be helpful to target the perceptions of the stigmatized group (i.e., veterans experiencing mental illness), it is also essential to target the stigmatizing beliefs among civilians and the entities that may be perpetuating the stigma surrounding military veterans. One central entity argued to perpetuate mental health stigma among military veterans is the media (Armstrong & Olutunji, 2009; Parrott, 2023; Roscoe & Anderson, 2019; Roscoe, 2023a).

Roscoe et al. (2024) argued that scholars must examine how various illness attributions can be represented in media in ways that preempt and potentially mitigate the transmission of stigma and proposed halo communication as a conceptual tool. Halo communication is an extension of MSC wherein the stigmatizing content cues (e.g., labels, marks, and etiology content) are adapted to disseminate prosocial messages about stigmatized groups. However, halo communication offers a *well-being enhancement cue* instead of a peril cue that communicates a threat to well-being (Roscoe et al., 2024). Although additional research is needed, halo communication would be one possible way in which media can transmit perceptions of grace and acceptance rather than the disgrace and disqualification associated with stigma communication (Roscoe et al., 2024).

Although challenging to achieve, accurate and non-stigmatizing representations of military veterans experiencing mental illness may help educate civilians. In previous research, military veterans have claimed that civilians have little understanding of military service, war, and PTS (Roscoe, 2021).

The Pew Research Center reports that around 8 in 10 say that the public does not understand the problems—such as the physical, social, or psychological difficulties—faced by those in the military (Morin, 2011). As a result, veterans may be less willing to open up to civilians due to their inability to understand—even when it is a romantic partner serving as an informal caregiver (Roscoe, 2023b). This lack of understanding may further the civilian–veteran divide and impact veterans' management of mental illness and associated stigma. This is another area for scholarly attention.

Conclusion

Military veterans with PTS experience stigma within the military (i.e., military stigma) and from members of society (i.e., public stigma). These veterans may then internalize stigma, endorsing negative perceptions of themselves (i.e., self-stigma). Due to mental health stigma, military veterans experiencing PTS often attempt to cope without seeking professional treatment (Hernandez et al., 2016; Roscoe, 2021). Veterans who forego professional help are at increased risk of substance abuse, severe depression, and suicide (Hoge et al., 2006). A better understanding of the role of mental health stigma is necessary in order to develop interventions that can reduce the prevalence of stigma and thereby facilitate treatment-seeking among military veterans. Using MSC (Smith, 2007) and SMC (Meisenbach, 2010), the current chapter analyzes the multifaceted stigma that deters many veterans from seeking help, as well as how they manage and cope with mental health stigma. Research must continue to interrogate the communication surrounding mental health stigma to minimize it, encourage veterans to seek professional help for mental illnesses, and ultimately, minimize health disparities.

Note

1 The use of post-traumatic stress (PTS) versus post-traumatic stress disorder (PTSD) is a purposeful choice by the author, as many veterans have described their disdain for calling the condition a disorder and argue that the use of the word further stigmatizes them. PTSD will be used when quoted by a research participant or another researcher.

Recommended Readings/Resources

Mittal, D., Drummond, K. L., Blevins, D., Curren, G., Corrigan, P., & Sullivan, G. (2013). Stigma associated with PTSD: Perceptions of treatment seeking combat veterans. *Psychiatric Rehabilitation Journal, 36*(2), 86–92. https://doi.org/10.1037/h0094976

Kulesza, M., Pederson, E., Corrigan, P., & Marshall, G. (2015). Help-seeking stigma and mental health treatment seeking among young adult veterans. *Military Behavioral Health, 3*(4), 230–239. https://doi.org/10.1080/21635781.2015.1055866

Roscoe, R. A. (2021). The battle against mental health stigma: Examining how veterans with PTSD communicatively manage stigma. *Health Communication, 36*(11), 1378–1387. https://doi.org/10.1080/10410236.2020.1754587

Roscoe, R. A. (2023). Stigma communication about invisible illness: Military and public stigma about veterans experiencing posttraumatic stress. *Communication Studies, 74*(5), 447–461. https://doi.org/10.1080/10510974.2023.2221702

Roscoe, R. A., Riles, J., & Schroeder, M. (2024, online first). News media portrayals of military- related posttraumatic stress: Influences of stigma and halo communication on support for government health intervention. *Journal of Health Communication, 29*(5), 319–326. https://doi.org/10.1080/10810730.2024.2339239

References

Acosta, J. D., Becker, A., Cerully, J. L., Fisher, M. P., Martin, L. T., Vardavas, R., Slaughter, M. E., & Schell, T. L. (2014). *Mental health stigma in the military.* RAND Corporation. https://www.rand.org/content/dam/rand/pubs/research_reports/RR400/RR426/RAND_RR 426.pdf

Armstrong, T., & Olatunji, B. (2009). PTSD in the media: A critical analysis of the portrayal of controversial issues. *Scientific Review of Mental Health Practice, 7*(1), 55–60. https://www.srmhp.org/

Britt, T. W., & Klinefelter, Z. (2022). Understanding and reducing the stigma of mental health problems and of treatment among military personnel. In. N. Wade & D. Vogel (Eds.), *Cambridge handbook of stigma and mental health* (pp. 302–325). Cambridge University Press. https://doi.org/10.1017/9781108920995

Corrigan, P. W. (2004). How stigma interferes with mental health care. *American Psychologist, 59*, 614–625. https://doi.org/10.1037/0003-066x.59.7.614

Corrigan, P. W., Bink, A. B., Schmidt, A., Jones, N., & Rüsch, N. (2016). What is the impact of internalized stigma? Loss of self-respect and the "why try" effect. *Journal of Mental Health, 25*(1), 10–15. https://doi.org/10.1002/j.2051–5545.2009.tb00218.x

Corrigan, P. W., & Rao, D. (2012). On the self-stigma of mental illness: Stages, disclosure, and strategies for change. *The Canadian Journal of Psychiatry*, *57*, 464–469. https://doi.org/10.1177/070674371205700804

Goffman, E. (1963). *Stigma: Notes on the management of spoiled identity*. Prentice Hall.

Hernandez, S. H. A., Morgan, B. J., & Parshall, M. B. (2016). A concept analysis of stigma perceived by military service members who seek mental health services. *Nursing Forum*, *52*(3), 188–195. https://doi.org/10.1111/nuf.12187

Hoge, C. W., Auchterlonie, J. L., & Milliken, C. S. (2006). Mental health problems, use of mental health services, and attrition from military service after returning from deployment to Iraq and Afghanistan. *Journal of the American Medical Association*, *295*(9), 1023–1032. https://doi.org/10.1001/jama.295.9.1023

Hoge, C. W., Castro, C. A., Messer, S. C., McGurk, D., Cotting, D. I., & Koffman, R. L. (2004). Combat duty in Iraq and Afghanistan, mental health problems, and barriers to care. *New England Journal of Medicine*, *35*(1), 13–22. https://doi.org/10.1056/NEJMoa040603

Howe, W. T., & Bisel, R. S. (2023). Veteran contempt for civilian communication scale: Development and validation. *Management Communication Quarterly*, *38*(2), 249–278. https://doi.org/10.1177/08933189231186149

Kulesza, M., Pederson, E., Corrigan, P., & Marshall, G. (2015). Help-seeking stigma and mental health treatment seeking among young adult veterans. *Military Behavioral Health*, *3*(4), 230–239. https://doi.org/10.1080/21635781.2015.1055866

Lebel, T. P. (2008). Perceptions of and responses to stigma. *Sociology Compass*, *2*(2), 409–432. https://doi.org/10.1111/j.1751-9020.2007.000081.x

Make the Connection. (n.d.). *Connect with stories of help and hope*. https://www.maketheconnection.net/

McElhinny, G. (2023). *Addressing the stigma of mental health issues among veterans*. National Veterans Homeless Support. https://nvhs.org/addressing-the-stigma-of-mental-health-issues-among-veterans/

Meisenbach, R. J. (2010). Stigma management communication: A theory and agenda for applied research on how individuals manage moments of stigmatized identity. *Journal of Applied Communication Research*, *38*(3), 268–292. https://doi.org/10.1080/00909882.2010.490841

Mittal, D., Drummond, K. L., Blevins, D., Curren, G., Corrigan, P., & Sullivan, G. (2013). Stigma associated with PTSD: Perceptions of treatment seeking combat veterans. *Psychiatric Rehabilitation Journal*, *36*(2), 86–92. https://doi.org/10.1037/h0094976

Momen, N., Strychacz, C. P., & Virre, E. (2012). Perceived stigma and barriers to mental health care in marines attending the combat operational stress control program. *Military Medicine*, *177*(10), 1143–1143. https://doi.org/137.216.185.143

Morin, R. (2011). *The difficult transition from military to civilian life.* Pew Research Center. https://www.pewresearch.org/social-trends/2011/12/08/the-difficult-transition-from-military-to-civilian-life/

National Academies of Sciences. (2018). *Evaluation of the Department of Veterans Affairs mental health services.* The National Academies Press. https://www.nap.edu/read/24915/chapter/1

Parrott, S., Albright, D. L., Eckhart, N., & Laha-Walsh, K. (2023). U.S. veterans and civilians describe military news coverage as mediocre, think stories affect others more than themselves. *Armed Forces & Society, 49*(3), 713–728. https://doi.org/10.1177/0095327X221080944

Reger, G. M., Bourassa, K., Norr, A. M., & Buck, B. (2020). The impact of therapy on stigma and mental health treatment attitudes among active duty U.S. soldiers with combat related PTSD. *Journal of Psychiatric Research, 126*, 98–104. https://doi.org/10.1016/j.jpsychires.2020.05.005

Rimal, R. N., & Real, K. (2005). How behaviors are influenced by perceived norms: A test of the theory of normative social behavior. *Communication Research, 32*(3), 389–414. https://doi.org/10.1177/0093650205275385

Roscoe, R. A. (2021). The battle against mental health stigma: Examining how veterans with PTSD communicatively manage stigma. *Health Communication, 36*(11), 1378–1387. https://doi.org/10.1080/10410236.2020.1754587

Roscoe, R. A. (2023a). Stigma communication about invisible illness: Military and public stigma about veterans experiencing posttraumatic stress. *Communication Studies, 74*(5), 447–461. https://doi.org/10.1080/10510974.2023.2221702

Roscoe, R. A. (2023b). *Narrating the sociocultural experience and management of stigma* [Paper presentation]. Central States Communication Association. Saint Louis, MO, United States.

Roscoe, R. A., & Anderson, J. (2019). Civilian and veteran perceptions of communicated stigma about veterans with PTSD. *Discourse: The Journal of the Speech Communication Association of South Dakota, 5*(1), 1–17. https://openprairie.sdstate.edu/discoursejournal/vol5/iss2/1/

Roscoe, R. A., Riles, J., & Schroeder, M. (2024, online first). News media portrayals of military- related posttraumatic stress: Influences of stigma and halo communication on support for government health intervention. *Journal of Health Communication 29*(5), 319–326. https://doi.org/10.1080/10810730.2024.2339239

Simmons, A., & Yoder, L. (2013). Military resilience: A concept analysis. *Nursing Forum, 48*(1), 17–25. https://doi.org/10.1111/nuf.12007

Smith, R. A. (2007). Language of the lost: An explication of stigma communication. *Communication Theory, 17*(4), 462–485. https://doi.org/10.1111/j.1468-2885.2007.00307.x

Spoont, M. R., Sayer, N., Friedemann-Sanchez, G., Parker, L. E., Murdoch, M., & Chiros, C. (2009). From trauma to PTSD: Beliefs about sensations, symptoms, and mental illness. *Qualitative Health Research*, *19*(10), 1456–1465. https://doi.org/10.1177/1049732309348370

Suitt, T. H. (2021). *High suicide rates among United States service members and veterans of post-9/11 wars.* Watson Institute. https://watson.brown.edu/costsofwar/files/cow/imce/papers/2021/Suitt_Suicides_Costs%20of%20War_June%2021%202021.pdf

True, G., Rigg, K. K., & Butler, A. (2014). Understanding barriers to mental health care for recent war veterans through photovoice. *Qualitative Health Research*, *25*(10), 1443–1455. https://doi.org/10.1177/1049732314562894

Veterans Affairs. (2019). *VA psychologists help veterans overcome self-stigma.* https://news.va.gov/64887/va-psychologists-help-veterans-overcome-self-stigma/

Veterans Affairs. (2021). *National veteran suicide prevention annual report.* Office of Mental Health and Suicide Prevention. https://www.mentalhealth.va.gov/docs/data-sheets/2021/2021-National-Veteran-Suicide-Prevention-Annual-Report-FINAL-9-8- 21.pdf

Veterans Affairs. (2022). *Combat exposure.* https://www.ptsd.va.gov/understand/types/combat_exposure.asp

West, M. L., Yanos, P. T., Smith, S. M., Roe, D., & Lysaker, P. H. (2011). Prevalence of internalized stigma among persons with severe mental illness. *Stigma Research and Action*, *1*(1), 3–10. https://doi.org/10.5463/sra.v1i1.9

Zhu, X., & Smith, R. A. (2021). Stigma, communication, and health. In T. L. Thompson & N. G. Harrington (Eds.), *The Routledge handbook of health communication* (3rd ed., pp. 77–90). Routledge. https://doi.org/10.4324/9781003043379-8

4

Communicating What Is Silent

Black Women Navigating Mental Health

Adrienne F. Muldrow and Karlene Cunningham

We acknowledge that structural barriers within research may limit our ability to report on the experience of those birth capable but not identifying as women. Where data exist, we will call out where differences arise for those with these intersecting identities.

Kay Matthew's story in her voice

For illustration, we used Kay Matthew's, a Black woman's, story because it is a typical one. She feels that with the mantra of being *strong,* she has to face the world with strength. She has to know all the answers. She has to be the one in *control.* When she does not feel in control of things, she must be the one to blame.

> During my pregnancy, I was at the height of my life, and that is really what matters . . . All the things were falling into place . . . a relationship, a baby, a job, all the things, right? . . . I honestly was not prepared, where life just spiraled without my control . . . I am the person who is always in control . . . When you don't have control over adverse things . . . I am to blame . . . (Gourrier, 2023)

Unfortunately, she feels that this notion of *being strong has led to more negativity* than confidence. She did not know where to turn. Close relatives did not fully understand her pain. She did not know what she needed. For example, she says,

> I think there are a lot of things that we [Black women] don't talk about until other people can truly identify . . . So, a lot of the things that I also attribute to being

> a strong Black woman . . . all um ended up being negative to me . . . the push through mentality that I was raised with or forced to implement in my everyday life . . . it was also the thing that brought me to my knees . . . [reminiscing upon the stillborn birth of her daughter, Troya Simone]. . .they [relatives] felt sad for me, but they couldn't necessarily help me in the way . . . I needed them to do, so it was a struggle for me when people would say, "Hey, do you need help?" And I would say, "I don't know." . . . That was because I didn't know exactly what I needed . . . .I know I needed something that I wasn't getting . . . (Gourrier, 2023)

Also, when she does not receive good healthcare services after an intense trauma, *she feels that she has to accept it,* try her best to find someone she is comfortable with in medical settings, and *try to work within the framework set by those in the dominant culture,* even if she cannot see women like herself thriving in that cultural outsider space. No one questions whether or not she fits in or if that mental health space is comfortable for her. For example, she says,

> When it was time for me to leave the hospital, I remember asking the nurse, "Where's my baby?" She responded, "So no one told you?" [Kay responded] "Told me what"? . . . [the nurse responded] "Let me figure it out." After a long wait, she [the nurse] came back with a piece of paper with an address and a phone number. . . . So, overall interactions within the hospital was [sic] so subpar. It was the first time that I realized that I was a Black woman in America. . . . They didn't necessarily give us good treatment. I felt like I was asked a plethora of questions that didn't have anything to do with anything. . . . So, it took me five years before I made an appointment to see her [the obstetrician] to tell her how much she impacted me with that statement ["she had never lost a baby in all her years of delivering babies"], and how [badly] her staff treated me when I came in for follow-ups, but I also wanted to let her know that she didn't alter my life in that way where it actually propelled me. It didn't alter me and shut me down . . . and I am sure that there are a lot of women out there suffering . . . the tone and the way they reacted in the postpartum period was different. That part was not even addressed . . . the [mental health care] help was subpar . . . postpartum depression, "What the hell are you talking about. Girl, you ain't got no baby." . . . [a long-term doctor's nursing staff] found support groups. No one in those support groups looked like me, and no one identified in my situation . . . yeah, I went a little, but this ain't working "so now what do I need to do?" (Gourrier, 2023)

Lastly, she eventually *finds her own voice* and sense of healing from trauma. She eventually finds healing by doing things that make her happy, stating, "[to heal] I just started journaling " (Gourrier, 2023, 02:42).

The World Health Organization (WHO) defines mental health as a state of mental well-being that enables people to cope with the stresses of life, realize their abilities, learn well and work well, and contribute to their community (World Health Organization, 2022, para. 1). This definition is more than just the absence of a mental disorder but exists across a spectrum that can be enhanced by both internal and external structures and supports. The WHO considers mental health to be a basic human right and underscores the role of social and structural determinants that impact the ability of any individual to optimize their mental health.

Problem Identification

Black women are triply disadvantaged due to race, gender, and class (Castelin & White, 2022; Gibbs & Fuery, 1994). Black women have been the matriarchs of the Black community (Parks, 2010). In addition to this responsibility, Black women have also "been victims,victims of discrimination, economic exploitation, and social rejection for over 370 years" (Gibbs & Fuery, 1994, p. 560). In other words, Black women may face intersectional oppression (Abrams et al., 2014). Taken together, Black women are situated differently in terms of social, economic, and political environments (Crenshaw, 1998).

Facing race, gender, and economic oppression (Collins, 2022), Black women face one of the most unprivileged intersections of factors which, in turn, opens them up to a plethora of "negative" psychological and social ramifications (Copeland, 1982). Some of these negative psychological and social ramifications range from suicidal ideation and heart disease to numerous stress-related health problems, up to and including adverse birth outcomes (Perry et al., 2012; U.S. Department of Health & Human Services, 2021; Woods-Giscombe & Lobel, 2008). This interplay of disadvantages has led Black women to have disparate experiences within the mental health sphere (e.g., Hall et al., 2024). Despite the vast array of intersectional challenges, Black women have demonstrated resilience in their resolve to push back against these various hardships (Parks, 2010).

Socio-economic and Structural Challenges

Black women have led in labor force participation. In 2020, 58.8 percent of Black women had the highest labor participation rate of any other female racial group in the United States. Black moms have a 76 percent participation rate. Again, this labor participation rate was the highest of all racial groups (Roux, 2021). Despite this immense contribution to the workforce, economic disparities remain. Notwithstanding, the Black population comprises 13 percent of the US population but accounts for 20 percent of the population that resides in poverty. This poverty rate stands at a ratio of 1.5, equal to that of Hispanic Americans and lower than the ratio of Native Americans and Alaska Natives (Shrider, 2023).

In 2022, despite working more, Black women found themselves earning less. An impressive 28.9 percent of Black women twenty-five years and over obtained at least a bachelor's degree, nearly doubling the rate of that of 2000. Yet, this educational advancement did not translate into higher earnings when compared to their White male counterparts. In 2020, Black women with bachelor's degrees earned just 65.4 percent of what White men earned, which is not that different than the 63 percent earned by Black women overall compared to White men (Lopez & Moslimani, 2024).

The Strong Black Woman in Media Representation

In line with an intersectional frame where gender and race intersect (Crenshaw, 1998), Black women are considered objectively disadvantaged, which may render them susceptible to disproportionate harm. Nevertheless, some have managed to maintain a reservoir of unbridled resilience. Some have hypothesized that Black women can overcome adverse actions because of their great multiplicities of strength, acknowledged in the literature as the *strong Black woman* (SBW). The SBW, as a gender construct, is defined as a "provider and caretaker who is resistant to vulnerability or dependency, displays strength, suppresses emotions, succeeds despite inadequate resources, and assumes responsibilities as a community agent" (Abrams et al., 2014, p. 504). This construct is well known because it is omnipresent in Black culture (Parks, 2010).

In a paradoxical twist, Black women's endorsement of the SBW schema, influenced by the intersectional lenses of gender and race, diminishes their capacity to cope effectively, ultimately contributing to unfavorable mental health outcomes (Abrams et al., 2014; Donovan & West, 2015). For example, in a qualitative study by Abrams et al. (2014), Black women describe the SBW as an ethnically proud, independent, strong, and resilient matriarch of her community who juggles multiple roles while being a woman of faith (Abrams et al., 2014). While, to some, the SBW acts as a coping mechanism that allows Black women as well as Black families and communities to survive and thrive (Abrams et al., 2014; Woods-Giscombe, 2010), it also opens the door to having Black women suppress, or disregard altogether, very real emotional pain, and deal with stress alone (Beauboeuf-Lafontant, 2007; Black & Peacock, 2011; Erving et al., 2024).

Media may be partially responsible for some level of psychological distress on the part of Black women through its portrayal of the strong Black woman schema/script (Black & Peacock, 2011; Stanton et al., 2017). The SBW is a combination of two popular stereotypical tropes of Black women: the mammy (a nonthreatening, selfless woman whose main obligation in life is to be of dutiful service to others at the expense of her own needs) and the superwoman (a relentlessly hard-working woman of strength who resists dependency on others and feels an obligation to suppress her own emotions); Abdullah, 1998; Collins, 2000; Woods-Giscombe, 2010). Moreover, women who internalize thoughts consistent with the SBW gender schema experience feelings of worthlessness and guilt, otherwise known as the Sisterella Complex (Jones & Shorter-Gooden, 2003). Unfortunately, these women remain silent rather than communicating to others that they need some appropriate mental health resources and services.

When this supposed mythology strength has to be utilized in real life, many complexities are revealed (Beauboeuf-Lafontant, 2005). In a study of 412 Black women, Stanton et al. (2017) found that frequent social media use and buying into the SBW ideal were associated with maladaptive mental health and lower self-esteem. Abdullah (1998) described women who simply acquiesced to acting as a real-life mammy tend to demonstrate self-alienation and mental confusion. Furthermore, Erving et al. (2024) found that the tenets of the obligation to help and emotional suppression are positively related to higher depressive symptoms. Moreover, this SBW script has been linked to depression, exhaustion, overeating, and, in the direst cases, suicide (Beauboeuf-Lafontant, 2007; Black & Peacock, 2011).

Mental Health during the Perinatal Period

The current call to action to address the perinatal morbidity and mortality crisis is reflective of a reckoning that every year the United States allows over a thousand women and other birthing people to die in their effort to reproduce and thousands more to experience serious impacts from their birthing experience. The perinatal period, often defined as the nine months of pregnancy up to one year postpartum, has historically and erroneously been regarded as a "protected" period for mental health. This cultural messaging around the perinatal period has made it difficult to gain a widespread understanding that perinatal mood and anxiety disorders are the number one complications of pregnancy.

In 2021, the perinatal mortality rate for non-Hispanic Black women was 69.9 deaths per 100,000 live births. This rate is nearly three times higher than that of women and other birthing people racialized as White (Hoyert, 2021). This undue burden on Black birthing bodies has become interwoven into the call to action and has highlighted how the medical system fails Black women when they should be at their most supported. With greater attention to the perinatal mortality crisis and its unique impact on the Black birthing body, the reasons "why" individuals were dying came into stark relief. The historically identified causes such as infection and hemorrhage are highlighted in the literature, but mental health factors have started to emerge as significant contributors to death in the postpartum period.

The Centers for Disease Control and Prevention (CDC, 2022) now lists mental health conditions as the leading underlying cause of pregnancy-related death, accounting for 23 percent of deaths during this period. While death by suicide has been more common among older non-Hispanic White women, between 2006 and 2017 there has been a near tripling of suicidal behaviors, inclusive of suicidal ideation and intent, among younger non-Hispanic Black women. The greatest increases in suicidal behavior have been found among Black women experiencing economic hardship and those with comorbid depression and anxiety (Admon et al., 2021; Chin et al., 2022). Lastly, significant inequities in the diagnosis, treatment, and achievement of remission for perinatal or postpartum mood and anxiety disorders (PMAD) exist for Black women.

Disparities in Mental Health Care during the Perinatal Period

The American College of Obstetricians and Gynecologists (ACOG) recommends between 12 and 15 visits during the perinatal period for an uncomplicated pregnancy (Demosthenes, 2021), with additional visits added depending on the severity of complications. This number far exceeds the average of 3.6 doctor visits attended by non-pregnant women of reproductive age (Ashman et al., 2023).

Despite increased contact with medical providers during this period, estimates of the postpartum depression treatment cascade—the most commonly diagnosed PMAD—suggest that only 31 percent of people experiencing symptoms of perinatal depression are diagnosed, 14–16 percent initiate treatment, and only 3–5 percent of women will achieve remission of symptoms. Examinations of Black women across this cascade are much worse. For example, James and colleagues' (2023) findings suggest that while the majority of the Black women in their sample reported PMAD symptoms both during and after pregnancy, only 12–15 percent received any mental health treatment. In their findings, having private insurance significantly increased the chances of receiving mental health treatment after delivery. Finally, Chan et al. (2021) found that hospital-based mental health treatment (i.e., acute care) most impacted Black women, thus highlighting the significant gap in providing less traumatic outpatient treatment and prevention. When more fully accounted for, Black women are at the highest risk of PMADs, receive less mental health care, and access care at more acute phases of impaired functioning.

Extraordinary Challenges: Obstetric Racism

As previously noted, mental health entails much more than the presence or absence of a mental disorder but encompasses the ability to handle the stressors of day-to-day life. However, the stressors experienced by Black women are different, especially when considering experiences of both anti-Black racism and sexism. Furthermore, the process of becoming pregnant, maintaining a pregnancy, delivery, and newborn care places Black women in contexts that may exacerbate these discriminatory experiences, specifically the increased contact with the medical establishment.

Obstetric racism, as defined by Davis (2019) is the intersection of obstetric violence and medical racism. Obstetric violence encompasses the violence that women experience solely because they are obstetric patients (gender-based). The concept originated in Latin America and the Caribbean, where significant efforts to improve the care of women during pregnancy remain a focus. The concept has gained global appeal, with rates estimated between 15 percent and 91 percent depending on the country (Martínez-Galiano et al., 2021). However, there remains hesitancy to use the label for the experiences of women in the United States, despite the United States being the only industrialized nation with an increasing perinatal mortality rate (Garcia, 2020). Organizations like Birth Monopoly track and document the impact of this kind of gendered violence in the United States (Birth Monopoly, 2023).

Medical racism is discrimination that persists against patients based on how they are racialized. As detailed by Harriet Washington (2006) in Medical Apartheid and further explored by Deirdre Cooper Owens (2017) in Medical Bondage, the founding of the specialty of obstetrics and gynecology is rooted in the experimentation and exploitation of Black women. Owens (2017) highlights how previously revered physicians like Marion Sims experimented on enslaved Black women, named Betsey, Anarcha, and Lucy, and later justified these actions through the development of racist and sexist ideas about their patients. These racist concepts persist and significantly contribute to the documented *advantage* of being racialized as White across a multitude of health indicators, including maternal mortality. Taken together, obstetric racism highlights the unique experience of Black women in the reproductive space and the multiple avenues of harm that can be inflicted during this experience. It also speaks to how the physical and mental health of Black women are put at risk because of the way that these systems and structures are built.

A persistent racist concept that contributes to medical bias is the myth that Black people, especially Black women, can withstand more pain, be it physical or emotional (Carrington, 2006; Johnson et al., 2019). Psychological distress and the accumulation of traumatic experiences are often strongly correlated with the development of a psychiatric disorder. However, a "mental health paradox" exists in the report of greater experiences of psychological distress and trauma by Black women with generally lower rates of diagnosis of disorders such as depression (Robinson et al., 2023). While there are structural factors that may account for the underdiagnosis of depression among Black women in general, there is evidence to suggest that the distress-disorder pathway may vary for some subgroups of Black women related to other resources and connections they have in their lives. Specifically, community and financial support appear to help engender resilience during distressing times.

Barriers: Insurance and Cost of Prenatal and Mental Health Care

The primary barriers to Black women having adequate mental health care surround issues of affordability, approachability, and availability of mental health care (Coombs et al., 2021). For affordability, cost can be an issue. Pregnancy and childbirth are costly events, with the average out-of-pocket cost of childbirth with commercial insurance at $4,569 in 2015. Some estimates suggest that costs have continued to increase after the pandemic.

Insurance can be a barrier to the approachability and availability of mental health services. While the majority of births (51.7%) in 2021 were covered by private insurance, 41.0 percent of births were supported by public insurance (i.e., Medicaid). According to Valenzuela and Osterman (2023), approximately 64 percent of Black women's deliveries in 2021 were covered by Medicare, making Medicaid the primary insurer of Black women during the perinatal period. While this coverage may help to defray costs during pregnancy and at delivery, before the availability of Medicaid expansion, postpartum persons would lose their pregnancy-related Medicaid sixty days after delivery. Requalification was difficult, as approximately 65 percent did not meet Medicaid criteria before pregnancy. With Medicaid expansion, more birthing people can qualify. To date, forty-one states have implemented Medicaid expansion. The American Rescue Plan Act of 2021 provided an additional way to support pregnant people by allowing provisions for postpartum care to extend to one year postpartum. A total of forty-six have extended the period of postpartum support to date (Kaiser Family Foundation, 2024). Margerison et al. (2021) found that in states with expanded Medicaid, there was a 16 percent decline in self-reported prepregnancy depressive symptoms, but it did not appear to affect depressive symptoms experienced during the perinatal period. Golberstein and Gonzales (2015) have suggested that Medicaid expansion reduces out-of-pocket costs related to mental health care but does not increase use. However, Walker and colleagues (2015) suggest that those with public insurance coverage are more likely to access mental health services if they need them, more so than those with private insurance. These mixed results suggest that there is more than just insurance coverage at play when considering engaging in mental health care, especially for Black women who have one of the lowest rates of engaging in treatment of all racialized groups.

Even if Black women find access to some mental health services, other services remain prohibitive. Mental health services such as therapy and medication management can be cost-prohibitive even with Medicaid. Out-of-pocket costs can range from fully covered ($0 copay) to approximately $25 per visit or more, depending on the percentage above the federal poverty line and the contracted rate (Centers for Medicare & Medicaid Services, n.d.). These rates are lower than the typical self-pay costs of $100 to $200 per session for psychotherapy in many areas, and even small copays may add up quickly for those with limited means.

Communication Intervention

Redefining the Narrative of the Black Perinatal Experience

Poor patient-provider communication often leaves Black women feeling misunderstood and disengaged, which can lead to a delay in adopting interventions and result in more severe episodes of mental illness. In contrast, good communication paves the way to redefine more beneficial cultural narratives (Bhui et al., 2015; Cameron et al., 2018). According to Bhui et al. (2015), "Effective communication is central to psychiatric assessment, diagnosis, engagement and treatment, and, ultimately, recovery" (p. 2). One type of effective communication is therapeutic "health" communication (Kirmayer et al., 2003). Therapeutic communication includes "all interactions that enable people in distress to resolve conflicts, divergent expectations, traumatic histories and adverse life events, and to take up and to overcome distress and also take up offers of help" (Bhui et al., 2013, p. 4). In other words, therapeutic communication can help maximize factors that encourage the access and use of existing services as well as minimize critical communication-based healthcare incidents in the future, possibly lessening troubling inequalities (Kirmayer et al., 2003; Lorenz & Chilingerian, 2011).

To be effective, therapeutic communication must be patient-centered and involve an effective exchange of ideas between the patient and the provider. Moreover, the provider of mental healthcare services must be able to use their expertise to positively influence the emotional well-being of the patient (Bhui et al., 2013). In the following section, we discuss the innovative ways that Black women can control their narratives and find their peace throughout the perinatal experience.

Despite the startling statistics concerning perinatal morbidity and mortality, Black women work to assure that other Black women know that there is joy during the perinatal experience. Kimberly Seals Allers has worked to reduce the exposure to birth trauma for Black women through the creation of a Yelp-like app, *Irth*, that allows Black women and the people who serve them to rate how effectively hospitals, providers, and birth workers contribute to their care of Black birthing women (IRTH, 2024). Her app's motto is *birth, but we dropped the B for bias*. Making this an online secure space allows the community to increase the birthing safety of Black women, but also creates an avenue for accountability for providers and hospitals. The app is celebrating its third anniversary and is broadening its reach and narrative through a new podcast, *Birthright*. Birthright is solely focused on amplifying the joy and healing in Black birth. This positivity is also infused into the free e-book available on the site.

Another example of narrative shifting within the Black birthing community is *Dem Black Mamas*, a podcast and online community focused on centering #BlackMamaMagic while encouraging the creation of a new story through personal healing and liberation. A central focus of their main page is the *Meditations By Mamas*, which features messages like *You are Enough* and *Rewriting the Script on Mental Health for Black Mothers*. This authentically curated and community-centered offering provides many of the ingredients highlighted as being effective mental health interventions. They guide practices such as diaphragmatic breathing, meditation, and "cognitive restructuring" (i.e., narrative shifting) that are cornerstones of coping interventions in traditional mental health but deliver them in a way that more easily establishes a connection to the content.

Power in Community

Creating spaces for collective voices to advocate and take action for reproductive justice has continued to gain strength in the last ten years. The reproductive justice movement and framework was initiated in 1994 by a group of Black women focused on (1) the right to have children, (2) the right not to have children, and (3) the right to nurture children we have in a safe and healthy environment. The reproductive framework and movement differ from reproductive rights that are predominantly centered on feminists racialized as White because they recognize the intersectionality of reproduction in America. Instead, reproductive justice pushes for the human right of bodily autonomy, shifting the narrative to access as not just choice, but expanding the focus beyond abortion rights toward comprehensive sexual education and personal well-being.

SisterSong is a southern-based organization that has spearheaded the reproductive justice movement and the recent expansion around Birth Justice specifically. In 2013, they partnered with the Center for Reproductive Rights to create the Black Mamas Matter Alliance, which has spent the last eleven years advocating for policy change around Black birth, inclusive of Black mental health care. These national organizations have also helped to create smaller local organizations such as Shades of Blue in Texas, focused on Black perinatal mental health, Birth in Color in Virginia, and the Perinatal Mental Health Alliance for People of Color, focused on increasing the number of therapists of color providing perinatal mental health care.

Institutional Support

The alarmingly negative experience of Black women during the perinatal period has also spurred more structural and institutional changes to improve the quality of care. The American College of Obstetricians and Gynecologists, the governing body of Obstetricians and Gynecologists (OBGYNs), recently released a new set of training modules to help train OBGYNs about what respectful care (American College of Obstetricians and Gynecologists, 2024) should look like, the historical understanding of the disparities, and the ways to move toward birth equity. The development of the modules was supported by a U.S. Department of Health and Human Services grant to the Maternal Health Learning and Innovation Center (MHLIC, 2024). The MHLIC has been tasked with eliminating maternal health inequities and has provided new resources for addressing harm.

A recent addition to the center is a planning tool to help providers center people with lived experiences when exploring solutions. Other tools include toolkits for perinatal mental health advocacy, intersectionality policymaking, and a Black Mamas Matter kit to promote respectful care. The Postnatal Patient Safety Learning Lab has rolled out brief animations of actual patient-provider interactions and training about how to change these behaviors (Our work–The Postnatal Patient Safety Learning Lab, n.d.). These efforts are starting to shift how providers interact with patients and may help to reduce the mistrust of the system. However, widespread adoption and integration into training requirements are needed for lasting institutional change.

Communication Tactics for Trust, Healing, and Re-engagement for Black Women

One of the most unique and beneficial ways to alleviate these barriers would be to enact music as music has always played a role in resistance for Black communities and has recently been pulled into the mental health healing space (Watson, 2021). As was seen with some of the previously described podcasts, meditation is touted as an evidence-based intervention to address mood and anxiety disorders, but the "evidence base" has not been tailored to the unique experience of Black people. That has changed with the merging of the typical quiet meditation with music and beats often popular across Black communities. Popular artists such as rapper Lil Jon and other Black musicians have created albums for general and collaborative release. Working with popular mental health apps like Headspace and Calm (Experts, 2023), this integration has helped to increase belonging and access to the wider community. SoulMed is another example of a space created for and by Black women who have infused music for its role in healing with their Dear Black Woman Daily meditation mixtape (SoulMed Holistic Health Collaborative, n.d.). Even when not focused on mental health specifically, there has been a shift in music lyrics that attempt to soften the stigma around accessing or needing mental health care (Kresovich et al., 2021). Effective communication interventions should have a goal of having healthcare providers identify with, understand, and empathize with Black women (e.g., Cameron et al., 2018; Elfenbein & Ambady, 2003). To accomplish this, healthcare professionals should learn to understand common metaphorical and symbolic language typically used by Black women (Tesone, 1996). For example, some people have referred to diabetes as having "sugar" (Daniels, 2016). Furthermore, healthcare professionals should learn the cultural expectations regarding preferred hierarchies and power structures, etc. (Rüdell et al., 2009). Within the realm of psychiatric care, healthcare interventions that are known to be effective for Black individuals include cultural consultation, ethnographic interviews (interviews that led the healthcare professional to be sensitive to one's ethnic background), cognitive behavioral therapy, assessment of explanatory models, and telepsychiatry (Bhui et al., 2015).

Communication Theories to Be Explored

Several theories might be helpful to communication researchers who wish to discuss the topic of vulnerable groups and mental health, as well as those who desire to research issues surrounding how a vulnerable group expresses their stories in their own way. All theories introduced in this section may not have been exclusively used in the communication discipline but may have wide applicability among many disciplines, while also being germane to a proper technique for uncovering what were once were silenced voices.

Standpoint Theory. According to standpoint theory, those in subordinate positions in society are best positioned to see a truer picture of *reality,* supposedly because they can know the positionality of those in the dominant group and the contradictions within their thoughts or standpoints contradict this dominant position (e.g., Collins, 1986; Harding, 1991; Wood, 2019). In this manner, those in subordinate groups view life with a less distorted view (Harding, 1991). In terms of power relations, being both Black and a woman puts Black women in at least two subordinate positions of power relations (Collins, 1986). Furthermore, adding more intersectionality, such as being poor or being part of a sexual minority, puts these Black women in an even more subordinate position (Harding, 1991), thus adding more clarity to their way of knowing.

Hallstein (1999), however, still believes that Black women have some agency despite these multiple subordinate positions. Hallstein (1999) asserts that Black women can still be active agents in their lives even if historical and social contexts do not work in their favor. An example of an empowered approach that Black women could take is to maximize their cultural health capital (CHC). Shim (2010) introduced the concept of cultural health capital (CHC) to account for how patient-provider interactions reduce healthcare disparities. She defines CHC as the cultural skills, verbal and nonverbal competencies, attitudes, and interactional styles that are developed by both patients and clinics to help optimize healthcare relationships.

There are ways that standpoint theory can be applied. For instance, qualitative communication researchers can work together with clinical mental health professionals or community health partners to produce papers and best practices for Black women to achieve more beneficial mental health outcomes. In the proper application of standpoint theory, the voices of Black women should be centered.

Intersectionality Theory. While standpoint theory recognizes that people in subordinate positions may be closer to seeing the true reality, intersectionality theory helps identify the types of intersections that may place Black women in these subordinate positions (Crenshaw, 2013). For example, many Black women exist in the realm of intersecting categories: race and gender, and some face issues dealing with other identities, such as class and immigrant status (Crenshaw, 2013; Viruell-Fuentes et al., 2012). These intersectional identity categories can seek to marginalize individuals, albeit in different directions. Even more problematic is the notion that not mentioning these intersections creates greater problems among that group. For example, not acknowledging problems that poor, Black trans women face in reliably obtaining mental health services may lead to intragroup conflict between them and the poor, heterosexual Black women. Moreover, more intersectional categories can be exposed. According to this book chapter, researchers should add age as an additional and relevant identity for intersectionality in the context of Black women and healthcare services, given that Black, younger women entering the healthcare system tend to rely more on a public source of funding.

The advantage of exploring the experiences and voices of vulnerable groups with an intersectional lens is that, on a micro level, it can help reveal daily encounters with discrimination and, on a macro level, reveal policies, rules, and regulations that were put into place that mold disparate outcomes for these groups (Viruell-Fuentes et al., 2012). The ultimate goal of identifying these identities is not to opine or dominate but to use this knowledge as a source of reconstruction and social empowerment (Crenshaw, 2013).

Co-cultural theory. Co-cultural theory provides an understanding of the process used by marginalized groups as they engage in communicative practices operating within a more dominant social order (Orbe, 1998). It is aptly named co-cultural as this disadvantaged group, such as Black women, must exist among many groups operating within an understood social ranking. Specifically, the theory discusses how individuals who find themselves marginalized by societal powers can find ways to manage, alter, or overcome this disadvantageous position (Orbe, 2005). Some strategies employed can range from mirroring and censorship, to outright confrontations (Orbe, 2005). In other words, co-cultural theory can help mental health providers understand how Black women choose to communicate and how this pattern of communication exists as they struggle to overcome an unfortunate social standing.

Some ways that communication researchers can use co-cultural theory to improve the lives of Black women include the following. With knowledge of co-cultural theory, communication researchers may want to discuss how the words used, different ways of speaking, and the pictures and wording on brochures in the medical environment impact Black women and their ongoing struggles within the medical landscape. Furthermore, researchers in any field can study the underlying array of economic and social conditions that Black women face so they are less likely to be stressed and depressed. In solidarity with Alang (2019), researchers should continue to produce anti-racism research to reduce disparities faced by Black women. Lastly, researchers can explore other ways, beyond culturally driven meditations and anxiety-reducing music therapy, to other forms of stress relief that might work better for other cultures, including writing, that Black women can use to alleviate forms of stress.

Suggested Research Areas in Mental Health Communication for Black Women

Black women's history with medical institutions in the United States cannot be divorced from present challenges. As such, Black women seeking mental health services arrive carrying harmful histories, potential damages, and, sometimes, thoughts about a hopeful future. In this respect, communication researchers must begin if they hope for Black women to thrive in their mental health issues. We list the types of interactions that can be studied by health communication researchers:

- *Individual/Provider*: Communication researchers should investigate which words and actions are still leading to unnecessary distrust or trauma on behalf of Black women. Additionally, researchers could conduct research jointly with clinical healthcare providers to better determine what is leading to these unnecessary deaths.
- *Individual/Community*: Communication researchers can study the communication process used by Black women-centered organizations, such as the Black Mamas Matter Alliance (see Appendix), among others. How are Black women's voices being centered in this area, but not in others?
- *Individual/Institution*: In an attempt for Black women to relate to institutions that should promote health equity, which in turn might reduce the need for additional mental health services, communication researchers can examine the interactions between Black women and providers to ensure that respectful care is given.
- *Individual/Culture*: In an attempt for Black women as individuals to relate to the broader culture, communication researchers could study the effects of online racism and discrimination on Black women's pursuit of health care.
- *Individual/Community/Culture*: Communication researchers can study whether spaces created for and by Black women, like SoulMed, are more beneficial and healing to Black women than spaces created by others outside of the community.

In addition, we propose a couple of research agendas for future communication researchers. Knowing that Black women should counter stereotypical images (i.e., SBW) with nonstereotypical images to challenge these maladaptive images (Collins, 2000; hooks, 1993), communication researchers could investigate the effect of not showing a fuller range of images than that of the SBW. As an extension, communication researchers in integrated communication or public relations should explore the best images to be placed on websites, in doctors' offices, outside of clinics, or on social media that would encourage Black women to seek mental health services. Also, communication researchers should find out how Black women find resilience and how this sense of resilience can be fostered by health practitioners without them resorting to using any SBW schemas.

Conclusion

Reducing stress and depressive symptoms among Black women can aid in addressing their mental health concerns. In essence, enacting health communication strategies needs to work in tandem with a vast awareness of sociocultural issues. One might not work as well without the other. Nevertheless, communication researchers can help by finding ways to mitigate the harm to Black women by exploring multiple facets of therapeutic communication and theories that can improve the mental health of Black women.

Ultimately, a worthy goal for the mental health system is not to be satisfied with delivering a level of basic services, but rather to find ways that Black women can heal from historical abuses of the medical system, to allow Black women to find spaces where they can fully trust mental health professionals, and where all professionals must actively re-engage with Black women so that they feel confident that their presence is validated. We need to hear their voices if we truly want Black women to thrive.

By adopting a social-ecological approach to wellness, clinicians and healthcare systems can offer more tailored wellness experiences that can alleviate the negative repercussions of perinatal mood and anxiety disorders as well as re-engage Black women with necessary care. It is imperative to recognize that not all treatment needs to be facilitated through the healthcare system. Community-based spaces, centering around Black women, provide avenues to reclaim their healing and liberation during difficult times, a true sense of resilience.

Collaboration between communication researchers and healthcare providers is pivotal in elevating and enhancing this positive and liberating messaging for greater healing. This combination of researchers and clinical personnel can be a powerful weapon in creating beneficial environments and supportive messaging to enhance Black women's mental health. We encourage all researchers to embark upon a journey where the Black-centered women's voice can resonate and be validated within the mental health space.

Recommended Readings/Resources

Black Mamas Matter Alliance (n.d.). *Home—Advancing Black maternal health, rights & justice.* https://blackmamasmatter.org

Dem Black Mamas. (n.d.). *Home—Raising free Black children—black mama magic. Black Mama.* https://demblackmamas.com

IRTH. (n.d.). *Join the movement to DroptheB.* https://irthapp.com

Shades of Blue Project (n.d). *Shades of Blue: Breaking maternal mental health barriers.* https://www.shadesofblueproject.org/

References

Abdullah, A. S. (1998). Mammy-ism: A diagnosis of psychological misorientation for women of African descent. *Journal of Black Psychology, 24*(2), 196–210. https://doi.org/10.1177/00957984980242009

Abrams, J. A., Maxwell, M., Pope, M., & Belgrave, F. Z. (2014). Carrying the world with the grace of a lady and the grit of a warrior: Deepening our understanding of the "Strong Black Woman" schema. *Psychology of Women Quarterly, 38*(4), 503–518. https://doi.org/10.1177/0361684314541418

Admon, L. K., Dalton, V. K., Kolenic, G. E., Ettner, S. L., Tilea, A., Haffajee, R. L., … & Zivin, K. (2021). Trends in suicidality 1 year before and after birth among commercially insured childbearing individuals in the United States, 2006–2017. *JAMA Psychiatry, 78*(2), 171–176. https://doi.org/10.1001/jamapsychiatry.2020.3550

Alang, S. (2019). Mental health care among Blacks in America: Confronting racism and constructing solutions. *Health Services Research, 54*(2). https://www.ncbi.nlm.nih.gov/pmc/articles/PMC6407345/

American College of Obstetricians and Gynecologists. (2024). *Respectful care eModules.* ACOG. Retrieved March 18, 2024, from https://www.acog.org/education-and-events/emodules/respectful-care

Ashman, J. J., Santo, L., & Okeyode, T. (2023). *Characteristics of office-based physician visits by age, 2019.* https://doi.org/10.15620/cdc:125462

Beauboeuf-Lafontant, T. (2005). Keeping up appearances, getting fed up: The embodiment of strength among African American women. *Meridians: Feminism, Race, Transnationalism, 5*(2), 104–123. https://doi.org/10.1353/mer.2005.0003

Beauboeuf-Lafontant, T. (2007). You have to show strength: An exploration of gender, race, and depression. *Gender & Society, 21*(1), 28–51. https://doi.org/10.1177/0891243206294108

Birth Monopoly. (2023, November 28). *Birth monopoly.* https://birthmonopoly.com/

Black, A. R., & Peacock, N. (2011). Pleasing the masses: Messages for daily life management in African American women's popular media sources. *American Journal of Public Health, 101*(1), 144–150. https://doi.org/10.2105/ajph.2009.167817

Bhui, K., Aslam, R. H. W., Palinski, A., McCabe, R., Johnson, M. R., Weich, S., ... & Szczepura, A. (2015). Interventions designed to improve therapeutic communications between Black and minority ethnic people and professionals working in psychiatric services: a systematic review of the evidence for their effectiveness. *Health Technology Assessment, 19*(31), 1–176. https://doi.org/10.3310/hta19310

Bhui, K., McCabe, R., Weich, S., Singh, S., Johnson, M., & Szczepura, A. (2013). THERACOM: a systematic review of the evidence base for interventions to improve Therapeutic Communications between Black and minority ethnic populations and staff in specialist mental health services. *Systematic Reviews, 2*, 1–11. http://dx.doi.org/10.1186/2046-4053-2-15

Cameron, N. O., Muldrow, A. F., & Stefani, W. (2018). The weight of things: Understanding African American women's perceptions of health, body image, and attractiveness. *Qualitative Health Research, 28*(8), 1242–1254. https://doi.org/10.1177/1049732317753

Carrington, C. H. (2006). Clinical depression in African American women: Diagnoses, treatment, and research. *Journal of Clinical Psychology, 62*(7), 779–791. https://doi.org/10.1002/jclp.20289

Castelin, S., & White, G. (2022). "I'm a strong independent Black woman": The strong Black woman schema and mental health in college-aged Black women. *Psychology of Women Quarterly, 46*(2), 196–208. https://doi.org/10.1177/03616843211067501

Centers for Disease Control and Prevention (CDC). (2022, September 19). One in 5 pregnancy- related deaths in the U.S. are preventable. *Centers for Disease Control and Prevention*. Retrieved March 17, 2024, from https://www.cdc.gov/media/releases/2022/p0919-pregnancy-related-deaths.html

Centers for Medicare & Medicaid Services. (n.d.). *Cost sharing out of pocket costs | Medicaid*. medicaid.gov. https://www.medicaid.gov/medicaid/cost-sharing/cost-sharing-out-pocket- costs/index.html

Chan, A. L., Guo, N., Popat, R., Robakis, T., Blumenfeld, Y. Y., Main, E., . . . & Butwick, A. J. (2021). Racial and ethnic disparities in hospital-based care associated with postpartum depression. *Journal of Racial and Ethnic Health Disparities, 8*, 220–229. https://doi.org/10.1007/s40615-020-00774-y

Chin, K., Wendt, A., Bennett, I. M., & Bhat, A. (2022). Suicide and maternal mortality. *Current Psychiatry Reports, 24*(4), 239–275. https://doi.org/10.1007/s11920-022-01334-3

Collins, P. H. (1986). Learning from the outsider within: The sociological significance of Black feminist thought. *Social problems, 33*(6), s14–s32. https://doi.org/10.1525/sp.1986.33.6.03a00020

Collins, P. H. (2000). *Black feminist thought: Knowledge, consciousness, and the politics of empowerment* (2nd ed.). Routledge.

Collins, P. H. (2022). *Black feminist thought: Knowledge, consciousness, and the politics of empowerment.* Routledge.

Coombs, N. C., Meriwether, W. E., Caringi, J., & Newcomer, S. R. (2021). Barriers to healthcare access among US adults with mental health challenges: a population-based study. *SSM- Population Health, 15,* 100847. https://doi.org/10.1016/j.ssmph.2021.100847

Copeland, E. J. (1982). Oppressed conditions and the mental health needs of low-income Black women: Barriers to services, strategies for change. *Women & Therapy, 1*(1), 13–26. https://doi.org/10.1300/j015v01n01_03

Crenshaw, K. W. (1998). Demarginalizing the intersection of race and sex: A Black Feminist critique of antidiscrimination doctrine, feminist theory, and antiracist politics. In *Oxford University Press eBooks* (pp. 314–343). https://doi.org/10.1093/oso/9780198782063.003.0016

Crenshaw, K. W. (2013). Mapping the margins: Intersectionality, identity politics, and violence against women of color. In *The public nature of private violence* (pp. 93–118). Routledge.

Daniels, P. (2016, October 31). *How diabetes got its name - MSU Extension.* MSU Extension. https://www.canr.msu.edu/news/howdiabetes_got_its_name

Davis, D. A. (2019). Obstetric racism: The racial politics of pregnancy, labor, and birthing. *Medical Anthropology, 38*(7), 560–573. https://doi.org/10.1080/01459740.2018.1549389

Demosthenes, L. (2021, June 25). *Expanding prenatal care options for Low-Risk patients.* ACOG. Retrieved March 17, 2024, from https://www.acog.org/education-and-events/creog/curriculum-resources/cases-in-high-value-care/expanding-prenatal-care-options-for-low-risk-patients#:~:text=Mandy%20is%20told%20that%20the,to%20minimize%20the%20chance%20of

Donovan, R. A., & West, L. M. (2015). Stress and mental health: Moderating role of the strong Black woman stereotype. *Journal of Black Psychology, 41*(4), 384–396. https://doi.org/10.1177/0095798414543014

Elfenbein, H. A., & Ambady, N. (2003). When familiarity breeds accuracy: cultural exposure and facial emotion recognition. *Journal of Personality and Social Psychology, 85*(2), 276–290. https://doi.org/10.1037/0022 3514.85.2.276

Erving, C. L., McKinnon, I. I., Thomas Tobin, C. S., Van Dyke, M. E., Murden, R., Moore, R. H., ... & Lewis, T. T. (2024). Black Women as superwomen? The mental health effects of superwoman schema, socioeconomic status, and financial strain. *Social Problems*, spae007. https://doi.org/10.1093/socpro/spae007

Experts, B. Y. H. M. (2023, October 19). Mindful Marauders: The rise of mental health in hip- hop. *Headspace.* https://www.headspace.com/articles/mental-health-hip-hop

Garcia, L. M. (2020, November). A concept analysis of obstetric violence in the United States of America. *Nursing Forum*, *55*(4), 654–663. https://doi.org/10.1111/nuf.12482
Gibbs, J. T., & Fuery, D. (1994). Mental health and well-being of black women: Toward strategies of empowerment. *American Journal of Community Psychology*, *22*(4), 559–582. https://doi.org/10.1007/bf02506893
Golberstein, E., & Gonzales, G. (2015). The effects of Medicaid eligibility on mental health services and out-of-pocket spending for mental health services. *Health Services Research*, *50*(6), 1734–1750. https://doi.org/10.1111/1475-6773.12399
Gourrier, L. (2023, February 4). 165: Shades of blue – Kay Matthews. *BSiC*. https://www.birthstoriesincolor.com/birth-story/2023/2/4/165-shades-of-blue-kay-matthews
Hall, S. V., Zivin, K., Piatt, G. A., Weaver, A., Tilea, A., Zhang, X., & Moyer, C. A. (2024). Racial disparities in diagnosis of postpartum mood and anxiety disorders among symptomatic Medicaid enrollees, 2012–2015. *Psychiatric Services*, *75*(2), 115–123. https://doi.org/10.1176/appi.ps.20230094
Hallstein, D. L. O. B. (1999). A postmodern caring: Feminist standpoint theories, revisioned caring, and communication ethics. *Western Journal of Communication*, *63*(1), 32–56. https://doi.org/10.1080/10570319909374627
Harding, S. (1991). *Whose science? Whose knowledge?: Thinking from women's lives.* Cornell University Press.
hooks, B. (1993). *Sisters of the yam: Black women and self-recovery*. South End.
Hoyert, D. (2021). Maternal mortality rates in the United States, 2021. In *cdc.gov*. NCHS Health E-Stats. https://www.cdc.gov/nchs/data/hestat/maternal-mortality/2021/maternal-mortality-rates-2021.htm#:~:text=In%202021%2C%20the%20maternal%20mortality,(Figure%201%20and%20Table)
IRTH. (2024, February 27). *Home · IRTH*. https://irthapp.com/
James, K. F., Klomhaus, A. M., Elliott, T., Mensah, M., Jeffers, K. S., & Choi, K. R. (2023). Structural factors in health care associated with the mental health needs of Black women in California during the perinatal period. *Journal of Obstetric, Gynecologic & Neonatal Nursing*, *52*(6), 481–490. https://doi.org/10.1016/j.jogn.2023.08.002
Johnson, J. D., Asiodu, I. V., McKenzie, C. P., Tucker, C., Tully, K. P., Bryant, K., . . . & Stuebe, A. M. (2019). Racial and ethnic inequities in postpartum pain evaluation and management. *Obstetrics & Gynecology*, *134*(6), 1155–1162. https://doi.org/10.1097/01.aoa.0000661376.92421.ee
Jones, C., & Shorter-Gooden, K. (2003). *Shifting: The double lives of Black women in America.* HarperCollins.
Kaiser Family Foundation. (2024, March 9). Medicaid Postpartum Coverage Extension Tracker | KFF. *KFF*. https://www.kff.org/medicaid/issue-brief/medicaid-postpartum-coverage-extension-tracker/
Kirmayer, L. J., Groleau, D., Guzder, J., Blake, C., & Jarvis, E. (2003). Cultural consultation: A model of mental health service for multicultural societies.

The Canadian Journal of Psychiatry, *48*(3), 145–153. https://doi.org/10.1177/070674370304800302

Kresovich, A., Collins, M. K. R., Riffe, D., & Carpentier, F. R. D. (2021). A content analysis of mental health discourse in popular rap music. *JAMA Pediatrics, 175(*3), 286–292. https://doi.org/10.1001/jamapediatrics.2020.5155

Lopez, M., & Moslimani, M. (2024, January 18). *Key facts about the nation's 47.9 million Black Americans.* Retrieved March 1, 2024, from https://www.pewresearch.org/short-reads/2024/01/18/key-facts-about-black-americans/

Lorenz, L. S., & Chilingerian, J. A. (2011). Using visual and narrative methods to achieve fair process in clinical care. *JoVE (Journal of Visualized Experiments)*, (48), e2342. https://doi.org/10.3791/2342

Margerison, C. E., Hettinger, K., Kaestner, R., Goldman-Mellor, S., & Gartner, D. (2021). Medicaid expansion associated with some improvements in perinatal mental health: Study examines Medicaid expansion and perinatal mental health. *Health Affairs*, *40*(10), 1605–1611. https://doi.org/10.1377/hlthaff.2021.00776

Martínez-Galiano, J. M., Martinez-Vazquez, S., Rodríguez-Almagro, J., & Hernández-Martinez, A. (2021). The magnitude of the problem of obstetric violence and its associated factors: A cross-sectional study. *Women and Birth*, *34*(5), e526–e536. https://doi.org/10.1016/j.wombi.2020.10.002

Maternal Health Learning and Innovation Center (MHLIC). (2024, February 20). Maternal Health Learning and Innovation Center - Accelerating innovative and evidence-informed interventions that improve maternal health and eliminate maternal health inequities. *Maternal Health Learning and Innovation Center.* https://maternalhealthlearning.org/

Orbe, M. P. (1998). From the standpoint (s) of traditionally muted groups: Explicating a co- cultural communication theoretical model. *Communication Theory*, *8*(1), 1–26. https://doi.org/10.1111/j.1468 2885.1998.tb00209.x

Orbe, M. P. (2005). Continuing the legacy of theorizing from the margins: Conceptualizations of co-cultural theory. *Women and Language*, *28*(2), 65–66. https://www.proquest.com/scholarly-journals/continuing-legacy-theorizing-margins/docview/198819607/se-2

Our work – Postnatal Patient Safety Learning Lab. (n.d.). *Postnatal Patient Safety Learning Lab.* https://www.postnatalsafety.com/our-work

Owens, D. C. (2017). *Medical Bondage: Race, gender, and the origins of American gynecology.* https://library.oapen.org/bitstream/20.500.12657/30659/1/644220.pdf

Parks, S. (2010). *Fierce angels: The strong Black woman in American life and culture.* One World/Ballantine Books.

Perry, B. L., Pullen, E. L., & Oser, C. B. (2012). Too much of a good thing? Psychosocial resources, gendered racism, and suicidal ideation among low socioeconomic status African American women. *Social Psychology Quarterly*, *75*(4), 334–359. https://doi.org/10.1177/0190272512455932

Robinson, M. N., Erving, C. L., & Thomas Tobin, C. S. (2023). Are distressed Black women also depressed? Implications for a mental health paradox. *Journal of Racial and Ethnic Health Disparities*, *10*(3), 1280–1292. https://doi.org/10.1007/s40615-022-01313-7

Roux, M. (2021, August 3). 5 facts about Black women in the labor force. *U.S. Department of Labor Blog*. Retrieved from https://blog.dol.gov/2021/08/03/5-facts-about-black-women-in-the-labor-force

Rüdell, K., Bhui, K., & Priebe, S. (2009). Concept, development and application of a new mixed method assessment of cultural variations in illness perceptions: Barts Explanatory Model Inventory. *Journal of Health Psychology*, *14*(2), 336–347. https://doi.org/10.1177/1359105308100218

Shim, J. K. (2010). Cultural health capital: A theoretical approach to understanding health care interactions and the dynamics of unequal treatment. *Journal of Health and Social Behavior*, *51*(1), 1–15. https://doi.org/10.1177/0022146509361185

Shrider, E. (2023, September 12). *Poverty rate for the Black* population fell below pre-pandemic levels. Retrieved March 1, 2024, from https://www.census.gov/library/stories/2023/09/black-poverty-rate.html

SoulMed Holistic Health Collaborative. (n.d.). *Dear Black Woman: Daily Meditation Mixtape (EP) — SoulMed Holistic Health Collaborative*. https://soulmed.co/shop/dear-black- woman-daily-meditation-mixtape-ep

Stanton, A. G., Jerald, M. C., Ward, L. M., & Avery, L. R. (2017). Social media contributions to strong Black woman ideal endorsement and Black women's mental health. *Psychology of Women Quarterly*, *41*(4), 465–478. https://doi.org/10.1177/0361684317732330

Tesone, J. E. (1996). Multi-lingualism, word-presentations, thing-presentations and psychic reality. *The International Journal of Psycho-Analysis*, *77*(5), 871–881. https://www.proquest.com/scholarly-journals/multi-lingualism-word-presentations-thing-psychic/docview/1298188221/se-2

Thomas, A. J., Witherspoon, K. M., & Speight, S. L. (2008). Gendered racism, psychological distress, and coping styles of African American women. *Cultural Diversity and Ethnic Minority Psychology*, *14*(4), 307–314. https://doi.org/10.1037/1099–9809.14.4.307

USAFacts. (2023, June 14). *The state of relationships, marriages, and living alone in the US*. USAFacts. https://usafacts.org/articles/state-relationships-marriages-and-living-alone-us/

U.S. Department of Health and Human Services (2021, February 25). Heart disease risk factors you can't control. *Office on Women's Health*. Retrieved February 24, 2024, from https://www.womenshealth.gov/heart-disease-and-stroke/heart-disease/heart-disease-risk-factors/cant-control

Valenzuela, C. P., & Osterman, M. J. (2023). Characteristics of mothers by source of payment for the delivery: United States, 2021. *NCHS Data Brief*, (468), 1–8. https://doi.org/10.15620/cdc:127266

Viruell-Fuentes, E. A., Miranda, P. Y., & Abdulrahim, S. (2012). More than culture: structural racism, intersectionality theory, and immigrant health. *Social Science & Medicine*, *75*(12), 2099–2106. https://doi.org/10.1016/j.socscimed.2011.12.037

Walker, E. R., Cummings, J. R., Hockenberry, J. M., & Druss, B. G. (2015). Insurance status, use of mental health services, and unmet need for mental health care in the United States. *Psychiatric Services*, *66*(6), 578–584. https://doi.org/10.1176/appi.ps.201400248

Washington, H. A. (2006). *Medical apartheid: The dark history of medical experimentation on Black Americans from colonial times to the present*. Doubleday Books.

Watson, E. (2021, March 14). Black musicians are creating soundtracks for popular meditation apps. *Okayplayer*. https://www.okayplayer.com/originals/meditation-apps-music-madlib- john-legend.html

Woods-Giscombé, C. L., & Lobel, M. (2008). Race and gender matter: A multidimensional approach to conceptualizing and measuring stress in African American women. *Cultural Diversity and Ethnic Minority Psychology*, *14*(3), 173–182. https://doi.org/10.1037/1099- 9809.14.3.173

Woods-Giscombé, C. L. (2010). Superwoman schema: African American women's views on stress, strength, and health. *Qualitative Health Research*, *20*, 668–683. https://doi.org/10.1177/1049732310361892

Wood, J. T., & Fixmer-Oraiz, N. (2019). *Gendered lives: Communication, gender, and culture*. Cengage.

World Health Organization. (2022, June 17). *Mental health*. Retrieved March 17, 2024, from https://www.who.int/news-room/fact-sheets/detail/mental-health-strengthening-our-response

5

Designing Mental Health Communication Strategies for Hispanic and Latino Populations in the United States

Do Kyun David Kim and Jin-Ae Kang

According to the U.S. Census Bureau (2023), the Hispanic population of the United States as of July 1, 2022, reached 63.7 million, making it the nation's largest racial or ethnic minority—19.1 percent of the total population. Thirteen states had more than 1 million Hispanic residents in 2022, including Arizona, California, Colorado, Florida, Georgia, Illinois, New Jersey, New Mexico, New York, North Carolina, Pennsylvania, Texas, and Washington. Eight specific Hispanic groups had populations of one million or more in 2020 (Peña et al., 2023): Mexican (35.9 million); Puerto Rican (5.6 million); Salvadoran (2.3 million); Cuban and Dominican (each at 2.2 million); Guatemalan (1.7 million); Colombian (1.3 million); and Honduran (1.1 million).

Each year, recognizing the contributions and influence of Hispanic Americans to the history, culture, and achievements of the United States, National Hispanic Heritage Month has been celebrated from September 15 to October 15 (Library of Congress, n.a.; Peña et al., 2023). This recognition started in 1968 as Hispanic Heritage Week under President Lyndon Johnson and was expanded by President Ronald Reagan in 1988 to cover a thirty-day period, enacted into law on August 17, 1988, with the approval of Public Law 100-402. The date September 15 is significant because it is the anniversary of the independence of several Latin American countries—Costa Rica, El Salvador, Guatemala, Honduras, and Nicaragua. In addition, Mexico and Chile celebrate their independence days on September 16 and September 18, respectively, and Columbus Day, or Día de la Raza on October 12. All these fall within this thirty-day period.

In terms of health situations, several health issues are more prevalent in Hispanic people than in the general population (Northwestern Medicine, n.d.), such as obesity, diabetes, hypertension (high blood pressure), chronic kidney disease, chronic liver disease, and cancer: Hispanic Americans are 1.2 times more likely to be obese than non-Hispanic Whites. This is especially important because obesity can lead to other health challenges. About 40 percent of Hispanic adults in the United States are expected to develop type 2 diabetes in their lifetime. Nearly 1 in 4 Hispanics have high blood pressure, which can be a precursor to a heart attack, stroke, kidney disease, or heart failure. Hispanics are 1.5 times more likely to have kidney failure compared to other Americans. In fact, 20 percent of people on the kidney transplant waiting list are Hispanic. Hispanics are also at higher risk of developing certain liver diseases. Internally within diverse Hispanic groups, Black Hispanic adults are more likely to report negative healthcare experiences than their non-Black Hispanic counterparts, highlighting disparities within the Hispanic community itself (Tyson & Lopez, 2023). Furthermore, many attributes have worsened health outcomes in their communities due to occupational and structural factors.

Although Hispanic Americans have notably higher health problems, most of them have lower rates of health insurance coverage than people of other racial and ethnic backgrounds. Given the seriousness and urgency of health promotion among Hispanic and Latino populations in the United States, this chapter focuses on issues related to mental health among Hispanic and Latino populations in the United States and suggests effective health communication strategies to promote mental health among these populations.

Urgency of Mental Health Promotion among Hispanic Populations

Mental health issues or disorders are prevalent among Hispanic individuals in the United States, including higher rates of anxiety, depression, and substance use disorders, and are influenced by several factors, such as socioeconomic status, cultural stigma, and access to care (SAMHSA, 2023). Notably, Mental Health America (2017) reports that Hispanic youth also face high rates of depressive symptoms and suicidal thoughts. Such serious mental health conditions are often exacerbated by social determinants such as poverty, discrimination, and immigration-related stress (Santiago et al., 2018).

According to Ramos-Olazagasti and Conway (2022), over one-third (37%) of Latino[1] parents have experienced a mental health disorder—depression, anxiety, substance use disorder, or PTSD—at some point in their lives. Interestingly, Hispanic parents who were born outside of the fifty states had a lower prevalence of mental health disorders than Latino parents born in the United States. Specifically, 29 percent of non-US state-born Hispanic parents had experienced a mental health disorder, compared to 51 percent of US state-born Latino parents. Parents of Puerto Rican heritage were more likely to have a mental health disorder at some point in their lives than parents whose ancestry was from Mexico, El Salvador, or other Central American countries. However, differences by heritage were no longer present after adjusting for place of birth, which generalizes the mental issues across different groups within the Hispanic populations.

Uscher-Pines and colleagues (2023), using simulated patients, contacted 386 safety-net clinics in California, which has one of the states having the largest Hispanic populations, and reported the challenges in accessing Spanish-based mental health services. They found that nearly 20 percent of Spanish-speaking callers were either hung up on or told that no one could assist them in Spanish. Despite a significant drop in telehealth usage for most post-pandemic medical care, it remains high for behavioral health services, with 64 percent of clinics offering both telehealth and in-person visits, 22 percent offering only telehealth, and 14 percent only in-person. Beyond California, Pro et al. (2022) found that, between 2014 and 2019, the availability of mental health services in Spanish declined by 18 percent, even as the Hispanic population in the United States grew by 4.5 percent (5.2 million people). About one-third of Hispanic Americans, including 58 percent of Hispanic immigrants, express a preference for Spanish-speaking healthcare providers (Tyson & Lopez, 2023).

As a result of mental health problems, suicide is a critical consequence of mental health problems within the Hispanic and Latino American communities, particularly among younger and middle-aged individuals. According to the Office of Minority Health (2021), in 2019, suicide was the second leading cause of death for Hispanics aged 15–34. Suicide attempts among Hispanic girls in grades 9–12 were 30 percent higher than among non-Hispanic White girls in the same age group in 2019. These alarming statistics underscore the urgent need for effective mental health interventions and support for adolescents and young adults in this demographic, highlighting significant gaps in existing mental health services and the necessity for mental wellness in Hispanic and Latino communities.

In terms of healthcare equity, Hispanics and Latinos tend to not receive proper treatment for their mental health issues. For example, in 2018, 56.8 percent of

Hispanic young adults aged 18–25 with serious mental illness did not receive treatment (Thornhill et al., 2022). In the racial comparison, Hispanic populations are much more marginalized than many other racial groups. According to the 2021 National Survey on Drug Use and Health (NSDUH), nearly 22 percent of Hispanic and Latino Americans reported having a mental illness (SAMHSA, 2022). However, only 36 percent of Hispanic and Latino Americans received mental health services compared to 52 percent of non-Hispanic Whites.

The media have also reported the persistent challenges in mental health care access for Latino communities. For example, Gamboa (2023), a national reporter for NBC Latino and NBCNews.com, well described the racial gap in mental health treatment in her article: Despite the trauma of a mass shooting in Uvalde, Texas, where nineteen children and two teachers lost their lives, many still struggle to access mental health services. While President Joe Biden recently proposed regulations to improve insurance coverage for mental health treatments, Latino, Black, and Asian people were widely disconnected from mental health services. Only 36.1 percent of Latino adults with mental illness received services in 2021, compared to 52.4 percent of Whites. The study pointed out that critical barriers that created the inequity in mental health care for Latinos (and other minorities) in comparison with Whites include poverty rates, language barriers, cultural stigmas, and a shortage of culturally trained mental health professionals.

Health Communication and Culture

Health communication and culture are intricately connected, as cultural factors significantly influence the effectiveness of health communication (Kreuter & McClure, 2004). More specifically, culture shapes health beliefs, practices, and behaviors, which in turn affect the effectiveness of health communication campaigns and interventions (Hernandez & Gibb, 2014). In addition, cultural beliefs about health and illness play a critical role in how individuals understand and manage their health. For example, cultural norms and values can determine how communities understand concepts of health and illness, which impacts how health information is delivered, perceived, and accepted (Kreuter & McClure, 2004). Therefore, it is important to understand the target populations' unique cultural beliefs and the relationship between health communication and culture to design effective mental health communication strategies for the Hispanic population.

Cultural factors also affect people's health literacy, which influences how individuals process and use health information. Some cultural groups may have lower health literacy due to historical, socioeconomic, or educational disparities, necessitating tailored communication strategies that account for such differences (Schiavo, 2013). Specifically, sources of health information and their perceived credibility can vary significantly across cultures. Trust in health information is often influenced by cultural norms and the credibility of the information source within the community. Related to this, cultural competence in health communication is important in designing messages that accommodate varying levels of health literacy, thus making health information accessible and understandable to diverse cultural groups (Dutta, 2007).

Health communicators must possess cultural competence to be able to adopt culturally acceptable and, therefore, effective health communication strategies (Dutta, 2007). Cultural competence involves understanding and respecting cultural differences and tailoring communication strategies accordingly. In other words, cultural competence ensures that health messages are not only understood but also culturally relevant and respectful, thereby increasing their effectiveness. Health communication literature also emphasizes the importance of cultural competence in health communication, advocating for approaches that are culturally sensitive and responsive to the needs of diverse populations (Shen et al., 2018).

Uniqueness in Hispanic and Latino Culture

Hispanics in the United States include a variety of origins, including Cuban, Mexican, Puerto Rican, South or Central American, or other Spanish origin. Therefore, significant diversity exists within the Hispanic population. Considering the diversity within them, this chapter identifies some shared cultural attributes that commonly affect health communication across different Hispanic populations, which constitutes a foundation for providing recommendations for mental health communication campaigns and interventions for Hispanic populations at large.

First, Hispanics generally have a collectivistic culture, emphasizing group harmony, cooperation, and shared responsibility, which is stressed more than individual function and responsibility (Gudykunst, 2004). Related to their collective culture, their traditional patriarchal structure grants authority to fathers or the oldest male relatives. In general, Hispanic/Latino populations place a strong emphasis on showing respect to those authority figures (Kemp & Rasbridge, 2004), and this respect often extends to other authority figures in their communities as well (Flores, 2000).

Food is another interesting cultural factor. The relationship between food and Hispanic cultures is multifaceted, encompassing material and symbolic aspects. First, food practices are integral to everyday life, and complex connections between food and Hispanic communities involve cultural, dietary, aesthetic, and hedonistic dimensions (Boutaud et al., 2016). Roland Barthes views gastronomy as a humanistic approach, considering it to be a total social fact (Symons, 2014). In his view, food primarily represents a cultural act, deeply tied to identity. According to Boutaud et al. (201), food embodies a dialectical tension between attachment to tradition and the desire for exploration and novelty. Advocating this relationship between food and culture, Taylor and O'Flynn (2020) argued that food intersects with colonial studies, ethnicity, gender, power dynamics, embodiment, and identity.

The artistic representations of Hispanic culture through architecture, painting, photography, film, posters, and textiles are multifaceted and rich. First, arts and music play a significant role in constructing and consolidating national culture and identities among Latin Americans (Fernández & Vila, 2017; Madrid, 2017). It provides valuable bibliographies and reference lists for specific subjects, such as Bolivian, Chilean, and Central American art, Andean weaving, Sandinista revolutionary posters, dramatic arts, and Latin music. Several Latin dances also represent their artistic and expressive nature, including salsa, tango, rumba, samba, cha-cha-cha, mambo, and so on. With a focus on contemporary popular culture, the American Latino Media Arts (ALMA) Award aims to promote fair, accurate, and balanced portrayals of Latinos in television, film, and music (Robinson, 1993).

Considerable Factors Affecting Mental Health Communication among the Hispanic Population

From the communication perspective, culture is a product of communication. Therefore, culture and communication are inseparable, and culture in the context of the theme of this chapter significantly influences mental health communication within the Hispanic population. Therefore, cultural and communication factors influencing mental health campaigns and interventions are key to effectively promoting mental health among the target populations, as those factors are also critical in addressing the healthcare disparities faced by Hispanic populations. Due to this feature of health communication applicable to the Hispanic community, several studies claim that integration of cultural preferences into mental health communication could enhance engagement and utilization of services (e.g., Alegría et al., 2016; Interian et al., 2011). Considering these cultural and communication aspects, formative research is needed to find factors affecting mental health communication campaigns and interventions. This section also explores systemic and social factors that affect or, most of the time, hinder the effectiveness of mental health communication campaigns and interventions.

First, language is a critical factor and a barrier, as many Hispanic individuals struggle to communicate with healthcare providers due to limited English proficiency, resulting in misunderstandings, reduced quality of care, and reluctance to seek medical help (Artiga et al., 2021; Betancourt et al., 2003). In multicultural health communication, language is often considered the most common communication and cultural factor affecting health communication, as health messages need to be correctly and comprehensively conveyed in a language that the target population can understand, consume, and follow. Several studies also highlight the need for culturally tailored health communication that takes into account both verbal and nonverbal communication practices prevalent in different cultures (Clayman et al., 2010).

As slightly mentioned above, in Hispanic culture, mental health issues have been stigmatized and often seen as a source of shame and personal weakness, which has been a significant barrier to operating health campaigns and interventions. Specifically, stigma around mental health within the Hispanic and Latino communities impedes individuals from acknowledging mental health issues and seeking professional help, exacerbating the difficulties in addressing their needs. Cabassa and colleagues (2008) also highlighted that the stigma attached to mental illness in Hispanic culture could lead to the underutilization of mental health services. Hence, Mendoza et al. (2015) pointed out the need for culturally sensitive interventions to reduce the stigma of mental health problems, and the efforts to reduce stigma must be culturally tailored to resonate with Hispanic values and beliefs.

As another cultural factor, Hispanic cultures often emphasize *respeto* (respect) and *simpatía* (kindness), which affect how mental health issues can be communicated. In Hispanic communities, there is a tendency for mental health discussions to be avoided or approached indirectly to maintain social harmony and avoid discomfort. Therefore, mental health communicators should be aware of this cultural norm and find supportive and respectful methods to encourage open dialogue, employing respectful and sincere methods to facilitate dialogue on mental health issues (Cardemil et al., 2020).

In terms of help-seeking behaviors, traditional beliefs and reliance on alternative medicine influence help-seeking behaviors in Hispanic communities. Many prefer seeking support from family, community, or religious leaders rather than professional mental health services. According to Cruz et al. (2022), Traditional healers (THs)—sobadores, yerberos, espiritualistas, and hueseros—often serve as the first point of contact for Latino individuals in the United States due to barriers in accessing the biomedical healthcare system. Their study reviewed 85 studies and found that the use of traditional healers among the Latine communities for their mental, physical, and spiritual health in the United States varies widely (6%–67.7%) and is driven by accessibility, affordability, and cultural/linguistic compatibility. Having these results, they argued the need to assess the efficacy and safety of TH treatments and explore coordination with biomedical health care to improve health equity for Latine individuals.

In Hispanic culture, family plays a crucial role, significantly impacting decisions related to mental health. However, family support can be both a facilitator and a barrier to seeking help. Therefore, involving family in mental health communication and providing family-focused interventions can improve the effectiveness of treatment (Streit et al., 2020). Recent literature also emphasizes the importance of family in mental health communication, suggesting that family-inclusive approaches are proven effective (Streit et al., 2020).

Inescapably, religion significantly influences the mental health of the Hispanic and Latino populations (Caplan, 2019). It impacts their utilization of mental health care, with cultural and religious values contributing to disparities in access. For example, as explained previously, stigma around mental illness often leads to denial among Hispanic and Latino populations unless symptoms severely disrupt their daily lives. However, religious coping mechanisms like prayer are seen as protective factors. Interestingly, a lack of religiosity correlates with increased depression and anxiety symptoms more in older adults than younger or middle-aged individuals (Lerman et al., 2018).

The level of acculturation and ethnic identity is also a factor that notably impacts mental health communication among Hispanics. According to Bekteshi and Bellamy (2024), those with higher levels of acculturation may be more open to seeking mental health services, while those with strong ties to traditional values might be more resistant. Acculturation, the process of adapting to a new culture, can lead to stress and mental health repercussions, known as acculturative stress. This stress can precipitate a number of clinical conditions (Alarcón, 2022). On the other hand, a strong ethnic identity, a sense of belonging to one's ethnic group, can serve as a protective factor against mental health disorders (Burnett-Zeigler et al., 2018). Individuals with a stronger ethnic identity are generally less likely to have a lifetime psychiatric disorder. However, more acculturated individuals are more likely to have a lifetime psychiatric disorder. These effects are compounded by the stigma associated with mental health in the Hispanic or Latino community, leading to prolonged suffering in silence. Therefore, understanding the role of acculturation and ethnic identity is crucial in addressing mental health issues in this population. Acknowledging this cultural attribute, several studies highlight that tailoring communication strategies to different levels of acculturation can improve their effectiveness (e.g., Moreno & Cardemil, 2018; Fox et al., 2017).

Hispanic and Latino Americans encounter significant structural and social barriers to accessing behavioral health services and care. Specifically, *racism and discrimination* can significantly impact the mental health of Hispanic and Latino individuals. Perceived racial and ethnic discrimination is associated with poor mental health outcomes such as depression and anxiety (Hwang & Goto, 2008). The public discourse over immigration can harm the mental health of Latino groups in the United States, including native-born citizens. Greater feelings of ethnic pride and belonging can attenuate the negative relationship between perceived discrimination and mental health (Andrade et al., 2021). However, disparities in mental health care exist by race and ethnicity, with White adults more likely to receive mental health services compared to Hispanic adults (Tyson & Lopez, 2023). Public policy and political rhetoric can also lead to feelings of threat and insecurity among Latinos, further exacerbating mental health issues (Roche et al., 2024) These findings underscore the need for culturally sensitive mental health services and policies that promote inclusivity and respect for all individuals, regardless of their race or ethnicity.

Current Mental Health Communication Strategies for Hispanic Immigrants

SAMHSA (Substance Abuse and Mental Health Services Administration) has been actively involved in addressing mental health disparities within the Hispanic and Latino populations. For example, the Accept/Ignore Campaign, created through collaboration between SAMHSA, the Ad Council, and the Hispanic/Latino advertising agency, Wing, aims to raise awareness about mental health problems in Hispanic/Latino communities (PR Newswire, 2010). The campaign includes in-language radio, print, outdoor, and web banner ads. It directs young adults to visit the campaign website, aceptarignorar.samhsa.gov, where they can find tools to support friends in the recovery process and access additional resources. In addition, SAMHSA offers a variety of Spanish-language resources and reports to support behavioral health equity for Hispanic/Latino populations.

Several non-governmental organizations have also done mental health communication research, campaigns, and interventions specifically tailored for Hispanic and Latino populations. The National Hispanic and Latino Addiction Technology Transfer Center (ATTC) serves as an international multidisciplinary resource for professionals in the addiction treatment and recovery services field. In addition, the National Hispanic and Latino Prevention Technology Transfer Center (PTTC) provides training and technical assistance services to the substance misuse prevention field, with a focus on Hispanic and Latino populations, and the National Hispanic and Latino Mental Health Technology Transfer Center (MHTTC) disseminates and implements evidence-based practices and promising practices for mental disorders within the field, specifically addressing the needs of Hispanic and Latino communities. These efforts aim to reduce barriers, combat stigma, and improve access to culturally competent mental health services.

Social Marketing and Diffusion of Innovations as Theoretical Frameworks

In order to provide evidence-based, theoretical, applicable, and feasible health communication recommendations, this chapter introduces social marketing and diffusion of innovations as theoretical frameworks to design health

Table 5.1 Considerable Resources for Mental Health Communication Campaigns and Interventions for Hispanic/Latino populations.

Increasing Cultural Connection with Hispanic and Latinx Clients (Source: https://mhttcnetwork.org/wp-content/uploads/2022/06/rNHLMHTTC_-Latino-Population-Region-10.Session-3.pdf) This presentation by the National Hispanic and Latino MHTTC covers culturally centered interventions and provides insights into working with this population. Accordingly, key objectives include applying culturally centered interventions, discussing eight areas of culturally centered interventions and identifying specific elements of the Hispanic and Latino population that may need special attention.
Successful Interventions in Latino Mental Health (Source: https://lbhcphila.org/learning-center/successful-interventions-in-latino-mental-health) The Latino Behavioral Health Coalition (LBHC) focuses on culturally sensitive interventions, integrating traditional Latino family values into therapy, and promoting community engagement to address mental health disparities. Their initiatives include educational outreach to demystify mental health issues and advocacy for policies that improve access to mental health services for Latinos. By emphasizing community-based solutions and culturally relevant education, LBHC aims to enhance mental health outcomes in the Latino community.
Tailored Treatment for Latino Immigrants: (Source: https://salud-america.org/mental-health-treatment-offers-new-path-for-latino-immigrants/) Researchers at Massachusetts General Hospital's Disparities Research Unit have developed the Integrated Intervention for Dual Problems and Early Action (IIDEA) program to address mental health and substance misuse among Latino immigrants. This culturally tailored therapy, tested in the United States and Spain, involves 10–12 weekly sessions incorporating cognitive behavioral therapy, mindfulness, and motivational interviewing. Results show significant reductions in mental health symptoms and substance use, especially for those with moderate to severe symptoms.
Community-Defined Solutions for Latino Mental Healthcare Disparities (UC Davis, 2012) (Source: https://health.ucdavis.edu/media-resources/crhd/documents/pdfs/community-defined-solutions-latino-mental-health-care-disparities-exec-summary.pdf) This report highlights the challenges faced by Latinos, such as stigma, cultural barriers, and lack of bilingual services, and proposes community-defined strategies to improve access and quality of mental health care. Key recommendations include increasing culturally and linguistically appropriate services, enhancing community outreach, and developing school-based mental health programs. The report emphasizes the importance of community involvement and collaboration to achieve better mental health outcomes for Latinos.
Support From Peers to Expand Access (SUPERA) (University of California—Irvine, Berkeley, and San Francisco) (Source: https://news.uci.edu/2022/10/03/nih-funds-collaboration-to-improve-mental-health-treatment-for-latinos/) The National Institutes of Health is funding a $4.7 million, five-year project by UC Irvine, Berkeley, and San Francisco to enhance mental health services for Latino patients with limited English proficiency. The study aims to integrate peer support with a digital cognitive behavioral therapy platform, SilverCloud, in primary care settings. This approach also aims to improve the accessibility and effectiveness of mental health care by addressing cultural and linguistic barriers, leveraging community health workers, and evaluating different implementation strategies.

(*Continued*)

Table 5.1 (Continued)

Confronted with Multiple Crises, Latinos Draw Upon Culture and Community (Enfrentando múltiples crisis, los latinos recurren a la cultura y a la comunidad) (Source: https://www.samhsa.gov/blog/confronted-multiple-crises-latinos-draw-upon-culture-community-enfrentando-multiples-crisis) (SAMHSA) The Latinx community has faced significant challenges in 2020, including the COVID-19 pandemic, economic slowdown, and racial unrest, which have exacerbated behavioral health issues. Hispanics report higher rates of anxiety, depression, and suicidal thoughts compared to other groups. Despite these difficulties, the community shows resilience through strong cultural and social support systems, such as faith-based organizations and in-language communication. These support systems provide hope and a sense of community, helping to counteract fear and isolation.
Life is Precious (LIP): A suicide prevention intervention geared toward Latina adolescents and young adults (Source: https://www.tandfonline.com/doi/full/10.1080/13811118.2016.1242442) Life is Precious (LIP), a community-based program in New York City, helps adolescents and families address risk factors facing Latinas. Participants are assessed for suicidal ideation, depressive and other psychiatric symptoms, and family functioning, at program entry and every 4 months during participation. Demographic characteristics and suicide attempts are also tracked. In the study period, there were no attempted or completed suicides in this high-risk population. Suicidal ideation, depressive symptoms, anger, and post-traumatic stress symptoms decreased significantly during participation.

communication campaigns and interventions to promote mental health among Hispanic and Latino populations in the United States.

Social Marketing

Social marketing in the context of health communication involves applying marketing principles and techniques to influence health behaviors for the benefit of individuals and communities (Cheng et al., 2009). It aims to promote voluntary behavior change by addressing health issues through strategic communication and engagement. There are some key aspects of social marketing in health communication.

First, social marketing focuses on encouraging positive health behaviors, such as smoking cessation, healthy eating, and regular exercise, by understanding and addressing the barriers and motivators for the target audience (Andreasen, 1995). To substantiate this goal, conducting formative research to understand the needs, preferences, and behaviors of the target audience is crucial. This helps in designing interventions that are relevant and effective. Specifically, social marketing involves segmenting the audience based on demographic, psychographic, and behavioral characteristics to tailor messages and interventions that resonate with specific groups (Evans, 2006). Based on the segment analysis, social marketing strategically utilizes the marketing mix (product, price, place, promotion) that can be adapted to health communication to design effective interventions. For example, promoting the benefits of a health service (product), making it affordable (price), ensuring it is accessible (place), and using appropriate channels to communicate the message (promotion) (Hastings & Haywood, 1991). Social marketing also emphasizes the importance of continuous monitoring and evaluation of social marketing campaigns, which is essential to assess their impact and make necessary adjustments (Cheng et al., 2009).

Diffusion of Innovations

The theory of diffusion of innovations (DOI) explains how an innovation, including new ideas, practices, or products, spreads within a society. This theory identifies several key elements in consideration of the adoption of an innovation: the innovation itself, communication channels, time, and the social system (Rogers, 2003). In DOI, the adoption process is typically visualized as an S-curve, where the rate of adoption starts slowly, accelerates, and then levels off as the innovation reaches the critical mass—the level of adoption at which the diffusion is self-sustaining. The process includes five stages: knowledge, persuasion, decision, implementation, and confirmation.

DOI has been globally applied to health communication campaigns and interventions for decades for several purposes. First, DOI has been used to promote new health behaviors. For example, campaigns to increase vaccination rates may use influential community leaders to spread positive messages about vaccines, thereby accelerating adoption (Zimmerman et al., 2021). It has also been used to reduce health disparities. Specifically, by understanding the social system and communication channels, health campaigns based on DOI can be tailored to reach underserved populations (Valente, 2010). In general, the theory helps in designing strategies to enhance the reach and impact of health programs (Kim et al., 2013).

Combining the diffusion of innovations theory with social marketing can enhance the dissemination of health interventions. According to Dearing et al. (2006), the integration of these two focuses on how new ideas and practices spread within a community (diffusion of innovations) and emphasizes understanding and meeting the needs of the target audience to promote behavior change (social marketing). In other words, this combined approach aims to create more impactful and sustainable health interventions by addressing both the social and structural factors that influence behavior change.

Health Communication Strategies for Enhancing Mental Health among Hispanics and Latinos

This chapter highlighted that addressing mental health challenges for Hispanics and Latinos requires a multifaceted approach, including increasing the availability of bilingual and culturally competent mental health professionals, improving access to health insurance, and conducting community outreach to reduce stigma and educate about mental health issues. Responding to the strong need for mental health campaigns and interventions for the target populations, programs and initiatives by organizations like SAMHSA and NIMH have attempted to improve mental health outcomes for Hispanic populations through targeted research and support services.

In response to the problems and needs identified above, some key areas should be commonly considered for mental health communication campaigns targeting Hispanic/Latino populations in the United States. According to Mental Health America (n.d.), mental health and mental illness in the Latinx/Hispanic community are often *stigmatized* topics, resulting in prolonged suffering in silence. Considering the high level of stigma surrounding mental health issues, mental health communication campaigns should aim to find ways to normalize conversations around mental health in this community. In addition, as Latinx/Hispanic communities are *diverse* and often set apart by their countries of origin, mental health communication campaigns should strive to ensure that materials are translated and adapted to reflect the various sub-groups that make up the Spanish-speaking community. The Latinx/Hispanic community also faces unique *institutional and systemic* barriers that may impede access to mental health services. Therefore, campaigns should work to reduce these barriers in society and promote help-seeking behaviors where individuals work and live. Uniquely, religion can be a protective factor for mental health in Latinx/Hispanic communities but can also increase the stigma against mental illness and treatment. Faith-based mental health communication campaigns with religious institutions would greatly help encourage good mental health and treatment-seeking among the target populations. Based on a report presented by the UC Davis Center for Reducing Health Disparities (n.d.), language is also a major factor that keeps many Latinos with mental illness from seeking services. Therefore, mental health communication campaigns should focus on establishing a program or system that allows Spanish-speaking individuals to comfortably communicate in their mother language in healthcare facilities and services.

To be more specific and feasible in designing mental health communication campaigns and interventions for Hispanic/Latino populations, this chapter suggests some evidence-based strategies that more deeply incorporate communication elements to be culturally relevant and easy to adopt. First, highlighting the importance of culture as a significant factor in dealing with mental health issues, campaigns strategically include collectivist values or group orientation that permeates Hispanic life. For example, Hispanics often look to one another for opinions. Therefore, a collectivist orientation may serve as a valuable asset for health promotion. Related to this attribute, the theory of diffusion of innovations (DOI) emphasizes the importance of opinion leaders in the process of information dissemination and adoption (Kim et al., 2013; Rogers, 2003). If change agents promoting mental health can identify opinion leaders among populations in a collectivistic culture, this opinion leader-based interpersonal communication strategy can be very effective in changing people's attitudes and behaviors regarding mental health issues. Many research studies and empirical health interventions support the idea that collaborating with culturally trusted figures, such as community leaders or traditional healers, can enhance the acceptance and effectiveness of health messages (Green et al., 2009). In some cultures, community leaders or traditional healers may be more trusted than medical professionals (Airhihenbuwa, 1995). Therefore, health communicators must identify and collaborate with trusted figures within the community to enhance the credibility and acceptance of health messages.

Second, entertainment-education (EE) is a strong evidence-based framework that can be easily practiced in the target populations from Central and South American countries. As a representative example, many studies and reports have proven the popularity of telenovelas in Spanish-speaking countries in those regions. A telenovela is a type of television serial drama or soap opera produced primarily in Latin America and can bring important agendas in communication into their daily lives. Telenovelas are often characterized by a continuing melodramatic storyline. They have a significant cultural impact, shaping social discussions, reflecting societal values, and even influencing fashion trends. Most importantly, many communication scholars and practitioners have employed telenovelas for educational purposes, which has become very successful. This EE can clearly be an evidence-based media strategy for mental health promotion for Hispanic and Latino populations. According to Dupont-Reyes (2021), mental health content in Latinx and Spanish-language media is virtually absent, and mental illness anti-stigma media campaigns have not yet reached Latinx and Spanish-language media and their consumers. Therefore, the inclusion of Latinx and Spanish-language media and its consumers in mental health stigma-reduction campaigns is critical to narrowing the gaps in mental healthcare service utilization among Latinx populations, which also promotes help-seeking among individuals with mental illness.

Hispanic consumers in the United States are known to be avid fans of various types of media and have unique patterns of consumption. They are more likely to use audio and video streaming services than other ethnic groups. Social media platforms play a significant role in their media consumption. In July 2023, Hispanic people spent 50.7 percent of their total TV viewing time on streamed content, which is 13 percentage points higher than the general population (PR Newswire, 2023). Platforms like Netflix and YouTube are particularly popular, with Hispanics spending 24 percent and 57 percent more time on these platforms, respectively, compared to non-Hispanic Whites (Nielsen, 2022). In terms of social media usage, as of July 2023, 85 percent of Hispanic Americans reported using social media to some extent, compared to 80 percent of non-Hispanic Americans (Shriber, 2023). These trends highlight the significant potential of the use of internet-based media for mental health communication campaigns. In other words, this also indicates that Hispanic consumers are adopting new technologies at a faster pace than other ethnic groups and are finding it easier to transition from traditional forms of media to new media. Combining their collectivistic values and heavy use of social media, this chapter suggests reaching them through social media such as Facebook and TikTok, which facilitate such collective sharing of information and communication. According to Acevedo (2024), nearly half of Hispanic adults use TikTok, based on a Pew Research survey conducted in 2023, and Facebook is a predominant social media, as 66 percent of Hispanics use Facebook.

In conclusion, mental health communication campaigns for the Latino/Hispanic population in the United States are crucial due to their urgency and unique needs and challenges, such as stigma associated with mental health, institutional and systemic barriers, language barriers, misperceptions about seeking professional therapy, and a lack of culturally relevant and linguistically accessible mental health services. Health communication plays a pivotal role in addressing these needs, challenges, and effective solutions as well, fostering open discussions, challenging prevailing stigmas, and building safe and communicable spaces for individuals to share their experiences. It also aids in educating the target populations by providing accurate information about mental health, available services, and recommendations and resources for culturally adaptable existing treatments. Thus, health communication is essential in promoting mental health among Latino/Hispanic populations and implementing accessible services, contributing to enhancing the understanding of mental health within their community.

Note

1 The terms "Hispanic" and "Latino" are often used interchangeably, but they have different origins and meanings: *Hispanic*: This term generally refers to people with a background in a Spanish-speaking country or who are descended from Spanish-speaking communities. *Latino*: This term is typically used to identify people who hail from Latin America, a politically defined region usually unified by the predominance of Romance languages. This definition usually includes Portuguese-speaking Brazil and French-speaking Haiti, but excludes Spain. It's important to remember that these categories refer only to a person's origin and ancestry. A Latino or Hispanic person can be of any race or color. (Source: University of California, https://www.universityofcalifornia.edu/news/choosing-the-right-word-hispanic-latino-and-latinx)

Recommended Readings/Resources

Centers for Disease Control and Prevention. (n.d.). *Cultural insights: Communicating with Hispanics/Latinos (cdc.gov)*. https://www.cdc.gov/healthcommunication/pdf/audience/audienceinsight_culturalinsights.pdf.

Mental Health America. (n.d.). *Latinx/Hispanic communities and mental health*. Mental Health America of Putnam County https://www.mhaopc.org/bipoc-mental-health-awareness- month/latinx-hispanic-communities-and-mental-health/

Office of Minority Health. (2021). *Mental and behavioral health – Hispanics*. https://minorityhealth.hhs.gov/mental-and-behavioral-health- hispanics#:~:text=In%20

2019%2C%20suicide%20was%20the,Hispanics%2C%20ages% 2015%20to% 2034.&text=Suicide%20attempts%20for%20Hispanic%20girls,same%20ag e%20 group%2C%20in%202019.

SAMHSA. (2023). *Hispanic and Latino Americans*. https://www.samhsa.gov/behavioral -health- equity/hispanic- latino#:~:text=According%20to%20the%202021%20Natio nal,non%2DHispanic%20Whi tes%20(52%25)

Santiago, C. D., Distel, L. M. L., Ros, A. M., Brewer, S. K., Torres, S. A., Papadakis, J. L., Fuller, A. K., & Bustos, Y. (2018). Mental health among Mexican-origin immigrant families: The roles of cumulative sociodemographic risk and immigrant-related stress. *Race and Social Problems, 10*, 235–247.

References

Acevedo, N. (2024, Feb. 2). *Nearly half of Hispanic adults are using TikTok, according to recent Pew survey*. NBC News.https://www.nbcnews.com/news/latino/tiktok-growth -hispanics-%20latinos-platforms-users-rcna136817.

Airhihenbuwa, C. O. (1995). *Health and culture: Beyond the Western paradigm*. Sage Publications.

Alarcón, R.D. (2022). The role of acculturation in the mental health of Hispanics. In R. Castilla-Puentes, & T. Falcone. (Eds.) *Mental health for Hispanic communities* (pp. 87–103). Springer. https://doi.org/10.1007/978-3-031-13195-0_7.

Alegría, M., Alvarez, K., Ishikawa, R. Z., DiMarzio, K., & McPeck, S. (2016). Removing obstacles to eliminating racial and ethnic disparities in behavioral health care. *Health Affairs, 38*(3), 446–454. https://doi.org/10.1377/hlthaff.2016.0029.

Andrade, N., Ford, A. D., & Alvarez, C. (2021). Discrimination and Latino health: A systematic review of risk and resilience. *Hispanic Health Care International, 19*(1), 5–16. https://doi.org/10.1177/1540415320921489

Andreasen, A. R. (1995). *Marketing social change: Changing behavior to promote health, social development, and the environment*. Jossey-Bass.

Artiga, S., Hamel, L., Kearney, A., Stokes, M., & Safarpour, A. (2021). *Health and health care experiences of Hispanic adults*. Kaiser Family Foundation. https://www.kff.org/coronavirus-covid-19/poll-finding/health-and-health-care-experiences-of-hispanic -adults/

Bekteshi, V., & Bellamy, J. L. (2024). Adapting for well-being: Examining acculturation strategies and mental health among Latina immigrants. *Social Sciences, 13*(3), 138. https://doi.org/10.3390/socsci13030138

Betancourt, J. R., Green, A. R., Carrillo, J. E., & Ananeh-Firempong, O. (2003). Defining cultural competence: A practical framework for addressing racial/ethnic disparities in health and health care. *Public Health Reports, 118*(4), 293–302. https://doi.org/10.1093/phr/118.4.293.

Boutaud, J., Becuţ, A., & Marinescu, A. (2016). Food and culture. Cultural patterns and practices related to food in everyday life. *International Journal of Reviews and Research in Social Sciences, 2016*(6 (1)), 1–3. https://doi.org/10.1515/IRSR-2016-0001.

Burnett-Zeigler, I., Lee, Y. & Bohnert, K.M. (2018). Ethnic identity, acculturation, and 12- month psychiatric service utilization among black and Hispanic adults in the U.S. *The Journal of Behavioral Health Services & Research, 45(1)*, 13–30. https://doi.org/10.1007/s11414-017-95578.

Cabassa, L. J., Hansen, M. C., Palinkas, L. A., & Ell, K. (2008). Azúcar y nervios: Explanatory models and treatment experiences of Hispanics with diabetes and depression. *Social Science & Medicine*, 66, 2413–2424. https://doi.org/10.1016/j.socscimed.2008.01.054.

Caplan, S. (2019). Intersection of cultural and religious beliefs about mental health: Latinos in the faith-based setting. *Hispanic Health Care International, 17*(1), 4–10. https://doi.org/10.1177/1540415319828265.

Cardemil, E. V., Millán, F., & Arkin, M. (2020). Diversity issues in depression: The relevance of culture in the assessment and treatment of Latina/o depression. In I. H. Gotlib & C. L. Hammen (Eds.), *Handbook of depression* (3rd ed., pp. 308–324). Guilford Publications.

Centers for Disease Control and Prevention. (n.d.). *Cultural insights: Communicating with Hispanics/Latinos (cdc.gov).* https://www.cdc.gov/healthcommunication/pdf/audience/audienceinsight_culturalinsights.pdf.

Cheng, H., Kotler, P., & Lee, N. (2009). *Social marketing for public health: Global trends and success stories.* Jones & Bartlett Learning.

Clayman, M. L., Manganello, J. A., Viswanath, K., Hesse, B. W., & Arora, N. K. (2010). Providing health messages to Hispanics/Latinos: understanding the importance of language, trust in health information sources, and media use. *Journal of Health Communication, 15* (Suppl 3), 252–263. https://doi.org/10.1080/10810730.2010.522697.

Cruz, M. L., Christie, S., Allen, E., Meza, E., Nápoles, A. M., & Mehta, K. M. (2022). Traditional healers as health care providers for the Latine community in the United States: A systematic review. *Health Equity, 6*(1), 412–426. https://doi.org/10.1089/heq.2021.0099.

Dearing, J. W., Maibach, E. W., & Buller, D. B. (2006). A convergent diffusion and social marketing approach for disseminating proven approaches to physical activity promotion. *American Journal of Preventive Medicine, 31*(4), S11–S23. https://doi.org/10.1016/j.amepre.2006.06.018.

DuPont-Reyes, M. J. (2021). Leveraging Latinx and Spanish-language media to achieve mental health equity. *Psychiatric Services, 73*(7). https://ps.psychiatryonline.org/doi/10.1176/appi.ps.202100147

Dutta, M. J. (2007). Communicating about culture and health: Theorizing culture-centered and cultural sensitivity approaches. *Communication Theory, 17*(3), 304–328. https://doi.org/10.1111/j.1468-2885.2007.00297.x.

Evans, W. D. (2006). How social marketing works in health care. *BMJ*, 332(7551), 1207–1210. https://doi.org/10.1136/bmj.332.7551.1207

Fernández L'Hoeste, H., & Vila, P. (Eds.). (2017). *Sound, image, and national imaginary in the construction of Latin/o American identities*. Lexington Books.

Flores, G. (2000). Culture and the patient-physician relationship: Achieving cultural competency in health care. *The Journal of Pediatrics, 136*(1), 14–23. https://doi.org/10.1016/s0022-3476(00)90043-x.

Fox, M., Thayer, Z., & Wadhwa, P. D. (2017). Acculturation and health: the moderating role of socio-cultural context. *American Anthropologist, 19*(3), 405–421. https://doi.org/10.1111/aman.12867.

Gamboa, S. (2023, July 28). A persistent gap in mental health aid has left Latino communities unprepared for crisis. *NBC News*. https://www.nbcnews.com/news/latino/latino-gap- mental-health-access-hispanic-lawmakers-bill-rcna96874

González, H. M., Tarraf, W., Whitfield, K. E., & Vega, W. A. (2010). The epidemiology of major depression and ethnicity in the United States. *Journal of psychiatric research*, 44(15), 1043–1051. https://doi.org/10.1016/j.jpsychires.2010.03.017.

Green, L. W., Ottoson, J. M., Garcia, C., & Hiatt, R. A. (2009). Diffusion theory and knowledge dissemination, utilization, and integration in public health. *Annual Review of Public Health, 30*(1), 151–174. https://doi.org/10.1146/annurev.publhealth.031308.100049

Gudykunst, W. B. (2004). *Bridging differences: Effective intergroup communication*. Sage Publications.

Hastings, G., & Haywood, A. (1991) Social marketing and communication in health promotion. *Health Promotion International, 6*(2), 135–145. https://doi.org/10.1093/heapro/6.2.135.

Hernandez, L. M., & Gibb, H. J. (2014). *Health literacy: Improving health, health systems, and health policy around the world: Workshop summary*. National Academies Press.

Hwang, W. C., & Goto, S. (2008). The impact of perceived racial discrimination on the mental health of Asian American and Latino college students. *Cultural Diversity and Ethnic Minority Psychology, 14*(4), 326–335. https://doi.org/10.1037/1099-9809.14.4.326.

Interian, A., Ang, A., Gara, M. A., Rodriguez, M. A., & Vega, W. A. (2011). The long-term trajectory of depression among Latinos in primary care and its relationship to depression care disparities. General hospital psychiatry, 33(2), 94–101. https://doi.org/10.1016/j.genhosppsych.2010.12.001.

Kemp, C. & Rasbridge, L. A. (2004). Mexico. In *Refugee and immigrant health: A handbook for health professionals.* Cambridge University Press.

Kim, D. K., Kreps, G., & Singhal, A. (2013). *Health communication: Strategies for developing global health programs.* Peter Lang.

Kotler, P., & Zaltman, G. (1971). Social marketing: An approach to planned social change. *Journal of Marketing, 35*(3), 3–12. https://doi.org/10.1177/00222429710350030.

Kreuter, M. W., & McClure, S. M. (2004). The role of culture in health communication. *Annual Review of Public Health, 25*, 439–455. https://doi.org/10.1146/annurev.publhealth.25.101802.123000.

Lerman, S., Jung, M., Arredondo, E. M., Barnhart, J. M., Cai, J., Castañeda, S. F., ... & Daviglus, M. L. (2018). Religiosity prevalence and its association with depression and anxiety symptoms among Hispanic/Latino adults. *PLoS ONE, 13*(2), e0185661

Library of Congress. (n.a.). *National Hispanic Heritage Month.* https://guides.loc.gov/national-hispanic-heritage-month-legal-resources#:~:text=Introduction-,National%20Hispanic%20Heritage%20Month%3A%20 A%20Commemorative%20Observances%20Legal%20Research%20Guide,15

Madrid, A. L. (2017). The role of sound and music in the formation of national identity in Latin America. In H. Fernández L'Hoeste & P. Vila (Eds.), *Sound, image, and national imaginary in the construction of Latin/o American identities* (pp. 1–20). Lexington Books.

Mendoza, H., Masuda, A., & Swartout, K. M. (2015). Mental health stigma and self-concealment as predictors of help-seeking attitudes among Latina/o college students in the United States. *International Journal for the Advancement of Counselling*, 37(3), 207–222. https://doi.org/10.1007/s10447-015-9237-4.

Mental Health America. (2017). *Mental health and Latino kids: A research review.* https://salud- america.org/wp-content/uploads/2017/09/FINAL-mental-health-research-review-9-12-17.pdf

Mental Health America. (n.d.). *Latinx/Hispanic communities and mental health.* Mental Health America of Putnam County. https://www.mhaopc.org/bipoc-mental-health-awareness- month/latinx-hispanic-communities-and-mental-health/

Moreno, O., & Cardemil, E. (2013). Religiosity and mental health services: An exploratory study of help seeking among Latinos. *Journal of Latina/o Psychology*, 1(1), 53–67. https://doi.org/10.1037/a0031376.

National Hispanic and Latino MHTTC. (2022). *Increasing cultural connection with Hispanic and Latinx Clients.* https://mhttcnetwork.org/wp-content/uploads/2022/06/rNHLMHTTC_-Latino-Population-Region-10.Session-3.pdf

Nielsen. (2022, September). *Let's talk about streaming and engaging the Latino audience.* https://www.nielsen.com/insights/2022/lets-talk-about-streaming-and-engaging-the- latino-audience/

Northwestern Medicine. (n.d.). *Common Hispanic health issues.* https://www.nm.org/healthbeat/healthy-tips/common-hispanic-health-issues

Office of Minority Health. (2021). *Mental and behavioral health – Hispanics.* https://minorityhealth.hhs.gov/mental-and-behavioral-health- hispanics#:~:text=In%20 2019%2C%20suicide%20was%20the,Hispanics%2C%20ages%2015%20to%2034 .&text=Suicide%20attempts%20for%20Hispanic%20girls,same%20ag e%20 group%2C%20in%202019

Peña, J. E., Lowe Jr., R. H., & Ríos-Vargas, M. (2023, September 26). Eight Hispanic groups each had a million or more population in 2020. *U.S. Census.* https://www .census.gov/library/stories/2023/09/2020-census-dhc-a-hispanic-population.html

PR Newswire. (2010, July 8). *SAMHSA and the Ad Council launch national campaign to raise awareness about mental health problems in Hispanic/Latino communities.* https://www.prnewswire.com/news-releases/samhsa-and-the-ad-council-launch -national-campaign-to-raise-awareness-about-mental-health-problems-in -hispaniclatino-communities-98017144.html

PR Newswire. (2023, September 12). *Streaming reaches milestone as top choice for U.S. Hispanic viewers; Spanish-language dominant audiences continue to embrace broadcast television.* https://www.prnewswire.com/news-releases/streaming-reaches -milestone-as-top-choice-for-us-hispanic-viewers-spanish-language-dominant -audiences-continue-to-embrace-broadcast-television-301923744.html

Pro, G., Brown, C., Rojo, M., Patel, J., Flax, C., & Haynes, T. (2022). Downward national trends in mental health treatment offered in Spanish: State differences by proportion of Hispanic residents. *Psychiatric Services, 73*(11), 1232–1238. https://doi.org/10 .1176/appi.ps.202100614.

Ramos-Olazagasti, M. A., & Conway, C. A. (2022). The prevalence of mental health disorders among Latino parents. *National Research Center on Hispanic Children & Families.* https://www.hispanicresearchcenter.org/research-resources/the-prevalence -of-mental-health-disorders-among-latino-parents/

Robinson, B. J. (1993). *Artistic representations of Latin American diversity: Sources and collections.* SALALM/University of New Mexico.

Roche, K. M., White, R. M.B., Partovi, R., Vaquera, E., & Little, T. D. (2024). US immigration policy stressors and Latinx youth mental health. *JAMA Pediatrics, 178*(7), 669–677. https://doi.org/10.1001/jamapediatrics.2024.1153.

Rodriguez, S. (2019). Why doesn't the Latin X community believe in mental health? *GALEO.* https://galeo.org/2019/07/why-doesnt-the-latin-x-community-believe-in -mental-health/

Rogers, E. M. (2003). Diffusion of innovations (5th ed.). *Free Press.*

SAMHSA. (2022). *National survey on drug use and health.* https://www.samhsa.gov/data/data-we-collect/nsduh-national-survey-drug-use-and-health

SAMHSA. (2023). *Hispanic and Latino Americans.* https://www.samhsa.gov/behavioral -health-equity/hispanic- latino#:~:text=According%20to%20the%202021%20Natio nal,non%2DHispanic%20Whi tes%20(52%25)

Santiago, C. D., Distel, L. M. L., Ros, A. M., Brewer, S. K., Torres, S. A., Papadakis, J. L., Fuller, A. K., & Bustos, Y. (2018). Mental health among Mexican-origin immigrant families: The roles of cumulative sociodemographic risk and immigrant-related stress. *Race and Social Problems*, *10*, 235–247. https://doi.org/10.1007/s12552-018-9236-2.

Schiavo, R. (2013). *Health communication: From theory to practice.* John Wiley & Sons.

Shen, M. J., Peterson, E. B., Costas-Muñiz, R., Hernandez, M. H., Jewell, S. T., Matsoukas, K., & Bylund, C. L. (2018). The effects of race and racial concordance on patient-physician communication: A systematic review of the literature. *Journal of racial and ethnic health disparities*, *5*, 117–140. https://doi.org/10.1007/s40615-017-0350-4.

Shriber, S. (2023). *Key social media insights among U.S. Hispanic adults.* Civic Science. https://civicscience.com/key-social-media-insights-among-u-s-hispanic-adults/

Streit, C., Carlo, G., & Killoren, S. E. (2020). Family support, respect, and empathy as correlates of U.S. Latino/Latina college students' prosocial behaviors toward different recipients. *Journal of Social and Personal Relationships*, *37*(5), 1513–1533. https://doi.org/10.1177/0265407520903805.

Symons, M. (2014). Brillat-savarin and food. In P. Thompson & D. Kaplan (Eds.), *Encyclopedia of food and agricultural ethics.* Springer.

Taylor, A. N., & O'Flynn, C. (2020, December 16). *Food is a cultural connection for Hispanics – especially when it's homemade.* https://insights.paramount.com/post/food-is-a-cultural- connection-for-hispanics-especially-when-its-homemade/

Thornhill, C. W., Castillo, L. G., Piña-Watson, B., Manzo, G., & Cano, M. Á. (2022). Mental health among Latinx emerging adults: Examining the role of familial accusations of assimilation and ethnic identity. *Journal of Clinical Psychology*, *78*(5), 892–912. https://doi.org/10.1002/jclp.23271

Tyson, A., & Lopez, M. H. (2023). *5 facts about Hispanic Americans and health care.* Pew Research Center. https://www.pewresearch.org/short-reads/2023/10/30/5-facts-about- hispanic-americans-and-health-care/

UC Davis Center for Reducing Health Disparities. (n.d.). *Community-defined solutions for Latino mental health care disparities.* https://health.ucdavis.edu/media- resources/crhd/documents/pdfs/community-defined-solutions-latino-mental-health-care- disparities-exec-summary.pdf

U.S. Census Bureau. (2023). *Hispanic heritage month: 2023.* https://www.census.gov/newsroom/facts-for-features/2023/hispanic-heritage- month.html#:~:text=63.7%20million,19.1%25%20of%20the%20total%20population

Uscher-Pines, L., Kapinos, K., Rodriguez, C., Pérez-Dávila, S., Raja, P., Rodriguez, J. A., Rabinowitz, M., Youdelman, M., & Sousa, J. L. (2023). Access challenges for patients with limited English proficiency: a secret-shopper study of in-person and telehealth behavioral health services in California safety-net clinics. *Health Affairs Scholar*, *1*(3), qxad033. https://doi.org/10.1093/haschl/qxad033

Valente, T. W. (2010). *Social networks and health: Models, methods, and applications.* Oxford University Press.

Zimmerman, S., Gaugler, J. E., & Nkimbeng, M. (2021). Covid-19 vaccination and implementation science: How one can benefit the other. *Journal of the American Medical Directors Association, 22*(11), 2223–2224. https://doi.org/10.1016/j.jamda.2021.09.018

6

Housing Instability and Homelessness in Memphis

Mental Health Literacy and Community-Based Research

Joy V. Goldsmith, Diana R. Humble,
Sachiko Terui, Tharwa Bilbeisi, and Regina Alabere

No matter where people live in the United States, they are likely to encounter individuals experiencing housing instability and homelessness (HIH). On a national scale, chronic patterns of homelessness grew between 2022 and 2023, and the unsheltered population increased by around 70,650 (12%) (U.S. Department of Housing and Urban Development, 2023). The Department of Housing and Urban Development (2023) reported 653,100 people navigating HIH in the United States; around 60 percent of these individuals were sheltered, and 40 percent unsheltered. In 2023, 59 percent of unhoused people resided in urban areas, 23 percent were in the suburbs, and the remaining 18 percent were in largely rural areas (U.S. Department of Housing and Urban Development, 2023). These populations are most concentrated in urban settings, like Memphis, Tennessee—the site of this chapter's study.

It is difficult to determine the exact number of individuals facing HIH in the greater Memphis area due to poor record-keeping and assessment strategies (Johnson, 2010), but in 2023, 1,292 people were found to be homeless in Memphis and Shelby County (CAFTH Memphis, 2023). This problem is especially pronounced in school-aged populations. The Shelby County School District (i.e., Memphis schools) identified 395 homeless students (kindergarten to 12th grade) in the first quarter of the 2020–1 school year; this number climbed by 36.4 percent to 539 students by the beginning of the 2021–2 school year (Hargrave & Ball-Johnson, 2022). By the start of the 2022–3 school year, this figure had grown by a staggering 179 percent to 1,504 homeless students. HIH is growing at an unprecedented rate in Memphis. There were more homeless children in Shelby County schools in 2022 than homeless individuals of all ages across the county in 2019.

These numbers are far too high as is, but youth underreporting may mean that actual counts are even higher. A 2017 study on HIH youth in America cited that one in three children between the ages of thirteen to seventeen and one in ten young adults between eighteen and twenty-five experienced some form of homelessness over a twelve-month period (Morton et al., 2017). The transient and hidden nature of youth homelessness further complicates the record-keeping of individuals who may have chosen to run away or were forcibly ejected from their homes. Some of this underreporting may be due to a phenomenon called "couch surfing," where persons temporarily stay in locations not defined as "home" to avoid sleeping in shelters, which means they are not accounted for by official homeless totals. Marginalized youths—especially those who are female-presenting, LGBTQ+, and non-Latinx people of color—engage in couch surfing at higher rates because many shelters lack culturally competent and gender-inclusive care initiatives. These reports also do not account for those utilizing rehabilitation facilities and other temporary housing and support services (Byrne et al., 2020).

The racial and ethnic makeup of urban HIH generally reflects the demographic composition of the geographic location. This disproportionately affects low-income communities of color who suffer the consequences of gentrified neighborhoods, redevelopment projects, and revised and up-priced housing (Olivet et al., 2021). Housing instability and homelessness are racialized issues in America that disproportionately affect Black Americans. Despite only comprising 13 percent of the US population, Black Americans account for 40 percent of reported persons experiencing homelessness (Edwards, 2021).

Correlations among race, homelessness, and discrimination—including healthcare discrimination—are difficult to prove. Those who report one domain of discrimination (such as racial discrimination) are also more likely to experience discrimination in the other two domains (homelessness and mental health discrimination) (Skosireva et al., 2014). Therefore, centering HIH conversations in "colorblind" terms fails to acknowledge the historical, systemic racism and socioeconomic plight that leaves Black and Brown Americans disadvantaged (Richard, 2023). "Race matters in addressing homelessness because racism matters in addressing homelessness" (Richard, 2023, p. 480). Studies examining race and implicit or perceived bias also report racial disadvantage and worse healthcare services and outcomes among homeless Black Americans (Fitzgerald & Hurst, 2017; Maina et al., 2018).

Seeing those with unstable housing can create discomfort and anxiety for a community, and a desire among those with stable housing to "fix the problem" (Koo et al., 2023). Narratives around HIH focus on the "problems" of *persons lacking housing.* Common images of HIH include loitering, sleeping on the streets, panhandling, and drug-affected figures passed out on park benches or in alleyways. However, these narratives fail to account for those experiencing housing instability while actively employed or receiving state/federal support (Lee et al., 2010). The negative perceptions and stereotypes that wider society has constructed around what it means to be homeless are known as "homeism" (Canham et al., 2022). Although most everyone wants to "solve the problem" of HIH, the widely held beliefs of society (e.g., people should be well-groomed and housed to earn respect) discriminate against those who experience HIH.

This chapter recounts a photovoice project that highlighted the stories of three Black men who frequented a faith-based HIH support site (Manna House Memphis, *Figure 6.1*) in inner-city Memphis, TN, during the height of the COVID-19 pandemic. This project sought to give those experiencing HIH the tools necessary to create new visual and textual narratives about HIH. The results helped the research team gain a greater understanding of the mental health literacy barriers and pathways of those experiencing HIH in Memphis. Research at the Manna House was approved by the primary institution's IRB.

Figure 6.1 The exterior of Manna House Memphis. Source: Photo by Joy V. Goldsmith.

This chapter draws upon the narrative paradigm and the performance of self as theory anchors for our collective inquiry into HIH and mental health literacy. The collection of participant narratives will be analyzed in a manner that overlays the narrative paradigm with Goffman's (1959) depiction of performance driven by context. Guests of the Manna House who joined this project as co-researcher participants exist at the intersections of class, race, ethnicity, physical and mental ability, sexual orientation, housing, and employment statuses. Their social realities are unknown to the public and to policymakers. Photovoice, like Freirean epistemologies, seeks to give voice to the voiceless and allows them to provide narratives outside of pre-scripted Eurocentric, colonialist systems (Latz, 2017).

Manna House

The Manna House of Memphis is a hospitality center that provides services to individuals facing HIH in the Memphis metropolitan area. The Manna House is volunteer-run and rooted in the Catholic Worker tradition. The center is not a shelter where HIH individuals sleep overnight or eat full meals, but offers morning hospitality in a way that respects each guest's dignity as a human. Other nearby services include a no-cost HIV/AIDS support center, a church charity offering one meal a day, and a large mission offering nightly meals and emergency shelter. The guests begin their days at the Manna House when the doors open at 8:00 a.m. with fresh coffee, a hot shower, and a change of clothes before pursuing other services and support.

The Manna House is set apart from its neighbors by its commitment to providing a communal space for companionship, conversation, and hygiene care. The Manna House welcomes guests regardless of race, gender, or health. Guests are not required to state their name or prove their need. A "no questions asked" policy is heralded. Health and other personal statuses (e.g., HIV positive or negative) are considered private, only to be disclosed at the guest's choosing. Manna House's services include "socks and soap" and a range of toiletries. In the winter months, hats, scarves, blankets, and hand warmers are also provided. A volunteer barber provides haircuts under the covered back porch several mornings each month (see *Figures 6.2–6.4*). Guests mingle in a fenced yard

Figure 6.2 Area for haircuts. Source: Photo by Joy V. Goldsmith.

among picnic tables. Some charge their phones, others await their turn for showers and fresh clothes, and all commune over fresh coffee.

Located east of downtown Memphis and adjacent to the medical district, most Manna House guests do not have established transportation. As a city, Memphis is highly reliant on individual modes of transportation. The sprawling metropolis' only public transportation is an underfunded, somewhat unreliable bus system. Riding the bus imposes a significant time commitment (buses often run late or entirely skip stops), creates safety concerns, demands passengers have the ability to walk to and from bus stops, and costs money (Henning-Smith, 2020; Rittner & Kirk, 1995). Guests frequenting the Manna House walk, bike, ride a bus, or receive a ride from a friend or neighbor from their temporary sleeping location, which may be sheltered (e.g., apartment, shelter, or other indoor lodgings) or unsheltered (e.g., on the street, outdoor location, or abandoned structures).

Figure 6.3 Side yard covered seating. Source: Photo by Joy V. Goldsmith.

Mental Health Literacy

Health literacy began as an assessment strategy to improve health outcomes for the individual, but has since expanded to explore entire populations and stakeholder factors in co-creating health literacy (Goldsmith & Terui, 2019; Peprah et al., 2023; Petkovic et al., 2023; Terui et al., 2023). Mental health literacy (MHL) is an integrated component of health literacy. MHL includes any knowledge and resource that benefit the mental health of a person. This could mean an understanding of what prevents mental illness, the ability to recognize emergent mental illness, identifying care strategies, or communicating about ways to achieve mental health care (Sampaio et al., 2022). Health literacy research guides and informs the evolving ideas around MHL, though the complexities of mental health are rarely studied or examined with health literacy models or measures.

Disadvantaged populations—which include those individuals facing HIH and those with mental health illness—are difficult for researchers to access and study. Across disciplines, groups with lower socioeconomic status are historically

Figure 6.4 Open air seating in the backyard. Source: Photo by Joy V. Goldsmith.

under-researched (Emery et al., 2023). The need for housing, provision of day-to-day health care, transportation, and social support make it easy for these individuals to quickly slip through the gaping holes in our society (Pope et al., 2018). Individuals struggling with mental health disorders like depression, schizophrenia, and bipolar disorder are at increased risk of contracting illnesses, chronic diseases, comorbidities, injury, and premature death (Daré et al., 2019; McGrath et al., 2020; Melo et al., 2022). Sadly, those with mental health challenges and illness are disproportionately represented among those who cannot afford to meet basic food, housing, and health needs (Wolfson et al., 2021).

Despite shifts in health literacy conceptualizations, few definitions reflect a multivariable perspective accounting for stakeholders beyond the patient (Duell et al., 2015; Terui et al., 2023). Prevailing health literacy concepts are still yoked with an individual's functional literacy (i.e., reading and writing) skills and understanding of health information (Nutbeam & Lloyd, 2021). This pushes patients to assume responsibility for their own health literacy (Cutilli & Bennett, 2009), which is a formidable barrier for those with low socioeconomic and educational achievements (Schillinger, 2021). Another challenge with current health literacy conceptualizations is that researchers and clinicians typically study individuals who are already accessing healthcare systems and are in contact with clinic staff. Such studies do not include those who do not or cannot interact within care systems (Gibson et al., 2022).

New voices in health literacy and health communication argue that health literacy involves not only patients' cognitive and functional skills but also the collaborative efforts among patients, caregivers, healthcare organizations, healthcare providers, and communities (Batterham et al., 2016; Chou et al., 2015). This collaborative view of health literacy identifies the impactful role that each stakeholder plays in reducing health literacy barriers and inequities/disparities across all groups. The deficiencies of existing health literacy models warrant a comprehensive model that is representative of the transactional nature of interactions among patients, caregivers, providers, system, and community (Batterham et al., 2016; Goldsmith & Terui, 2018; Terui et al., 2023; Young et al., 2017). Most recently, mental health literacy research has identified social determinants of health as stronger predictors of a person's mental health literacy than their income, employment, education level, or racial and ethnic groups (Kutcher et al., 2016). Mental health literacy research continues to inform the study of health literacy by challenging demographic linkages to health literacy levels. Long-standing assumptions about who experiences low levels of mental health literacy have been dismantled in more recent mental health literacy research (Rosenblad et al., 2024).

Conceptual Lenses

Narrative Paradigm

To share and listen to stories is a fundamental piece of the human experience. Developed by communication scholar Walter Fisher, the narrative paradigm believes that humans are storytellers by nature and that each story's meaning can be derived from its use of symbolic words or actions (Griffin et al., 2019). Fisher found the rational worldview limiting in its explanation of logical human decision-making; he rebuffed the notion that all decisions were argument-driven. In its place, he offered a framework that situated rationality in a historical and cultural context driven by the coherence and quality of the stories people tell. He stated that shared values and experiences also hold sway over an audience. By adding dimensions of praxis, the narrative paradigm advances methods to determine if discourses are dependable and produce constructive thought or action (Fisher, 1985).

The paradigm's concern with communicative exchanges extends beyond the traditions of logic and narrative rationality. While the narrative paradigm may serve as a foundation for rhetorical analysis and interpretation, it invites humanistic theories—such as hermeneutics—to fill in the nuances created by complicated human circumstances, like homelessness and housing instability. People can be difficult to predict; the logic and reasoning behind their actions are formed characteristically, culturally, historically, linguistically, and through interaction (Fisher 1985, 1989). There is meaning in all human discourse, even the mundane (Fisher 1985). Moreover, Fisher describes that the production of knowledge (around reliability, truth, or "good reason[s]") exists in relation to the chosen form of communication, which does not require expert analysis and transpires between individuals daily, even in the most banal of dealings (Fisher, 1985, 1989). The following study seeks to examine the mundane visual and oral communication of those experiencing HIH. Narrative, or the story, is thus the precursor for the research endeavor.

Goffman and Performance

Erving Goffman's sociological theories reveal his fascination with the projection of self, community interaction, inequalities, and deviant behavior through which any social setting might be explored. In *The Presentation of Self in Everyday Life* (1959), Goffman conceptualized *dramaturgy* as an approach that explains all social activity as a performance people enact within a specific setting. This could include their failures in executing those performances, performance teams, regional behavior (the parts we play depending on our location within the social scene), realigning work mid- and post-conflict, and communicating out of character given the context.

Erving Goffman's *dramaturgy* approaches human communication from a perspective of theatrical performance and describes social interactions as derived from principles of drama. Goffman explores the behaviors of individuals in everyday situations and reasons that their physical and symbolic actions—verbal and nonverbal—are crafted as performances that differ based on the setting and audience. In the absence of a stage and the third-party presence of an audience, the co-communicators fulfill the role of presenter or actor and "audience" member even in interpersonal exchanges. Goffman claims that people are proverbial characters in performances whose purpose is to continuously negotiate—in exchanges with others—public identity and establish a persona within the state of present events (Griffin et al., 2019). Such negotiations are often fragile, temporal, or adhere to understandings of normalcy and sociopolitical hegemonies. Goffman provides examples of people "acting" in certain mannerisms that are either at odds with their abilities, in line with expectations, or performed to manipulate a situation in pursuit of a desired outcome.

Community-Based Research Approach

As part of community-based collaborative partnerships, research participants join as co-researchers in sharing their knowledge through the qualitative methodologies of narrative inquiry, photovoice, and ethnography. To engage the individual and community-influenced health beliefs of HIH, this project implemented the methodology of photovoice. This project sought to give those experiencing HIH the tools necessary to create new visual and textual narratives about HIH.

Ethnomethodology helps researchers identify meaning that is made and understood in context. Ethnomethodology invites researchers to situate themselves as ordinary participants in the situational context (or *the field*) to observe and engage as part of the learning opportunity (Schindler, 2018). This work requires the researchers to lessen controls over the project's direction and devote a considerable commitment of time to collecting and analyzing data. Ethnomethodology—such as community-based fieldwork—invites the analysis of field notes, interviews, and narratives, and self-reflections (Goodall, 2000).

Photovoice

Photovoice is a form of community-based research that engages directly with members of the community being examined. It enables the larger public to learn about the struggles of members who are rarely given a voice and offers them the opportunity to capture representations of barriers and pathways related to their underrepresented lived experience. Photovoice produces member-generated images and narratives that reveal competence, strength, and a will to endure. In this work, *participants become co-researchers*. Photovoice is practical (capturing images) and collaborative (sharing descriptions of photos and how they represent the barriers and pathways related to HIH) (Kemmis & McTaggart, 2007). It is a social scientific method that encourages those most afflicted by community issues to link their identified needs directly to potential solutions (Wang & Burris, 1997).

Photovoice is an applied research methodology that is narrative-based, community-based, and often in contrast with conventional research models (Latz, 2017). Photovoice incorporates aspects of the observational mode of filmmaking by relinquishing image control to the subject; the participatory model emphasizes the interactive relationship between the participant and researcher collaboration (Nichols, 2001). Representation, as a goal of the research, challenges notions of a singular "truth" or "reality." This makes photovoice inherently political, feminist, and in opposition to traditional empirically based research methods (Goodall, 2000). Instead of objectivity, photovoice research encourages participants to self-represent and challenge notions of "truth" while filling in the gaps left behind by empirical researchers (Goodall, 2000; Latz, 2017). Photovoice borrows from the conceptual teachings of Freirean pedagogy and uplifts community empowerment, cultural sensitivity/humility, and praxis (Gadotti & Torres, 2009; Latz, 2017; Lekas et al., 2020). As a form of resistance to institutionalized power and rejection of the student–teacher authoritarian paradigm, Freire's teachings affirm individuals' agency for reclaiming authority over their lives (Gadotti & Torres, 2009).

In this photovoice project, guests at the Manna House were invited to join the research team. If they agreed, they were responsible for collecting images of barriers and pathways related to mental health, housing instability, and the impact of COVID-19. Once they had filled their disposable cameras with twenty images (*Figure 6.5*), the co-researcher participants returned the cameras to the research team. In the final stage of the project, participant-researchers narrated each developed photo, explained why they felt called to capture that moment, and unpacked its symbolism.

Photovoice Picture Tracker

Barriers O O O O O O

Pathways O O O O O O

COVID-19 Impact on Your Life O O O O O O

Your Choice O O O O O O

Figure 6.5 Adaptation of the sticker affixed to the back of each camera for co-researcher participants to track photos taken. Source: Created by authors.

Table 6.1 Photovoice Overview at the Manna House

Collection	Description		Nature of Data
IMAGES	Photos captured by participants, driven by barrier and pathway themes.	280 images	Images taken using disposable camera.
Formal Recorded interviews	Recorded and transcribed interviews about photos.	N=14	Participant narrative descriptions of photos.
Informal discussions	Non-transcribed, unstructured conversations with shelter guests.	Over 12 months	Notations of conversations with those who participated in full or partial capacity.
Field notes	Notations of shelter visits.	Over 12 months	Notes describing people, events, and happenings at the shelter. Includes notes of incidences and conversations.

Table 6.2 Demographic Characteristics of Participants

Name	Race/Age	Sheltered/UN	Medical Access/ Condition	COVID-19 Vaccine	Relationship Status
Isaiah	Black/43	UN	N/A	Yes	Single
Bobby	Black/48	UN	HIV+	Yes	Partnered
Gerald	Black/40-50	Apt	HIV+	Yes	Single

Three Photovoice Cases: Isaiah, Bobby, and Gerald

Of the fourteen participants who were part of the larger project, this chapter highlights the perspectives of three Black men—using the pseudonyms of Isaiah, Bobby, and Gerald (*Table 6.2*)—who experienced HIH. We include a selection of their photographs (which were digitally enhanced and turned to grayscale from color for publishing purposes) and transcripts in the following pages. In their experiences of HIH, these men experience various MHL barriers resulting from their high exposure to violence, an absence of privacy, and stigma. However, they also narrate three MHL pathways: (1) embracing the status of homelessness, (2) saving face, and (3) demonstrating pride and responsibility.

Isaiah: Embracing the Status of Homelessness

Isaiah dedicates his life to his religious beliefs. He sees himself as a person of God, and his mission in life is to be in the service of the Lord. He carries a Bible with him everywhere and often reads from it when there is no one to talk to or to fill idle time (*Figure 6.6*). Isaiah is always at the property early in the morning; he is usually waiting for the doors to open even before the volunteers arrive at 7:30 a.m. He is often the last to leave.

Isaiah lives unsheltered and carries his belongings with him. His heavy winter coat and multiple layers hide his relatively lean frame, which is revealed in the summer months when his overcoat is finally removed. Isaiah is 43, a middle-aged Black man with some college education. He studied engineering and worked in architectural design until job losses made it impossible for him to maintain a residence.

Isaiah is perhaps the quintessential "homeless by choice" person. He's in no hurry to get off the streets, prefers this life of "contentment" over the stressors of the alternative, and finds purpose in helping others find their way to "God." Isaiah is almost without fail always at the Manna House during its operating hours. He is friendly with all the guests and is there should anyone ever need him. We witnessed him holding prayer for the guests, even placing his hand on a woman's head once to pray for her and her health.

Isaiah was knowledgeable about the entire community and served as a resource regarding the status of those who had not been to the Manna House

Figure 6.6 Isaiah's Bible. Source: Photo by co-research participant Isaiah.

for a while. He was always there to offer his thoughts, philosophizing about life and even about the pandemic. He was a sounding board and a litmus test for broaching specific topics. Isaiah was open, yet careful and guarded. He presented as always "being busy" with something, but we noticed he, too, was in observation of others. At times he would be listening in on conversations between other guests or even between one of our team members and other volunteers. He would often chuckle at something funny or add his perspective. He never talked much about his family or friends. Despite his social shrewdness, Isaiah was very independent. He never refused a question but demonstrated a mastery of deflection. He would often answer in abstractions, never dwelling on the particularities of his own family or life. Isaiah is a guide—a medium to connect and help others navigate the volatile life on the streets of Memphis—yet still felt worn down by a life on the streets.

> I took a picture of that cause that's my hands. And my feet, you know. I have my hands—I *feel* cold. Calluses and stuff from carrying bags and on my feet that had this long walk. So, I believe the hardest part of my body is in the feet (*Figure 6.7*).

> A lot of us have had a lot of lonely roads out here. A lot of us, we don't have no friends out here and it's difficult to get through today. And this, you know, a lot of people are isolated from love. A lot of us are isolated because of drugs and alcohol. It just looked like a lonely path (*Figure 6.8*).

Figure 6.7 Isaiah's gloves and feet. Source: Photo by co-research participant Isaiah.

Figure 6.8 Isaiah's lonely road. Source: Photo by co-research participant Isaiah.

> It's difficult to speed through your process out here. So, it's difficult to speed through homelessness. I think right now it's difficult to get a home. I think it makes the process even slower, you know, because it's difficult to meet with people like Catholic charities, the most famous group that gets people into homes, but then you got to wait 60 days to meet with the counselor. Then they give you something else you fill out. Yeah. I picked that one because there's no privacy out here, just a private parking sign and there's no privacy (*Figure 6.9*). So, it was for a lot of homeless, isolated [inaudible] you don't have nowhere to go. You got to be very creative.

Isaiah accepted his HIH status while emphasizing significant gaps between society's misconstrued, stigmatized framing of the homeless identity and the "real" homeless identity. He embodies a life that chooses to veer away from more socially accepted pathways. Isaiah's narratives challenge the stigma of homeless framing, redirecting notions of responsibility and misunderstanding back onto the non-homeless population. Many participants experienced difficult interpersonal relationships before and after coming to live on the streets. Isaiah describes finding meaning and safety in being homeless, in spiritual enhancement, and in achieving a non-traditional quality of life. Isaiah described regaining a sense of control by reframing social isolation as a personal choice.

Figure 6.9 A private parking sign Isaiah encountered. Source: Photo by co-research participant Isaiah.

Homeless spaces and contexts, in Isaiah's narratives, are spaces for coping with mental health challenges and losses.

Bobby: Face Saving

Bobby is lean and stands about 5'8" or 5'9". He's talkative and can be coy or intentionally evasive at times. He was immediately receptive to our presence at the shelter and was happy to sit and talk. Each time we saw him, Bobby eagerly came over to talk about the day, the weather, and his next endeavor. He often had a prop to exemplify his pursuits of a better life (e.g., a tablet, a phone, a job application, a new work uniform, etc.). Bobby reveals bits about himself over time and shows a docile side at the shelter. His photo contributions and interviews featured blight, and the economic and social effects of the pandemic on the local poor and homeless populations. In our first meeting with him, he carried a tablet claiming he was enrolling in academic courses for the next term. He claimed the device was offered by the school and would enable him to attend classes online via an internet connection provided by the local library branch. Over the next few weeks, it became clear that this was not the case. Bobby was skilled at performing the life of a person striving to achieve the recognizable social markers of education, employment, and housing, yet lacked the ability or desire to do so.

Almost a year after we first met Bobby, he began to reveal stories about his past. Bobby had been a prostitute. He would cross-dress and wear wigs in his interchangeable wardrobe. He shared about the potential dangers of the work and how he was attacked with a screwdriver by a man who presented as a client. We would overhear conversations between him and other guests in which it was clear that he was no pushover. He chose to present himself in a way that was nonthreatening and buoyant. In observing him with others, Bobby had the wit, charm, and chameleon-like ability to reinvent himself. His one constant was his ability to suggest a less stigmatized self.

Bobby appeared to be the alpha in the relationship with a "friend," Frankie, who would accompany him on occasion. Bobby presented as though he had housing, but as time passed, it became clear that he and Frankie stayed in an abandoned structure without running water, electricity, or heat. At the time of his interview, Bobby claimed that he had a job at McDonald's. He would arrive at the Manna House with an apron as evidence of his employment—a prop, much like the tablet that demonstrated he was a student. For a large portion of his photovoice interview, he spoke about the place he "used to live," which turns out to be the place he is currently living.

Bobby: Yeah. And this is, uh, my old apartment building (*Figure 6.10*). They shut it down due to the COVID-19 because a lot of people, you know, couldn't pay any money and couldn't afford. So, the landlord had to end up closing the building down. Now they're getting ready to tear the whole building down. You have seen, cause this used to be my old apartment right here. And you can see everything is . . .

Interviewer: It's empty-

Bobby: Yeah, it's slowly, slowly being . . . Actually, it was a big apartment building because he's had apartments sit on both sides. Yeah. And this is my old apartment.

Interviewer: Is that a window?

Bobby: Yup, it's the window (*Figure 6.11*).

Interviewer: And the door was just open . . . the door. Is there anybody still living in there?

Bobby: There's a couple of homeless people that still stay in, you know, in the building and the landlord is letting them stay there. 'Cause he gave them four months before he's going to tear it down.

Interviewer: Is there, um, is there any heat in there? Is there like power or light? Or warmth?

Bobby: No. 'Cause all the warmth they have is their extra blankets. Yep. The owners are slowly moving this stuff out of it. Like the hardware, and the wood, and the windows and things like that.

Figure 6.10 Bobby's living conditions. Graffiti is visible on the right wall. Source: Photo by co-research participant Bobby.

Figure 6.11 A broken window that exposes the apartment to the elements. Source: Photo by co-research participant Bobby.

Figure 6.12 The hallway to Bobby's kitchen. Source: Photo by co-research participant Bobby.

Bobby: And a small kitchen entry right there (*Figure 6.12*).

Interviewer: And we can see some kitchen, and a really pretty archway into the kitchen. What does it make you think when you think about your old place?

Bobby: It makes me think that if it wasn't due to the COVID-19, I'd probably be still living there right now. Uh, the reason why I'm not in there because, um, he had to, you know, shut the building down because a lot of people wasn't paying the rent.

Interviewer: He didn't have a means to pay it.

Bobby: Yeah, the means to pay it. So, he eventually part sold it to this other room rental and leasing company. And they're getting ready to tear the building down and build, start over.

In this interview about his photos, Bobby remarks, "Cause all the warmth they have, is their extra blankets." He never acknowledged that the "they" is him and Frankie. The intense stigma connected to his profession, his dependence on substances, his health, and his housing combined to generate a face-saving dimension to his presentation of the self. The truth goes against the status quo and would heighten the stigma he already struggles to navigate. Instead, Bobby performs that he has more resources and financial prospects than he actually does.

Gerald: Pride and Responsibility

Gerald is a tall, lanky man of about forty to fifty years. He walks with a spring in his step. Gerald is a Dallas Cowboys fan, and football is a topic that excites him. On Monday mornings, he and many other guests often huddle around, talking about the last night's game, exchanging predictions, and arguing about the best plays or players. Gerald is upbeat and social; he mainly visits the Manna House to grab a cup of coffee and mingle, but he will also get on the supply list to get some extra socks or a new t-shirt. His health was improving since he got back on antiretroviral drug therapy for HIV; Gerald received treatment from a neighboring organization that supports individuals in Memphis with HIV. He is grateful to the organization and credits them with his healthful "undetected" status. Gerald also expressed gratitude to the organization for providing a non-judgmental space to talk (seek counseling), access to technological devices (e.g., computers and internet use) free of charge, and securing a small apartment for him. Gerald was homeless before and is an unofficial Manna House ambassador for getting and staying in HIV care. He was always sending friends of his who were also HIV positive to the support organization.

Gerald talks about race and its role in discrimination, as well as the stigma of HIV. Many of the pictures he provided show his local area and its safety.

> I took a picture down the street, that street down there [pointing]. You know what? The neighborhood, how it look, you see (*Figure 6.13*)? There ain't no stragglers or nothing like that. Cause people say Midtown is a bad neighborhood or whatever. But you see, I took that picture. You don't see nobody on the sidewalk. It ain't all about people, places, or things. It's what's in your heart, you know? So, ain't no excuses really, ain't no excuses.

In other conversations, Gerald told us about being incarcerated for drug possession but that he was "not doing that anymore." Having been homeless and in and out of prison, Gerald was happy to live a quiet life and enjoy his health. Gerald spoke of the vulnerable, open spaces he once relied on for sleep and rest.

> This is a picture of a place where some of us used to sleep (*Figure 6.14*). See cardboard boxes up in there? No, not allowed. As long as we kept it clean, we could sleep up in there. Get up in the morning, go in at night, get up in the morning, clean up, or whatever.

Gerald testifies to the benefits of positive social support for those in precarious living situations. His close friendship with other Manna House guests was

Figure 6.13 An empty and safe street in Gerald's neighborhood. Source: Photo by co-research participant Gerald.

Figure 6.14 A covered archway with a cardboard box by the front door. Source: Photo by co-research participant Gerald.

evidence of a fundamental human need to connect. Their shared hardships were, for some, safe topics to share and explore in the context of the Manna House. Gerald credited a local HIV agency for his recent improvement in health. He depicts a different approach from Bobby; Gerald openly shares his shortcomings as well as his advancements in seeking help.

> This is where it all started. Friends for Life (*Figure 6.15*). That organization helps people with HIV. And I can say they are my friends. They are my friends because I was homeless before I got my own apartment. I want you to know, I'm on my medicine. And somebody introduced me to them. It's been going steady for two years now. I've still got my place. You can go there, get on a computer, look for a job or whatever. They've got case workers there. You need someone to talk to that feeds you? They give you a food pantry, but you got to fit the criteria to get all of that. Can't just anybody go up in there. You know, you gotta fit the criteria. An organization that helps people with their homeless situation. All kinds of people. Whether you get an HIV check or whatever. They'll help you if you applied—you got to apply yourself, though. You can't be out there missing phone calls or missing your appointments. And if you stay with them, they'll stay with you. You work with them, they'll work with you.
>
> And this picture right here, it's an empty apartment (*Figure 6.16*). Somebody is out there—homeless, living with HIV—that can be in that apartment, you know?

Figure 6.15 The Friends for Life building. Source: Photo by co-research participant Gerald.

> That whole apartment building, it's for people like me, you know? I tell people all the time, you know, I'm getting a check. They pay my rent, pay my light bill. Now, it ain't much, but it's mine. I know the difference, you know, between HIV and AIDS, you know, cause you're living with the results. No, I'm not happy about it. But life goes on. Life goes on and I'm going to keep putting one foot in front of the other. There is life with HIV. There's *life* with HIV. And as long as the person is kept in the right frame of mind that "I can do this," they can do it.

This emphasis on individual responsibility and participation seems to drive Gerald to maintain motivation and a sense of control over his life circumstances. In contrast to Bobby, Gerald does not put up any facades of grandeur or victimhood. He understands that life was never meant to be a fair game, and that he must play the hand he was dealt. Gerald does not ruminate on the past; instead, he is intent on developing a brighter future.

Recommendations to Support Mental Health Literacy among the Homeless

As evidenced by the co-researcher participants in these three cases, HIH is a byproduct of complex societal levels of economic instability, mental healthcare access, addiction, stigmatization, challenges related to race, and

Figure 6.16 Apartment building for people living with HIV. Source: Photo by co-research participant Gerald.

access to resources in America. The discomfort around housing instability and homelessness is often explained away by the housed as a stigmatized individual's weakness, but most Americans are closer than they would imagine—a single paycheck away—from being challenged in ways similar to Isaiah, Bobby, and Gerald. The process of regaining resources and housing stability, once lost, is exponentially more complex for those facing MHL barriers.

As each of the co-researcher participants indicated, homelessness is inherently isolating. Because of the stigmatization and discrimination against unhoused people, it can be difficult for individuals facing HIH to know whom they can trust. Older data conservatively estimates that around 20 percent of individuals facing HIH have experienced a violent attack (Meinbresse et al., 2014), but it cannot account for all the emotional traumas and microaggressions experienced on a daily and nightly basis. Despite this trauma, each of these participants tried to connect with the research team to offer insight into the complexities of the barriers and pathways they experienced. Based on this photovoice research and the lenses of Fisher and Goffman, we recommend the following actions for allied health workers, communication researchers, and all interdisciplinary social support partners to advance the mental health literacy of those surviving housing instability and homelessness:

- Prioritize the creation of mobile mental health resources. Those with housing instability are likely not to have transportation to fixed locations.
- Prioritize the identification and implementation of trauma-informed health workers/providers to deliver place-based mental health care.
- Prioritize Wi-Fi and charging stations at support settings. This digital pathway is required to interact with virtual mental health settings, access care portals, field calls from agencies, and seek social support.
- Include trauma-related training for volunteers and community members who work with shelter clients.
- Include spiritual support and care in shelter sites. Spiritual well-being is linked to higher mental health literacy.
- Identify gender-related resources to offer appropriate mental health support for clients who endure fragmented and uncoordinated services geared toward male-gendered people living with housing instability.
- Create narrative outlets for those with housing instability and homelessness to share their stories.
- Engage students to staff support sites for clients with housing instability and homelessness.

Conclusion

Offering time and space to facilitate collective connections reduces the differences among the housed and unhoused and elevates their shared losses and goals. By sharing in a warm cup of coffee, gathering in community, and receiving the support of others, people at the Manna House get a break from the stigma they endure in other spaces in Memphis. At the Manna House, there is no distinction between those who are housed and unhoused or HIV positive and HIV negative. People are allowed to connect, share, and learn about one another without traditional barriers.

Researchers in communal spaces akin to the site of this project should be prepared to be participant observers first. Knowing the people, practices, and policies within the space is the first step to identifying with the context. Interacting with others from a place of genuine interest and graciousness—brewing the coffee, dumping the trash, sharing stories, and deeply listening—is the first step toward finding common ground in a space like the Manna House.

Within the realm of communication research, the perspectives of marginalized and unhoused voices have been historically underrepresented. Using community-based research methods—especially photovoice—to narrate the homeless experience endows participants with a sense of agency and buy-in. As Isaiah noted, to be unhoused is to be without privacy. Giving these participants the *choice* to share their lived experiences and allow others to see through their eyes can be empowering. Fisher's work focuses on the narrative credibility of the narrator. Granting the voice of the person living in homelessness or unstable housing narrative agency lends value to their lived experiences, attention to their challenges, and support for their successes. The voices of our co-researchers are the most credible interpreters of this reality.

Approaching each participant as a *person*—one who has walked a lonely road to reach their current point in life—will give them the freedom to share their truth. Communication research can serve as a change agent. Gerald demonstrated this in his final thoughts with the research team. The interviewer inquired if there was anything else he wanted to share; teary-eyed, he said:

> Yeah, there is one thing—one more thing I'd like to say. You know, it's people like y'all that give me inspiration. You know, to let me know that there is hope and help out there for others. Because y'all show up. Y'all show it. And it's touching.

To be a researcher is to be in pursuit of understanding and knowledge. In this case, understanding and knowledge are complicated without a clear set of solutions. Each person facing HIH bears their own unique challenge in relation to living without stable shelter. Together, their voices are the most credible source in identifying pathways to physical safety and mental health support.

Recommended Readings/Resources

Richard, M. K. (2023). Race matters in addressing homelessness: A scoping review and call for critical research. *American Journal of Community Psychology*, *72*(3–4), 464–485.

Rosenblad, A. K., Klarare, A., Rapaport, P., Mattsson, E., & Gaber, S. N. (2024). Health literacy and its association with mental and spiritual well-being among women experiencing homelessness. *Health Promotion International*, *39*(2), daae019.

References

Batterham, R. W., Hawkins, M., Collins, P. A., Buchbinder, R., & Osborne, R. H. (2016). Health literacy: Applying current concepts to improve health services and reduce health inequalities. *Public Health*, *132*, 3–12. https://doi.org/http://dx.doi.org/10.1016/j.puhe.2016.01.001

Byrne, T., Baggett, T., Land, T., Bernson, D., Hood, M. E., Kennedy-Perez, C., Monterrey, R., Smelson, D., Dones, M., & Bharel, M. (2020). A classification model of homelessness using integrated administrative data: Implications for targeting interventions to improve the housing status, health and well-being of a highly vulnerable population. *PloS one*, *15*(8), e0237905. https://doi.org/10.1371/journal.pone.0237905

CAFTH Memphis. (2023). *2023 Memphis/Shelby County Point-in-Time summary*. Point In Time Count. Retrieved from https://www.cafth.org/point-in-time-count/

Canham, S. L., Moore, P., Custodio, K., & Bosma, H. (2022). Homeism: Naming the stigmatization and discrimination of persons experiencing homelessness. *Housing, Theory and Society*, *39*(5), 507–523. https://doi.org/10.1080/14036096.2021.2014558

Chou, W.-y. S., Gaysynsky, A., Persoskie, A., & Ragan, S. L. (2015). Health literacy and communication in palliative care. In E. Wittenberg, B. R. Ferrell, J. Goldsmith, T. Smith, M. Glajchen, & G. F. Handzo (Eds.), *Textbook of palliative care communication* (pp. 90–101). Oxford University Press. https://doi.org/10.1093/med/9780190201708.003.0012

Cutilli, C. C., & Bennett, I. M. (2009). Understanding the health literacy of America results of the National Assessment of Adult Literacy. *Orthopaedic Nursing*, *28*(1), 27–34. https://doi.org/10.1097/01.NOR.0000345852.22122.d6

Daré, L. O., Bruand, P. E., Gérard, D., Marin, B., Lameyre, V., Boumédiène, F., & Preux, P. M. (2019). Co-morbidities of mental disorders and chronic physical diseases in developing and emerging countries: A meta-analysis. *BMC Public Health*, *19*(1), 304. https://doi.org/10.1186/s12889-019-6623-6

Duell, P., Wright, D., Renzaho, A. M. N., & Bhattacharya, D. (2015). Optimal health literacy measurement for the clinical setting: A systematic review. *Patient Education and Counseling, 98*(11), 1295–1307. https://doi.org/https://doi.org/10.1016/j.pec.2015.04.003

Edwards, E. J. (2021). Who are the homeless? Centering Anti-Black racism and the consequences of colorblind homeless policies. *Social Sciences*, *10*(9), 340. https://doi.org/10.3390/socsci10090340

Emery, L. F., Silverman, D. M., & Carey, R. M. (2023). Conducting research with people in lower-socioeconomic-status contexts. *Advances in Methods and Practices in Psychological Science*, *6*(4), 25152459231193044. https://doi.org/10.1177/25152459231193044

Fisher, W. R. (1985). The narrative paradigm: An elaboration. *Communication Monographs*, *52*(4), 347–367. https://doi.org/10.1080/03637758509376117

Fisher, W. R. (1989). Clarifying the narrative paradigm. *Communication Monographs*, *56*(1), 55–58. https://doi.org/10.1080/03637758909390249

Fitzgerald, C., & Hurst, S. (2017). Implicit bias in healthcare professionals: A systematic review. *BMC Medical Ethics*, *18*(1), 19. https://doi.org/10.1186/s12910-017-0179-8

Gadotti, M., & Torres, C. A. (2009). Paulo Freire: Education for development. *Development and Change*, *40*(6), 1255–1267. https://doi.org/10.1111/j.1467-7660.2009.01606.x

Gibson, C., Smith, D., & Morrison, A. K. (2022). Improving health literacy knowledge, behaviors, and confidence with interactive training. *Health Literacy Research and Practice*, *6*(2), e113–e120. https://doi.org/10.3928/24748307-20220420-01

Goffman, E. (1959). *The presentation of self in everyday life.* Anchor.

Goldsmith, J., & Terui, S. (2018). Family oncology caregivers and relational health literacy. *Challenges*, *9*(35), 1–10. https://doi.org/10.3390/challe9020035

Goldsmith, J., & Terui, S. (2019). Mental health literacy at the house of grace: Advancing relational health literacy as a conceptual model. In R. H. L. Lippert, A. Miller-Ott, & D. Cochece Davis (Eds.), *Communicating mental health: History, concepts, and perspectives*. Lexington Press.

Goodall, H. L. (2000). *Writing the new ethnography.* AltaMira Press.

Griffin, E. A., Ledbetter, A., & Sparks, G. G. (2019). *A first look at communication theory* (Tenth ed.). McGraw-Hill Education.

Hargrave, A., & Ball-Johnson, K. (2022). *Q1 homeless enrollment updates, Shelby County School District, November 2022 academic committee meeting.* Retrieved from https://go.boarddocs.com/tn/scsk12/Board.nsf/files/CL2UWN7E1079/$file/November%202022%20Academic%20Performance%20Comm%20Mtg%20(1).pdf

Henning-Smith, C. (2020). The public health case for addressing transportation-related barriers to care. *American Journal of Public Health, 110*(6), 763–764. https://doi.org/10.2105/AJPH.2020.305638

Johnson, R. A. (2010). African Americans and homelessness: Moving through history. *Journal of Black Studies, 40*(4), 583–605. https://doi.org/10.1177/0021934708315487

Kemmis, S., & McTaggart, R. (2007). *The action research planner: Doing critical participatory action research.* Sage Publications.

Koo, H. J., Piff, P. K., & Shariff, A. F. (2023). If I could do it, so can they: Among the rich, those with humbler origins are less sensitive to the difficulties of the poor. *Social Psychology and Personal Science, 14*(3), 333–341. https://doi.org/10.1177/19485506221098921

Kutcher, S., Wei, Y., & Coniglio, C. (2016). Mental health literacy: Past, present, and future. *Canadian Journal of Psychiatry, 61*(3), 154–158. https://doi.org/10.1177/0706743715616609

Latz, A. O. (2017). *Photovoice research in education and beyond: a practical guide from theory to exhibition.* Routledge, Taylor & Francis Group.

Lee, B. A., Tyler, K. A., & Wright, J. D. (2010). The new homelessness revisited. *Annual Review of Sociology, 36*(1), 501–521. https://doi.org/10.1146/annurev-soc-070308-115940

Lekas, H.-M., Pahl, K., & Fuller Lewis, C. (2020). Rethinking cultural competence: Shifting to cultural humility. *Health Services Insights, 13,* 117863292097058. https://doi.org/10.1177/1178632920970580

Maina, I. W., Belton, T. D., Ginzberg, S., Singh, A., & Johnson, T. J. (2018). A decade of studying implicit racial/ethnic bias in healthcare providers using the implicit association test. *Social Science & Medicine, 199,* 219–229. https://doi.org/10.1016/j.socscimed.2017.05.009

Meinbresse, M., Brinkley-Rubinstein, L., Grassette, A., Benson, J., Hamilton, R., Malott, M., & Jenkins, D. (2014). Exploring the experiences of violence among individuals who are homeless using a consumer-led approach. *Violence and Victims, 29*(1), 122–136. https://doi.org/10.1891/0886–6708.vv-d-12-00069

McGrath, J. J., Lim, C. C. W., Plana-Ripoll, O., Holtz, Y., Agerbo, E., Momen, N. C., Mortensen, P. B., Pedersen, C. B., Abdulmalik, J., Aguilar-Gaxiola, S., Al-Hamzawi, A., Alonso, J., Bromet, E. J., Bruffaerts, R., Bunting, B., de Almeida, J. M. C., de Girolamo, G., De Vries, Y. A., Florescu, S., Gureje, O., Haro, J. M.,

Harris, M. G., Hu, C., Karam, E. G., Kawakami, N., Kiejna, A., Kovess-Masfety, V., Lee, S., Mneimneh, Z., Navarro- Mateu, F., Orozco, R., Posada-Villa, J., Roest, A. M., Saha, S., Scott, K. M., Stagnaro, J. C., Stein, D. J., Torres, Y., Viana, M. C., Ziv, Y., Kessler, R. C., & de Jonge, P. (2020). Comorbidity within mental disorders: A comprehensive analysis based on 145, 990 survey respondents from 27 countries. *Epidemiological and Psychiatric Sciences*, *29*, e153. https://doi.org/10.1017/s2045796020000633

Melo, A. P. S., Dippenaar, I. N., Johnson, S. C., Weaver, N. D., de Assis Acurcio, F., Malta, D. C., Ribeiro, A. L. P., Júnior, A. A. G., Wool, E. E., Naghavi, M., & Cherchiglia, M. L. (2022). All-cause and cause-specific mortality among people with severe mental illness in Brazil's public health system, 2000–15: A retrospective study. *The Lancet Psychiatry*, *9*(10), 771–781. https://doi.org/10.1016/S2215-0366(22)00237-1

Mgbako, O., Conard, R., Mellins, C. A., Dacus, J.-d., & Remien, R. H. (2022). A systematic review of factors critical for HIV health literacy, art adherence and retention in care in the U.S. for racial and ethnic minorities. *AIDS and Behavior*, *26*(11), 3480–3493. https://doi.org/10.1007/s10461-022-03680-y

Morton, M., Dworsky, A., & Samuels, G. (2017). Missed opportunities: Youth homelessness in America. *National Estimates.* Retrieved from https://voicesofyouthcount.org/wp- content/uploads/2017/11/VoYC-National-Estimates-Brief-Chapin-Hall-2017.pdf

Nichols, B. (2001). *Introduction to documentary.* Indiana University Press.

Nutbeam, D., & Lloyd, J. E. (2021). Understanding and responding to health literacy as a social determinant of health. *Annual Review of Public Health*, *42*(1), 159–173.

Olivet, J., Wilkey, C., Richard, M., Dones, M., Tripp, J., Beit-Arie, M., Yampolskaya, S., & Cannon, R. (2021). Racial inequity and homelessness: Findings from the SPARC study. *The ANNALS of the American Academy of Political and Social Science*, *693*(1), 82–100. https://doi.org/10.1177/0002716221991040

Peprah, P., Lloyd, J., & Harris, M. (2023). Health literacy and cultural responsiveness of primary health care systems and services in Australia: Reflections from service providers, stakeholders, and people from refugee backgrounds. *BMC Public Health*, *23*(1), 2557. https://doi.org/10.1186/s12889-023-17448-z

Petkovic, J., Magwood, O., Lytvyn, L., Khabsa, J., Concannon, T. W., Welch, V., Todhunter- Brown, A., Palm, M. E., Akl, E. A., Mbuagbaw, L., Arayssi, T., Avey, M. T., Marusic, A., Morley, R., Saginur, M., Slingers, N., Texeira, L., Ben Brahem, A., Bhaumik, S., Bou Akl, I., Crowe, S., Dormer, L., Ekanem, C., Lang, E., Kianzad, B., Kuchenmüller, T., Moja, L., Pottie, K., Schünemann, H., & Tugwell, P. (2023). Key issues for stakeholder engagement in the development of health and healthcare guidelines. *Research Involvement and Engagement*, *9*(1), 27. https://doi.org/10.1186/s40900-023-00433-6

Pope, M. A., Malla, A. K., & Iyer, S. N. (2018). Who should be responsible for supporting individuals with mental health problems? A critical literature review. *The International Journal of Social Psychiatry*, *64*(3), 293–302. https://doi.org/10.1177/0020764017752019

Reynolds, R., Smoller, S., Allen, A., & Nicholas, P. K. (2019). Health literacy and health outcomes in persons living with HIV disease: A systematic review. *AIDS and Behavior*, *23*(11), 3024–3043. https://doi.org/10.1007/s10461-019-02432-9

Richard, M. K. (2023). Race matters in addressing homelessness: A scoping review and call for critical research. *American Journal of Community Psychology*, *72*(3–4), 464–485. https://doi.org/https://doi.org/10.1002/ajcp.12700

Rittner, B., & Kirk, A. B. (1995). Health care and public transportation use by poor and frail elderly people. *Social Work*, *40*(3), 365–373. https://www.ncbi.nlm.nih.gov/pubmed/7761923

Rosenblad, A. K., Klarare, A., Rapaport, P., Mattsson, E., & Gaber, S. N. (2024). Health literacy and its association with mental and spiritual well-being among women experiencing homelessness. *Health Promotion International*, *39*(2), daae019. https://doi.org/10.1093/heapro/daae019

Sampaio, F., Gonçalves, P., & Sequeira, C. (2022). Mental health literacy: It is now time to put knowledge into practice. *International Journal of Environmental Research in Public Health*, *19*(12), 7030. https://doi.org/10.3390/ijerph19127030

Schillinger, D. (2021). Social determinants, health literacy, and disparities: Intersections and controversies. *HLRP: Health Literacy Research and Practice*, *5*(3), e234–e243. https://doi.org/doi:10.3928/24748307-20210712-01

Schindler, L. (2018). The ethnomethods of ethnography: A trans-situational approach to the epistemology of qualitative research. *Human Studies*, *41*(1), 103–120. https://doi.org/10.1007/s10746-017-9449-1

Skosireva, A., O'Campo, P., Zerger, S., Chambers, C., Gapka, S., & Stergiopoulos, V. (2014). Different faces of discrimination: Perceived discrimination among homeless adults with mental illness in healthcare settings. *BMC Health Services Research*, *14*(1), 376. https://doi.org/10.1186/1472-6963-14-376

Terui, S., Goldsmith, J. V., Huang, J., Yang, C.-C., Yu, X., Deng, L. Y., & Wicke, R. (2023). Validating the communicating care needs tool for HIV (CCNT-HIV). *Journal of Health Communication*. https://doi.org/10.1080/10810730.2023.2271876

U.S. Department of Housing and Urban Development. (2023). *The 2023 Annual Homelessness Assessment Report (AHAR) to Congress, Part 1: Point-in-Time estimates of homelessness*. Retrieved from www.huduser.gov/portal/sites/default/files/pdf/2023-AHAR-Part-1.pdf

Wang, C., & Burris, M. A. (1997). Photovoice: Concept, methodology, and use for participatory needs assessment. *Health Education & Behavior*, *24*(3), 369–387. https://doi.org/10.1177/109019819702400309

Wolfson, J. A., Garcia, T., & Leung, C. W. (2021). Food insecurity is associated with depression, anxiety, and stress: Evidence from the early days of the COVID-19 Pandemic in the United States. *Health Equity*, *5*(1), 64–71. https://doi.org/10.1089/heq.2020.0059

Young, A. J., Stephens, E., & Goldsmith, J. V. (2017). Family caregiver communication in the ICU: Toward a relational view of health literacy. *Journal of Family Communication*, *17*(2), 137–152. https://doi.org/10.1080/15267431.2016.1247845

7

e-Mental Health Intervention Strategies for the Low-Income Population

A Communicative Approach

Kyung Jung Han

eHealth interventions are the interventions delivered via websites, mobile phone applications, or other various online programs or tools using electronic devices (Han et al., 2024; Kupila et al., 2023). It includes mHealth (mobile health) and partially with technology-based interventions indicating both intervention programs running online and offline. Specifically, when considering eHealth interventions, there are different types of intervention features based on communication. That is, eHealth interventions including the Web 1.0 modality are designed with one-way communication (website only), whereas Web 2.0 eHealth interventions allow participants with mental health issues to interact with other participants or mental health providers through two-way communication (website plus interaction). These days, many eHealth interventions are designed using a mixture of Web 2.0 and 3.0 (customized media modalities) via different media channels (website plus interactive apps with different social media platforms) compatible with various media devices including wearable devices (Han et al., 2024).

Although the eHealth intervention strategies for mental health (or e-mental health interventions) are adopted as the technology changes, it is not unusual to exclude participants from specific contexts, such as low-income populations and ethnically identified minorities, in conducting and reviewing the eHealth intervention programs. The low-income population itself is regarded as an additional variable to consider for mental health interventions. Thus, the low-income population is a specific group when designing any mental health interventions, and the feasibility of e-mental health interventions should be also assessed for this target group. The population can be identified in many ways: Medicaid (a program that supports people in the United States who may not have enough money to pay for their medical expenses) beneficiaries in the US context or the population group with lower socioeconomic status (SES) (e.g., education and household income). By tracking the situational context of the low-income population, it will be easier to find better ways to succeed in eHealth intervention strategies for mental health and wellness.

Particularly in health communication, it is important to understand that many mental health interventions or health campaign programs have different health goals with 3S perspectives: (1) selecting appropriate intervention modality or media channel and platform (i.e., apps, web-based, texting, in-person, etc.), (2) sharing intervention messages or target health education content, and (3) supporting various communication directions (one-way or two-way communication between other participants and with health providers).

For example, an eBody project (Stice et al., 2017) examined various modalities for the intervention (clinician-led/in-person, peer-led/in-person, self-driven/internet-based, and educational/a weblink shared video) with different communicative messages depending on assigned groups (with a clinician, with peers, with self-driven web modules, and with an educational video), allowing either one- or two-way communication to prevent eating disorders. As a result, risk factors (thin-ideal internalization, body dissatisfaction, negative affect) for eating disorders and eating disorder symptoms were reduced in the clinician-led and peer-led groups. It calls for the need to develop more successful strategies with e-mental health interventions, questioning how to replace clinician and peer support.

As another example, *Mom-Net*, an internet-facilitated cognitive treatment for depression, was tailored to low-income mothers of young children (Sheeber et al., 2017). In the intervention, the selected modalities were both coach supported (allowing direct phone calls and online education programs) and shortened program sessions from twelve to eight modules with specific message content such as training for behavioral activation, cognitive skills, and interpersonal skills, considering the challenges of mothers to maintain the e-mental health over longer periods. The intervention outcomes were very promising, with a significant reduction in depression. It shows the benefits of e-mental health intervention with a more strategic design for the intervention platform, content, and communication allowances for patients with health providers.

As such, this chapter will discuss successful prevention and treatment strategies for e-mental health interventions targeting low-income populations. More specifically, it will discuss challenges to succeed in e-mental health interventions, applicable theories for developing the interventions, and effective strategies for implementing e-mental health interventions with a communicative approach for low-income populations.

Challenges to Succeed in e-Mental Health Interventions with a Communicative Approach

Although previous studies (Armaou et al., 2020; Linardon et al., 2020) have attempted to investigate effective communication strategies in e-mental health intervention programs for low-income populations, some challenges, such as the lack of assessment for health and technology literacy and no tailoring or target-oriented intervention development for low-income populations, and a lack of references to reflect in the intervention planning, remain as homework for communication specialists. The details for each challenge will be discussed in the next part.

Mental Health Literacy and eHealth Literacy

To understand the content of the intervention and delivered messages by other peers and health providers, a certain level of mental health literacy and eHealth literacy is required. However, not many program developers consider the levels of mental health literacy and eHealth literacy. Besides, the low-income population sometimes has different priorities for spending their daily lives for their families and to reduce their financial burden (Kaltman et al., 2016). Thus, attention to their specific mental health literacy and eHealth literacy is suggested.

In general, health literacy has been assessed in many intervention studies so far. More specifically, depending on the context, mental health literacy (Seedaket et al., 2020) or general health literacy assessment during the COVID-19 (Ayaz-Alkaya & Dülger, 2022) was considered to understand the challenges in behavioral changes or meeting a health goal. However, for the low-income population, although health literacy could be a barrier to succeeding in intervention programs (Cheng et al., 2020), not many studies assessed participants' health literacy levels in their intervention programs. In Cheng et al. (2020)'s systematic review study, there are few studies targeting socially disadvantaged groups that assessed/discussed health literacy perspectives. Only three out of forty-eight interventions considered the health literacy component (Miller et al., 2018). Meanwhile, eHealth literacy matters in using eHealth intervention technology, understanding health terms, engaging with the intervention program through digital services, and feeling safe and in control with digital services. It also relates to the motivation and online privacy concerns of the involved participants (Cheng et al., 2020). Therefore, it will be one of the prioritized factors to consider in e-mental health interventions for successful communication strategies.

Lack of Target-Oriented Interventions for the Low-Income Population

Understanding different target audiences for an intervention program is essential for public health promotion campaigns and interventions in general. It is also one of the important components in strategic communication in selecting the appropriate media outlet or modality and the message content and applies to e-mental health intervention development as well. A full understanding of different ethnicities (cultural differences), variations in ages, and their preferences in selecting intervention modality, frequency of intervention exposure, eHealth literacy, and technology literacy could be considered from the intervention development phase. In some previous intervention studies, the reasons for insignificant results between intervention and control groups or limitations for the studies, such as no investigation of participating parents (Coker et al., 2023), short-term results (Palacios et al., 2018), and intervention tailoring issues (Wang & Miller, 2020) were discussed. Matching the situation of low SES, longer term interventions are still challenging. Thus, how to fulfill the needs of low-income patients with mental health problems matters.

Lack of References Considering Mental Health, Low-Income, and Communicative Perspectives

A lack of guidelines for developing eHealth interventions for low-income people is another barrier (Al-Dhahir et al., 2023). In a recent systematic review study by Cheng et al. (2020), previous interventions were investigated. However, those samples could not proceed to meta-analysis to compare statistical differences between interventions due to a lack of samples and reported articles to assess the differences. It is also due to a lack of guidelines or a rubric/protocol to analyze eHealth interventions, particularly targeting low SES population. Under the situation, communication components based on 3S (selecting intervention modality, sharing mental health promoting messages, and supporting various communication directions) will be examined together.

Applicable Theories for Successful e-Mental Health Interventions to Execute Effective Communication Strategies

Theories are selected by systematic search from five databases (CINAHL, Cochrane Library, PsycINFO, PUBMED, and Web of Science) including technology or web-based health intervention studies targeting low-income populations and reporting any theory or model. The theories explained in this chapter are intended to help understand the logic of e-mental health interventions and their structure/features based on theories, not randomly developed intervention implementation. When reviewing each theory, consideration for the feasibility of low-income population studies is still suggested.

Social Learning Theory

Social Learning Theory focuses on *learning* in a social context by observing others' behaviors and the consequences of those behaviors (Bandura, 1963, 1969). According to Bandura (1977), Social Learning Theory has four processes: attention to goal/issue, retention (self-motivating), production (practicing/getting feedback), and motivation (reinforcing/getting rewards). Goals do not automatically activate unless a self-evaluative process or observation occurs and leads to any performance. The effectiveness of intention in controlling self-behaviors depends on the likelihood of the projected outcomes. Intentional control of behavior works with two cognitive sources of motivation: the capacity to represent projected consequences in the future and intervention progress by goals and self-evaluation of one's performance. Individuals can have two goals in practicing the intervention: end goals and subgoals. End goals could be recommended by health providers or self-set goals. It is the ultimate goal of the intervention. On the other hand, subgoals are more immediate goals that may be challenging but achievable with extra effort. One can be motivated and satisfied by attaining those subgoals.

For example, Social Learning Theory is applicable to interpret children's mental health issues or their violent behaviors. Children learn many things about how to behave from their friends, family, and others from direct and indirect (media) contexts. Children's observation of parents' behaviors affects their relationships with the parents, imitation, and definitions of specific behaviors like conflict and violence (Sellers et al., 2005). A child imitates the physical force used by a parent in his or her experience to get what they want from how their parents resolve and engage in conflict between parents. They might interpret violence as the solution to end conflicts (Sterrett-Hong et al., 2018). Such observation can be found through their discourse. In finding the reasons for mental problems or encouraging positive health goals, the Social Learning Theory approach could be utilized. Additionally, the theory can be applied to educational programs and the communication content or shared messages of e-mental health intervention modules to find better solutions to the mental issues the participants are facing.

Self-regulation Theory

Self-regulation theory is about personal, conscious control of one's behaviors, thoughts, and feelings to reach goals. In a self-regulation process, individuals are affected by internal and external motivation. It leads to certain outcome to feel (psychological), behave (behavioral), and think (cognitive). Individuals can reflect on themselves, monitor their behaviors, and evaluate their performances (Bandura & Simon, 1977). Individuals decide to change their current behaviors or to learn more about the risks of current health problems. Self-regulation is a metatheory or paradigm for thinking about motivation, which has broader definitions and mechanisms (Deshon & Ranch, 2009). An *intention* is defined as the determinant of performing activities or attaining future conditions. *Goal proximity* is the most critical factor in the self-regulation of behaviors with intentions. Compared to the distal goal-setting condition, the proximal goal condition had better outcomes in controlling personal eating behaviors.

For example, Buckner et al. (2009) examined the association of self-regulation with adaptive functioning among 155 youth aged eight to eighteen years from families of very low income. The results show that self-regulation is strongly associated with various outcome measures of mental health, behavioral and academic achievement, and social competence. Youth with better self-regulation skills reported more adaptive responses both in terms of their coping behaviors with past stressful life events and engagement with hypothetical stressors. Likewise, setting a realistic goal for any intervention program can be supported by the self-regulation theory (Laing et al., 2014). Designing e-mental health interventions is meaningful, based on self-regulation theory, as low-income participants can engage in the intervention program to manage and improve their emotional control skills at home. The population can reduce the burden on families and additional schedules to visit mental health clinics (time and transportation costs). Thus, selecting appropriate communication platforms for the low-income population to implement self-regulation-based e-mental health interventions, such as a portal, and social media, can be prioritized (Linardon et al., 2020).

Social Cognitive Theory

Albert Bandura proposed the Social Cognitive Theory[1] as a culmination of his work on social learning theory. According to his theory (Bandura, 1986), individuals learn new habits by observing others. Social Cognitive Theory regards human behaviors as the product of the interplay of personal, environmental, and behavioral factors (Bandura, 1986). Cognitive and environmental components interact to determine whether observed actions will be repeated. Key components of Social Cognitive Theory are *knowledge, self-efficacy, goals, outcome expectations, and perceived facilitators and impediments* (Bandura, 2004). In particular, *knowledge* is more relevant to health literacy or the information level of the potential health risks and benefits under a particular health-related context. Self-efficacy—the essential determinant of Social Cognitive Theory—is a personal belief in one's capacity or controllability to attain one's health goals. *Goals* are the direct antecedent to following health behaviors and are associated with *intentions to behave as* in the Theory of Perceived Behaviors (Ajzen, 1991). *Intention* by Bandura (2004) is the proximal goal because *aiming to* do something is identical to *intending* to do something. *Facilitators* and *impediments* of health behaviors are explained by perceived social (interacting with family or peers) and structural factors (accessing the technology to get support or to get information). Check Bandura's book for the details of the initial model (1999).

Compared to the previous two theories (social learning theory and self-regulation theory), social cognitive theory has a broader theoretical scope as it discusses a conceptualization of humans as subjects capable of shaping their environment and self-regulation (Whitham et al., 2013). Social cognitive theory emphasizes the major role of cognition interplaying in encoding and performing individuals' actions. Children, for instance, learn social norms through observing and imitating their parents, teachers, and classmates.

As a case, type 2 diabetes patients living in low-income countries have common challenges to manage themselves at home due to their mental health issues and lack of family support. Based on the social cognitive theory approach, the *¡Sí, Yo Puedo Vivir Sano Con Diabetes!* program included group-based interactive processes in sessions and daily text/picture messages for the participants so they can be reminded of peers' and health providers' support (Whittemore et al., 2020). Such interactive communication is effective in reducing depression symptoms and other mental health issues through social support. In the case of Social Cognitive Theory-based mental health intervention, self-efficacy was taught through animation, that is, about the benefits and effectiveness of treating depression and the positive impact of overcoming this psychological problem with a female student who managed to overcome her depression and transfer her positive experience.

Motivational Interviewing Theory

Motivational interviewing (MI) is a collaborative effort between a counselor and client/patient to elicit and evoke motivation for change (Miller & Rollnick, 2009). MI was first developed from Miller's experience in the treatment of alcohol disorders. However, it has been used in a variety of contexts, from chronic pain management to mental health treatment (Rollnick et al., 2008). It is a more internal approach to exploring and resolving ambivalence and focuses on motivational processes to facilitate change. It does not enforce change based on the individual's values, beliefs, or wishes through externally driven methods; rather, it rather supports change by stimulating congruent personal values and concerns (Miller & Rollnick, 2009). MI has some key components. Building rapport is important at the beginning. It moves into conversations about change through counseling, therapy, consultation, or even general communication. It is possible to proceed with collaboration between the client and counselor (partnership).

As MI is not only a theory for research but also a guide for practice, understanding the details of MI training is still important. MI is a core communication style that physicians apply in conversations with patients (Flaum, 2022). MI skills require the physician to execute patient-centered communication in mental health treatment (Reinauer, et al., 2018). It is frequently used to treat mental health symptoms by general healthcare practitioners. For example, prevention efforts for depressive symptoms in adolescents were tested with a computerized single-session intervention using MI at three, six, and twelve-month follow-ups (Ranney et al., 2017). MI itself is possible when two parties—doctor and patient—agree to develop their conversation and continue the session through two-way communication. In particular, for low-income young digital generation, e-mental health interventions via apps may increase mental healthcare accessibility (Domhardt et al., 2021; Reinauer et al., 2021). Utilizing MI for mental disorder mitigation is also effective. Through systematic MI, intervention programs have proven efficacy in reducing the frequency and quantity of cannabis use in adults but not in adolescents to mitigate the disorder symptoms (Calomarde-Gómez et al., 2021). Therefore, MI is applicable in leading self-awareness of current status, benefits, and risks of health behaviors even though it is uneasy (Miller & Rollnick, 2009).

Uses and Gratification and User-Centered Principles

Uses and Gratification Theory is more popular in mass communications, but the user-centered approach is more familiar within the design discipline as *user-centered design*. As the e-mental health intervention program itself is interdisciplinary, both communicative and design approaches will be discussed together. Uses and Gratification Theory emphasizes the role of the audience; thus, the theory includes five assumptions: the audience is conceived as active;

in media consumption, the audience selects media to initiate gratification; the media competes with other sources of satisfaction; the goals of media use can be derived from individual audience members; and value judgments about the cultural significance of mass communication should be considered while audience orientations are valued (Katz et al., 1973). In detail, the goals of media use include education, situational identification, entertainment, social interaction, and stress relief (McQuail, 2010).

This theory is useful to understand the individual needs and preferences in intervention participation and retention. For example, what drives users to engage in the regular intentional or habitual use of media or physical activity can be investigated with the uses and gratification approach (Blumler & Katz, 1974). Furthermore, in fitness app development, gender-specific gratifications and determinants of app usage can be identified (Klenk et al., 2017). Social media disorders and mental health issues during the COVID-19 pandemic in using media can be investigated with the uses and gratification theory (Cleofas, 2022).

As another approach to value the audience or intervention participants, user-centered (design) principles are applicable. It is more common in design from the point of view of the user (Norman, 1986) with users' needs, goals, and feedback to create highly usable and accessible websites and apps (Cheng et al., 2020; Mathur et al., 2021). In the intervention development stage, Wang et al. (2023) enabled the research team to align their research goals with users' needs and rapidly revise the mental health and medication intervention features for HIV patients to increase contextual appropriateness, acceptability, and feasibility of the intervention. Similarly, message tailoring or patient-tailored intervention is based on the user-centered approach (Casu et al., 2021; Cheng et al., 2020). As the result of implementing the user-centered approach in the iDecide program for diabetes management, the intervention differed by literacy levels and media modality preference. The educational content and interactive discussion method were tailored with a more graphical style for low-literacy patients.

Information-Motivation-Behavioral Skills Model

The Information-Motivation-Behavioral Skills (IMB) model consists of three key components: information, motivation, and behavioral skills (Rongkavilit et al., 2010). Fisher et al. (1996) discussed the principle of the IMB model.

Information includes relevant knowledge of risks, benefits, and processes of any health behaviors; *Motivation* includes both personal and social motivation. *Personal* motivation is derived from internal attitudes (positive or negative) toward complying with any suggested health behaviors. On the other hand, *social* motivation comes from self-perception or awareness learned through social support and interaction; and *Behavioral skills* include both the individual's objective ability to perform the suggested tasks and one's self-efficacy to comply with the task. The IMB model assumes mutual feedback between information and motivation, with a linear relationship between these two constructs, behavioral skills, and actual behavior (Fisher et al., 2006). The model can be used to understand, predict, and promote any health behaviors. The IMB model assumes that if individuals have the information, are willing to perform the healthy behavior, and have the qualified behavioral skills, they are likely to comply with the suggested behaviors (DeBate et al., 2018).

For example, DeBate et al. (2018) assessed the relationship between the determinants of help-seeking behaviors regarding mental health-relevant concerns among male college students. The IMB model was based on understanding the importance of mental health literacy as a prerequisite for any changes in behaviors or help-seeking behaviors. Then, motivation included attitudes toward help-seeking and normative beliefs about help-seeking behaviors. As the last prerequisite for behavior changes, individuals' perceived objective skills and self-efficacy to engage in help-seeking behaviors were examined. Meanwhile, the IMB model applies to anxiety prevention intervention programs for primary school-aged children. Understanding the current level of anxiety, emotions and their intensity, triggers, effects, emotional regulation, empathy skills, and self-esteem can help children handle any unexpected or gradual anxiety concerns (Ab Ghaffar et al., 2019).

Likewise, the IMB model facilitates any suggested behavior changes focusing on the way to improve behavioral skills and increase the perceived self-efficacy level (Fisher et al., 2003). This theory applies to understanding the importance of the inclusion of informative, motivational, and skill-building content in intervention programs to succeed in any mental health behavior change goals. When reviewing the communication content for patients, this logic can be applied to create, organize, and deliver e-mental health intervention modules. Successful information strategies reflecting key factors for target participants can stimulate patients to mitigate their ongoing health symptoms (Han & Kim, 2019).

TransTheoretical Model

TransTheoretical Model (TTM) focuses on the stages of change, not as a single decision-making result, and is intended to provide a comprehensive conceptual model of how and why changes occur with multiple behavioral change phases (Prochaska et al., 1996). Following the literal meaning of *Trans-Theories*, TTM uses the stages of change to integrate processes and principles of change from different theories (Prochaska & Velicer, 1997). This complicated model includes six stages of change, ten processes of change (e.g., consciousness-raising, dramatic relief, self-reevaluation, etc.), pros and cons of changing self-efficacy, and temptation with a measure of the target behavior. Additionally, TTM assumes seven statements as follows: no single theory can account for the complicated behavioral change; behavior change is a process that occurs over time as a sequence of stages; stages are both stable and open to change; without planned interventions, people will remain stuck in the early stages; they will not be served by existing traditional prevention programs; specific strategies need to be applied at appropriate stages if progress occurs; and chronic behavior patterns involve some combinations of biological, social, and self-control (Prochaska & Velicer, 1997). As one of the core constructs, the six stages of change help us understand *change* as a process. The phases are pre-contemplation, contemplation, preparation, action, maintenance, and termination. Understanding the adoption process of any technology, thinking about any change, preparing, and taking action take time. A one-time change is not a genuine change. It should last for a while. Check Prochaska and Velicer's article (1997) for the details of each stage.

In terms of recruiting and retention communication strategies for participants, for instance, a short message service (SMS) can be sent as a part of intervention content to encourage health behavior changes. Using one-way communication methods by texting, low-income pregnant and postpartum women to maintain mental and physical health conditions according to the TTM (Evans et al., 2012). Although they implemented one-way communication, depending on the target, two-way communication or interactive formatting might work for e-mental health intervention participants. Considering the TTM will work well to understand the current status of the target audiences and to build appropriate communication strategies to approach specific target audiences. Even when targeting low-income populations, individuals' diversity and their needs can vary. As another example, social marketers used the TTM of change to enhance their web-based campaigns promoting mental health during the COVID pandemic (Akdaş & Cismaru, 2022). They commented that behavioral change is not a simple vote—select or not select—but a process of behavioral modification by individuals. Over months or years, for those who face situational crises that affect mental health, the TTM is applicable to understand the audience more accurately and to determine appropriate communication content for boosting retention and recruitment strategies.

e-Mental Health Intervention Strategies Strengthening Communication Effectiveness for Low-Income Population

As successful strategies to conduct and review e-mental health intervention programs for low-income populations, there are four main perspectives to consider before proceeding with any practices and research as follows: the matter of intervention quality and risk of bias, strategic design of intervention features, target-oriented modalities selection and message delivery, and systematic assessment of key components in the interventions.

1. Criteria to Design e-Mental Health Interventions with Communicative Components: Intervention Quality and Risk of Bias

Important is the selection of qualified exemplars to review and modify. To develop more qualified or comparable e-mental health interventions, systematic consideration for intervention quality, free from risk of bias, and communicative intervention features.

For intervention quality, many studies used different types of intervention quality evaluation, but unified or overlapping quality assessment will be helpful to cross-check between different review studies. It will also be applied to *inclusion* and *exclusion* criteria for data selection or the overall sampling process. The Grading of Recommendations Assessment, Development, and Evaluation (GRADE) is a transparent framework for evidence-based guideline development targeting clinical intervention and guideline developers and systematic reviewers (Guyatt et al., 2011). The GRADE Domains to assess include *risk of bias* (i.e., study limitation), *imprecision* (i.e., absolute effect by 95% confidence interval), *inconsistency* (i.e., similarity of point estimates, the overlap of their confidence intervals, and heterogeneity test by the I^2 and chi-squared test), *indirectness* (i.e., comparability between interventions of interest with the population of interest), and *publication bias* (i.e., making inferences about missing evidence in observed data) (Siemieniuk & Guyatt, 2019). Regarding the *Risk of Bias*, it is easy to adopt an existing template to evaluate selected studies by Ameratunga (2023). It includes five domains to evaluate: randomization process, deviations from intended interventions, missing outcome data, measurement of outcome, and selection of the reported results (Guidelines available at https://www.riskofbias.info/).

As an additional framework to review the quality of studies, Miller et al. (2003)'s Methodological Quality Rating Scale (11 criteria: group allocation, quality control, follow-up rate and length, contact, collaterals, objective, attrition, independent, analyses, and multisite) and Harenberg et al. (2025)'s Health and Wellness Coaching Research Design Rubric (15 criteria: participant recruitment, random allocation, allocation concealment, assessor blinding, exclusion/inclusion criteria, withdrawal reporting, sample characteristics, sample size determination, active controls, baseline, intent-to-treat, quality of outcome, statistical analyses, covariate control, and confounding treatment) are examples of utilizing a quality evaluation tool.

Although the purpose of e-mental health intervention is more focused on confirming the effectiveness of a digital-based intervention platform as a tool for communication, without assessing the quality of the study to inspect the internal and external validity of the intervention studies and risk of bias, it will be hard to justify the effectiveness of the intervention. To promote mutual health communication in e-mental health intervention with appropriate communication content in the intervention, researchers and health providers should eliminate other risk factors to prevent the direct effects of health communication strategies.

2. Strategic Design of e-Mental Health Intervention Features for Low-income Population with Successful Communication Practice

As discussed in "Challenges to Succeed in e-Mental Health Interventions with a Communicative Approach" above, training and educating health professionals and developers on more effective communication skills and strategies are recommended due to limited knowledge of people with a low SES by the planners of interventions (Al-Dhahir et al., 2023) and a lack of systematic and financial support to hire professional health communicators. In designing interventions, itemizing appropriate intervention features for effective health communication matters. Neve et al. (2010) initially assessed online intervention features (general information, individualized or tailored information, goal setting, self-monitoring (no feedback), self-monitoring (feedback), online meeting, professional contact, interacting with peers, and so on). Recalling 3S perspectives in e-mental health interventions (selecting a modality, sharing messages, and supporting various communication directions), researchers can assess whether the designed intervention includes the appropriate communication environment and content for both patients and doctors.

For a more effective relational building to promote successful communication via e-mental health intervention, the suggested theories earlier can be recalled in planning the intervention platform. *Social Cognitive Theory* can support the inclusion of some intervention features like self-monitoring, goal setting, and social support by counselors and peers having similar symptoms. *Motivational Interviewing* can be used to facilitate successful conversations between patients and doctors. It can serve as a guide to build rapport and develop doctor-patient conversations, promoting motivation to mitigate risky behaviors affected by mental health symptoms. Additionally, the Information-Motivation-Behavioral (IMB) model approach can be referred to develop necessary intervention features. In Chang et al. (2014), IMB features were systematically reviewed from selected interventions, and the study found that the most frequent intervention strategy for the *Information* domain is distributing instructional pamphlets; for the *motivation* domain is to use motivational interview skills; and for *behavioral skills* domain is to give direct instruction or role-playing during interventions.

From a communicative perspective, intervention is *a mediated* tool to communicate, and the way of communication and the communication content are the areas of interest. Message tailoring is very critical (Casu et al., 2021; Cheng et al., 2020). Lack of tailoring is discussed as one of the frequent reasons for failing to support intervention assumptions (Coker et al., 2023). There are many ways to tailor the message content and intervention delivery, such as population context, modality, content, frequency, group/community-based, or individual intervention. User-centered design and uses and gratification approach can help create more effective intervention features and content (Klenk et al., 2017; Wang et al., 2023). It is particularly helpful to understand the motives for selecting specific interventions and to attain or quit the intervention program before the planned period ends.

3. Target-oriented Intervention Modalities and Message Delivery for Low-Income Population

Not only counting a specific focus area of prevention and management for e-mental health intervention but also caring for the target group is crucial. Overlapped components between theories such as Social Cognitive, Social Learning, and Self-Regulation Theory value individuals' cognitive, psychological, and behavioral stances and their changes. In Social Cognitive Theory (Whitham et al., 2013), individuals are the agents shaping their environment and controlling themselves if needed. According to Social Learning Theory (Bandura, 1977), individuals intentionally control their behavior through cognitive awareness of the necessary conditions for motivation, as well as through awareness of the consequences when evaluating their own performance. All evaluations and motivations to behave come from self-driven observation and determination. Similarly, Self-regulation Theory (Deshon & Rench, 2009) works by internal and external motivation. Given this property of the theories, understanding the proximal goal or immediate goal to achieve is important. In other words, the role of health communicators is to help patients or target people to be aware of highly potential outcomes or benefits of their behavioral changes by sharing appropriate information through the most accessible intervention platform and supporting more effective communication between doctors and patients regarding mental health problems.

The general e-mental health interventions are designed to utilize wearables, mobile apps, patient portals, or social media, but this is possible only when participants have appropriate access to use them and the ability to understand and control (Lee et al., 2022). However, in many cases, the limitations of e-mental health interventions arise from low literacy/numeracy, internet access issues, intervention capability, and so on. This is frequent for low-income individuals. They are not sufficiently motivated or stimulated to engage in ehealth interventions (Al-Dhahir et al., 2023). With a user-centered approach, satisfying usability, privacy concerns, and other challenges are expected to be overcome.

As a broader scope of e-mental health interventions, designing hybrid modalities for more effective health communication will be effective. It is consistent with the logistics of the Transtheoretical Model (TTM). From promoting a self-care lifestyle to addressing user-specific barriers to overcome, text messages, interactive communication, and follow-ups can be implemented with low-income populations (Palacios et al., 2018). It has been tested during the COVID-19 pandemic to promote mental health through a web-based intervention program and proved its effectiveness (Akdaş & Cismaru, 2022).

Mental health communication experts need to be ready to respond to participants' concerns or feedback. For instance, multiple intervention modalities can be prepared or designed to test the specific group of people participating in the e-mental health intervention programs. If needed, financial incentives can also work, or adjusting the number of site/in-person visits may work better (Clark et al., 2023). In other words, e-mental health interventions have been studied with various intervention ideas (Cheng et al., 2020; Clark et al., 2023), but the reason for having few studies qualified to review e-mental health intervention reports with low-income populations may come from barriers or a realistic status that low-income people have in participating in e-mental health interventions to prevent and mitigate their health symptoms (Al-Dhahir et al., 2023).

4. Assessment of Key Communication Components in e-Mental Health Interventions for Low-Income Populations

Before designing any intervention program, a needs assessment should come first. Additionally, assessment is essential in follow-ups. It is not simply to measure the behavior change of participants, but other assessments include their satisfaction level, attitudes toward the suggested behavior changes, and the intervention program, including health communication messages and allowable communication direction with health providers and peers. Adding to the general evaluation of the outcomes of e-mental health interventions, a survey is needed to listen to the participants' feedback and confirm the communicative goals of the intervention (e.g., recruiting appropriate audiences for the study, monitoring the retention rate with effective communication strategies to give reminders, boost and maintain motivation levels, and allow two-way communication with health providers and peers as participants recognize *social* and *relational support*).

The issue with no consideration for health literacy or eHealth literacy was discussed in Cheng et al.'s systematic review study (2020). In particular, needs assessment for community-based intervention programs is required because it helps mental health communicators understand the specific context of the community and the need to adjust the general intervention features/programs (Wang et al., 2023). Meanwhile, needs assessment can be also approached by the transtheoretical model of behavior change stages. To understand if participants are ready to change or have enough knowledge to change, the identification of behavioral change stages (pre-contemplation, contemplation, and preparation) can be analyzed and applied in the new intervention development (Ghahramani, et al., 2022). For low-income populations, understanding the accurate level of eHealth literacy and monitoring their special needs or facilitators and barriers of e-mental health interventions should be considered from the beginning of the intervention planning to the end of the intervention assessment (Al-Dhahir et al., 2023; Carter et al., 2021).

Therefore, e-mental health interventions will be implemented in multisteps, starting with a systematic review to understand the general trend and health communication needs in the target area (Chang et al., 2014; Cheng et al., 2020). Then, various assessments based on the key components with relevant theories will proceed. The 3S perspectives: Selecting appropriate intervention modality or media channel and platform (i.e., apps, web-based, texting, in-person, etc.); Sharing intervention messages or target health education content; and Supporting various communication directions (one-way or two-way communication between other participants and with health providers) will be key factors to consider in communication-oriented e-mental health interventions. After conducting a pilot test and survey/interview with the target population or low-income individuals, e-mental health intervention programs can be implemented. It is comparatively a long journey, so engaging multiple stakeholders (Lee et al., 2022) and balancing the research and practice are suggested.

Notes

1 More information about Social Cognitive Theory can be found at https://www.sciencedirect.com/topics/medicine-and-dentistry/social-cognitive-theory

Recommended Readings/Resources

Al-Dhahir, I., Breeman, L. D., Faber, J. S., Reijnders, T., van den Berg-Emons, H. J. G., van der Vaart, R., ... & Evers, A. W. (2023). An overview of facilitators and barriers in the development of eHealth interventions for people of low socioeconomic position: A Delphi study. *International Journal of Medical Informatics*, *177*, 105160. https://doi.org/10.1016/j.ijmedinf.2023.105160

Carter, H., Araya, R., Anjur, K., Deng, D., & Naslund, J. A. (2021). The emergence of digital mental health in low-income and middle-income countries: A review of recent advances and implications for the treatment and prevention of mental disorders. *Journal of Psychiatric Research*, *133*, 223–246. https://doi.org/10.1016/j.jpsychires.2020.12.016

Stice, E., Rohde, P., Shaw, H., & Gau, J. M. (2017). Clinician-led, peer-led, and internet-delivered dissonance-based eating disorder prevention programs: Acute effectiveness of these delivery modalities. *Journal of Consulting and Clinical Psychology*, *85*(9), 883. https://doi.org/10.1037/ccp0000211

Wang, L., & Miller, L. C. (2020). Just-in-the-moment adaptive interventions (JITAI): a meta-analytical review. *Health Communication*, *35*(12), 1531–1544. https://doi.org/10.1080/10410236.2019.1652388

Yeo, G., Reich, S. M., Liaw, N. A., & Chia, E. Y. M. (2024). The effect of digital mental health literacy interventions on mental health: Systematic review and meta-analysis. *Journal of Medical Internet Research*, *26*, e51268.

References

Ab Ghaffar, S. F., Mohd Sidik, S., Ibrahim, N., Awang, H., & Gyanchand Rampal, L. R. (2019). Effect of a school-based anxiety prevention program among primary school children. *International Journal of Environmental Research and Public Health*, *16*(24), 4913.

Ajzen, I. (1991). The theory of planned behavior. *Organizational Behavior and Human Decision Processes*, *50*, 179–211.

Akdaş, O., & Cismaru, M. (2022). Promoting mental health during the COVID-19 pandemic: the transtheoretical model of change and social marketing approach. *International Review on Public and Nonprofit Marketing*, *19*(3), 447–474. https://doi.org/10.1007/s12208-021- 00307-1

Al-Dhahir, I., Breeman, L. D., Faber, J. S., Reijnders, T., van den Berg-Emons, H. J. G., van der Vaart, R., ... & Evers, A. W. (2023). An overview of facilitators and barriers in the development of eHealth interventions for people of low socioeconomic position: A Delphi study. *International Journal of Medical Informatics*, *177*, 105160. https://doi.org/10.1016/j.ijmedinf.2023.105160

Ameratunga, D. (2023). ROB2_IRPG_beta_v9.xlsm. figshare. Dataset. https://doi.org/10.6084/m9.figshare.22300303.v1

Armaou, M., Araviaki, E., & Musikanski, L. (2020). eHealth and mHealth interventions for ethnic minority and historically underserved populations in developed countries: An umbrella review. *International Journal of Community Well-Being*, *3*(2), 193–221.

Ayaz-Alkaya, S., & Dülger, H. (2022). Fear of coronavirus and health literacy levels of older adults during the COVID-19 pandemic. Geriatric nursing, 43, 45–50.

Bandura, A. (1963). *Social learning and personality development.* Holt Rinehart and Winston.

Bandura, A. (1969). Social-learning theory of identificatory processes. In D. Goslin (Ed.), *Handbook of socialization theory and research.* Rand McNally.

Bandura, A. (1977). *Social learning theory.* Prentice-Hall.

Bandura, A. (1986). *Social foundations of thought and action: A social cognitive theory.* Prentice-Hall.

Bandura, A. (1999). Social cognitive theory of personality. *Handbook of Personality, 2,* 154–196.

Bandura, A. (2004). Health promotion by social cognitive means. *Health Education and Behavior, 31*(2), 143–164.

Bandura, A., & Simon, K. M. (1977). The role of proximal intentions in self-regulation of refractory behavior. *Cognitive Therapy and Research, 1*(3), 177–193.

Blumler, J. G., & Katz, E. (1974). *The uses of mass communications: Current perspectives on gratifications research.* SAGE.

Buckner, J. C., Mezzacappa, E., & Beardslee, W. R. (2009). Self-regulation and its relations to adaptive functioning in low income youths. *American Journal of Orthopsychiatry, 79*(1), 19–30.

Calomarde-Gómez, C., Jiménez-Fernández, B., Balcells-Oliveró, M., Gual, A., & López-Pelayo, H. (2021). Motivational interviewing for cannabis use disorders: a systematic review and meta-analysis. *European Addiction Research, 27*(6), 413–427.

Carter, H., Araya, R., Anjur, K., Deng, D., & Naslund, J. A. (2021). The emergence of digital mental health in low-income and middle-income countries: A review of recent advances and implications for the treatment and prevention of mental disorders. *Journal of Psychiatric Research, 133,* 223–246. https://doi.org/10.1016/j.jpsychires.2020.12.016

Casu, G., Hlebec, V., Boccaletti, L., Bolko, I., Manattini, A., & Hanson, E. (2021). Promoting mental health and Well-being among adolescent young carers in Europe: A randomized controlled trial protocol. *International Journal of Environmental Research and Public Health, 18*(4), 2045.

Chang, S. J., Choi, S., Kim, S. A., & Song, M. (2014). Intervention strategies based on information-motivation-behavioral skills model for health behavior change: A systematic review. *Asian Nursing Research, 8*(3), 172–181.

Cheng, C., Beauchamp, A., Elsworth, G. R., & Osborne, R. H. (2020). Applying the electronic health literacy lens: Systematic review of electronic health interventions targeted at socially disadvantaged groups. *Journal of Medical Internet Research, 22*(8), e18476.

Clark, T. L., Savin, K. L., Perez-Ramirez, P., Valdez, T., Toba, G., & Gallo, L. C. (2023). eHealth weight loss interventions for adults with low income: A systematic review. *Health Psychology, 42*(6), 353–367. https://doi.org/10.1037/hea0001278

Cleofas, J. V. (2022). Social media disorder during community quarantine: A mixed methods study among rural young college students during the COVID-19 pandemic. *Archives of Psychiatric Nursing*, *40*, 97–105.

Coker, T. R., Mitchell, S. J., Lowry, S. J., Klein, E. J., Stout, J. W., Brown, J. C., Liljenquist, K. S., Wingfield, E., & Horn, I. B. (2023). Text2Breathe: Text-Message intervention for parent communication and pediatric asthma. *Academic Pediatrics*, *23*(1), 123–129. https://doi.org/10.1016/j.acap.2022.05.004

DeBate, R. D., Gatto, A., & Rafal, G. (2018). The effects of stigma on determinants of mental health help-seeking behaviors among male college students: An application of the information-motivation-behavioral skills model. *American Journal of Men's Health*, *12*(5), 1286–1296.

DeShon, R. P., & Rench, T. A. (2009). Clarifying the notion of self-regulation in organizational behavior. In G. P. Hodgkinson & J. K. Ford (Eds.), *International review of industrial and organizational psychology* (pp. 217–247). Wiley-Blackwell.

Domhardt, M., Schröder, A., Geirhos, A., Steubl, L., & Baumeister, H. (2021). Efficacy of digital health interventions in youth with chronic medical conditions: a meta-analysis. *Internet Interventions*, *24*, 100373. https://doi.org/10.1016/j.invent.2021.100373

Evans, W. D., Wallace, J. L., & Snider, J. (2012). Pilot evaluation of the text4baby mobile health program. *BMC Public Health*, *12*, 1–10. https://doi.org/10.1186/1471-2458-12-1031

Fisher, C. D. (2003). Why do lay people believe that satisfaction and performance are correlated? Possible sources of a commonsense theory. Journal of Organizational Behavior: The International Journal of Industrial, Occupational and Organizational Psychology and Behavior, 24(6), 753–777.

Fisher, J. D., Fisher, W. A., Amico, K. R., & Harman, J. J. (2006). An information-motivation- behavioral skills model of adherence to antiretroviral therapy. *Health Psychology*, *25*(4), 462.

Fisher, J. D., Fisher, W. A., Misovich, S. J., Kimble, D. L., & Malloy, T. E. (1996). Changing AIDS risk behavior: Effects of an intervention emphasizing AIDS risk reduction information, motivation, and behavioral skills in a college student population. *Health Psychology*, *15*(2), 114.

Flaum, M. (2022). Motivational interviewing as a core communication style. In W. E. Sowers, H. L. McQuistion, J. M. Ranz, J. M. Feldman, & P. S. Runnels (Eds.), *Textbook of community psychiatry* (pp. 101–115). Springer. https://doi.org/10.1007/978-3-031-10239-4_9

Ghahramani, A., de Courten, M., & Prokofieva, M. (2022). The potential of social media in health promotion beyond creating awareness: An integrative review. *BMC Public Health*, *22*(1), 1–13.

Guyatt, G., Oxman, A. D., Akl, E. A., Kunz, R., Vist, G., Brozek, J., ... & Schünemann, H. J. (2011). GRADE guidelines: 1. Introduction—GRADE evidence profiles and summary of findings tables. *Journal of Clinical Epidemiology*, *64*(4), 383–394.

Han, K. J., & Kim, S. (2019). Toward more persuasive diabetes messages: Effects of personal value orientation and freedom threat on psychological reactance and behavioral intention. *Journal of Health Communication*, *24*(2), 95–110. https://doi.org/10.1080/10810730.2019.1581304

Harenberg, S., Sforzo, G., Hunter, R., Jackson, E., & Moore, M. (2025). The Well-Being Coaching Inventory (WCI): Questionnaire Development and Validation. American Journal of Lifestyle Medicine, 15598276251320573.

Han, K. J., Yu, M., & Kehinde, O (2024). Effectiveness of different online intervention modalities for middle-aged adults with overweight and obesity: A 20-year systematic review and meta-analysis. *Journal of Prevention*, *45*, 123–157. https://doi.org/10.1007/s10935-023-00761-z

Kaltman, S., Hurtado de Mendoza, A., Serrano, A., & Gonzales, F. A. (2016). A mental health intervention strategy for low-income, trauma-exposed Latina immigrants in primary care: A preliminary study. *American Journal of Orthopsychiatry*, *86*(3), 345.

Katz, E., Blumler, J. G., & Gurevitch, M. (1973). Uses and gratifications research. *The Public Opinion Quarterly*, *37*(4), 509–523. https://doi.org/10.1086/268109

Klenk, S., Reifegerste, D., & Renatus, R. (2017). Gender differences in gratifications from fitness app use and implications for health interventions. *Mobile Media & Communication*, *5*(2), 178–193.

Kupila, S. K., Joki, A., Suojanen, L. U., & Pietil.inen, K. H. (2023). The effectiveness of ehealth interventions for weight loss and weight loss maintenance in adults with overweight or obesity: A systematic review of systematic reviews. *Current Obesity Reports*, *12*, 371–394.

Laing, B. Y., Mangione, C. M., Tseng, C. H., Leng, M., Vaisberg, E., Mahida, M., ... & Bell, D. S. (2014). Effectiveness of a smartphone application for weight loss compared with usual care in overweight primary care patients: A randomized, controlled trial. *Annals of Internal Medicine*, *161*(10_Supplement), S5–S12.

Lee, E. W., McCloud, R. F., & Viswanath, K. (2022). Designing effective eHealth interventions for underserved groups: Five lessons from a decade of eHealth intervention design and deployment. *Journal of Medical Internet Research*, *24*(1), e25419

Linardon, J., Shatte, A., Messer, M., Firth, J., & Fuller-Tyszkiewicz, M. (2020). E-mental health interventions for the treatment and prevention of eating disorders: An updated systematic review and meta-analysis. *Journal of Consulting and Clinical Psychology*, *88*(11), 994.

Mathur, S., Janaudis-Ferreira, T., Hemphill, J., Cafazzo, J. A., Hart, D., Holdsworth, S., Lovas, M., & Wickerson, L. (2021). User-centered design features for digital health applications to support physical activity behaviors in solid organ transplant recipients: A qualitative study. *Clinical Transplantation, 35*(12), e14472. https://doi.org/10.1111/ctr.14472

McQuail, D. (2010). *Mass communication theory: An introduction.* SAGE Publications.

Miller, W. R., Wilbourne, P. L., & Hettema, J. E. (2003). What Works? A summary of alcohol treatment outcome research. In R. K. Hester & W. R. Miller (Eds.), Handbook of alcoholism treatment approaches: Effective alternatives (3rd ed.). Allyn & Bacon.

Miller Jr, D. P., Denizard-Thompson, N., Weaver, K. E., Case, L. D., Troyer, J. L., Spangler, J. G., ... & Pignone, M. P. (2018). Effect of a digital health intervention on receipt of colorectal cancer screening in vulnerable patients: A randomized controlled trial. *Annals of Internal Medicine, 168*(8), 550–557. https://doi.org/10.7326/M17-2315

Miller, W. R., & Rollnick, S. (2009). Ten things that motivational interviewing is not. *Behavioural and Cognitive Psychotherapy, 37*(2), 129–140. https://orca.cardiff.ac.uk/id/eprint/30246/1/MILLER%202009.PDF

Neve, M., Morgan, P. J., Jones, P., & Collins, C. (2010). Effectiveness of web-based interventions in achieving weight loss and weight loss maintenance in overweight and obese adults: A systematic review with meta-analysis. *Obesity Reviews, 11*(4), 306–321. https://doi.org/10.1111/j.1467-789X.2009.00646.x

Norman, D. A. (1986). *User-centered system design: New perspectives on human-computer interaction.* Lawrence Erlbaum Associates.

Palacios, C., Campos, M., Gibby, C., Meléndez, M., Lee, J. E., & Banna, J. (2018). Effect of a multi-site trial using short message service (SMS) on infant feeding practices and weight gain in low-income minorities. *Journal of the American College of Nutrition, 37*(7), 605–613.

Prochaska, J. O., Redding, C. A., & Evers, K. E. (1996). The transtheoretical model and stages of change. In K. Glanz, F. M. Lewis, & B. K. Rimer (Eds.), *Health behavior and health education: Theory, research, and practice* (2nd ed., pp. 60–84). Jossey-Bass.

Prochaska, J. O., & Velicer, W. F. (1997). The transtheoretical model of health behavior change. *American Journal of Health Promotion, 12*(1), 38–48.

Ranney, M. L., Goldstick, J., Eisman, A., Carter, P. M., Walton, M., & Cunningham, R. M. (2017). Effects of a brief ED-based alcohol and violence intervention on depressive symptoms. *General Hospital Psychiatry, 46,* 44–48. https://doi.org/10.1016/j.genhosppsych.2017.01.008

Reinauer, C., Platzbecker, A. L., Viermann, R., Domhardt, M., Baumeister, H., Foertsch, K., ... & Meissner, T. (2021). Efficacy of motivational interviewing to improve utilization of mental health services among youths with chronic medical conditions: A cluster randomized clinical trial. *JAMA Network Open, 4*(10), e2127622–e2127622. https://doi.org/10.1001/jamanetworkopen.2021.27622

Reinauer, C., Viermann, R., Förtsch, K., Linderskamp, H., Warschburger, P., Holl, R. W., ... & COACH consortium. (2018). Motivational Interviewing as a tool to enhance access to mental health treatment in adolescents with chronic medical conditions and need for psychological support (COACH-MI): Study protocol for a clusterrandomised controlled trial. *Trials, 19*, 1–9. https://doi.org/10.1186/s13063-018-2997-5

Rollnick, S., Miller, W. R., & Butler, C. C. (2008). *Motivational Interviewing in Health Care: Helping Patients Change Behavior.* Guilford Press.

Rongkavilit, C., Naar-King, S., Kaljee, L. M., Panthong, A., Koken, J. A., Bunupuradah, T., & Parsons, J. T. (2010). Applying the information-motivation-behavioral skills model in medication adherence among Thai youth living with HIV: A qualitative study. *AIDS Patient Care and STDs, 24*(12), 787–794. https://doi.org/10.1089/apc.2010.0069

Seedaket, S., Turnbull, N., Phajan, T., & Wanchai, A. (2020). Improving mental health literacy in adolescents: systematic review of supporting intervention studies. Tropical Medicine & International Health, 25(9), 1055–1064.

Sellers, C. S., Cochran, J. K., & Branch, K. A. (2005). Social learning theory and partner violence: A research note. *Deviant Behavior, 26*(4), 379–395.

Sheeber, L. B., Feil, E. G., Seeley, J. R., Leve, C., Gau, J. M., Davis, B., Sorensen, E., & Allan, S. (2017). Mom-Net: Evaluation of an Internet-facilitated cognitive behavioral intervention for low-income depressed mothers. *Journal of Consulting and Clinical Psychology, 85*(4), 355–366. https://doi.org/10.1037/ccp0000175

Siemieniuk, R., & Guyatt, G. (2019). What is GRADE? *BMJ J Best Practice* (10). https://bestpractice.bmj.com/info/us/toolkit/learn-ebm/what-is-grade/

Sterrett-Hong, E., Antle, B., Nalley, B., & Adams, M. (2018). Changes in couple relationship dynamics among low-income parents in a relationship education program are associated with decreases in their children's mental health symptoms. *Children, 5*(7), 90.

Stice, E., Rohde, P., Shaw, H., & Gau, J. M. (2017). Clinician-led, peer-led, and internet-delivered dissonance-based eating disorder prevention programs: Acute effectiveness of these delivery modalities. *Journal of Consulting and Clinical Psychology, 85*(9), 883. https://doi.org/10.1037/ccp0000211

Wang, L., Yuwen, W., Hua, W., Chen, L., Forsythe Cox, V., Zheng, H., ... & Simoni, J. M. (2023). Enhancing mental health and medication adherence among men who have sex with men recently diagnosed with HIV with a dialectical behavior therapy–informed intervention incorporating mHealth, online skills training, and phone coaching: Development study using human-centered design approach. *JMIR Formative Research, 7*, e47903.

Whitham, S., Sterling, L., Lin, C. E., & Wood, J. J. (2013). Social cognitive learning theory. In F. R. Volkmar (Eds.), *Encyclopedia of autism spectrum disorders.* Springer. https://doi.org/10.1007/978-1-4419-1698-3_484

Whittemore, R., Vilar-Compte, M., Burrola-Méndez, S., Lozano-Marrufo, A., Delvy, R., Pardo- Carrillo, M., ... & Pérez-Escamilla, R. (2020). Development of a diabetes self- management+ mHealth program: Tailoring the intervention for a pilot study in a low- income setting in Mexico. *Pilot and Feasibility Studies*, 6, 1–10. https://doi.org/10.1186/s40814-020-0558-7

8

Addressing Mental Health Issues of Older Adults for Healthy Aging

Jin-Ae Kang and Do Kyun David Kim

McKay's Story

My name is McKay. I'm an 82-year-old Black woman living alone in Dorchester. My health isn't great—I've got high blood pressure, diabetes, and arthritis. And then there's my leg—it's just a stump now, after an accident years ago. I used to be active and went to church all the time. But lately, I've been stuck in this apartment, letting the mail pile up, surrounded by a mess of my own making.

The lady who runs my place, the resident services coordinator, says I seem depressed. She suggested seeing my doctor, so I did. My primary care doctor told me that I looked okay and returned in six months. However, the resident service coordinator recommended the local hospital's outpatient psychiatric clinic for mental health treatment. A hospital clinic? No way. Isn't it normal for an old lady to be gloomy sometimes? But then the coordinator mentioned a social worker coming to my place. I figured, why not? Truth is, I'm lonely. That accident when I was only in my 20s. It ruined more than my leg. My fiancé left. I have never tried to get married since then. My only family, my niece, recently moved far away. Now I belong nowhere. Sometimes, I think no one would even notice if I disappeared. It's a scary thought.

But now, I have felt much better since I met a social worker, Lori. She's different. She comes every week, right on time. We talked to her about everything that I never shared with anyone—the accident, losing my fiancé, feeling like no one cared. Slowly, things are changing. I started going to the senior center and joined a quilting group. Church again too. I still see my social worker, but not as often. Life's getting better (Kuhn, 2015).

Aging, *getting old,* is a complex process in which every human experiences various changes ranging from mental acuity to physical robustness. Aging is commonly measured by chronological age, although the definition of "old adults" could connote other perspectives such as biological, psychological, cultural, and societal perspectives (CDC, 2024). In general, a person aged 65 years or older is often referred to as an "older adult", and several sub-groups are identified as "young-old" (aged 65–74), middle-old (aged 75–84), and oldest-old (85+). Although the subcategories are identified as chronological age again, lifestyles or the way people adapt themselves to senior life vary. Some people remain active well into their nineties while others show visible signs of aging in their emotional or physical status as early as their sixties. The quality of life older people does not necessarily follow chronological age.

In any society, *getting old* implies both positive and negative connotations. From a positive perspective, older adults often report greater wisdom, stronger and denser social connections, and a deeper appreciation for life (Taylor et al., 2009). Seniors are relieved from family responsibilities, spending more time on hobbies, volunteer work, or even starting a second career (Taylor et al., 2009). Negative perceptions, however, are mainly associated with physical and mental decline such as illness, memory loss, and inability to drive. Older people often suffer from depression and anxiety caused by deteriorating physical health, loneliness, absence of a meaningful role in social life, marginalization in social relationships, financial insecurity, and so on (World Health Organization, 2023b).

Such negative issues associated with aging have become a societal issue since population aging has become a global phenomenon. The United Nations defines "population aging" as a summary term for shifts in the age distribution of a population toward older ages (Scherbov & Sanderson, 2019). The population above the age of sixty-five years is growing more rapidly than the population below that age. The UN reported that the percentage of the global population aged sixty-five and above is expected to rise from 10 percent in 2022 to 16 percent by 2050. The number of individuals aged sixty-five years or above across the world will be twice the number of children under age five and almost equivalent to the number of children under twelve years (UN Department of Economic and Social Affairs, Population Division, 2022).

Although the extension of lifespan is regarded as a triumph of modern medical advances such as access to better treatments and preventative therapies, many older people are at risk of developing mental health problems (WHO,

2023b). The Global Health Estimates (WHO, 2020) reported that 14 percent of adults aged sixty and over live with a mental disorder. What makes things worse is that the mental health issues of older people are under-recognized. Even if aware, the mental health issues of older people are neglected and often misrepresented as a normal part of the aging process. Moreover, several mental health issues of older people, such as dementia, and elder abuse, need urgent attention and systemic support at the public health policy level, because the societal cost—i.e., healthcare expenses, loss of labor force, and volunteerism that sustain civil society—are too much when the problems are not addressed. Therefore, there is a need for attention to aging-related mental health issues and to promote supportive norms and policies/programs for dealing with aging at a societal level.

This chapter will broadly address the mental health problems that older people experience as they face a new stage of life and explore health communication intervention strategies using several theoretical frameworks.

Problem Identification

World Health Organization (2022) defines mental health as "a state of well-being in which the individual realizes his or her own abilities, can cope with normal stresses of life, can work productively and fruitfully, and can make contributions to his or her community." It is used to describe either a level of cognitive or emotional well-being or an absence of a mental disorder.

From the holistic approaches, however, mental health does not only indicate an absence of a mental disorder but also includes an individual's ability to enjoy life and procure a balance between life activities and efforts to achieve psychological resilience (Snyder et al., 2011). This section addresses both mental disorders (i.e., dementia and depression) and socio-psychological distresses (i.e., ageism, isolation, and loneliness) for problem identification.

Dementia

Dementia is one of the most feared health problems of older people in many countries (i.e., Watson, et al., 2023). Dementia refers to a group of diseases characterized by a progressive and generally irreversible loss of mental capabilities that include memory loss, confusion, and inappropriate social behavior (Dementia Society of America, n.d.). Several examples include Alzheimer's disease, vascular dementia, and Lewy body dementia, among others. People with dementia experience changes in their ability to communicate with other people throughout the progression of the disease. Symptoms include difficulty finding the right words, loss of a train of thought, using familiar words repeatedly, relying on gestures more than speaking, and so on. As a result, older people are likely to be isolated, losing social interaction and independence.

The dementia population increases as longevity extends. The risk of dementia increases significantly with age. As of March 2023, over 55 million people worldwide live with dementia (WHO, 2023a). Approximately one in nine people aged sixty-five and older (10.9%) has Alzheimer's. The percentage of people with Alzheimer's dementia increases with age: 5 percent of people aged sixty-five to seventy-four, 13.2 percent of people aged seventy-five to eighty-four, and 33.4 percent of people aged eighty-five and older have Alzheimer's dementia (Alzheimer's Association, 2024). The number of people living with dementia will almost double every twenty years, reaching 78 million in 2030 and 139 million by 2050, with the most significant increase in developing countries (Alzheimer's Disease International, n.d.).

Such an increasing rate of dementia becomes an enormous burden to public health services at the societal level, not only because of the increasing healthcare costs but also because of the loss of valuable workforces and volunteer manpower that senior citizens would provide in their communities. In addition, the mental health of caregivers is one of the most concerning topics of dementia-related issues. Caring for people with dementia is regarded as an emotional, physical, and sometimes financial burden on the family caregivers, which would add another layer of mental health concerns for caregivers in society.

Loneliness and Isolation

A lack of communication with social support groups such as family, friends, colleagues, and community members is centered on the feeling of isolation and loneliness among older adults. Loneliness is defined as a subjective feeling of lack or loss of companionship, separated or apart from others, which arises from an imbalance between desired social contacts and actual social contacts (Ernst & Cacioppo, 1999). In many cases, loneliness is perceived as an intense feeling of emptiness or abandonment. The feeling of loneliness in older adults seems prevalent. According to the National Poll on Healthy Aging conducted by the University of Michigan Institute for Healthcare Policy and Innovation (2023), one in three adults (34%) aged fifty to eighty reported feeling isolated from others in 2023, and 37 percent of older adults also reported feeling a lack of companionship. Reduced social interaction caused by loss of physical capabilities (e.g., mobility, hearing, sight, mental functioning, intelligence, memory) and by retirement from work is most likely to reinforce these feelings and may lead to further social withdrawal and segregation (Cohen-Mansfield & Parpura-Gill, 2007). Research has reported that loneliness, caused by isolation has a positive association with more serious mental health issues such as depression symptoms, insomnia, cognitive decline, and even suicide attempts (National Academies of Sciences, Engineering, and Medicine, 2020).

The COVID-19 pandemic worsened the negative effects of isolation and loneliness (NCOA: National Council on Aging, 2021). One in five US adults aged fifty to eighty expressed depression, anxiety, insomnia, or substance abuse since the COVID-19 pandemic began (Institute for Healthcare Policy and Innovation, 2023). Older people, who reported poorer physical health were more likely to report worse mental health since chronic illness and social isolation often go together. Stricter restrictions on social interaction further isolated older people during the pandemic. There was fear of catching the virus—or fear that a loved one would—exacerbate the feelings of confinement, loneliness, uncertainty, and anxiety.

The feeling of loneliness also impacts physical health. For older people, loneliness exacerbates stress levels, resulting in elevated cortisol and blood pressure (Hawkley, Thisted, Masi & Cacioppo, 2010; Singer, 2018). In sum, struggles to adjust oneself to changes in life and physical condition result in the loneliness of older people, which causes various mental health issues and physical challenges in return.

Depression

Late-life depression refers to the occurrence of major depressive disorder in adults sixty years of age or older (Taylor, 2014). Approximately 6 to 9 percent of adults over sixty-five in the United States are reported to experience major depressive disorder, and the number goes up to 25 percent in long-term care facilities (Husain-Krautter & Ellison, 2021). Despite the increasing numbers, late-life depression seems to be often neglected since people tend to perceive that depression is a normal part of aging, which is not true (National Institute on Aging, 2021). Depression in older adults is not just a psychological reaction but is caused by factors in psychological issues (loneliness and isolation, reduced sense of purpose due to retirement or physical limitations), health problems (illness, disability, chronic pain, or damage to body image due to surgery or disease), medications, fear of death, anxiety, or recent bereavement (the death of friends, family members, or loss of a spouse or partner).

While significant advances have been made in understanding and treating depression in older people, late-life depression is a symptom that requires more attention from researchers and experts in health communication. According to a meta-analysis by Haigh et al. (2018) examining the mental health of older people over twenty years (2007–2017), five myths regarding depression symptoms in older adults have emerged from empirical studies conducted during the period. Among the five myths, two items can be addressed from a communication perspective. First, the myth that depression in late life is more difficult to treat than depression at younger ages is not accurate. A substantial body of literature supports the efficacy of treatment for depression in older adults (Haigh et al., 2018). However, depression symptoms in older people are underdiagnosed and are easily perceived as a normal part of aging by family members, caregivers, or even older people themselves. Enhancing the mental health literacy of family members and older people themselves and facilitating family communication would help older people seek help in the early stage of depression. Health communication campaigns for healthy aging could also intervene to correct such myths in society. Second, the myth that depression in late life is merely a psychological reaction to the challenges of aging is inaccurate. Studies have found that psychological factors may serve more as protectors than causes of depression in older adults (Blazer, 2005). For example, perceived social support from strong relationships with family, friends, and community members provides emotional support and a buffer against depression (Uchino, 2006). Quality communication is essential for emotional support and is strong enough to defeat negative thought processes.

These findings of myths demonstrate the need for a holistic effort to understand the underdiagnoses of late-life depression from a societal context that goes beyond mere medical factors (i.e., mental health history, medication, and lack of access to mental health care services). A deeper understanding of societal issues such as ageism, stigma toward aging and mental disorders, and elder abuse would advance our understanding of mental health issues of older people and further suggest communication interventions.

Ageism

Ageism, aka age discrimination, refers to stereotypes, prejudice, and discrimination toward others or oneself based on chronological age (WHO, 2021), which can be observed as cognitive (how we think), affective (how we feel), and behavioral (how we act) components (WHO, 2021; Iversen et al., 2009). Age stereotypes contribute to assumptions about a person's physical and mental capabilities, social skills, political and religious beliefs, and other traits based on their perceived association with a particular group (WHO, 2021). Age prejudice is one of the most socially vocalized and institutionalized prejudices in many segments of society, and it is disregarded in numerous aspects of social life (Kang & Kim, 2022). Although ageism can be theoretically directed toward any age group, older adults are one of the two most studied groups regarding research on ageism along with late adolescents (Nelson, 2005).

Ageism Among Mental Health Clinicians and Patients

Ageism in a clinical setting is typically revealed in doctor-patient communication. These biases against older patients appear to be formed well before mental healthcare professionals enter the professional world (Bodner, Palgi, & Wyman, 2018). As there is a misperception toward older people's mental health problems (i.e., depression), several studies have found negative views regarding the aging process and a preference against working with older patients. Psychologists describe older people as being rigid, having difficulties in learning new material, and lacking the required energy and resilience for therapeutic growth. Several studies have found that psychologists consistently gave less favorable prognoses than their younger counterparts and perceived older patients as less ideal for therapy (i.e., Shmotkin, Eyal & Lomranz, 1992). Aharon et al (2024) found that Israeli mental health professionals were less interested in treating older adults with suicidal intentions than they were in treating younger patients with identical problems, which would indicate that ageism is still deep-rooted among healthcare professionals. Because of these issues, mental health problems or depression in older people are less likely to be diagnosed and cared for.

In summary, such evidence demonstrated that many mental healthcare professionals are less willing to work with older adults, have negative assumptions about the effectiveness of psychotherapy with older adults, and lack professional knowledge of the geriatric population. The bias results in the systematic negligence of mental health issues of older people. A norm change along with curriculum changes in geriatric mental health are demanded at a societal level.

Intersectionality of Ageism in a Mental Health Context

Ageism is a complicated issue. It is sometimes experienced in a multi-layered marginalized context with gender, race, culture, or immigration status. For example, older immigrants who arrived in their host countries in good health and after years of hard manual work, problematic living conditions, an insecure legal status, limited welfare, and pension in the host countries developed health problems, which is called the "*exhausted migrant effect*" (Dolberg, Sigurðardóttir & Trummer, 2018, p.208). While their marginalized social status already negatively affects physical health, mental health issues could add more hardship. On top of this, there is double stigmatization. Negative attitudes toward both old age and mental health problems can cause older people to withdraw from seeking help (Werner et al. 2009). Such multi-layered stigmatization creates a problem when those stigmas are internalized by those who are the target of the stigmatization (Rush et al. 2005 & Smith, 2011). Therefore, the ageism issue in a mental health context must be addressed in a way that prevents the internalization of the multi-layered stigmatization and helps older people secure their human dignity. Thus, communication interventions must reduce such stigmatization of aging that older people would have toward themselves, and younger people would have toward older people (Magsamen- Conrad et al., 2013). Improving mental health literacy is indispensable to changing negative perceptions toward aging, mental health, and the intersectionality of the ageism issue.

Elder Abuse

The last mental health problem of older people is elder abuse. Elder abuse is defined as "a single, or repeated act, or lack of appropriate action, occurring within any relationship where there is an expectation of trust, which causes harm or distress to an older person" (WHO, 2024). The scope of elder abuse (Herman, 2023) is wide from physical abuse (i.e., hitting, confining, and withholding necessary medical care), emotional or psychological abuse through problematic communication style (i.e., yelling, isolating an older adult from friends or family, gaslighting, or manipulating), financial exploitation (i.e., misusing or stealing money or property), neglect (i.e., neglecting hygiene and grooming, and leaving an older adult alone for extended periods), and sexual abuse (i.e., any unwanted sexual contact, and rape/sexual assault).

Elder abuse reported is increasing as the older adult population is growing faster in the United States than are younger population (Centers for Disease Control, 2024). Acierno et al (2010) reported that, in their survey, approximately one in ten older adults who are sixty or older and live at home experience some form of abuse such as neglect, exploitation, and mistreatment. According to the fifteen-year trend research (Logan et al., 2019), the nonfatal assault rate against older people (aged 60+) increased by 75.4 percent among men (2002–16) and 35.4 percent among women (2007–16). The estimated homicide rate for men increased by 7.1 percent from 2010 to 2016.

The causes of elder abuse are complicated and multifaceted, often stemming from a combination of individual, relational, and societal factors (National Institute of Justice, 2013). First, caregivers' stress is one of the noteworthy individual factors of elder abuse. The increasing number of people with dementia often involves family members as primary caregivers, since licensed caregivers are not always accessible due to multiple reasons (i.e., financial burden or the lack of certified caregivers). Second, relational factors of elder abuse remain in a private part of individual or personal life. Sometimes, older adults who need care are frail and too dependent on their caregivers. Another case is when a family member who has a history of conflict with the older person becomes a caregiver, and the relationship turns oppressive in the context of extended conflict. Third, at the societal level, ageism and the lack of social support for caregivers can cause elder abuse.

Elder abuse causes serious mental health consequences such as depression, anxiety, low self-esteem, and even post-traumatic stress disorder (PTSD) to the victims (National Council on Aging, 2024). Such consequences can also affect the families of the victims who witness the problematic behaviors and outcomes. Moreover, the destructive consequences do not remain in the individual domain but bring societal repercussions such as increased healthcare costs and stains on the social safety net.

In sum, the causes and consequences of mental health issues of older people are deeply intertwined with communication issues at the individual level (e.g., lack of knowledge in mental health, internalization of ageism and stigma) interpersonal contexts (e.g., abusive family communication, elder abuse), and a social system level (e.g., negative social norms about aging, ageism of mental healthcare professionals against older people). Communication interventions must be made to improve older people's mental health conditions at all levels.

Recommendations for Communication Intervention Strategies

Health communication plays a crucial role in distributing accurate information about mental health issues, correcting ageism and stigma toward older people, and creating positive social norms of healthy aging. In this sense, this section will suggest several communication intervention strategies. First, mental health literacy will be discussed to empower older adults to understand, manage, and seek help for mental health concerns. Second, online and offline social support will be addressed as measures to buffering the mental distress that older people may experience. Lastly, health communication campaigns will be introduced to showcase how campaigns effectively create awareness and promote a positive lifestyle for healthy aging and dementia prevention.

Enhancing Mental Health Literacy (MHL)

Mental health literacy (MHL), or the "knowledge and beliefs about mental health disorders which aid their recognition, management, and prevention (Jorm et al, 1997, p.182)," is an indispensable element for enhancing mental well-being. A lack of mental health hinders older people from helping themselves. Failure to recognize mental health problems results in ignorance until the problem turns into a severe condition. Poor mental health literacy also makes it difficult for older adults to relieve distress or seek help, since they do not know how to manage mental distress. Older people with low mental health literacy are less likely to adopt preventative behaviors for dementia or other mental disorders from a young age.

Although mental health literacy indicates the individual capability to comprehend health information, the interpersonal communication process is at the center of mental health literacy enhancement interventions (Caban, Makos & Thompson, 2023). Knowledge transfer processes such as lectures and group discussions inherently incorporate interpersonal interaction. Seeking help and exchanging social support also involve the interpersonal communication process. Therefore, we suggest improving the communication competence of older people to enhance mental health literacy.

Social Support and Mental Health

Mental distress such as social isolation and loneliness is caused by reduced interpersonal interaction at first. Therefore, it is crucial to remember the value of traditional interpersonal communication in supporting older people. The communication process is at the center of social support. Social support is defined as the network of relationships and resources that people have available to them through their relationships with others, which includes emotional, informational, and practical support from family, friends, and community (Langford, Bowsher, Maloney, & Lillis, 1997). Social support plays a crucial role in mental health by providing emotional comfort, validation, and a sense of belonging. It also helps individuals cope with stress, reduce feelings of loneliness and isolation, and enhance their overall psychological well- being (Brummett et al., 2005; Tajvar, Fletcher & Grundy, 2016).

However, social support alone is not sufficient; the belief in the existence of social support plays a critical role (Marmot & Wilkinson, 2005). Knowing that there are people who can care about them and are willing to listen and provide help can significantly buffer against the negative psychological effects of situations and mental health challenges, which is proven by many empirical studies (i.e., Harandi et al., 2017, Okabayashi et al., 2004).

Older people tend to experience losses of social networks and support more often than other age groups due to retirement, decline of physical health, and even deaths of friends and family. Therefore, it is necessary to facilitate social support for older people through institutionalized social support programs. For example, Winningham and Pike (2007) run a 3- month, group-based intervention program that provides various activities to facilitate social interactions in an assisted living facility and help older adults increase and maintain their social connectivity. Programs such as group discussions, memory games, paired activities, family days, games, and resident ambassador programs help the participants stay active and maintain the quality of their social networks, which leads to enhanced cognitive functioning, decreased depression, and feelings of isolation, as well as improved quality of life (Winningham & Pike, 2007). Interpersonal communication components that such intervention programs include can help older adults express themselves, develop coping mechanisms, and build social relationships (Substance Abuse and Mental Health Services Administration, 2021).

Technological Intervention and Online Social Support

Communication technologies such as the internet, online communities, and social media have the potential to prevent social isolation and enhance the social connectivity of older adults, especially for those at high risk of isolation who have mobility restrictions, live alone, or live in rural locations. Although there are mixed results regarding the efficacy of using communication technology to enhance older adults' quality of life and mental well-being, there is a body of literature that demonstrates the effect of communication technology on enhancing social interaction and reducing feelings of loneliness.

PRISM (Personal Reminder Information and Social Management System) can be a good example of communication technology used for mental health intervention. Czaja et al. (2018) developed PRISM, a computer system that is specially designed for older people, and evaluated its efficacy. PRISM is a software application designed for older adults, where they find mental health resources, make friends with other users, and enjoy leisure activities. The users of the application enhanced their social connectivity and decreased social isolation in six months. A meta-analysis of fiftyt-two research articles regarding online social networking and mental health among older adults (Chen, Wood & Ysseldyk, 2022) also identified that online social networking enhances communication with family and friends, feelings of independence and self-efficacy, creates a sense of (online) community, and decreases depressive symptoms. Those positive outcomes improve the subjective well-being and life satisfaction of older adults. Therefore, it is important to improve older adults' proficiency in using communication technologies, which will be an underlying condition to sustain the positive impact of digital communication technologies to enhance older people's social connectivity.

Emerging Media and Senior Mental Health Care

The potential of using communication technologies in alleviating mental health issues has been proven by creating online social support. Now, researchers are reviewing the potential of emerging media to enhance mental well-being. Emerging media refers to newer and innovative communication technologies that are characterized by their interactivity, integration of various media forms, and technological evolution (Li et al., 2016). Examples of emerging media in general include social media platforms, live streaming services, interactive applications, virtual reality (VR), augmented reality (AR), and arguably, socially assistive robots.

Regarding addressing mental health, researchers and clinicians have tried to explore the potential of emerging media on mental health and have brought both opportunities and areas for improvement. For example, Skurla, et al. (2022) report virtual reality (VR) is being tested for its potential to enhance care for older adults with cognitive and affective disorders, but calls for further research on refining diagnostic specificity and addressing important issues such as usability, data privacy, and confidentiality. According to Scoglio et al (2019)'s meta-analysis on researchers regarding the use of socially assistive robots on mental health outcomes, studies are so far at the level of pilot studies and have shown weak external validity, with lab interventions mostly involving dementia patients. Nevertheless, Scoglio et al (2019) suggest the feasibility of using socially assistive robots in mental health care. Overall, new technologies such as humanoid robots could provide older people with useful assistance to enhance social connectivity and companionship (i.e., Lima et al., 2021).

Health Communication Campaigns

Another recommendation for health communication intervention is to execute a health communication campaign on the topic of the mental health of older people. A campaign is a carefully coordinated effort that involves various communication strategies and tactics to achieve goals at a cognitive, attitudinal, and behavioral level among the target publics (Kaur-Gill & Dutta, 2021). A well-designed communication campaign is powerful enough not only to inform the publics of new ideas but also to create a positive attitude toward the new idea and motivate the target publics to adopt desirable behaviors, which would lead to social change in the long run. In terms of mental health for older people, there must be a sustained effort to create a positive attitude toward aging, combat ageism, reduce stigma toward aging and mental disorders, and motivate the publics to be involved in preventative lifestyles for healthy aging. The following three campaign examples provide insights into how campaigns reshape the human mind to advocate mental health.

Case 1: Make Your Way® Campaign

The US Office of Disease Prevention and Health Promotion initiated *the Move Your Way®* campaign to promote healthy aging with physical activity among the US population as part of the Healthy People 2030 project (U.S. Department of Health and Human Services, n.d.). In the initiative, older adults are identified as one of the core target publics, and the campaign provides appropriate information such as the recommended amount of physical activity, types of activities, and intensity levels, creating desirable behaviors. The campaign emphasizes the importance of maintaining physical health since physical health is closely linked to mental well-being, and vice versa. Physical activity also keeps older adults from isolation and prevents loneliness, since physical activities and exercise are usually conducted in a group setting or through interpersonal interaction with another person (i.e., trainer). Overall, the Healthy Aging Campaign is a good example of a publicity-focused campaign tactic for informing key publics.

Case 2: Mental Healthiness Aging Initiative (MHAI)

The Mental Healthiness Aging Initiative (MHAI) intervention program provides a good example of blending interpersonal communication tactics and media campaigns to target double-barrier populations: older adults in rural areas (Zanjani et al., 2012). The objective of the intervention campaign is to increase knowledge surrounding mental health and aging, based on the information diffusion process (Rogers, 2003). Therefore, creating conversations regarding mental health and aging at the community level is an essential part of the campaign strategies. Targeting older adults in rural areas (aged 65+) as the primary key public, but also including younger generations from the region, the program develops community partnerships with Family Consumer Science (FCS) extension agents and implements a community mental health and aging awareness intervention program. Interventions include multiple focus groups, extension agent training sessions, and a mass media campaign.

To measure the effectiveness of the intervention program, particularly of the training program through the extension agents, the research team divided the states of Kentucky into three sub-groups: one for the full intervention (research-based training program through extension agents and TV-based campaigns), another for the partial intervention (only TV-based campaign), and a control group (no intervention). The primary messages of the intervention program are (1) mental illness is not a normal part of aging, and (2) when signs of mental illness are present, prompt management is important.

The campaign reached out to the younger public and created intergenerational communication to address older people's mental health. Several interesting ideas emerged from focus group interviews conducted by the research team: For healthy aging, (a) maintaining independence and (b) promoting emotional health are important. Therefore, the intervention training needs to (c) include intergenerational activities, (d) encourage older adults to share their life history, remain active and engaged, and (e) educate younger community members about aging and encourage respect for older adults. Thus, the training sessions reflected those findings with three key components: facts and information through a TV-based social marketing campaign, an application exercise entitled PALS (Pay attention, Ask questions, Listen actively, and Show support), and community tools (communication packets, pamphlets, magnets, checklist, etc.).

Although the TV-based media campaign is regarded as an outdated strategy nowadays, it still implies the important lesson of distributing health information to target audiences through the right channels. Indeed, this initiative provides a good example of community interventions on mental health awareness and the importance of partnerships with local agents in rural regions such as Extension Agents for promoting mental health and healthy aging.

Case 3: SaniMemorix—Dementia Awareness Campaign

The dementia awareness campaign (Van Asbroeck et al., 2021), *SaniMemorix*, showcases various communication strategies to target not only older adults (aged 40–75) but also the younger public (aged 20+). A previous survey found that people tend to believe that dementia is a normal, non-preventable part of aging (Steyaert et al., 2021), and are not aware of ways to reduce dementia risk (i.e., Livingston et al., 2020). Thus, the Flanders Center of Expertise on Dementia in Belgium launched a large-scale health education campaign to raise awareness of dementia risk reduction (DRR) strategies, partnering with regional organizations including the Flemish Pharmacist Network, the Flemish Institute on Healthy Living, and the Alzheimer Liga. The campaign initiation timing was also strategically set from World Alzheimer's Day (Sep. 21, 2018) until March 2019 to gain maximum media spotlight.

Future health communicators who design dementia awareness campaigns can take several lessons from *SaniMemorix*. First, the campaign adopted various communication strategies to raise awareness, such as publicity (press release), social media posting with partnering organizations, and creating a website where all campaign materials are referenced and people could complete an online screening tool that assessed the twelve "Lifestyle for BRAin health" (LIBRA), which scores modifiable risk and protective factors for dementia and showed individuals their personalized room for improvement.

One of the most creative parts of the campaign strategies was to distribute the *Vaccine Boxes against Box*. The boxes contained an empty blister pack that symbolized the 12 LIBRA (Lifestyle of BRAin health) factors and a leaflet with more detailed information. The leaflet also displayed personal messages from opinion leaders such as well-known Flemish individuals, health experts, and scientists. The boxes also contained a packet of unsalted nuts, symbolizing the importance of a brain-healthy diet because of their vascular and cognitive health benefits. Approximately 40,000 boxes were distributed in public places such as train stations, local markets, and pharmacies. Overall, the campaign enhances individuals' knowledge regarding dementia risk and protective factors.

Second, future dementia awareness campaigns would benefit from the accompanying survey of the *SaniMemorix* Campaign. The survey suggests that the preference for information sources about dementia differs by socioeconomic status in the population. Overall, general practitioners were the most preferred primary source of information. Individuals of sixty-one to seventy-five years favored the general practitioners more than their younger counterparts (40–50 years old). Younger counterparts preferred the internet. A government-supported or non profit organization's website that provides information about dementia prevention was popular among highly educated individuals but less so among intermediate- and low-educated individuals. Smartphone apps were also favorably perceived as a good information source to improve brain health across all ages. Digital communication strategies such as smartphone application development are highly recommended for future intervention.

The SaniMemorix campaign demonstrates that effective public awareness campaigns regarding dementia risk reduction are feasible. In addition, creating international partnerships can be a doable communication intervention. The campaign was inspired by a previous campaign conducted in another country, the Netherlands. Effective campaigns across nations to enhance global awareness of dementia can contribute to reducing the risks of dementia.

Conclusion

Mental health issues in older people are as complex as aging itself. The causes and consequences of mental health problems among older people are deeply intertwined with one another. Feelings of loneliness can lead to isolation and depression, and loneliness itself can become a serious mental health issue for older people. Dementia is one of the most critical mental health problems that needs public health policy and program-level intervention. It is also closely connected with the mental well-being of the caregivers. Both covert and overt ageism are prevalent, hindering older individuals from seeking help when facing mental health issues. Additionally, elder abuse is another important issue that cannot be ignored, as its consequences affect not only the victims but also their families.

To explore solutions for alleviating mental health problems in older people, this chapter suggests communication interventions. Enhancing mental health literacy reduces self-stigmatization and motivates older people to seek help. Social support strengthens the social connections of older people and facilitates intergenerational communication. Lastly, health communication campaigns can contribute to reshaping societal norms about aging, combating ageism, reducing stigma toward dementia, and creating supportive networks. Sustained efforts will continue to enhance the mental well-being of older people.

Recommended Readings/Resources

Ayalon, L., & Tesch-Römer, C. (Eds.). (2018). *Contemporary perspectives on ageism.* Springer Open. https://doi.org/10.1007/978-3-319-73820-8

Caban, S., Makos, S., & Thompson, C. M. (2023). The role of interpersonal communication in mental health literacy interventions for young people: A theoretical review. *Health Communication, 38*(13), 2818–2832. https://doi:10.1080/10410236.2022.2121473

Haigh, E. A., Bogucki, O. E., Sigmon, S. T., & Blazer, D. G. (2018). Depression among older adults: a 20-year update on five common myths and misconceptions. *The American Journal of Geriatric Psychiatry, 26*(1), 107–122. https://www.sciencedirect.com/science/article/abs/pii/S1064748117303573

Magsamen-Conrad, K., Hanasono, L. K., & Billotte Verhoff, C. (2013). Health communication in the context of aging: The development of an Intergenerational Communication Intervention to reduce biases and discrimination. In *Applications in Health Communication: Emerging Trends* (pp. 101–125). Kendall Hunt.

Van Asbroeck, S., van Boxtel, M. P., Steyaert, J., Köhler, S., Heger, I., de Vugt, Verhey, F., & Deckers, K. (2021). Increasing knowledge on dementia risk reduction in the general population: Results of a public awareness campaign. *Preventive Medicine, 147*, 106522. https://doi.org/10.1016/j.ypmed.2021.106522

References

Acierno, R., Hernandez, M. A., Amstadter, A. B., Resnick, H. S., Steve, K., Muzzy, W., & Kilpatrick, D. G. (2010). Prevalence and correlates of emotional, physical, sexual, and financial abuse and potential neglect in the United States: The National Elder Mistreatment Study. *American Journal of Public Health, 100*(2), 292–297. https://doi.org/10.2105/AJPH.2009.163089

Aharon, O. N., Aisenberg-Shafran, D., & Levi-Belz, Y. (2024). The effect of suicide severity and patient's age on mental health professionals' willingness to treat: The moderating effect of ageism. *Death Studies, 48*(7), 652–662. https://doi.org/10.1080/07481187.2023.2255854

Alzheimer's Association (2024). *2024 Alzheimer's disease facts and figures.* https://www.alz.org/media/Documents/alzheimers-facts-and-figures.pdf

Alzheimer's Disease International. (n.d.) *Dementia statistics.* https://www.alzint.org/about/dementia-facts-figures/dementiastatistics/#:~:text=Someone%20in%20the%20world%20develops,will%20be%20in%20developing%20countries.

Blazer, D. G., & Hybels, C. F. (2005). Origins of depression in later life. *Psychological Medicine, 35*(9), 1241–1252. https://doi.org/10.1017/S0033291705004411

Bodner, E., Palgi, Y., & Wyman, M. F. (2018). Ageism in mental health assessment and treatment of older adults. In L. Ayalon & C. Tesch-Römer (Eds.), *Contemporary perspectives on ageism* (pp. 241–262). Springer Open. https://doi.org/10.1007/978-3-319-73820-8

Brummett, B. H., Mark, D. B., Siegler, I. C., Williams, R. B., Babyak, M. A., Clapp-Channing, N. E., & Barefoot, J. C. (2005). Perceived social support as a predictor of mortality in coronary patients: Effects of smoking, sedentary behavior, and depressive symptoms. *Psychosomatic Medicine, 67*(1), 40–45. https://doi.org/10.1097/01.psy.0000149257.74854.b7

Caban, S., Makos, S., & Thompson, C. M. (2023). The role of interpersonal communication in mental health literacy interventions for young people: A theoretical review. *Health Communication, 38*(13), 2818–2832. https://doi:10.1080/10410236.2022.2121473

Centers for Disease Control (2024, May 15). About abuse of older persons. https://www.cdc.gov/elder-abuse/about/?CDC_AAref_Val=https://www.cdc.gov/violenceprevention/elderabuse/fastfact.html

Chen, E., Wood, D., & Ysseldyk, R. (2022). Online social networking and mental health among older adults: A scoping review. *Canadian Journal on Ageing / La Revue canadienne du vieillissement, 41*(1), 26–39. https://doi:10.1017/S0714980821000040

Cohen-Mansfield, J., & Parpura-Gill, A. (2007). Loneliness in older persons: A theoretical model and empirical findings. *International Psychogeriatrics, 19*(2), 279–294. https://doi.org/10.1017/S1041610206004200

Czaja, S. J., Boot, W. R., Charness, N., Rogers, W. A., & Sharit, J. (2018). Improving social support for older adults through technology: Findings from the PRISM randomized controlled trial. *The Gerontologist*, *58*(3), 467–477. https://doi.org/10.1093/geront/gnw249

Dementia Society of America. (n.d.). *Definitions.* https://www.dementiasociety.org/definitions?gad_source=1&gclid=Cj0KCQjwtZK1BhDuARIsAAy2VztkWZ6rY78bG6z1esOD5qQirVpTHpO9t_wZaZMI1wJaiREBRKZJrgaAlHXEALw_wcB

Dolberg, P., Sigurðardóttir, S. H., & Trummer, U. (2018). Ageism and older immigrants. In L. Ayalon & C. Tesch-Römer (Eds.), *Contemporary perspectives on ageism* (pp. 177–191). Springer Open. https://doi.org/10.1007/978-3-319-73820-8

Ernst, J. M., & Cacioppo, J. T. (1999). Lonely hearts: Psychological perspectives on loneliness. *Applied and Preventive Psychology*, *8*(1), 1–22. https://doi.org/10.1016/S0962-1849(99)80008-0

Haigh, E. A., Bogucki, O. E., Sigmon, S. T., & Blazer, D. G. (2018). Depression among older adults: A 20-year update on five common myths and misconceptions. *The American Journal of Geriatric Psychiatry*, *26*(1), 107–122. https://doi.org/10.1016/j.jagp.2017.06.011

Harandi, T. F., Taghinasab, M. M., & Nayeri, T. D. (2017). The correlation of social support with mental health: A meta-analysis. *Electronic Physician*, *9*(9), 5212–5222. https://doi:10.19082/5212

Hawkley, L. C., Thisted, R. A., Masi, C. M., & Cacioppo, J. T. (2010). Loneliness predicts increased blood pressure: 5-year cross-lagged analyses in middle-aged and older adults. *Psychology and Aging*, *25*(1), 132–141. https://doi.org/10.1037/a0017805

Herman, L. (2023 March 6). Seven forms of elder abuse and how to recognize the abuse of seniors. *Safer Senior Care.* https://saferseniorcare.com/types-of-elder-abuse/

Husain-Krautter, S., & Ellison, J. M. (2021). Late life depression: The essentials and the essential distinctions. *Focus*, *19*(3), 282–293. https://doi.org/10.1176/appi.focus.20210006

Institute for Healthcare Policy and Innovation (2023, March). *Trends in loneliness among older adults from 2018–2023.* https://deepblue.lib.umich.edu/bitstream/handle/2027.42/175971/0300_NPHA-Loneliness-report-FINAL-doifinal.pdf?sequence=4&isAllowed=y

Iversen, T. N., Larsen, L., & Solem, P. E. (2009). A conceptual analysis of ageism. *Nordic Psychology*, *61*(3), 4–22. https://doi.org/10.1027/1901 2276.61.3.4

Jorm, A. F., Korten, A. E., Jacomb, P. A., Rodgers, B., Pollitt, P., Christensen, H., & Henderson, S. (1997). Helpfulness of interventions for mental disorders: Beliefs of health professionals compared with the general public. *British Journal of Psychiatry*, 171, 233–237. https://doi.org/10.1192/bjp.171.3.233

Kang, H., & Kim, H. (2022). Ageism and psychological well-being among older adults: A systematic review. *Gerontology and Geriatric Medicine*, *8*, 23337214221087023. https://doi.org/10.1177/2333721422108702

Kaur-Gill, S., & Dutta, M. J. (2021). Strategic communication campaigns in health. In C. H. Botan (Ed.), *The handbook of strategic communication* (pp. 309–319). Wiley-Blackwell.

Kuhn, K. (2015, January 23). *"It's my fault and I just need to get over it": The story of Ms. McKay's depression.* Massachusetts Healthy Aging Collaborative. https://mahealthyagingcollaborative.org/stories/its-my-fault-and-i-just-need-to-get-over-it-the-story-of-ms-mckays-depression/

Langford, C. P. H., Bowsher, J., Maloney, J. P., & Lillis, P. P. (1997). Social support: A conceptual analysis. *Journal of Advanced Nursing, 25*(1), 95–100. https://doi.org/10.1046/j.1365 2648.1997.1997025095.x

Li, X., Liu, X., Liu, Y., Nergadze, N., Yao, M., & Zeng, L. (2016). *Emerging media: Uses and dynamics.* Routledge.

Lima, M. R., Wairagkar, M., Natarajan, N., Vaitheswaran, S., & Vaidyanathan, R. (2021). Robotic telemedicine for mental health: A multimodal approach to improve human-robot engagement. *Frontiers in Robotics and AI, 8*, 618866. https://doi.org/10.3389/frobt.2021.618866

Livingston, G., Huntley, J., Sommerlad, A., Ames, D., Ballard, C., Banerjee, S., Brayne, C., Burns, A., Cohen-Mansfield, J., et al. (2020). Dementia prevention, intervention, and care: 2020 report of the Lancet Commission. *Lancet, 396*, 413–446. https://doi.org/10.1016/S0140-6736(20)30367-6

Logan, J. E., Haileyesus, T., Ertl, A., Rostad, W. L., & Herbst, J. H. (2019, April 5). Nonfatal assaults and homicides among adults aged ≥60 years — United States, 2002–2016. *MMWR Morbidity and Mortal Weekly Report, 68*, (13). 297–302. http://dx.doi.org/10.15585/mmwr.mm6813a1.

Magsamen-Conrad, K., Hanasono, L. K., & Billotte Verhoff, C. (2013). Health communication in the context of aging: The development of an Intergenerational Communication Intervention to reduce biases and discrimination. In *Applications in health communication: Emerging trends* (pp. 101–125). Kendall Hunt.

Marmot, M., & Wilkinson, R. (Eds.). (2005). *Social determinants of health.* OUP Oxford.

National Academies of Sciences, Engineering, and Medicine. (2020). *Social isolation and loneliness in older adults: Opportunities for the health care system.* National Academies Press. https://www.ncbi.nlm.nih.gov/books/NBK557974/

National Council on Aging. (2021, March 21). *COVID-driven isolation can be dangerous for older adults.* https://www.ncoa.org/article/covid-driven-isolation-can-be-dangerous-for-older-adults

National Council on Aging. (2024, July 8). Get the facts on elder abuse. https://www.ncoa.org/article/get-the-facts-on-elder-abuse

National Institute on Aging. (2021 July 7). *Depression and older adults.* https://www.nia.nih.gov/health/mental-and-emotional-health/depression-and-older-adults

National Institute of Justice. (2013). *Causes and characteristics of elder abuse.* https://nij.ojp.gov/topics/articles/causes-and-characteristics-elder-abuse

Nelson, T. D. (2005). Ageism: Prejudice against our feared future self. *Journal of Social Issues*, *61*(2), 207–221. https://doi.org/10.1111/j.1540 4560.2005.00402.x

Okabayashi, H., Liang, J., Krause, N., Akiyama, H., & Sugisawa, H. (2004). Mental health among older adults in Japan: Do sources of social support and negative interaction make a difference? *Social Science & Medicine*, *59*(11), 2259–2270. https://doi.org/10.1016/j.socscimed.2004.02.024

Rogers, E. M. (2003). *Diffusion of innovations* (5th ed.). Free Press.

Rush, N., Angermeyer, M. C., & Corrigan, P. W. (2005). Mental illness stigma: Concepts, consequences, and initiatives to reduce stigma. *European Psychiatry*, *20*(8), 529–539. https://doi.org/10.1016/j.eurpsy.2005.04.004

Scherbov, S., & Sanderson, W. (2019, February 25–26). *New measures of population aging: Bridging research and policy. International Institute for Applied Systems Analysis.* https://www.un.org/development/desa/pd/sites/www.un.org.development.desa.pd/files/unpd_egm_201902_s1_sergeischerbov.pdf

Scoglio, A. A., Reilly, E. D., Gorman, J. A., & Drebing, C. E. (2019). Use of social robots in mental health and well-being research: Systematic review. *Journal of Medical Internet Research*, *21*(7), e13322. https://doi.org/doi:10.2196/13322

Shmotkin, D., Eyal, N., & Lomranz, J. (1992). Motivations and attitudes of clinical psychologists regarding treatment of the elderly. *Educational Gerontology: An International Quarterly*, 18(2), 177–192. https://doi.org/10.1080/0360127920180205

Singer, C. (2018). Health effects of social isolation and loneliness. *Journal of Aging Life Care*, *28*(1), 4–8.

Skurla, M. D., Rahman, A. T., Salcone, S., Mathias, L., Shah, B., Forester, B. P., & Vahia, I. V. (2022). Virtual reality and mental health in older adults: A systematic review. *International Psychogeriatrics*, *34*(2), 143–155. https://doi.org/10.1017/S104161022100017X

Smith, R. A. (2011). Stigma, communication, and health. In T. L. Thompson, R. Parrott, & J. F. Nussbaum (Eds.), *The Routledge handbook of health communication* (pp. 480–493). Routledge. https://doi.org/10.4324/9780203846063

Snyder, C. R., Lopez, S. J. & Pedrotti, T. (2011). *Positive psychology: The scientific and practical explorations of human strengths* (2nd ed.). SAGE.

Steyaert, J., Deckers, K., Smits, C., Fox, C., Thyrian, R., Jeon, Y. H., ... & Interdem Taskforce on Prevention of Dementia. (2021). Putting primary prevention of dementia on everybody's agenda. *Aging & Mental Health*, *25*(8), 1376–1380. https://doi.org/10.1080/13607863.2020.1783514

Substance Abuse and Mental Health Services Administration (2021). *Psychological interventions for older adults with serious mental illness.* https://store.samhsa.gov/product/psychosocial-interventions-older-adults-serious-mental-illness/pep21-06-05-001

Tajvar, M., Fletcher, A., & Grundy, E. (2016). Exploring associations between social support and mental health in older people: A systematic narrative review. *International Journal of Ageing Developing Countries*, *1*(2), 174–193.

Taylor, P., Morin, R., Parker, K., Cohn, D., & Wang, W. (2009, June 29). *Growing old in America: Expectations vs. reality.* Pew Research Center: A Social & Demographic Trends Report. https://www.pewresearch.org/social-trends/2009/06/29/growing-old-in-america-expectations-vs-reality/

Taylor, W. D. (2014). Depression in the elderly. *New England Journal of Medicine, 371*(13), 1228–1236. https://doi.org/10.1056/NEJMcp1402180

Uchino, B. N. (2006). Social support and health: A review of physiological processes potentially underlying links to disease outcomes. *Journal of Behavioral Medicine, 29*, 377–387. https://doi.org/10.1007/s10865-006-9056-5

United Nations Department of Economic and Social Affairs, Population Division. (2022). *World population prospects 2022: Summary of results.* UN DESA/POP/2022/TR/NO. 3. https://www.un.org/en/global-issues/ageing

U.S. Department of Health and Human Services. (n.d.). *Materials for older adults.* https://health.gov/our-work/nutrition-physical-activity/move-your-way-community-resources/campaign-materials/materials-older-adults

Van Asbroeck, S., van Boxtel, M. P., Steyaert, J., Köhler, S., Heger, I., de Vugt, M., ... & Deckers, K. (2021). Increasing knowledge on dementia risk reduction in the general population: Results of a public awareness campaign. *Preventive Medicine, 147*, 106522. https://doi.org/10.1016/j.ypmed.2021.106522

Watson, R., Sanson-Fisher, R., Bryant, J., & Mansfield, E. (2023). Dementia is the second most feared condition among Australian health service consumers: Results of a cross-sectional survey. *BMC Public Health, 23*(1), 876. https://doi.org/10.1186/s12889-023-15772-y

Werner, P., Stein-Shvachman, I., & Heinik, J. (2009). Perceptions of self-stigma and its correlates among older adults with depression: A preliminary study. *International Psychogeriatrics, 21*(06), 1180–1189. https://doi.org/10.1017/s1041610209990470

Winningham, R. G., & Pike, N. L. (2007). A cognitive intervention to enhance institutionalized older adults' social support networks and decrease loneliness. *Aging & Mental Health, 11*(6), 716–721. https://doi.org/10.1080/13607860701366228

World Health Organization. (2020, December). *Global health estimates* 2019. World Health Organization. https://view.officeapps.live.com/op/view.aspx?src=https%3A%2F%2Fcdn.who.int%2Fmedia%2Fdocs%2Fdefault-source%2Fgho-documents%2Fglobal-health-estimates%2Fghe2019_yld_global_2000_2019c417f68b-841d-4a7a-9e5c-f087f9f86e48_4a694273-e334-4099-975e-8534ea25feb9.xlsx%3Fsfvrsn%3Ddac29788_7&wdOrigin=BROWSELINK

World Health Organization. (2021, March 18). *Ageing: Ageism* https://www.who.int/news-room/questions-and-answers/item/ageing-ageism

World Health Organization. (2022, June 17). *Mental health.* https://www.who.int/news-room/fact-sheets/detail/mental-health-strengthening-our-response

World Health Organization. (2023a, March 15). *Dementia.* https://www.who.int/news-room/fact-sheets/detail/dementia

World Health Organization. (2023b, October 20). *Mental health of older adults.* https://www.who.int/news-room/fact-sheets/detail/mental-health-of-older-adults

World Health Organization. (2024, June 15). *Abuse of older people.* https://www.who.int/news-room/fact-sheets/detail/abuse-of-older-people

Zanjani, F., Kruger, T., & Murray, D. (2012). Evaluation of the mental healthiness aging initiative: Community program to promote awareness about mental health and aging issues. *Community Mental Health Journal, 48*, 193–201. https://doi.org/10.1007/s10597-011-9373-1

9

Mental Health Communication for Religious Minorities

Jacob Watson, Jorge Seifert, and John Parrish-Sprowl

Case Description

Flooded with fear, Sana assumed the worst. Sana, a young mother, was going through bouts of depression and could not seem to reconcile it with her faith. Friends of hers alluded to having weak faith and that her state was a result of that. She needed to pray more and read the Qur'an to restore her faith. The direction she received from friends was simple and as expected, leaving her feeling even more hopeless. Regardless, she contemplated suicide and felt that Allah might not forgive her for her ingratitude. Not being able to bond with her children during this time led her to believe that suicide was the best option, a way to escape from her feelings of despair. As a teacher of the Islamic sciences and a lawyer no less, she was perplexed that she felt suicide was her best option. Typically full of joy and happy to engage personally, Sana was overwhelmed by feelings of guilt and darkness. On the day that Sana was going to commit suicide, a friend who had just completed a suicide response training reached out. Noticing the red flags evident in Sana, she managed to get Sana to have a psychiatric evaluation. It was only then that they learned that her depression was postpartum. She was told that her symptoms and overall feelings of unease had nothing to do with her level of faith or education. This comforted Sana and contributed to saving her life.

Mehran Nazir was experiencing the hell of a depressive episode. From legal proceedings to emergency room visits, Nazir struggled heavily. On top of this, he experienced the death of loved ones while being involuntarily unemployed. He became consumed with intrusive thoughts that were neither helpful nor wanted. They were destructive and hopeless in nature. He imagined his plane crashing on the way to its destination or falling asleep while driving. Usually outgoing and full of life, Nazir became complacent to the point of paralysis, lying in bed for hours on end while terminating plans with friends. Finally, Nazir felt that suicide was what he had to do. He put together a will and planned its location in writing. Through this, however, Nazir found solace in his writing in the form of journaling. He then shared what he wrote online, finding many others who were going through similar occurrences. Nazir remarked that this was not a unique circumstance but one that was prevalent in the Muslim community. Nazir was right, as numbers show the escalating and pervasive number of suicides that occur in the Islamic community. Stories such as these are all too common, and much needs to be done to reduce the occurrence of such situations.

Mental Health Problems in Religious Minority Communities

Cases such as those above[1] are indexical of the mental health challenges confronting the Muslim community. Although circumstances such as the stories above are experienced across all groups, as explored elsewhere in this volume, it should be recognized that there is a unique interplay between mental health experience and religious beliefs. For many, the thoughts and feelings associated with poor mental health are as much about their faith as they are about their body and mind. This can potentially exacerbate the problem by leading one to feel like a spiritual failure and often means avoiding seeking help.

While such is the case for many faith communities, in this chapter we will particularly focus on a Muslim community as a case study of how mental health might be addressed given the complexities of the intertwined aspects of health and faith. This case may serve as an example that may apply to similar Muslim communities and to other faith communities as well. Mental, physical, and social well-being is a challenge in all communities, including those of the Islamic faith. The focus here will be on mental illness stigma, depression, and anxiety; not seeking care due to religious convictions; encounters with racism and Islamophobia when seeking care; the cultural sensitivity of healthcare professionals; and heightened levels of stress.

Mental Illness Stigma

The Islamic promotion of mental well-being recognizes intrinsic human defects and emotional shortcomings and calls for constructive enactments to overcome them (Baasher, 2001). Baasher (2001) also notes that the problem of suicide in the Quran is pronounced with clear and firm directives. This provides advice to Muslims, laying out a course of action if concerns arise. Stigma can develop, as evidenced in Sana's story, where we find that prescriptive directives by friends were insufficient to manage the complexity of her mental health status. Al-Adawi et al., (2002) found that participants believed mental illness was caused by spirits, rejecting genetics or environmental factors as significant contributors to mental health conditions. Abu-Ras et al. (2008) found that 84 percent of the respondents in Muslim communities believed in the devil's possession of the mentally ill person and 98 percent of the respondents agreed that life stressors are a test of one's faith. In another study, participants noted that the Muslim community contains powerful narratives of shame and stigma connected to accessing mental health services (Weatherhead & Daiches, 2010). This is in addition to the treatment that Muslims receive for their faith alone, such as being characterized based on negative stereotypes, poor public image, profiling, and affronts that equate Islam with radicalism (Afridi, 2001).

Stigma is a pervasive health communication problem concerning mental illness but is especially prevalent when attributed to a population that already suffers from stigmatizing stereotypes. Muslims must navigate cultural and religious dilemmas that make sharing their struggles inherently difficult, often further isolating them as they attempt to manage anxiety, depression, addiction, suicidal thoughts, and other mental health challenges. Since the Quran has ascriptions and even directives for managing one's internal state, it is apparent that sharing one's mental struggle with others becomes difficult when it carries the burden of stigma and a sense of spiritual failure.

The powerful narratives of shame and stigma stem from a culture that may not discuss such issues openly due to widespread beliefs that mitigate against seeking treatment from mental health providers. Weatherhead and Daiches (2010) further comment that participants felt that professional assistance was less of a need if one has a strong faith and that many expressed the view that accessing mental healthcare services felt like a betrayal of their religion and was a secular way of dealing with what should be considered issues of faith. Stigma from within the community that inhibits ameliorative action exacerbates debilitating mental health challenges.

Depression and Anxiety

Depression and anxiety are the most common mental health conditions that affect daily life around the world. Gorman (1996) found that 85 percent of Muslim patients with depression also experience symptoms of anxiety and comorbid depression is prevalent in 90 percent of patients with anxiety disorders. From a health communication standpoint, it can be posited that depression and anxiety are contagious (Wainberg et al., 2018, Yapko, 2016) and in that sense, they have little difference from the common cold. Familial communicability facilitates the risks associated with having family members manifest psychiatric illnesses, including genetic, behavioral, and developmental pathways (Wainberg et al., 2018). Also, social disadvantage and structural discrimination are found to be common risk factors for psychiatric illness (Allen et al., 2014). In the Islamic community, suicide is twice as likely compared to other religious groups (Awaad & Kouser, 2021), which often stems from prior depression. Due to the allostatic load of being part of an underserved population, there is a higher chance that these conditions will manifest (Geronimus, 2006). However, it is important to note that contagion (communicability) may also depend on one's own mental health, where individuals with poorer mental health may be more susceptible because they cannot manage their stress when being around somebody else with poor mental health (Eisenberg et al., 2013).

Although perceiving depression and anxiety as communicable has not been fully adopted, it is often viewed as a springboard for leading people to isolation (Lombrozo, 2015), it is important to note the systemic and community-level effects that mental health problems have within these groups. If depression and anxiety are potentially communicable within an underserved population, specifically a Muslim community, the question we could ask is in what ways could the "spread" be curtailed? How this will be addressed from a communication complex perspective will be outlined in the communication strategies section.

Not Seeking Care

Playing into the larger notion of stigma within the Muslim community, many individuals with mental illness fail to seek care. Reputation, questioning of their faith, or overall distrust in mental healthcare providers can lead a mentally ill Muslim to handle their condition on their own. Muslims with mental health issues can interpret symptoms as a punishment from God and can view seeking psychiatric services as showing spiritual weakness (Abu-Ras et al., 2008). Additionally, Islam emphasizes the preservation of one's intellect, distinguishing competency from incompetency, where one who is mentally incompetent is excluded from religious duties (Abbasi & Paulsen, n.d.) Therefore, Muslims may feel uncomfortable seeking psychiatric help to avoid conflicting with their religious beliefs (Sabry & Vohra, 2013).

If help is sought, whether for individual, emotional or relationship problems, Muslims most often see their religious leaders first. Some may seek counseling within the faith or may seek help from imams who are not trained in counseling but do deal with family and marital problems (Johansen, 2005). Followers of the Islamic faith are responsible for caring for their minds and bodies, which includes seeking appropriate help, although this tends to be overlooked with respect to mental health (Awaad & Kouser, 2023). However, if the prevailing notion of seeking mental health services is a negative one, then it can be difficult to change the conversation. Therefore, it is important to recognize the source from which the stigma and false conceptions arise.

Problem Identifications: Racism and Islamophobia from Healthcare Providers

Issues of racism and discrimination are strong contributors to the challenge of dealing with mental health problems for Muslim communities. Khan (2022) notes that even with the need for commitment to values of compassion, social justice, and cultural humility within the healthcare professions, many doctors and other professionals continue to harbor deep-seated prejudice toward those of the Islamic faith, often appearing in derogatory statements about Muslim colleagues or patients. Fear or stigma toward those of the Islamic faith is known as *Islamophobia*, which has a negative influence on one's health through the disruption of several different systems such as individual, interpersonal, and structural pathways (Samari, 2016). Inhorn and Fakih (2006) found through a qualitative study of Iraqi refugees that participants described healthcare workers as unhelpful, patronizing, and having stereotypical attitudes toward Muslim women, believing that they are pious, have many children, and are under oppression by their husbands. Aronson et al. (2013) found that Islamophobia-based stereotype threats can adversely affect the patient-provider relationship by creating inept interactions, distrust of medical advice, or failure to obtain medical care.

Martin (2015) indicates that anti-Muslim discrimination crosses over from society to the healthcare setting in the United States, where nearly one-third of the study participants perceived they were discriminated against in this setting. Feeling excluded or ignored was the most frequent type of discrimination, followed by problems related to the use of Muslim clothing, offensive or insensitive verbal remarks, and problems related to Islamic holidays, prayer rituals, and physical assault, respectively (Martin, 2015). However, despite these circumstances, a lack of health literature regarding Islamophobia makes it difficult to assess its incidence, thereby limiting our understanding of the multiple sources of discrimination for Muslims in the United States (Samari, 2016).

While racism and minority discrimination are not new to contemporary discourse, it is important to highlight how particular aspects of Islamophobia influence those within the medical profession as well as those outside. By recognizing that Islamophobia and racism lead to impaired health care, practitioners can be better prepared to implement communication interventions to mitigate its prevalence. Muslims, as a minority group in the United States, face frequent discrimination, in general, and it is likely to be much more stressful if this occurs within health contexts.

Insufficient Cultural Sensitivity of Healthcare Providers

Healthcare providers often have a unique perspective that can lead to a focus on the body and not on the person as a whole, which can give rise to insufficient cultural sensitivity when dealing with those from cultures separate from their own. With Islamic patients, however, cultural sensitivity is an important consideration regarding the provision of healthcare, especially concerning mental health. Furthermore, complicating the issue is that even culturally aware interactions with healthcare professionals face the challenge of stigmatization within Muslim communities (Jamil, 2020). It is incumbent on healthcare professionals to be aware of the cultural and community concerns of all their patients, including the Islamic population (Attum et al., 2023). Another way to promote culturally aware communication patterns is to learn about restrictions and allowances in the faith such as being aware of modesty during physical examinations (Attum et al., 2023). As noted by Tackett et al. (2018) Islamic women generally want culturally appropriate interaction with healthcare providers that includes respect for modesty, body privacy, and a preference for the same gender of provider. Additionally, Muslim women feel best about their provider when they demonstrate an understanding of the need to maintain religious practices during illness, insight into Muslim family patterns of caring, the cultural tendency toward a sense of fatalism along with belief in predestination, and sensitivity to the fear of stereotyping that gives rise to discrimination.

Muslims, like all religious communities, take varied approaches to life based on their understanding of the Quran. That said, a practicing Muslim wants their beliefs to be acknowledged and respected in healthcare settings. It is critical to note that with important periods of observance such as Ramadan, there may be challenges when fasting is required by faith, but a patient may suffer from diabetes, which makes this impractical and even dangerous. Healthcare workers face additional challenges in communicating with Muslim patients who may be adamant about not circumventing their faith practices. If a Muslim patient expects that a healthcare worker will not consider their faith appropriately, then they are more likely to limit seeking care or fail to follow through with care instructions.

That is a critical issue concerning the cultural sensitivity of healthcare workers serving Muslims, as expectations of disregard lead to an inherent distrust and presupposition that they will not consider how their faith is intertwined with their health needs. This becomes a treatment issue when nearly one-third of Muslim Americans perceive discrimination in healthcare settings, including being excluded or ignored, which are the most frequently conveyed types of discrimination (Martin, 2015). Also, a lack of understanding or knowledge about the religious beliefs, customs, or rituals of Muslim patients by non-Muslim healthcare providers serves as an obstacle to establishing a productive therapeutic relationship. Finally, existing data show high rates of adjustment disorder experienced by Muslim Americans seeking mental health treatment, which may be suggestive of the challenges of cultural integration, as well as discrimination and marginalization in society (Mental Health America, n.d.).

Stress

Research has consistently supported the conclusion that stress can adversely impact our health as well as our ability to retain and recall information (Siegel, 2010; Vogel, 2016). In addition, research suggests that stress can have an intergenerational impact, especially if the mother is unduly stressed during pregnancy (Siegel, 2010). The challenge with stress is not that we need strategies to avoid it, that is impossible. What is needed is an ability to identify unnecessary stress and to develop the means of managing stress to minimize adverse impacts on our mental, physical, and social health. Stigma related to mental health can often prevent people from having the necessary conversations to better manage stress, and this enables small challenges to grow into larger, more pervasive problems for people. In addition to stigma, discrimination also plays a role in adding stressors to Muslims in the United States. For immigrants, language barriers and cultural differences may exacerbate stress in ways that impact not only the individuals but the entire family and, by extension the community.

Even in Muslim-dominant countries, political and economic circumstances may cause difficulty in managing stress levels. Recent armed conflicts in Syria, Libya, Lebanon, Gaza, Yemen, and elsewhere can create unduly stressful circumstances for those trying to manage life with constant threats of death and destruction. For those who have immigrated to the West, the stress is still manifest due to friends and family who have been left behind. The recent outbreak of violence between Hamas and Israel not only impacts those trying to live amid the fighting, but it has also led to fear for loved ones, angst regarding their culture under attack, and increased violence and discrimination in their new countries. For many, it is difficult to reconcile their faith and fighting, adding to the burden. All these stressors are manifest in a Muslim school in the Midwest, and such stress sets the context for everyone's ability to manage the mental health of Muslim communities in the United States.

Theory

Communication Complex

Arguably, communication theories have largely ignored issues related to mental health until recent years. This is a bit surprising given that as early as 1951 Ruesch and Bateson (1951) stated unequivocally that *all psychiatry is communication* and that Watzlawick, Beavin, and Jackson, in their seminal work *The Pragmatics of Human Communication* (1967) which has been widely read and cited in the communication literature, also addresses issues of mental health. There are myriad reasons for this, such as the search for biological roots of mental health that has dominated the framing of and research into mental health in the United States for a century (Harrington, 2019). Yet, increasingly many are beginning to recognize communication as a locus of origin for much of mental health (Parrish-Sprowl et al., 2020; Cozolino, 2014; Yapko, 2016). Indeed, neuroscientists Hasson et al. (2011) note that "cognition materializes in an interpersonal space" (p. 114). One approach to communication theory that addresses mental health, which draws from these theorists and others, is that of Communication Complex, a meta-theoretical gathering of multiple communication theories, neuroscience, and other scientific research (Parrish-Sprowl et al., 2020; Parrish-Sprowl & Parrish-Sprowl, 2014a, 2014b).

Communication Complex (CC) emerges from a quantum paradigm which, in contrast to a traditional Newtonian approach, presumes that everything is created in relations between, and not by the objects themselves (Cooper, 2017; Parrish-Sprowl & Parrish-Sprowl, 2023; Rovelli, 2021; Zohar, 2022). Although social constructionism has a rich literature born of an epistemological position that social worlds are made in interaction, it has rarely been intertwined with the neuroscience research that suggests that social interaction does more than make meaning; it also creates and shapes biology as well (Cozolino, 2014; Seigel, 2020).

CC engages the theory and theoretical perspectives of Ruesch and Bateson (1951), Watzlawick et al. (1967), Pearce and Cronen (1980), Pearce (1989, 2007), Seigel (2020), and others to develop a meta-theoretical approach to communication that embraces and intertwines within the quantum paradigm, social constructionism, systemic approaches to communication, and neuroscience as a way of understanding human communication in general and within that mental health. Thus, CC is more science than social science-based and draws on a large and growing number of studies that lead us to the realization that communication is both bioactive and systemic.

CC provides the conceptualization that frames the Communication for Whole Health (CWH) approach to enabling people to engage with each other in ways that can improve mental, physical, and social health (Parrish-Sprowl, 2020; Rascon, 2022). More specifically, Parrish-Sprowl and Parrish-Sprowl (2014b) addressed post-traumatic growth from a CC perspective and later implemented clinic-wide Mental Health and Psychosocial Support (MHPSS) in Jordan in facilities that provided health services to refugees (Parrish-Sprowl et al., 2020). CWH promotes ways of interacting that can facilitate healthy meaning and sense-making, along with activating healthy biological functioning and a neurological sense of safety necessary for healthful social engagement (Parrish-Sprowl, et al, 2020; Parrish-Sprowl & Parrish-Sprowl, 2023; Porges, 2017, 2021). Currently, CWH-informed projects are taking place in multiple countries with a special effort to promote community-wide improvements in mental health. Two of these projects are focused on Muslim-majority communities.

In Jordan, qualitative data offers multiple instances where mental health was improved among refugees, clinic staff, and their families when CWH approaches are taken based on the idea of the Communication Complex (Parrish-Sprowl et al., 2020). Although the science that supports CWH is substantial, it is important to demonstrate efficacy in how the science can engage to perturb patterns of interaction among people to improve mental health. It is not enough to simply know that interaction gives rise to better health; it is important to develop the facility to interact in ways that achieve this in the daily lives of people within a group or community. Ongoing research continues to shape our understanding of how interaction can be a vehicle for promoting health and what strategies might be engaged to achieve this in different communities.

Intervention Strategies

According to quantum theory, any engagement holds the potential to perturb a pattern of action. Given this, a mantra developed during the project in Jordan: "Every interaction is an intervention" (Parrish-Sprowl et al., 2020, p. 7). Whether we avoid, ignore, smile, nod, talk at them, or exchange messages, there is potential to create differing patterns of interaction among people. In Jordan, the intervention team conducted brief training sessions for everyone working in the clinic regarding the impact of trauma histories, power differences, and other aspects of interaction that can impact mental health. Multiple people reported examples of where they engaged in this training in interaction with patients, family, or among patients and their families that positively impacted mental health (Parrish-Sprowl et al., 2020). On the first visit, one member of the team provided some breathing exercises that can lead to calming feelings and interaction. One of the individuals disclosed that based on that interaction, they practiced this activity every day, often multiple times, and that it made a real difference in stress levels. One interaction made a great difference. Everyone should consider how each interaction might promote better mental health both in themselves and in the others involved in the conversation.

Although every interaction holds potential for change, it is often necessary to repeat interactions multiple times to alter patterns, whether this diminishes mental health or bolsters it. For example, stigma related to mental health (and anything else) rarely emerges from a single statement that one person shares with another. Instead, it is born from a repetition of messages that in turn instantiate in our brains and biology, forming the basis for reactions that might include shame, guilt, anger, or fear. In contrast, if we interact in ways that help people feel safe and receptive, then we promote mental health. As Porges (2017) notes:

> The critical point is that the neural circuit regulating social interaction and social engagement behaviors is the same neural circuit that supports health, growth, and restoration . . . . the most important thing to our nervous system is that we are safe. When we're safe, magical things occur. They occur on multiple levels, not merely in terms of social relations, but also in the accessibility of certain areas of the brain, certain areas of feeling pleasure—being expansive, being creative, and being very positive as well. (p. 141)

Thus, we need to create an environment or communication ecology that, through repetition, promotes good mental health. Every interaction is an intervention that can alter patterns, while multiple interactions give rise to patterns that can diminish or strengthen mental health.

Research demonstrates that many people benefit from psychotherapy and/or pharmacological interventions. Both approaches to improving mental health are necessary to provide support for people who are suffering from poor mental health or mental illness. In the cases at the beginning of the chapter, each of the individuals had mental health concerns that had progressed to the point of debilitation. At that point, they may well need either therapy, pharmacological tools, or both interventions. Yet, this could have been avoided if they lived in a different communication ecology, one that promoted better mental health in most interactions. As Yapko (2009) noted:

> You can't catch depression in the same way you catch a cold, but the latest research in neuroscience, social psychology, epidemiology, and genetics provides overwhelming support that moods spread through social conditions. Our social lives directly shape our brain chemistry and powerfully affect the way we think and feel. . . . In fact, brains can change as much with social circumstances as with medication. Drugs may address some of depression's symptoms, but they cannot change the social factors that cause and perpetuate it. (p. 2)

From a practical perspective, while encouraging everyone who can benefit from therapy to seek it out seems like a good idea, the reality is that there are simply not enough therapists in any country, including the United States, to meet the needs of the whole population (Weiner, 2022). When you have special concerns related to being a member of a faith community such as the Islamic one, the pool of qualified therapists who will not either purposefully or inadvertently discriminate is even smaller with respect to the size of the population it needs to serve. Instead of therapy, people are often prescribed antidepressants or anti-anxiety medication without any other treatment. As Yapko (2009) noted above, this may or may not relieve symptoms, but it does not address the social interaction that often gives rise to depression or anxiety in any given individual.

None of this is to say that therapy and pharmacy are not valuable in efforts to improve mental health and deal with mental illness. However, from a CC framework, there is much that can be done to both improve mental health and mitigate the number of people who need more specialized treatment. This involves a constellation of strategies that includes:

- Providing community members with some understanding of the relationship between how we interact with each other and the development of depression and anxiety. This includes an understanding of how intergenerational stress and trauma, as well as current circumstances, can lead to unhealthy interaction.
- Providing people with ongoing support until new, more mentally healthful ways of interacting become normative in each family, organization, or community. People need reminders, nudges, and advice regarding how they might interact differently to both achieve the instrumental goals of a conversation and to do so in a healthy manner.
- Providing interventions that enable members of a community to be healthy in their interactions in ways that are consonant with their values and faith.
- Reminding people that everyone has mental health, all people can develop mental illness, and most people can manage or even emerge from such illness. There is no stigma attached to having a cold, COVID-19, or other debilitating ailments; this should be the case for mental health as well.

Improving mental health in individuals, couples, families, organizations, and communities is not a rapid process. Furthermore, since every interaction is an intervention, progress can be undermined in any conversational episode. It can also be repaired in any conversational episode.

Case Study Example

To illustrate a CC-framed strategy, we offer an example from an ongoing intervention. A Muslim Community Association (MCA) in a midwestern city approached the communication center at a local university with a suggestion that we work together to improve the health of the community, especially mental health. The MCA board was aware of the Communication for Whole Health (CWH) approach and believed it might be helpful to all of their community members. This community includes people from across the economic spectrum, people originally born and raised in the United States, and a large immigrant segment from multiple countries and cultures. The commonality of all members is their faith.

The university interventionists (UI) spent over a year building relationships with the MCA and various community members, and together we decided to focus our efforts on their private K-12 school as a central hub where we can reach teachers, parents, and students from across the population. From this point, the UI began expanding into the community more each day in various ways. At the time of this writing, the process is ongoing and entering its third year. To offer a sense of how the CC approach conceptualizes change in the world, we share a conversation held at the school that juxtaposes the CC perspective with more classical, Newtonian, and foundationalist thinking in a way that illustrates some key differences.

The school has been experiencing high teacher turnover for some time; people are always coming and going, even in the middle of the school year, and it can be stressful for everyone. Several members of the team (which included both UI and community members) were noodling it out and discussing the issue deeply with the staff when someone suggested that the solution was essentially to *attract the right people*; that is, keep looking for teachers and staff with what we might call grit, who can withstand the various issues in the context that lead to teachers leaving. This is a good example of foundationalist thinking, where the world exists as objects—and here, people are also conceptualized and treated as objects—with specific discrete and enduring properties. This is not an uncommon notion, and it has good face appeal—someone with the right personality can ostensibly deal with the situation better than others. But, as Watzlawick et al. suggested in 1967, we are who we are in relation to who we communicate with. The context and the relationships change the nature of the interaction and the individual.

So, instead of looking at people as objects to treat, CC looks at the connections, the relationships, and asks what can change to mitigate mental health issues in individuals. Following Pearce (2007), CC asks a fundamental question: what are we (those in conversation) making here? People are always in the process of making something when interacting with others. This doesn't just mean the type of relationships created between people (such as friendship, partnership, etc.), but how everything in the communication ecology is systemically interlinked with everything else, including our biology. So, instead of trying to attract the right people—not that disposition has no bearing on the matter—the UI suggested that we start with the communication ecology within the school. By investigating how people talk with one another, what kind of vibe or atmosphere is being created, and how people treat each other and deal with stress, the UI could work with teachers and staff to identify patterns and where we might perturb them. The UI agreed to start in the classrooms most directly, putting researchers in place to observe and share with the rest of the team. The UI also established weekly office hours in the teachers' lounge where UI members can listen, give advice if it makes sense, troubleshoot specific issues, etc. A large part of that is, of course, just being present to build relationships and rapport with folks.

Often, interventions framed by classical (Newtonian) onto-epistemological thinking take the form of pre-made training, leading to something one member of the UI team refers to as the BuzzFeed approach: "Do these 7 things and you'll be healthier," "5 proven skills of effective employees," etc. These approaches also tend to focus on messages, announcements, checklists, rules, and training; that is, if we tell people to do these things, they will ostensibly be healthier and such—even if the actions recommended do not necessarily fit the context. This is a key difference from CC and why the UI works so hard to build relationships—because they can learn what people are actually doing and what they need, and work with them to make change, rather than imposing something already made. The UI attempts to maintain the patterns that are working well and tries to make more of that happen. The UI also began to find people open to suggestions because the UI members were no longer strangers.

An overarching goal of this approach is to foster what the UI team refers to as a culture of receptivity. This is more than just being friendly or open-minded; it is not just a social-psychological construct, nor is it simply about avoiding conflict or accepting whatever happens with a smile. Creating a culture of receptivity requires conscious choices that account for the nervous systems of people with one another. By treating every interaction as an intervention that takes place within the context of communicative bioactivity, we set the stage for better whole health—physical, mental, and social—because safety and receptivity *as a nervous system* state foster less stress, which is not only better for our health but allows us to process information more effectively. In other words, whatever messages are deemed important come after building good, safe connections and are likely to be more effective, given that information processing is poor under conditions of nervous system reactivity, as noted earlier.

A large body of scientific evidence demonstrates how to achieve this by regulating ourselves, for example with breathing exercises, and by talking with others in particular ways. This is what the UI team is trying to bring to the school and the community: perturbing the patterns of interaction in the communication ecology, as opposed to *finding* folks who *fit* or have grit. Over time, the UI will help people develop skills to notice and regulate the state of their biology and to choose to speak in conversation with others in ways that invite more receptive states in all conversational participants. By accounting for stress, by recognizing, and engaging their understanding of the bioactivity of communication, people learn to be gentle with themselves, as well as with each other, leading to healthier conversational patterns. In the process, participants deal with new information, messages, and training more effectively than they otherwise would, leading to a sustainable ecology across the community.

When you change the conversation, it literally changes the people—which is different from expecting certain kinds of people, based on personality traits, to change the structure of the conversational milieu. In this way, social construction serves as both a meaning-making and biological process. This process is gradually helping in the transformation of people in the community. Quite simply, changing communication among people can make a difference in the incidence of mental health issues within the community. It is not simple or easy, but it is doable and cost-effective.

Conclusion

At the beginning of the chapter, cases are presented that illustrate the challenges in managing mental health issues within the Muslim community due to stigma and fear. This often provides an additional obstacle in seeking treatment beyond spiritual advice. This can limit access to medication, psychotherapy, and the need for social support that gives rise to healthier feelings.

Many Muslim communities share the spiritual challenges and stigma related to mental health. The focus on the Muslim community serves not only to examine this case but also to highlight the issues that arise from the interconnection of faith and mental health. The pervasiveness of Islamophobia can make matters more difficult, not only from the general issues arising from discrimination but also from the specific problems that occur in a healthcare setting. Healthcare providers must develop the ability to interact with sensitivity to the practices and concerns of those in the Muslim community. In addition, those in the faith community can do much to mitigate the challenges to mental health by developing community-wide interaction patterns that enable good mental health on a routine basis.

Communication Complex is a useful meta-theoretical framework for understanding how patterns of interaction can lead to better individual and community health. Based on a large and growing body of science that recognizes both the meaning-making and biological constructionist communication perspectives, CC helps to guide us to perturb patterns that facilitate poor mental health and in turn learn to interact in ways that lead us to better overall health, including the physical, mental, and social dimensions. In this case, we describe how one Muslim community is engaging this perspective to improve mental health across its population. This ranges from simple practices such as breath awareness that can facilitate better interaction to more conceptual understanding that enables people to see the importance of relationships in the construction of individual mental health. The CC-informed approach is inherently culturally adapted because the members of the community decide the content of the interaction. CC is more concerned with how we talk than what we say. Members of the Muslim community can interact with each other and those outside of their faith in ways that are consistent with both their spiritual and mental health. Most faith communities, including Islam, believe that people should take care of their bodies and minds. CC enables faith communities to find ways of developing healthy patterns of interaction that are consistent with beliefs and spiritual practices.

Creating a space where these ideas can take root is likely to be a gradual process, especially when done so on a community-wide basis. Quick fixes often provide temporary relief at best but can fall short of the sustainable change needed to support better mental health in daily interactions. This approach has the advantages of being cost-effective, biologically safer, and more nuanced than traditional approaches. Mental health can be addressed across groups and done so within the parameters of the faith community. We can address mental health in daily interactions, which in turn can reduce the demands on what is often a limited number of mental health professionals. Faith can and should be a source of sustenance, not a constraint to healthy living. A communication perspective can help faith communities reconcile faith and health.

Note

1 These stories are adapted from (Awaad & Kouser, 2022) and (Faheid, 2021) respectively.

Recommended Readings/Resources

Abbasi, F., & Paulsen, E. (n.d.). *Working with Muslim patients.* American Psychiatric Association. https://www.psychiatry.org/psychiatrists/diversity/education/best-practice-highlights/working-with-muslim-patients#:~:text=Muslims percent20with%20mental%20illness%20may,demarcates%20between%20competency%20and%20incompetency

Khan, A. A. (2022). Encountering Islamophobia in the medical profession. *CMAJ: Canadian Medical Association Journal, 194*(23), E815–E816. https://doi.org/10.1503/cmaj.220455

Parrish-Sprowl, S., Parrish-Sprowl, J., & Alajlouni, S. (2020). Innovations in addressing mental health needs in humanitarian settings: A complexity informed action research case study. *Frontiers in Communication, 5*(601792), 1–15. https://doi.org/10.3389/fcomm.2020.601792

Parrish-Sprowl, J., & Parrish-Sprowl, S. (2023). A case for a quantum informed approach to health communication research. *Frontiers in Communication, 8,* 1232616. https://doi.org/10.3389/fcomm.2023.1232616

Samari, G. (2016). Islamophobia and public health in the United States. *American Journal of Public Health, 106*(11), 1920–1925. https://doi.org/10.2105/AJPH.2016.303374

References

Abbasi, F., & Paulsen, E. (n.d.). *Working with Muslim patients.* American Psychiatric Association. https://www.psychiatry.org/psychiatrists/diversity/education/best

-practice-highlights/working-with-muslim:patients#:~:text=Muslims%20with %20mental%20illness%20may,demarcates%20between%20competency%20and %20incompetency

Abu-Ras, W., Gheith, A., & Cournos, F. (2008). The Imam's role in mental health promotion: A study of 22 mosques in New York City's Muslim community. *Journal of Muslim Mental Health, 3*(2), 155–176. https://doi.org/10.1080/15564900802487576

Afridi, S. (2001). *Muslims in America: Identity, diversity and the challenge of understanding*. Carnegie Corporation of New York. https://www.carnegie.org/publications/muslims-in-america/

Al-Adawi, S., Dorvlo, A. S., Al- Ismaily, S. S. et al. (2002). Perception of and attitude towards mental illness in Oman. *The International Journal of Social Psychiatry, 48*, 305–317. http://dx.doi.org/10.1177/002076402128783334

Allen, J., Balfour, R., Bell, R., & Marmot, M. (2014). Social determinants of mental health. *International Review of Psychiatry, 26*(4), 392–407. http://www.tandfonline.com/doi/abs/10.3109/09540261.2014.928270

Aronson, J., Burgess, D., Phelan, S. M., & Juarez, L. (2013). Unhealthy interactions: The role of stereotype threat in health disparities. *American journal of Public Health, 103*(1), 50–56. https://doi.org/10.2105/AJPH.2012.300828

Attum B., Hafiz S., Malik A., & Shamoon, Z. (2023). *Cultural competence in the care of Muslim patients and their families*. StatPearls Publishing. https://www.ncbi.nlm.nih.gov/books/NBK499933/

Awaad, R., El-Gabalawy, O., Jackson-Shaheed, E., Zia, B., Keshavarzi, H., Mogahed, D., & Altalib, H. (2021). Suicide attempts of Muslims compared with other religious groups in the US. *JAMA Psychiatry, 78*(9), 1041–1044. https://doi.org/10.1001/jamapsychiatry.2021.1813

Awaad, R., & Kouser, T. (2022, January 02). *Muslims face a suicide crisis in America. The taboo of talking about it must end*. USA Today. https://www.usatoday.com/story/opinion/2022/01/02/american-muslims-must-break-taboo-confronting-suicide/9043880002/

Awaad, R., & Kouser, T. (2023). *How faith can get in the way of seeking mental health care*. Washington Post. https://www.washingtonpost.com/wellness/2023/05/26/faith-mental-health-strategies-spiritual-bypassing/

Baasher, T. A. (2001). Islam and mental health. *La Revue de Santé de la Méditerranée orientale, 7*(3), 372–376.

Cooper, B. (2017). *The quantum turn in social science*. Medium. https://medium.com/the-abs-tract-organization/the-quantum-turn-in-social-science-4dad9f92a6a5/

Cozolino, L. (2014). *The neuroscience of human relationships: Attachment and the developing social brain* (2nd ed.). W.W. Norton & Company.

Eisenberg, D., Golberstein, E., Whitlock, J. L., & Downs, M. F. (2013). Social contagion of mental health: Evidence from college roommates. *Health Economics, 22*(8), 965–986. https://doi.org/10.1002/hec.2873

Faheid, D. (August 10, 2021). *American Muslims are 2 times more likely to have attempted suicide than other groups.* NPR. https://www.npr.org/2021/08/10/1025430083/muslims-suicide-attempts-study-religion-american

Geronimus, A., Hicken, M., Keene, D., & Bound, J. (2006). "Weathering" and age patterns of allostatic load scores among Blacks and Whites in the United States. *Research and Practice, 96*(5), 826–833.

Gorman, J. M. (1996). Comorbid depression and anxiety spectrum disorders. *Depression and Anxiety, 4*(4), 160–168. https://doi.org/10.1002/(SICI)1520-6394(1996)4:4<160::AID-DA2>3.0.CO;2-J

Harrington, A. (2019). *Mind fixers: Psychiatry's troubled search for the biology of mental illness.* W. W. Norton & Company.

Hasson, U., Ghazanfar, A. A., Galantucci, B., Garrod, S., & Keysers, C. (2011). Brain-to-brain coupling: A mechanism for creating and sharing a social world. *Trends in Cognitive Sciences, 16*(2), 114–121. https://doi.org/10.1016/j.tics.2011.12.007

Inhorn, M. C., & Fakih, M. H. (2006). Arab Americans, African Americans, and infertility: Barriers to reproduction and medical care. *Disparity in Infertility Treatment, 85*(4), 844–852. https://doi.org/10.1016/j.fertnstert.2005.10.029

Jamil, N. (2020). #depression: Singaporean muslim women navigating mental health on social media. *International Journal of Communication, 14*(2020), 669–696. https://ijoc.org/index.php/ijoc/article/view/11742/2949

Johansen, T. M. (2005). Applying individual psychology to work with clients of the Islamic faith. *Journal of Individual Psychology, 61*(2), 174–184.

Khan, A. A. (2022). Encountering Islamophobia in the medical profession. *CMAJ: Canadian Medical Association Journal, 194*(23), E815–E816. https://doi.org/10.1503/cmaj.220455

Lombrozo, T. (2015). *Belief that mental illness can be contagious contributes to isolation.* NPR. https://www.npr.org/sections/13.7/2015/08/17/432541935/belief-that-mental-illness-can-be-contagious-contributes-to-isolation

Martin, M. B. (2015). Perceived discrimination of Muslims in health care. *Journal of Muslim Mental Health, 9*(2). https://doi.org/10.3998/jmmh.10381607.0009.203

Mental Health America (n.d.). *Overview of mental health issues in Arab/Middle Eastern/Muslim/South Asian communities.* https://mhanational.org/issues/overview-mental-health-issues-arabmiddle-easternmuslimsouth-asian-communities

Parrish-Sprowl, J. (2014a). Communication complex. In T. L. Thompson (Ed.), *Encyclopedia of health communication* (Vol. 3, pp. 211–213). SAGE. http://dx.doi.org/10.4135/9781483346427.n78

Parrish-Sprowl, J., & Parrish-Sprowl, S. (2014b). Suggestions for a heuristic turn in the conversation on posttraumatic growth. *Transformative Learning Conference Proceedings* (787–792), Columbia University, New York.

Parrish-Sprowl, S., Parrish-Sprowl, J., & Alajlouni, S. (2020). Innovations in addressing mental health needs in humanitarian settings: A complexity informed action research case study. *Frontiers in Communication, 5*(601792), 1–15. https://doi.org/10.3389/fcomm.2020.601792

Parrish-Sprowl, J., & Parrish-Sprowl, S. (2023). A case for a quantum informed approach to health communication research. *Frontiers in Communication, 8*(1232616). https://doi.org/10.3389/fcomm.2023.1232616

Pearce, W. B., & Cronen, V. E. (1980). *Communication, action, and meaning: The creation of social realities*. Praeger.

Pearce, W. B. (1989). *Communication and the human condition*. Southern Illinois University.

Pearce, W. B. (2007). *Making social worlds: A communication perspective*. Blackwell publishing.

Porges, S. (2017). *The pocket guide to polyvagal theory: The transformative power of feeling safe*. W. W. Norton & Company.

Porges, S. (2021). *Polyvagal safety: Attachment, communication and self-regulation*. WW Norton.

Rascon, N. A. (2022). A communication complex approach to Autism awareness training within first response systems in Indiana. *Frontiers in Communication, 7*(610012). https://doi.org/10.3389/fcomm.2022.610012

Rovelli, C. (2021). *Helgoland: Making sense of the quantum revolution*. Riverhead Books

Ruesch, J., & Bateson, G. (1951). *Communication: The social matrix of psychiatry*. W.W. Norton & Company.

Sabry, W. M., & Vohra, A. (2013). Role of Islam in the management of psychiatric disorders. *Indian Journal of Psychiatry, 55*(Suppl 2), S205–S214. https://doi.org/10.4103/0019–5545.105534

Samari, G. (2016). Islamophobia and public health in the United States. *American Journal of Public Health, 106*(11), 1920–1925. https://doi.org/10.2105/AJPH.2016.303374

Siegel, D. (2020). The Developing Mind: How Relationships and the Brain Interact to Shape Who We Are, 3rd Edn. New York, NY: Guilford.

Siegel, D. (2010). *The developing mind: How relationships and the brain interact to shape who we are* (2nd ed.). The Guilford Press.

Tackett, J., Young, H. J., Putman, S., Wiener, C., Deruggiero, K., & Bayram, J. (2018). Barriers to healthcare among Muslim women: A narrative review of the literature. *Women's Studies International Forum, 69*, 190–194. https://doi.org/10.1016/j.wsif.2018.02.009

Vogel, S., & Schwabe, L. (2016). Learning and memory under stress: Implications for the classroom. *NPJ Sci Learn, 1*, 16011. https://doi.org/10.1038/npjscilearn.2016.11

Wainberg, M. L., Helpman, L., Duarte, C. S., Vermund, S. H., Mootz, J. J., Gouveia, L., Oquendo, M. A., McKinnon, K., & Cournos, F. (2018). Curtailing the communicability of psychiatric disorders. *The Lancet Psychiatry, 5*(11), 940–944. https://doi.org/10.1016/S2215-0366(18)30342-0

Watzlawick, P., Beavin, J. H., & Jackson, D. D. (1967). *Pragmatics of human communication: A study of interactional patterns, pathologies, and paradoxes*. W. W. Norton & Company.

Weatherhead, S., & Daiches, A. (2010). Muslim views on mental health and psychotherapy. *Psychology and Psychotherapy: Theory, Research and Practice*, *83*(1), 75–89. https://doi.org/10.1348/147608309X467807

Weiner, S. (August, 2022). *A growing psychiatrist shortage and an enormous demand for mental health services*. Association of American Medical Colleges. https://www.aamc.org/news/growing-psychiatrist-shortage-enormous-demand-mental-health-services

Yapko, M. (2009). *Depression is contagious: How the most common mood disorder is spreading around the world and how to stop it*. Atria Books. Kindle Edition.

Yapko, M. (2016). The *keys to unlocking depression*. Yapko publications.

Zohar, D. (2022). *Zero distance: Management in the quantum age*. Palgrave Macmillan.

10

Mental Health Communication Strategies for Individuals with Disabilities

Applying a Socio-Ecological Framework

Jaehyun Kim

An estimated 1.3 billion people, comprising 16 percent of the global population, experience significant disabilities today (World Health Organization, 2023a). This number continues to rise due to increases in noncommunicable diseases and life expectancy. The United States reflects a similar trend in disability prevalence, with approximately 20 percent of the population, nearly 57 million people, reporting disabilities. The most common types of disabilities among US citizens are associated with physical challenges, including difficulty walking or using stairs. About two-thirds (66%) of adults with a disability or health condition reported a higher level of mental distress in comparison to the 34 percent of those without a disability (Pew Research Center, 2023). During the COVID-19 pandemic, social isolation, disrupted daily routines, and reduced access to health services have significantly impacted the mental health of people with disabilities (Centers for Disease Control and Prevention, 2023). The development of effective health communication strategies is essential for addressing the multifaceted environmental, social, and psychological factors that influence behavior and health. These strategies, by effectively conveying health information and promoting behavior change, have the potential to improve health outcomes, reduce health disparities, and enhance the overall well-being of individuals living with disabilities.

Physical Disabilities

Definition

The World Health Organization (WHO) (1976) has defined physical disability as "an existing difficulty in performing one or more activities which, in accordance with a person's age, sex, and normative social role, are generally accepted as essential components of daily living, such as self-care, social relations, and economic activity." This definition describes a condition where the ability to perform social and work roles is diminished, which in turn affects personal fulfillment and satisfaction.

Types of Physical Disability

This section introduces the three most common physical disabilities worldwide: arthritis, spinal cord injuries, and sensory impairments.

Arthritis

Arthritis refers to inflammation of the joints in individuals across all age groups. In 2019, approximately 528 million people worldwide were living with osteoarthritis, marking a 113 percent increase since 1990 (WHO, 2023b). About 73 percent of individuals living with osteoarthritis are older than 55 years, with females comprising 60 percent of cases. The knee has the highest prevalence, affecting 365 million people, followed by the hip and the hand (Long et al., 2022). In the same year, 18 million people worldwide were living with rheumatoid arthritis (WHO, 2023c). Approximately 70 percent of those with rheumatoid arthritis are women, and 55 percent are older than fifty-five years (WHO, 2023c). Among them, 13 million experience severity levels (moderate or severe) that could benefit from rehabilitation (Cieza et al., 2020). These statistics highlight that arthritis is not solely an inevitable consequence of aging.

The most prevalent type of arthritis is osteoarthritis, which manifests as swelling in joints such as the hands, knees, hips, feet, and ankles, aggravated by weight-bearing or prolonged standing. Rheumatoid arthritis, on the other hand, is a chronic and progressive condition characterized by periods of remission and flare-ups, resulting in deteriorating symptoms affecting not only the joints but also organs and tissues like the heart and muscles. With over 100 variants of the disease, symptoms include pain, swelling, stiffness, discoloration, reduced mobility, limited range of motion, discomfort, and loss of work productivity (Bullock & Mahon, 2000).

Spinal Cord Injury (SCI)

The term "spinal cord injury" refers to damage to the spinal cord resulting from various causes such as trauma (e.g., car accidents) or diseases like cancer. According to a systematic review covering studies from 2000 to 2016, the global incidence of SCI is approximately 10.5 cases per 100,000 people, leading to an estimated 768,473 new cases each year (Kumar et al., 2018). SCI can be categorized based on its severity (complete or incomplete) and the level at which the injury occurs (quadriplegia or paraplegia), and the symptoms experienced by individuals with SCI vary depending on these factors.

According to the American Spinal Cord Injury Association (ASIA), a lesion is classified as complete when a total loss of voluntary and sensory motor activity occurs in the S4–S5 segment. Conversely, if there is any preservation of motor activity or sensory function in the sacral segment S4–S5, the lesion is considered incomplete. In terms of the level of injury occurrence, quadriplegia is defined as the loss of function in the trunk, upper limbs, and lower limbs, while paraplegia is characterized by the loss of function in the trunk and lower limbs (Roberts et al., 2017). Regardless of the cause and classification, SCI can significantly affect both physical and mental health, as well as overall quality of life.

Sensory Impairment

Globally, in 2020, there were 1.1 billion people living with vision loss, comprising 43 million individuals who were blind, 295 million with moderate to severe visual impairment (VI), 258 million with mild VI, and 510 million with near vision issues (Hashemi et al., 2024; WHO, 2021). These numbers are expected to rise significantly in the future due to population aging and shifts in lifestyle. According to the International Classification of Diseases, 9th Revision, Clinical Modification (ICD-9-CM), "low vision" is defined as visual acuity ranging from 20/70 to 20/400, with optimal correction, or a visual field of 20° or less. "Blindness" is characterized by visual acuity worse than 20/400, with the best possible correction, or a visual field of 10° or less.

According to the WHO, an individual who cannot hear as well as someone with normal hearing—defined as hearing thresholds of 20 dB or better in both ears—is considered to have hearing loss. This condition can manifest as mild, moderate, severe, or profound and may affect one or both ears, resulting in difficulties in hearing conversational speech or loud sounds. Currently, over 5 percent of the global population, totaling 430 million individuals (including 34 million children), require rehabilitation to address their disabling hearing loss. Projections suggest that by 2050, the number of people with disabling hearing loss will surpass 700 million, affecting approximately 1 in every 10 individuals.

Physical Disability and Mental Health

Mental well-being is an essential aspect of overall health, "defined as a state of mental well-being that enables people to cope with the stresses of life, realize their abilities, learn well and work well, and contribute to their community" (WHO, 2022). Therefore, mental health extends beyond the mere absence of mental disorders or impairments and serves as a cornerstone for enhancing the overall quality of life. The prevalence of mental illness is a growing concern in global public health. According to WHO (2013), for example, depression alone accounts for 4.3 percent of the worldwide disease burden and is widely recognized as one of the most significant single causes of disability worldwide.

Fundamentally, mental and physical health are closely linked. It is well-documented that individuals with chronic physical conditions are more likely to be at risk of developing poor mental health. Prior studies have reported that adults with disabilities report experiencing more mental distress than those without disabilities. For example, in 2018, an estimated 17.4 million adults with disabilities reported experiencing mental distress, or mentally unhealthy status, for at least 14 days within the past 30 days (Cree et al., 2020). This figure is approximately five times higher than that for individuals without disabilities.

Scott et al. (2007) investigated the correlation between ten chronic physical conditions and depressive and anxiety disorders, utilizing data from eighteen surveys in the World Mental Health Surveys. Despite significant diversity across the seventeen surveyed countries in demographics, socioeconomic status, and health patterns, the combined international results consistently reveal that depressive and anxiety disorders are independently and similarly linked to various chronic physical conditions. This study indicated that heart disease and chronic pain conditions exhibit the strongest associations with depressive and anxiety disorders, aligning with prior research identifying the robust connections between these physical conditions and major depressive disorder (Evans et al., 2005).

Despite the common belief that physical disability complicates the attainment and preservation of mental well-being, there has not been a comprehensive work summarizing specific evidence on the correlation between physical disability and mental distress among individuals with physical disabilities. To address this gap, the following section outlines general trends in the mental health of individuals with physical disabilities.

Mental Health Among People with Arthritis

Arthritis is a leading classification among long-lasting musculoskeletal and joint conditions. There has been a growing focus on the mental well-being of arthritis patients, particularly regarding depression and anxiety. In particular, mental health conditions often coincide with osteoarthritis (OA) and rheumatoid arthritis (RA). Stang et al. (2006) utilized data from the National Comorbidity Survey Replication, a nationally representative household survey conducted between 2001 and 2003, with 9,282 respondents aged eighteen and older. Among these respondents, 27.3 percent reported arthritis, and of those, 80.9 percent also reported at least one additional physical or mental disorder. The authors emphasized that "Comorbidity is the rule rather than the exception among people with arthritis" (Stang et al., 2006, p. 152).

An examination of thirty-eight studies investigating anxiety and depression in OA patients revealed a high prevalence of anxiety and/or depression among this group (Sharmar et al., 2016). In particular, individuals diagnosed with OA and these accompanying mental health issues reported higher pain levels, increased hospital visits, and greater medication use. That is, anxiety and depression are interconnected with pain and physical limitation, which are the two key symptoms of OA. Additionally, the authors suggested that these psychological comorbidities can substantially impair patients' quality of life. They emphasized the importance of educating physicians about the timely identification of psychosocial factors such as anxiety and depression among OA patients during early rehabilitation treatment, as this can enhance their quality of life. Matcham et al. (2013) found that 17 percent of people with RA diagnoses have depressive symptoms in seventy-two reviewed studies with a total of 13,189 patients; this prevalence estimate is significantly greater than those observed in the general population.

Overall, previous research suggests that, compared to the general population, those with OA and RA frequently have higher levels of depression and anxiety. This suggests that when treating individuals with OA, physicians and other caregivers should consider offering a holistic, individualized management approach that integrates physical examinations with mental state assessments and psychiatric evaluations.

Mental Health Among Individuals with Spinal Cord Injury

Spinal cord injury (SCI) occurs when the spinal cord is damaged, often due to traumatic injury, leading to partial or complete loss of motor and/or sensory function below the level of injury (Hearn et al., 2020). Persons with SCI are at a heightened risk of developing secondary health complications, including cardiovascular disease, insulin resistance, diabetes mellitus, and obesity (Williams, 2015). In addition to an increased risk of physical health complications, individuals with SCI often experience mental disorders. A recent meta-analysis study indicated that the prevalence of depression after SCI is substantially higher than that in the general medical population (Boldt et al., 2014). Moreover, studies across various European, American, and Asian countries have consistently shown that individuals with SCI tend to have lower mental health and quality of life compared to the general population (Post et al., 2012; Williams, 2015). More recently, Peterson et al. (2020) found that adults with SCIs had a higher incidence of psychogenic pain (1.0% vs 0.2%), anxiety disorders (19.3% vs 14.1%), depressive disorders (29.3% vs 9.3%), alcohol dependence (2.4% vs 1.0%), drug dependence (2.3% vs 0.8%), and insomnia (10.9% vs 7.2%), as compared with adults without SCIs.

Previous studies have identified negative mental health outcomes that individuals with SCI might experience, including fear of pain, anxiety, depression, post-traumatic stress disorder, low life satisfaction, and diminished quality of life. Such psychological comorbidity has been linked to poorer self-reported health, reduced physical function, and an increased risk of early mortality (Krause et al., 2008). Some studies have indicated a higher prevalence of psychological morbidity and suicide among individuals with SCI (Craig et al., 2009). The suicide mortality rate among individuals with SCI is nearly five times higher than that of the general population (Krause, 1998).

Previous research has provided evidence that the presence and severity of negative psychological outcomes are influenced by various individual and environmental factors. For instance, positive psychological and social resources, such as self-efficacy, resilience, and social support, play a significant role in promoting health and can potentially alleviate adverse effects. Despite sufficient evidence of negative mental health outcomes caused by SCI, such as depression and anxiety, relatively fewer studies have examined positive/protective or negative factors that might affect mental health among individuals with SCI.

Mental Health Among Individuals with Sensory Impairments

About 43.2 million people were blind in 2020, while 295.3 million had moderate to severe visual impairment and 257.3 million had mild (Pardhan et al., 2021). Age-related vision and hearing problems are prevalent, especially in Western societies. According to Goman and Lin (2016), approximately 30 million persons in the United States who are 60 years of age or older suffer from bilateral hearing impairment. The prevalence of hearing loss increases twofold with each decade of life, with approximately two-thirds of older adults experiencing hearing impairment by the age of 70 (Lin et al., 2011).

Hearing impairment has been linked to various mental health issues, including heightened feelings of loneliness (Sung et al., 2016), depression (Garnefski & Kraaij, 2012; Shin & Hwang, 2017), anxiety (Garnefski et al., 2012; Monzani et al., 2008), mental distress (Kobayashi et al., 2015), increased suicide risk (Kim, Kwak, & Kim, 2015; Shin et al., 2017), and decreased quality of life (Dalton et al., 2003; Sano et al., 2013). Blindness affects 0.10 percent of the US population aged eighteen to thirty-nine years and 2.41 percent of those aged sixty-five years and older (Wittenborn & Rein, 2013), with a substantial rise to 7 percent in individuals older than eighty years. Vision impairment (excluding blindness) increases from 1.1 percent in ages sixty-five to sixty-nine years to 16.7 percent in those aged eighty years and older (Congdon et al., 2004). Vision loss has been associated with depression (Carrière et al., 2013; Eramudugolla et al., 2013), symptoms of anxiety (Y. Li et al., 2011), suicide (Kim et al., 2015), and poor self-perceived health (Harada et al., 2008).

Dual sensory impairment (DSI) refers to the simultaneous loss of vision and hearing (Diehl, 1998). Around 20 percent of US adults aged seventy and above reported experiencing both hearing and vision impairments (Brennan et al., 2006). DSI is linked to lower self-rated health (Crews & Campbell, 2004), decreased health-related quality of life (Khil et al., 2015), suicidal thoughts (Kim et al., 2015), and reduced social interaction, potentially leading to feelings of loneliness (Gopinath et al., 2012). Moreover, DSI increased the risk of depression by 20 percent among older adults (Guthrie et al., 2016). These findings highlight the importance of screening older adults with sensory impairments for depression and anxiety in identifying more effective treatment opportunities to improve overall health and well- being (Simning et al., 2019).

Although there are likely multiple pathways linking physical disability to the onset of mental health symptoms, the connection has not been thoroughly explored. Therefore, the following section outlines various factors influencing the mental health of individuals with physical disabilities from a social-ecological perspective.

Socio-Ecological Factors of Mental Health Among People with Disabilities

The socio-ecological model incorporates a wide range of personal and environmental influences on individuals' health-promoting behavior and health, rather than focusing solely on their demographic or psychological aspects. The term "ecology" originated from biological science, emphasizing the interrelationships of organisms (e.g., plants and animals) with their biological and physical environments (Sallis et al., 2015). In the fields of behavioral sciences and public health, ecological models have particularly focused on socio cultural and physical environments and their effects on human health behaviors and outcomes (Stokols, 1992). These models specifically consider a wide array of human environments surrounding individuals, such as social networks, neighborhoods, communities, organizations, and policies, to better understand health-related behaviors and health. Therefore, this socio-ecological approach will help better understand the relationships between individual and environmental factors and mental health among individuals with physical disabilities.

Disabilities impact individuals at various levels—personal, social, economic, societal/structural, cultural, and political (Noonan et al., 2004; Yorkston et al., 2003). Therefore, stressors encountered by individuals with physical disabilities often tend to have a more complex and varied nature, considerably affecting one's health, well-being, and quality of life (Janssen, Schuengel, & Stolk, 2002). Iwasaki and Mactavish (2005) explored the nature of stress encountered by individuals with disabilities in their daily lives. In the proposed conceptual model, eight key stressors that could lead to social exclusion among individuals with disabilities were identified. These stressors are further subdivided into individual-level stressors and systemic/environmental-level stressors. Four individual-level stressors comprise (1) disability, involving increased demands in daily living and the complexities of disability and aging, (2) physical and mental health, (3) interpersonal relationships, and (4) the inability to meet expectations, which may lead to feelings of shame, low self-esteem, and dependency. Four systemic/environmental stressors include (1) exclusionary social systems/structures (e.g., negative public attitudes and behaviors), (2) physical accessibility, (3) employment accessibility (e.g., labor market exclusion), and (4) economic marginality (e.g., poor housing).

In summary, evidence suggests that the mental well-being of individuals with disabilities is influenced by multiple domains, including biological, social, psychological, and environmental factors, and their interplay. Therefore, it is imperative to explore potential factors influencing various mental health outcomes (e.g., depression, anxiety, life satisfaction, and quality of life) among individuals with diverse physical disabling conditions (e.g., arthritis, spinal cord injury, and sensory impairment). In this regard, the following sections provide a summary of various personal and environmental factors that could impact mental health outcomes among people with physical disabilities. This comprehensive approach to mental health and its disorders will provide practical insights for health communication strategies to promote mental well-being among individuals with physical disabilities across individual, social, community, and policy levels.

Personal Predictors of Mental Distress

Demographic Factors

1. *Arthritis:* Previous studies have provided evidence that demographic factors are associated with mental health among people with arthritis. For example, van't Land et al. (2010) found that the incidence of any psychiatric disorder was significantly higher among younger individuals (<45 years) with arthritis compared to their peers without arthritis. Several

studies have also found that depression among patients with rheumatoid arthritis is significantly higher in females, homemakers, and individuals with a low education level (Enginar & Nur, 2023; Khan et al., 2021). Additionally, Enginar et al. (2023) reported that anxiety was significantly higher in blue-collar workers with rheumatoid arthritis compared to retired patients. A personal characteristic, pre-existing arthritis, was found to increase the likelihood of developing any mood disorder (van't Land et al., 2010).

2. *Spinal Cord Injury:* For individuals with spinal cord injury (SCI), studies also found that some demographic factors significantly influence the mental health outcomes of individuals with SCI. For example, female patients with SCI, particularly those with tetraplegia rather than paraplegia, tended to report higher levels of depressed mood (Adhikari et al., 2020). SCI Patients who had lower educational levels and longer injury durations tended to report higher levels of depressed mood (Adhikari et al., 2020).
3. *Sensory Impairments:* Prior research has indicated that people with sensory impairments who have certain demographic characteristics are more vulnerable to mental disorders. Pardhan et al. (2021) found that the prevalence of depression and anxiety was more than twice as high in women with sensory impairments compared to men with those conditions. Additionally, those with dual sensory impairment (hearing and vision) were more likely to report higher levels of depression and anxiety compared to single sensory impairment (Pardhan et al., 2021). Shen et al. (2017) found that the likelihood of developing depressive symptoms generally decreases with age among individuals with sensory impairments, while women with sensory disabilities have a higher incidence of depression compared to men. The study also showed that individuals with more severe sensory disabilities have a higher incidence of depression, with the highest rates among those with severe disabilities. Additionally, people with sensory impairments and lower socioeconomic status face an elevated risk of depression due to limited access to resources, healthcare, and social support.

Psychosocial Factors

Arthritis: Several psychosocial factors have been identified as predictors of mental disorders among people with arthritis. For example, higher levels of relatedness and autonomy significantly predicted lower depression among people with RA (Ryan & McGuire, 2016). The unpredictability of disease progression, persistent pain, and perceived mobility restrictions contribute to an increased risk of clinically severe emotional states, such as anxiety (Treharne et al., 2005). The perceived severity of RA was associated with increased levels of mental distress (Euesden et al., 2017).

Spinal Cord Injury: For individuals with SCI, higher self-efficacy and self-esteem correlate with improved mental health and overall quality of life (Peter et al., 2012). Similarly, a systematic review revealed that stronger social support, both in terms of quantity (e.g., network size and availability of support sources) and quality (e.g., perceived support resources), is associated with enhanced mental well-being and overall quality of life (Müller et al., 2012). Those with SCI who demonstrate greater acceptance of their disability consistently report higher quality of life, life satisfaction, well-being, and better mental health, along with lower levels of depression and anxiety (Aaby et al., 2020). Reduced resilience (i.e., the ability to adapt and rebound in the face of challenges) and concerns about medical rationing and financial issues predict increased anxiety symptoms among people with SCI (Mikolajczyk et al., 2021).

Sensory Impairments: Among individuals residing in nursing homes, hearing loss and visual impairment were associated with reduced social engagement and decreased participation in social activities, particularly among those with more severe impairment levels (Resnick et al., 1997). The social stigma associated with both hearing loss and visual impairment likely contributes to the limitations in social participation experienced by individuals with dual sensory loss (Munoz-Baell & Ruiz, 2000). Frequent communication breakdowns led to reduced socialization, whereas staying socially connected was related to enhancing their quality of life among older adults with sensory loss (Heine & Browning, 2004).

Environmental Predictors of Mental Distress

Arthritis: Several social and physical environmental factors are associated with mental health among arthritis patients. For example, individuals with RA exhibit significantly lower levels of social support compared to age- and sex-matched healthy controls (Khan et al., 2021). Similarly, reduced participation in social activities and community engagement is linked to mental distress in arthritis populations (Meek et al., 2018). Social isolation stemming from RA progression contributes to depressed mood (Fitzpatrick et al., 1991), while a lack of emotional support from significant others predicts poorer psychosocial adjustment (Smith & Wallston, 1992). Regarding physical environmental predictors, access to healthcare services has been identified as influencing mental health outcomes in arthritis populations (Loyola-Sanchez et al., 2016).

Spinal Cord Injury: For individuals with SCI, perceived social isolation predicted increased depressive symptoms (Mikolajczyk et al., 2021). Higher proportions of greenspace in communities are associated with better self-rated health (Botticello et al., 2015). Architectural features such as ramps, elevators, and accessible restrooms, along with transportation options and barriers like public transit and accessible vehicles, can influence the psychological well-being and mobility of users of mobility assistive devices (Kapsalis et al., 2024).

Sensory Impairments: For people with sensory impairments, communication difficulties resulting from sensory impairments can restrict engagement in social activities, diminish satisfaction in fulfilling social roles, and exacerbate challenges in maintaining social connections (Broese van Groenou et al., 2013). Moreover, reduced participation in social activities and networks could worsen psychological health issues among individuals with sensory impairments (Vink et al., 2008). Sufficient social support networks are identified as protective factors against depressive symptoms in this population. Conversely, social isolation and restricted social networks correlate with an elevated risk of depression (Papadopoulos et al., 2014). Physical and environmental barriers, such as inaccessible transportation and lack of access to technological aids, can lead to social exclusion and limit participation in social activities (Jaiswal et al., 2020), potentially increasing the risk of depression (Desrosiers et al., 2009).

Strategic Mental Health Communication for People with Disabilities: A Socio-Ecological Framework

This chapter outlined general trends in the mental health of individuals with physical disabilities and provided a summary of personal and environmental factors that could impact their mental health. Building upon the social-ecological framework discussed earlier, the following section offers practical suggestions and implications on how to design and develop strategies to enhance the mental health of individuals with physical disabilities. It is suggested that interventions for people with physical disabilities should address the holistic well-being of individuals, encompassing physical, mental, and social aspects. By collectively considering individual needs and their social and physical environment, health interventions could be more effective in improving health outcomes and overall quality of life for people with physical disabilities.

From a broader viewpoint, policy considerations are also pivotal in ensuring fair access to healthcare services. Policies should emphasize inclusive practices that address the unique needs of individuals with physical disabilities, including provisions for accessible facilities, transportation, and communication. The following section outlines specific recommendations for health communication strategies aimed at promoting the mental health of individuals with physical disabilities across individual, social, community, and policy levels.

1. Health Communication Strategies: *Individual and Social Domains*
   - Expressive Therapy: Recreation therapists can provide patients with diverse options for creative engagement, including expressive art therapy, journaling, music therapy, and dance/movement therapy. These recreational activities serve as valuable means of mental health communication, allowing individuals with physical disabilities to express their emotions, experiences, and inner thoughts nonverbally, thereby alleviating stress and enhancing mental well-being.
   - Pain Management Interventions: Pain is a common issue among individuals with physical disabilities. Non-pharmacological interventions for pain management, such as recreation therapy programs and biofeedback therapy, may include a range of physical modalities and psychosocial approaches, which can contribute to mental health.
   - Physical and Movement Interventions: Generally, physical exercise has been identified as an effective tool for mental health promotion and quality of life in individuals with any types of physical disabilities addressed in this chapter. For example, strength training is a strategy to promote physical health, mental health, and quality of life, as it presents positive results in different aspects, such as improving muscle strength and functional capacity, reducing symptoms of anxiety and depression, and increasing the general indicators of quality of life in people with SCI (Rodrigues et al., 2020). For individuals with sensory impairments, more specific intervention considerations

will be necessary, particularly concerning their communication and social skills, as well as the development of effective orientation (i.e., the ability to know location in various settings) and mobility skills (i.e., the ability to travel safely and independently in different environmental settings).

- Mindfulness-based Interventions: Incorporating mindfulness components into interventions is essential for addressing emotional well-being and mental health challenges. Mindfulness interventions, such as biofeedback, meditation, progressive muscle relaxation exercises, yoga, and Tai Chi, have been found to be effective in improving pain management and reducing depression and anxiety among people with physical disabilities.
- Peer Support Programs: Health professionals can provide peer support programs tailored to individuals with physical disabilities, where they can connect with others facing similar challenges and receive emotional support. "Peer support interventions" is an umbrella term used to describe a range of ancillary services provided by people with disabilities to people with disabilities, including peer mentoring, peer health education, and peer health navigation. A growing body of research has provided evidence that peer support interventions are effective in providing people with disabilities with informal, social, and emotional support (Magasi & Papadimitriou, 2021). Health professionals can offer peer support programs tailored to individuals with physical disabilities, enabling them to connect with others confronting similar challenges and receive emotional support. The qualitative findings from this review study emphasized various positive experiences, including increased empathy, enriched understanding of the individual's chronic condition, enhanced access to information, and a heightened sense of empowerment. Therefore, fostering communication channels between individuals through interventions will benefit the mental health of people with physical disabilities.

2. Health Communication Strategies: *Community and Policy Domains*
   - Public Awareness Campaigns: All discussions presented in this chapter underscore the necessity of allocating resources to community-based support programs that provide social activities, recreational opportunities, and counseling services tailored to the needs of

individuals with physical disabilities. From a health communication perspective, clear and accessible communication channels are essential for disseminating important health information to people with physical disabilities with different characteristics within a community. Effective community health campaigns, for example, may include utilizing various mediums, such as social media, traditional media, and community events, to meet the different needs of different demographic groups. For example, the use of social media platforms for mental health communication is growing. People exchange personal accounts, links, and advice about how to deal with mental health issues. Through online forums, live chats, and hashtags, people can connect, provide support, and spread awareness about mental health concerns globally.

- Community Integration Services: For individuals with physical disabilities, who often experience social isolation, facilitating interventions that promote community integration and social participation is essential. This may involve organizing individual and/or group outings, providing family training outings, and assisting this population in transferring various skills learned in hospital or rehabilitation settings to real-world situations (Porter, 2015). Mock et al. (2010) suggested that community integration services can increase the sense of belonging compared to staying in a hospital or institution, which can lead to better mental health among people with RA. In many cases, services include home visits and field trips into the community, enabling health professionals to assess and address patients' or clients' real-world functioning. During these services, healthcare professionals should recognize obstacles to reintegration and help individuals master the skills necessary for home-based daily life and community involvement. Such efforts toward community integration will help promote mental health among individuals with physical disabilities.
- Accessibility of Mental Health Services: Given the significant comorbidity between chronic physical conditions and mental disorders among individuals with physical disabilities, enacting policies that ensure more accessible mental health services for this population is crucial. Specific efforts may include creating policies aimed at enhancing the physical accessibility of mental health facilities

and accommodating the communication and mobility needs of individuals with physical disabilities, particularly those with sensory impairments.

- Integrated Care: As indicated earlier, given the notable comorbidity between chronic physical conditions and mental disorders, it is essential to establish policies that advocate for integrated care models, where mental health services are integrated into primary care settings or rehabilitation programs for individuals with physical disabilities. Additionally, it is important to take a person-centered approach, understanding the unique needs, preferences, and abilities of each individual. Tailoring interventions to accommodate diverse disabilities, including mental or cognitive challenges, along with physical disabilities, will ensure effectiveness and promote empowerment. Thus, collaboration among multidisciplinary teams, including medical professionals, therapists, social workers, and community support services, is essential for providing comprehensive care. This approach will allow for a holistic assessment of the diverse needs of individuals with physical disabilities.
- Engaging the Community in Policy Development: Engaging community members in the development and implementation of health policies is crucial for promoting transparency, trust, and community support. By utilizing participatory communication methods to involve stakeholders, healthcare practitioners, and policymakers can gather valuable insights into community needs and preferences, ultimately leading to the creation of more relevant and impactful health policies.
- Research and Data Collection: Further investment in research initiatives is necessary to enhance our understanding of the mental health needs and experiences of individuals with physical disabilities. Increased evidence will facilitate the development of more targeted policies and interventions.

Recommended Readings/Resources

American Foundation for the Blind. (n.d.). Retrieved from https://www.afb.org
American Spinal Injury Association. (n.d.). Retrieved from https://asia-spinalinjury.org

Arthritis Foundation. (n.d.). Retrieved from https://www.arthritis.org
Communication Services for the Deaf, Inc. (n.d.). Retrieved from https://csd.org
National Institutes of Health. (n.d.). Retrieved from https://www.nih.gov

References

Aaby, A., Ravn, S. L., Kasch, H., & Andersen, T. E. (2020). The associations of acceptance with quality of life and mental health following spinal cord injury: A systematic review. *Spinal Cord*, *58*(2), 130–148.

Adhikari, S. P., Gurung, G., Khadka, B., & Rana, C. (2020). Factors influencing depression in individuals with traumatic spinal cord injury and caregivers' perceived burden in a low-income country: A cross-sectional study. *Spinal Cord*, *58*(10), 1112–1118.

Boldt, I., Eriks-Hoogland, I., Brinkhof, M. W., de Bie, R., Joggi, D., & Von Elm, E. (2014). Non-pharmacological interventions for chronic pain in people with spinal cord injury. *Cochrane Database of Systematic Reviews*, 11, CD009177

Botticello, A. L., Rohrbach, T., & Cobbold, N. (2015). Differences in the community built environment influence poor perceived health among persons with spinal cord injury. *Archives of Physical Medicine and Rehabilitation*, *96*(9), 1583–1590.

Brennan, M., Su, Y. P., & Horowitz, A. (2006). Longitudinal associations between dual sensory impairment and everyday competence among older adults. *Journal of Rehabilitation Research & Development*, *43*(6), 777–792.

Broese van Groenou, M., Hoogendijk, E. O., & Van Tilburg, T. G. (2013). Continued and new personal relationships in later life: Differential effects of health. *Journal of Aging and Health*, *25*(2), 274–295.

Bullock, C. C., & Mahon, M. J. (2000). *Introduction to recreation services for people with disabilities: A person-centered approach.* Sagamore Publishing.

Carrière, I., Delcourt, C., Daien, V., Pérès, K., Féart, C., Berr, C., . . . & Ritchie, K. (2013). A prospective study of the bi-directional association between vision loss and depression in the elderly. *Journal of Affective Disorders*, *151*(1), 164–170.

Centers for Disease Control and Prevention. (2023). *The mental health of people with disabilities.* https://www.cdc.gov/ncbddd/disabilityandhealth/features/mental-health -for- all.html

Cieza, A., Causey, K., Kamenov, K., Hanson, S. W., Chatterji, S., & Vos, T. (2020). Global estimates of the need for rehabilitation based on the global burden of disease study 2019: A systematic analysis for the Global Burden of Disease Study 2019. *The Lancet*, *396*(10267), 2006–2017.

Congdon, N., O'Colmain, B., Klaver, C. C., Klein, R., Muñoz, B., Friedman, D. S., ... & Mitchell, P. (2004). Causes and prevalence of visual impairment among adults in the United States. *Archives of Ophthalmology (Chicago, Ill.: 1960)*, *122*(4), 477–485.

Craig, A., Tran, Y., & Middleton, J. (2009). Psychological morbidity and spinal cord injury: A systematic review. *Spinal Cord, 47*(2), 108–114.

Cree, R. A. (2020). Frequent mental distress among adults, by disability status, disability type, and selected characteristics—United States, 2018. *MMWR. Morbidity and mortality weekly report, 69.*

Crews, J. E., & Campbell, V. A. (2004). Vision impairment and hearing loss among community-dwelling older Americans: Implications for health and functioning. *American Journal of Public Health, 94*(5), 823–829.

Dalton, D. S., Cruickshanks, K. J., Klein, B. E., Klein, R., Wiley, T. L., & Nondahl, D. M. (2003). The impact of hearing loss on quality of life in older adults. *The Gerontologist, 43*(5), 661–668.

Desrosiers, J., Wanet-Defalque, M. C., Témisjian, K., Gresset, J., Dubois, M. F., Renaud, J., ... & Overbury, O. (2009). Participation in daily activities and social roles of older adults with visual impairment. *Disability and Rehabilitation, 31*(15), 1227–1234.

Diehl, M. (1998). Everyday competence in later life: Current status and future directions. *The Gerontologist, 38*(4), 422–433.

Enginar, A. U., & Nur, H. (2023). The frequency and factors affecting anxiety and depression in patients with rheumatoid arthritis. *Reumatologia, 61*(1), 30.

Eramudugolla, R., Wood, J., & Anstey, K. J. (2013). Co-morbidity of depression and anxiety in common age-related eye diseases: A population-based study of 662 adults. *Frontiers in Aging Neuroscience, 5*, 1–9.

Euesden, J., Matcham, F., Hotopf, M., Steer, S., Cope, A. P., Lewis, C. M., & Scott, I. C. (2017). The relationship between mental health, disease severity, and genetic risk for depression in early rheumatoid arthritis. *Psychosomatic Medicine, 79*(6), 638–645.

Evans, D. L., Charney, D. S., Lewis, L., Golden, R. N., Gorman, J. M., Krishnan, K. R. R., ... & Valvo, W. J. (2005). Mood disorders in the medically ill: Scientific review and recommendations. *Biological Psychiatry, 58*(3), 175–189.

Fitzpatrick, R., Ziebland, S., Jenkinson, C., Mowat, A., & Mowat, A. (1991). The social dimension of health status measures in rheumatoid arthritis. *International Disability Studies, 13*(2), 34–37.

Garnefski, N., & Kraaij, V. (2012). Cognitive coping and goal adjustment are associated with symptoms of depression and anxiety in people with acquired hearing loss. *International Journal of Audiology, 51*(7), 545–550.

Goman, A. M., & Lin, F. R. (2016). Prevalence of hearing loss by severity in the United States. *American Journal of Public Health, 106*, 1820–1822.

Gopinath, B., Schneider, J., McMahon, C. M., Teber, E., Leeder, S. R., & Mitchell, P. (2012). Severity of age-related hearing loss is associated with impaired activities of daily living. *Age and Ageing, 41*(2), 195–200.

Guthrie, D. M., Thériault, É. R., & Davidson, J. G. (2016). Self-rated health, cognition, and dual sensory impairment are important predictors of depression among home care clients in Ontario. *Home Health Care Management & Practice, 28*(1), 35–43.

Harada, S., Nishiwaki, Y., Michikawa, T., Kikuchi, Y., Iwasawa, S., Nakano, M., ... & Takebayashi, T. (2008). Gender difference in the relationships between vision and hearing impairments and negative well-being. *Preventive Medicine, 47*(4), 433–437.

Hashemi, A., Hashemi, H., Jamali, A., Ghasemi, H., Ghazizadeh Hashemi, F., & Khabazkhoob, M. (2024). The association between visual impairment and mental disorders. *Scientific Reports, 14*(1), 2301.

Hearn, J. H., & Cross, A. (2020). Mindfulness for pain, depression, anxiety, and quality of life in people with spinal cord injury: A systematic review. *BMC Neurology, 20*, 1–11.

Heine, C., & Browning, C. J. (2004). The communication and psychosocial perceptions of older adults with sensory loss: A qualitative study. *Ageing & Society, 24*(1), 113–130.

Iwasaki, Y., & Mactavish, J. B. (2005). Ubiquitous yet unique: Perspectives of people with disabilities on stress. *Rehabilitation Counseling Bulletin, 48*(4), 194–208.

Jaiswal, A., Fraser, S., & Wittich, W. (2020). Barriers and facilitators that influence social participation in older adults with dual sensory impairment. *Frontiers in Education, 5*, 1–11.

Janssen, C. G. C., Schuengel, C., & Stolk, J. (2002). Understanding challenging behaviour in people with severe and profound intellectual disability: A stress-attachment model. *Journal of Intellectual Disability Research, 46*(6), 445–453.

Kapsalis, E., Jaeger, N., & Hale, J. (2024). Disabled-by-design: Effects of inaccessible urban public spaces on users of mobility assistive devices–a systematic review. *Disability and Rehabilitation: Assistive Technology, 19*(3), 604–622.

Khan, A., Pooja, V., Chaudhury, S., Bhatt, V., & Saldanha, D. (2021). Assessment of depression, anxiety, stress, and quality of life in rheumatoid arthritis patients and comparison with healthy individuals. *Industrial Psychiatry Journal, 30*(1), S195–S200.

Khil, L., Wellmann, J., & Berger, K. (2015). Impact of combined sensory impairments on health-related quality of life. Quality of Life Research, 24(9), 2099-2103.

Kim, Y., Kwak, Y., & Kim, J. S. (2015). The association between suicide ideation and sensory impairment among elderly Koreans. *Aging & Mental Health, 19*(7), 658–665.

Kobayashi, Y., Tamiya, N., Moriyama, Y., & Nishi, A. (2015). Triple difficulties in Japanese women with hearing loss: Marriage, smoking, and mental health issues. *PloS one, 10*(2), e0116648.

Kramer, S. E., Kapteyn, T. S., Kuik, D. J., & Deeg, D. J. (2002). The association of hearing impairment and chronic diseases with psychosocial health status in older age. *Journal of Aging and Health, 14*(1), 122–137.

Krause, J. S. (1998). Intercorrelations between secondary conditions and life adjustment in people with spinal cord injury. *SCI Psychosocial Process, 11*, 3–7.

Krause, J. S., Carter, R. E., Pickelsimer, E. E., & Wilson, D. (2008). A prospective study of health and risk of mortality after spinal cord injury. *Archives of Physical Medicine and Rehabilitation, 89*(8), 1482–1491.

Kumar, R., Lim, J., Mekary, R. A., Rattani, A., Dewan, M. C., Sharif, S. Y., . . . & Park, K. B. (2018). Traumatic spinal injury: Global epidemiology and worldwide volume. *World Neurosurgery, 113*, e345–e363.

Li, Y., Crews, J. E., Elam-Evans, L. D., Fan, A. Z., Zhang, X., Elliott, A. F., & Balluz, L. (2011). Visual impairment and health-related quality of life among elderly adults with age-related eye diseases. *Quality of Life Research, 20*, 845–852.

Lin, F. R., Niparko, J. K., & Ferrucci, L. (2011). Hearing loss prevalence in the United States. *Archives of Internal Medicine, 171*(20), 1851–1853.

Long, H., Liu, Q., Yin, H., Wang, K., Diao, N., Zhang, Y., ... & Guo, A. (2022). Prevalence trends of site-specific osteoarthritis from 1990 to 2019: Findings from the global burden of disease study 2019. *Arthritis & Rheumatology, 74*(7), 1172–1183.

Loyola-Sanchez, A., Richardson, J., Wilkins, S., Lavis, J. N., Wilson, M. G., Alvarez-Nemegyei, J., & Pelaez-Ballestas, I. (2016). Barriers to accessing the culturally sensitive healthcare that could decrease the disabling effects of arthritis in a rural Mayan community: A qualitative inquiry. *Clinical Rheumatology, 35*, 1287–1298.

Magasi, S., & Papadimitriou, C. (2021). Peer support interventions in physical medicine and rehabilitation: A framework to advance the field. *Archives of Physical Medicine and Rehabilitation, 103*(7), S222–S229.

Matcham, F., Rayner, L., Steer, S., & Hotopf, M. (2013). The prevalence of depression in rheumatoid arthritis: A systematic review and meta-analysis. *Rheumatology, 52*(12), 2136–2148.

Meek, K. P., Bergeron, C. D., Towne Jr, S. D., Ahn, S., Ory, M. G., & Smith, M. L. (2018). Restricted social engagement among adults living with chronic conditions. *International Journal of Environmental Research and Public Health, 15*(1), 158.

Mikolajczyk, B., Draganich, C., Philippus, A., Goldstein, R., Andrews, E., Pilarski, C., . . . & Monden, K. R. (2021). Resilience and mental health in individuals with spinal cord injury during the COVID-19 pandemic. *Spinal Cord, 59*(12), 1261–1267.

Mock, S. E., Fraser, C., Knutson, S., & Prier, A. (2010). Physical leisure participation and the well-being of adults with rheumatoid arthritis: The role of sense of belonging. *Activities, Adaptation & Aging, 34*(4), 292–302.

Monzani, D., Galeazzi, G. M., Genovese, E., Marrara, A., & Martini, A. (2008). Psychological profile and social behaviour of working adults with mild or moderate hearing loss. *Acta Otorhinolaryngologica Italica, 28*(2), 61.

Müller, R., Peter, C., Cieza, A., & Geyh, S. (2012). The role of social support and social skills in people with spinal cord injury—A systematic review of the literature. *Spinal Cord, 50*(2), 94–106.

Munoz-Baell, I. M., & Ruiz, M. T. (2000). Empowering the deaf. Let the deaf be deaf. *Journal of Epidemiology & Community Health, 54*(1), 40–44.

Noonan, B. M., Gallor, S. M., Hensler-McGinnis, N. F., Fassinger, R. E., Wang, S., & Goodman, J. (2004). Challenge and success: A qualitative study of the career development of highly achieving women with physical and sensory disabilities. *Journal of Counseling Psychology*, *51*(1), 68–80.

Papadopoulos, K., Papakonstantinou, D., Montgomery, A., & Solomou, A. (2014). Social support and depression of adults with visual impairments. *Research in Developmental Disabilities*, *35*(7), 1734–1741.

Pardhan, S., Lopez Sanchez, G. F., Bourne, R., Davis, A., Leveziel, N., Koyanagi, A., & Smith, L. (2021). Visual, hearing, and dual sensory impairment are associated with higher depression and anxiety in women. *International Journal of Geriatric Psychiatry*, *36*(9), 1378–1385.

Peter, C., Müller, R., Cieza, A., & Geyh, S. (2012). Psychological resources in spinal cord injury: A systematic literature review. *Spinal Cord*, *50*(3), 188–201.

Peterson, M. D., Kamdar, N., Chiodo, A., & Tate, D. G. (2020, May). Psychological morbidity and chronic disease among adults with traumatic spinal cord injuries: A longitudinal cohort study of privately insured beneficiaries. *Mayo Clinic Proceedings*, *95*(5), 920–928.

Peterson, M. D., Kamdar, N., Whitney, D. G., Ng, S., Chiodo, A., & Tate, D. G. (2019). Psychological morbidity and chronic disease among adults with nontraumatic spinal cord injuries: A cohort study of privately insured beneficiaries. *The Spine Journal*, *19*(10), 1680–1686.

Pew Research Center. (2023). *8 facts about Americans with disabilities*. Retrieved from https://www.pewresearch.org/short-reads/2023/07/24/8-facts-about-americans -with- disabilities/#:~:text=Some%2046%25%20of%20Americans%20ages,8%25%20 of%20ad ults%20under%2035.

Pope, A. M., & Tarlov, A. R. (1991). *Disability in America: Toward a national agenda for prevention*. National Academies Press.

Porter, H. R. (Ed.). (2015). *Recreation therapy for specific diagnoses and conditions*. Idyll Arbor.

Post, M. W. M., & van Leeuwen, C. M. (2012). Psychosocial issues in spinal cord injury: A review. *Spinal Cord*, *50*(5), 382–389.

Resnick, H. E., Fries, B. E., & Verbrugge, L. M. (1997). Windows to their world: The effect of sensory impairments on social engagement and activity time in nursing home residents. *The Journals of Gerontology Series B: Psychological Sciences and Social Sciences*, *52*(3), S135–S144.

Roberts, T. T., Leonard, G. R., & Cepela, D. J. (2017). Classifications in brief: American Spinal Injury Association (ASIA) impairment scale. *Clinical Orthopaedics and Related Research*, *475*(5), 1499–1504.

Rodrigues, J. A., Pereira, E. T., de Oliveira, C. E. P., & Moreira, O. C. (2020). Effect of strength training on physical and mental health and quality of life of people with spinal cord injury: A literature review. *Archivos de Medicina Deport*, *37*(3), 192–196.

Ryan, S., & McGuire, B. (2016). Psychological predictors of pain severity, pain interference, depression, and anxiety in rheumatoid arthritis patients with chronic pain. *British Journal of Health Psychology*, *21*(2), 336–350.

Sallis, J. F., Owen, N., & Fisher, E. (2015). Ecological models of health behavior. *Health Behavior: Theory, Research, and Practice*, *5*, 43–64.

Sano, H., Okamoto, M., Ohhashi, K., Iwasaki, S., & Ogawa, K. (2013). Quality of life reported by patients with idiopathic sudden sensorineural hearing loss. *Otology & Neurotology*, *34*(1), 36–40.

Scott, K. M., Bruffaerts, R., Tsang, A., Ormel, J., Alonso, J., Angermeyer, M. C., ... & Von Korff, M. (2007). Depression–anxiety relationships with chronic physical conditions: Results from the World Mental Health Surveys. *Journal of Affective Disorders*, *103*(1–3), 113–120.

Sharma, A., Kudesia, P., Shi, Q., & Gandhi, R. (2016). Anxiety and depression in patients with osteoarthritis: Impact and management challenges. *Open Access Rheumatology: Research and Reviews*, *8*, 103–113.

Shen, S. C., Huang, K. H., Kung, P. T., Chiu, L. T., & Tsai, W. C. (2017). Incidence, risk, and associated factors of depression in adults with physical and sensory disabilities: A nationwide population-based study. *PLoS One*, *12*(3), e0175141.

Shin, H. Y., & Hwang, H. J. (2017). Mental health of the people with hearing impairment in Korea: A population-based cross-sectional study. *Korean Journal of Family Medicine*, *38*(2), 57.

Simning, A., Fox, M. L., Barnett, S. L., Sorensen, S., & Conwell, Y. (2019). Depressive and anxiety symptoms in older adults with auditory, vision, and dual sensory impairment. *Journal of Aging and Health*, *31*(8), 1353–1375.

Smith, C. A., & Wallston, K. A. (1992). Adaptation in patients with chronic rheumatoid arthritis: Application of a general model. *Health Psychology*, *11*(3), 151.

Stang, P. E., Brandenburg, N. A., Lane, M. C., Merikangas, K. R., Von Korff, M. R., & Kessler, R. C. (2006). Mental and physical comorbid conditions and days in role among persons with arthritis. *Psychosomatic Medicine*, *68*(1), 152–158.

Stokols, D. (1992). Environmental quality, human development, and health: An ecological view. *Journal of Applied Developmental Psychology*, *13*(2), 121–124.

Sung, Y. K., Li, L., Blake, C., Betz, J., & Lin, F. R. (2016). Association of hearing loss and loneliness in older adults. *Journal of Aging and Health*, *28*(6), 979–994.

Treharne, G. J., Hale, E. D., Lyons, A. C., Booth, D. A., Banks, M. J., Erb, N., ... & Kitas, G. D. (2005). Cardiovascular disease and psychological morbidity among rheumatoid arthritis patients. *Rheumatology*, *44*(2), 241–246.

van't Land, H., Verdurmen, J., Ten Have, M., van Dorsselaer, S., Beekman, A., & de Graaf, R. (2010). The association between arthritis and psychiatric disorders; Results from a longitudinal population-based study. *Journal of Psychosomatic Research*, *68*(2), 187–193.

Vink, D., Aartsen, M. J., & Schoevers, R. A. (2008). Risk factors for anxiety and depression in the elderly: A review. *Journal of Affective Disorders*, *106*(1–2), 29–44.

Williams, R., & Murray, A. (2015). Prevalence of depression after spinal cord injury: A meta-analysis. *Archives of Physical Medicine and Rehabilitation*, *96*(1), 133–140.

Wittenborn, J., & Rein, D. (2013). *Cost of vision problems: The economic burden of vision loss and eye disorders in the United States.* National Opinion Research Center.

World Health Organization (1976). *Disability prevention and rehabilitation: Reports of specific technical matters.* Twenty-Ninth World Health Assembly.

World Health Organization. (2013). *Mental health action plan 2013–2020.* Retrieved from https://www.who.int/publications/i/item/9789241506021

World Health Organization. (2021). *Governments commit to accelerate action to improve access to eye care services.* Retrieved from https://www.who.int/news/item/23-07-2021-governments-commit-to-accelerate-action-to-improve-access-to-eye-care-services#:~:text=Over%202%20billion%20people%20globally,%2Dsightedness%2C%20 glaucoma%20and%20cataract

World Health Organization. (2022). *Mental health.* Retrieved from https://www.who.int/news- room/fact-sheets/detail/mental-health-strengthening-our-response

World Health Organization. (2022, June 17). Mental health: Strengthening our response. World Health Organization. https://www.who.int/news-room/fact-sheets/detail/mental-health-strengthening-our-response

World Health Organization. (2023a). *Disability.* Retrieved from https://www.who.int/news- room/fact-sheets/detail/disability-and-health

World Health Organization. (2023b). *Osteoarthritis.* Retrieved from https://www.who.int/news- room/fact-sheets/detail/osteoarthritis

World Health Organization. (2023c). Rheumatoid arthritis. World Health Organization. https://www.who.int/news-room/fact-sheets/detail/rheumatoid-arthritis

Yorkston, K., Johnson, K., Klasner, E., Amtmann, D., Kuehn, C., & Dudgeon, B. (2003). Getting the work done: A qualitative study of individuals with multiple sclerosis. *Disability and Rehabilitation, 25*(8), 369–379.

11

Communication in Substance Use Counseling

The Role of Aggressive Communication

Theodore A. Avtgis and Veronica Nuzzolo

The study of aggressive communication has commanded an abundance of attention from scholars for over forty years (see Rancer & Avtgis, 2006, 2014). Scores of studies have analyzed differences in the communication trait of verbal aggressiveness (Infante & Wigley, 1986) in virtually every communication context (e.g., health, family, organizational). In fact, this communication trait is the most investigated of all the communication predispositions. However, given that this construct is considered trait-like in nature, it has been almost exclusively investigated using normative subjects such as college students and the general public as opposed to assessing marginalized or stigmatized groups such as those in need of behavioral health services.

Overwhelmingly, research has revealed many negative relational outcomes associated with the use of aggressive communication. For example, verbal aggressiveness has been identified as a precursor to pre-assaultive states as well as physically violent episodes within healthcare (see, e.g., Avtgis & Madlock, 2008). However, little research has been conducted within the realm of behavioral health and behavioral health disorders regarding the influence and role that aggressive communication plays in such situations. The paucity of this type of research, in the post-COVID-19 world, has revealed a huge chasm that needs to be the focus for research efforts moving forward. This chapter will introduce the concept of aggressive communication in the creation and maintenance of stigma, focusing specifically on the influence that aggressive communication has on the therapeutic process. Furthermore, suggestions for both researchers and practitioners for better understanding the role that aggressive communication plays in behavioral health practice specific to addiction will be forwarded.

Aggressive Communication

To understand the role of aggressive communication in marginalized populations, there must be a discussion regarding the evolution of the construct and how such construct development can be particularly useful in explaining and predicting behavior in marginalized populations, such as people struggling with substance use disorder. Infante (1987) defined aggression in interpersonal communication in the following way:

> An interpersonal behavior may be considered aggressive if it applies force physically or symbolically in order, minimally, to dominate and perhaps damage or, maximally, to defeat and perhaps destroy the locus of attack. The locus of attack in interpersonal communication can be a person's body, material possessions, self-concept, positions on topics of communication, or behavior. (p. 158)

There are a variety of verbally aggressive messages that researchers have identified as unique in their locus of attack. These messages consist of *competence attacks* (i.e., verbal attacks directed at a person's ability to do something), *character attacks* (i.e., verbal attacks directed at a person's character), *profanity* (i.e., use of obscene words, epithets, and vulgarities), *teasing and ridicule* (i.e., mock or make fun of another individual), *maledictions* (i.e., messages that wish someone harm), *threats* (i.e., threaten someone with an intention to inflict physical or psychological pain), *non verbal verbal aggression* (i.e., speech-independent gestures which are also known as emblems), *negative comparison* (i.e., compare the person to others held in low stature), *significant others* (i.e., attacking people who are important to the person), *background attacks* (bring up past failure or bad experiences), and *disconfirmation* (i.e., completely ignore the other person) (Rancer & Avtgis, 2006, 2014).

The development of the predisposition (i.e., trait) of aggressive communication is believed to be developed in a variety of ways. The *social learning* explanation holds that verbal aggressiveness is developed as a result of constant exposure to verbally aggressive interactions and thus becomes a regular part of the person's communication repertoire. *Disdain* is another explanation that contends a deep-seated dislike or hatred will trigger a person to engage in verbally aggressive behavior. The skills deficiency approach holds that people who lack the communication skills to effectively express themselves revert to aggressive messages prompted by the lack of communication ability to formulate arguments and the resulting frustration such a deficiency brings about. The final explanation for aggressive communication is that of *psychopathology* and assumes that a person expresses repressed hostility as a result of past negative experiences (Infante & Wigley, 1986). When dealing with a marginalized or stigmatized population such as people suffering from substance use disorder, one can easily see influences from all of the explanations for verbally aggressive expression being present in the treatment of the substance-addicted person.

It is important to discuss the effects of neurobiological processes involved in verbal aggressiveness when considering substance use and the resulting effects on the brain. A plethora of theories and research have indicated particular brain structures that are involved in and predispose people to verbal aggression. Beatty and McCroskey (2001) forwarded their Communibiological paradigm of communication behavior. They argued, similarly to the psychobiological explanation of human behavior, that all communication behavior is, to a large extent, a function of genetics and heredity. Basing this perspective on the Three-Factor Model of Personality (Eysenk & Eysenk, 1985), communication behavior could be explained as a function of three super-factors of personality: *psychoticism, neuroticism, and extraversion.* Psychoticism is associated with a lack of feeling and empathy, being unconcerned with and possibly hostile to others, disregarding social conventions, and exhibiting inappropriate emotional expression.

Neuroticism is associated with worry, quickness to anger, and difficulty coping with stress. Extraversion is associated with being outgoing, friendly, and gregarious. The long-term effects of substance use on the brain have been well established (Vik et al., 2004).

Several studies investigating the validity of the communibiological paradigm and verbal aggressiveness indicated a clear and distinct relationship between psychoticism and verbal aggressiveness, as well as a mediating relationship between verbal aggression and extraversion (Beatty & McCroskey, 2001; Beatty et al., 1999; Heisel et al., 2003; Valencic et al., 1998). In terms of linking specific physiological processes and aggressive communication, several findings show a high level of verbal aggressiveness is related to asymmetrical processing in the pre- frontal cortex (Heisel, 2010) and amygdala activation (Avtgis et al., 2010).

Taken as a whole, aggressive communication in general and verbal aggression in particular have been shown to have social-psychological and bio-psychological antecedents and manifestations. When one couples this with the social-psychological and bio-psychological factors associated with addiction and substance use, the confounding relationships and possible influence between addiction and verbally aggressive communication become a fertile and relatively unexplored area for researchers and scholars alike (Polcin et al., 2010, 2012).

Communication, Addiction, and Stigma

The last two decades have seen a dramatic increase in people suffering from negative consequences associated with substance use. For example, opioid use disorder (OUD) and resulting overdose deaths are steadily increasing with each passing year, not to mention the increasing incidences of alcohol-related injuries, deaths, and people reporting suffering from alcohol use disorder (AUD). OUD and AUD are but two of the many addictions and dependencies that fall under the rubric of *substance use disorder (SUD)*. A SUD, as defined in the fifth edition of the *Diagnostic and Statistical Manual of Mental Disorders* (DSM- 1) "involves patterns of symptoms caused by using a substance that an individual continues taking despite its negative effects. Levels of severity are classified as mild, moderate, or severe" (2013, p. 541). SUD and co-occurring disorders (e.g., anxiety, depression) are characterized by dysregulated neurobiology and compulsive behaviors. There is no single root cause that activates the neurobiological pathway toward illness or dependence, and more importantly, there is no one standardized treatment modality that addresses these behavioral health issues.

The American Psychological Association (APA), the American Society of Addiction Medicine (ASAM), the National Institute on Drug Abuse (NIDA), and the Association for Addiction Professionals (NAADAC) concur that for treatment to be effective, a variety of approaches are necessary. Such approaches include communication strategies, early intervention, counseling/psychotherapy, medication-assisted treatments, recovery support systems, community support systems, and peer-led support groups, among others. To establish productive and trusting relationships, providers must continually assess all communication through risk management, ethical, and legal lenses (APA, NIDA, & NAADAC, n.d.). According to the Centers for Disease Control (CDC) (2024a), 40.3 million Americans aged twelve years and older have suffered from substance use disorder (SUD) in the past year. Looking specifically at overdose deaths, national statistics (2021) report that 71,000 Americans died from fentanyl; 33,000 from methamphetamine; 24,000 from cocaine; 9,000 from heroin; and 52,000 from alcohol (a 34 percent increase from pre-pandemic levels) (CDC, 2024b). As if not alarming enough, between 1999 and2021, 280,000 Americans died from abusing legally prescribed medications. It is in these staggering numbers that communication scholars and researchers cannot ignore the potential impact that aggressive communication plays in the addiction process and, in the best of situations, the recovery process.

When discussing marginalized populations, one cannot ignore the influence that stigma exerts on that population and how such stigma can have deleterious effects on change and the change process. This effect is also prevalent when addressing issues of addiction and treatment. Stigma can be defined as a characteristic associated with disgrace or something that is unacceptable (Avtgis et al., 2024). There are generally two types of stigma: physical and social. *Physical stigma* is a physical attribute that is usually visible and serves to marginalize a person solely based on this physical characteristic (e.g., needle marks on the arm, looking jaundiced, lack of hygiene). *Social stigma* reflects societal attributes that serve to marginalize a person solely based on whom they associate with (e.g., group membership, affiliations).

Focusing specifically on health-related stigma, there are biomedical and social dimensions where the meaning and experience of health conditions are formed by both cultural and social systems (Conrad & Barker, 2010). Wright and Rains (2013) defined health-related stigma as an "individual's perception that her or his health conditions represent a mark of discredit" (p. 310). Such discredit is detrimental to a person's physical and mental health (Rains, 2018). This "spoiled identity" can vary in severity based on the cultural significance placed on the particular characteristic (Goffman, 1963). Spoiled identity refers to a characteristic of a person's identity, either self-derived or other-derived, which causes them to experience stigma. For example, consider conditions such as lupus, type 1 diabetes, type 2 diabetes, cancer, etc. All of these conditions conjure up different interpretations of "spoiled identity." Health stigmas can be visible (i.e., obvious outward manifestations of the condition or state of the person) or concealable (i.e., not obvious to people in everyday life without some sort of disclosure from the bearer of the stigma). While such stigma manifests differently in interpersonal interactions, both types of stigma are sources of stress for the individual (Chaudoir et al., 2013).

The most relevant form of stigma related to addiction and dependency concerns mental-behavioral problems. By mental-behavioral problems, we are referring to issues such as SUD, anxiety, attention deficit disorder, etc. These types of stigmas are perceived as being onset-controllable or, simply put, due to a person's own choices and free will (Avtgis et al., 2024; Goffman, 1963). As a direct result of this perception, there is a fear of social isolation and rejection (Link et al., 1989) as well as disapproval, anger, and global disconfirmation from both significant and non-significant others (Weiner et al., 1988). Furthermore, such attributes concern mental-behavioral issues and carry the added burden of being perceived as unpredictable and dangerous (Avtgis et al., 2024). One of the most adversely affected populations by this perception is people suffering from substance use disorder.

The negative impact of stigma on behavioral health treatment is well established.

However, the relationship between communication and stigma in relation to proactive engagement in the treatment of SUD is largely unexamined. Effective communication is essential when treating individuals with SUD and co-occurring disorders. "Support and empathy from providers can help maintain the therapeutic alliance, increase client motivation, and assist with medication adherence" (SAMHSA TIP 42, p.1).

Aggressive Communication in the Therapeutic Relationship Historically, research indicates that aggressive communication is a confrontational communication style or tactic used to force or pressure people with SUD into treatment. More recently, aggressive communication or confrontational styles have been interpreted as a brutally honest approach, attempt, warning, or harm reduction technique for high-risk individuals regarding harmful behaviors (Polcin et al., 2010, 2012).

To gain insight into the dynamics of aggressive/confrontational communication, Polcin et al. (2012) asked participants suffering from SUD to recall and describe experiences of helpful versus unhelpful communication that they received while they were using substances as well as communication they received when abstinent. Helpful and unhelpful communication refers to messages associated with the act of considering, engaging in, or maintaining recovery. The most consistent theme regarding unhelpful aggressive confrontations concerned hypocrisy on the part of confronters. Participants reported disrespectful tone and constant reminders of the past as demoralizing and counterproductive. This was particularly true if there was blame and if confronters did not offer encouragement, support, or helpful suggestions.

For example, Polcin et al. illustrate the following responses from participants recovering from SUD:

> Just the blame game. Just when people constantly you know, it doesn't help those situations when you bring up the past constantly. You're not supposed to forget your past but if it's constantly thrown in your face, you know telling you the negative things you've done, I don't think that helps with your recovery. It makes me angry, you know, it's like how long do you have to be sober before people—maybe it's never but it seems like they could cut you some slack after a few years you know . . . It gets me a little upset because I'm on the right path; got a good job you know, [I'm] a good father. It's like how much do you have to do before you don't hear that . . . My thing is if you're gonna talk to me, talk to me in a respectful [way] and don't just sit there and tell me what I need to do because you're not me. I know what I have to do. You know what I mean? I'm my own person. Don't say "you need to do this". . . . Come at me in a respectful manner and I'll come back at you respectfully; that's my whole thing on it . . . You're not my mom, you're not my dad. Don't tell me what to do. (pp. 144–152)

Building a positive therapeutic alliance is a cornerstone of effective, high-quality, person-centered care for all clients. The ability to effectively communicate allows providers and patients the ability to form and maintain healthy therapeutic relationships. Individuals with SUD often have trouble articulating their needs, which can be misinterpreted as aggressive communication and/or problematic behavior. Participants indicated that they found it easier to engage with others when the communicator made an attempt to negate perceptions of moral superiority, "offered hope and practical support, encouragement, and perhaps most importantly, a sense of hope that change is possible" (Polcin et al., 2012, pp. 144–152).

Communication, Stigma, and Caregivers

Communication is a vital part of any relationship and can be especially challenging to navigate when dealing with individuals suffering from SUD. To communicate effectively, one must listen, be kind, show empathy and understanding, choose words thoughtfully and respectfully, and, most importantly, remember that language matters. For normatively functioning individuals, these characteristics are termed communication competence. Simply put, competent communication entails the ability to communicate effectively (i.e., the ability to achieve a desired goal) and do so in a socially appropriate manner (i.e., the ability to avoid diverging from social and relational norms) (Spitzberg & Cupach, 1984). Werder et al. (2021) reported that despite increased access to medication-assisted treatments for SUD, specifically opioid use, "less than 20 percent of individuals with SUD receive treatment. Stigmatizing language has been identified as a potential trigger for explicit and implicit biases that may adversely affect treatment enrollment and quality of care for persons with an SUD" (pp. 9–22). Stone et al. (2021) reported high rates of stigma from healthcare professionals targeted toward individuals with SUD, resulting in great barriers to effective treatment (DeFlavio et al., 2015; Kennedy-Hendricks et al., 2016; van Boekel et al., 2014). A 2016 national survey of 1010 US primary care physicians found that the majority of participants/respondents believed addiction to prescription opioids was the fault of the individual and believed that people with SUD presented a greater danger to society than the general population (Kennedy-Hendricks et al., 2016).

NIDA (n.d.) reported that such collective bodies of research on biases in perceptions, communication, and the resulting treatment of people with SUD are more prevalent than one would think. Volkow (2020) described stigma against people with SUD as negative attitudes and stereotypes that can create obstacles and barriers to treatment and can make the patient's condition worse. More specifically:

> Beliefs or assumptions about personal responsibility and the false belief that willpower should be sufficient to stop drug use—are never entirely absent from most people's thoughts when they interact with someone with a drug problem. Healthcare professionals are not immune to these assumptions. Indeed, they may hold stigmatizing views of people with addictions that may even lead them to withhold care. In emergency departments, for instance, healthcare professionals may be dismissive of someone with an alcohol or drug problem because they don't view it as a medical condition and therefore don't see its treatment as part of their job. People who inject drugs are sometimes denied care in emergency departments and other hospital settings because they are believed to be drug-seeking. (pp. 1289–1290)

The DeFlavio et al. (2015) study regarding the adoption of evidence-based medication-assisted treatments in rural areas concluded that these types of barriers to treatment continue. Their study presented a review of barriers to treatment among primary care physicians in rural areas. An anonymous survey of healthcare providers in New Hampshire and Vermont, two rural states, was conducted with a total of 180 healthcare providers. Common themes identified by healthcare providers regarding SUD included limited knowledge, time, interest, a general mistrust of people with SUD, the use of medication-assisted treatment, and the perception of a difficult patient population. That is, patients with addiction are difficult to manage. Furthermore, treating patients with drug addiction is also considered to be high-maintenance, stressful, and challenging when compared to other patient populations. The results of the study suggested that primary care physicians were excellent candidates to provide services. However, significant barriers remain, such as limited access, inadequate staff training, lack of access to SUD specialists, and perceived efficacy of medication-assisted treatments (2015). Overall, the results of the DeFlavio et al. study indicated that roughly 10 percent of the healthcare respondents were medication-assisted treatment prescribers. While more than 80 percent regularly saw patients with SUD, 70 percent felt that as the primary care provider, they were responsible for treating their patients with SUD. Perhaps one of the more alarming aspects regarding care for treating people with SUD is the ability to create a vital relational connection or strong therapeutic alliance. This therapeutic alliance is almost entirely developed and maintained by communication. For example, the ability of the provider to establish trust, goodwill, security, and credibility (i.e., therapeutic ethos) is one of the most central factors in treatment success.

Need for Education and Training

Historically, bedside manner has always been an important aspect of the patient-provider relationship (see Avtgis et al., 2024). Trying to communicate with disgruntled patients isn't easy, but neither is dealing with disgruntled healthcare providers. Contributing to these negative relational climates is the societal perception of SUD, which has been documented since SUD's identification as a disorder (Cazalis et al., 2023; Schomerus et al., 2011; Yang et al., 2017). Furthermore, the fact that the medical community has not been supportive, empathetic, or respectful of patients with SUD only serves to further negatively affect an already toxic environment. The continued stigmatization of this population, along with a lack of compassion, understanding, and provider education, only exacerbates healthcare provider perceptions of people with SUD. Such perceptions and personal emotions often result in discriminatory clinical care. A Massachusetts survey conducted by Davidson et al., (2019), a public-private partnership dedicated to finding solutions that end the overdose crisis in the United States, found that 24 percent of healthcare professionals practicing emergency, family, and internal medicine report their practices would attract less desirable patients if they actively practiced treatment on individuals with SUD. In addition, further studies conducted by Kennedy-Hendricks et al. (2016) indicated that negative attitudes and aggressive communication toward people with SUD remain prevalent in healthcare. Stigma not only impedes care delivery but serves to exacerbate the problem. When internalized, stigma creates many obstacles to treatment, the most critical being guilt, shame, and isolation, resulting in an increase in substance use. Which, in turn, further exacerbates the disease. It is well documented in aggressive communication literature that a low self-concept (i.e., low self-esteem) is an important factor in the expression of verbal aggression. For example, a person with a poor self-concept is more likely to see any critique or feedback as being a personal attack, and thus, respond in an aggressive manner (Kinney & Segrin, 1998). Understanding that stigma is not the only contributing factor impeding treatment for people with SUD, providers must also ensure that the system at large will not penalize people who suffer from SUD, let alone people who are actively engaged in their own recovery efforts.

Volkow (2020) suggested that efforts to promote SUD awareness include the education of providers emphasizing that addiction is a chronic and treatable disease. Training initiatives should include effective communication skills training by promoting an understanding of the disease and behaviors associated with the disease. Improving treatment in healthcare settings will require training of all staff, including physicians, nurses, and clinicians, on how to provide compassionate care to patients who may display aggressiveness or other behaviors associated with withdrawal symptoms, as well as general personality predispositions to be verbally aggressive.

Kelly et al. (2015) recommended that the medical community needs to better train health professionals on how to communicate and treat patients with SUD, as communication skills training, especially regarding aggressive communication that has been found to be extremely successful within general healthcare settings (Avtgis et al., 2024). Training begins with ensuring healthcare professionals understand that addiction is a treatable health condition, and using appropriate language that reflects this fact is crucial for success. Related to their earlier recommendations, Kelly et al. (2016) suggested that replacing stigmatizing language is an important step toward effective communication by eliminating stigma and replacing stigmatizing language with empowering language that does not have negative connotations or interfere with the therapeutic relationship.

For decades, communication scholars have distinguished between affirming communication (i.e., communication that validates the self-concept of the other person) and non-affirming communication (i.e., communication that negates the self-concept of the other person) (Norton, 1978). Research findings clearly endorsed the positive and negative relational outcomes associated with each type of communication (see, e.g., Avtgis & Rancer, 2023).

There is ample evidence indicating that the use of stigmatizing and judgmental language affects how providers and the general public react to individuals with SUD. Simply put, words and labels matter. For example, when a provider refers to an individual with SUD as a "substance abuser, addict, or junkie" versus a person with a "substance use disorder," the result of such language is the perception that a person's substance use is a moral failing and an outcome of willful misconduct and thus, something worthy of stigma (e.g., junkie) as opposed to something that is a treatable medical condition that needs to be managed similar to any other chronic illness (e.g., substance use disorder) (Kelly et al., 2010, 2016). NIDA (n.d.) has developed and made available guides for both healthcare providers and the general public on non-stigmatizing language called "Words Matter: Preferred Language for Talking About Addiction" (NIDA). Understanding the differences between communication styles is imperative when treating individuals with SUD. Aggressive communication theory suggests that verbal aggressiveness is considered destructive in nature and leads to negative relational climates that can result in detrimental personal and relational outcomes. Volkow (2020) described a personal account:

> While visiting a makeshift heroin "shooting gallery" in San Juan, Puerto Rico, I urged a man who had what appeared to be a massive abscess in his leg to go to an emergency room to get it treated. He refused to even consider it and told me that when he had previously sought medical help, he had been so badly mistreated that he was frightened of returning. He would rather jeopardize his life or risk a leg amputation than endure being dismissed as a "drug addict." (pp. 1289–1290)

Further data regarding stigma in healthcare based on interviews with intravenous drug users revealed interesting findings as to how stigma is processed by people with SUD and how such processing significantly impacts their willingness to seek out emergency care (Paquette et al., 2018). Consider the following respondent experiences:

Robert, age sixty-two and from Kern, described the following:

> Interviewer: What happens when people do know that you use drugs? What does that look like?
>
> Robert: . . . You're a nobody . . . You're just on the back burner to them. For example, people get abscesses and stuff like that, and they go to the hospital, and once the doctors . . . realize that you're a drug user, they sit you on the back side and they'll take that person in front of you . . . Yeah, you get treated a lot different.

Melissa, thirty-eight years old and from Kern, knew multiple people who injected substances and died from injection-related infections because they were afraid to go to a hospital:

> Melissa: When you go to a hospital, and you're a drug addict—or an IV drug user, especially—you are treated horribly. . . . Your life isn't as valuable, you're a second- or third-class citizen, and it's sad. . . . [T]hey [PWID] don't want to go and have someone go and look down their nose and tell them what a piece of crap you are. You already know. Most people using a needle know. They've hit rock bottom. They know that they're down there pretty far. A lot of people just won't go. They'd literally rather die than face that. It's sad. It's really sad, it happens. I get it. I never would have understood, I'm like, just go to the doctor, that's stupid, but I get it now. I understand. (Paquette et al., 2018, pp. 104–110)

The attitude of a healthcare professional regarding SUD may negatively affect the delivery of SUD services, resulting in delayed treatment, ending treatment services prematurely thus increasing the potential for relapse (Ball et al., 2006; Eaton 2004). Previous studies conducted by Luoma et al. (2007) and Schomerus et al. (2011) demonstrated that the outcomes associated with stigma experiences resulted in negative effects on the treatment of SUD. More specifically, these effects included noncompliance with treatment recommendations, hindered recovery, and decreased perceptions of self-efficacy. The researchers concluded that negative attitudes of healthcare providers toward patients with SUD are known to lead to poor communication between provider and patient, diminished therapeutic alliance, and misattribution of physical illness symptoms to substance use problems, which may influence diagnoses, treatment, and rehabilitation of SUD (Luoma et al., 2007; Schomerus et al., 2011).

van Boekel et al. (2013) conducted a systematic review to assess the impact of healthcare provider attitudes toward patients with SUD and healthcare delivery. Results indicated that, in general, healthcare providers held negative perceptions and attitudes toward patients with SUD. The providers perceived individuals with SUD as violent, manipulative, and having low motivation. Providers also reported these perceptions as impeding factors in the healthcare delivery for these patients. Furthermore, healthcare providers lacked adequate education and communication skills when working with this population. The conclusion of this study revealed that the negative attitudes of healthcare providers diminished patients' feelings of empowerment and subsequent treatment outcomes. Healthcare providers are less involved with SUD patients and take a more task-oriented approach in the delivery of treatment, resulting in less personal engagement and diminished empathy (van Boekel et al. 2013). It becomes clear from this and many other findings that a lack of competent communication skills, especially with marginalized populations, can have deleterious effects.

Assertive versus Aggressive Communication

In a healthcare/behavioral health setting, the trait of assertive communication has been associated with positive results such as decreased anxiety and decreased substance use, which are crucial in the treatment of SUD and co-occurring disorders. Assertive communication has been described as a style of communication that affords the opportunity for a person to express their thoughts, feelings, opinions, and needs in an articulate, honest, and respectful manner (Rancer & Avtgis, 2006, 2014). Assertive communication can be viewed as a healthy midpoint between passive communication and aggressive communication. Richard et al. (2023) suggest that assertiveness enables healthcare providers to share their expertise with confidence without presenting as authoritarian. Interpersonal communication skills such as assertiveness help the provider express knowledge and opinions when sharing scientific information while simultaneously respecting the patient's person, ideas, and autonomy. Healthcare providers who are skilled in assertive communication can assist the patient in connecting the patient's beliefs and values with the practice of evidence-based medicine. While the concept of assertiveness may be easy to understand, training in assertive communication remains a challenge in everyday clinical practice. Richard et al. argued that the communication difficulties that providers encounter stem from their misunderstanding of this communication style. A healthcare provider skilled in assertive communication also understands the importance of maintaining an attitude of benevolence and respect for others. These skilled providers allow and encourage patient engagement and participation.

The assertive provider combines firmness and clarity of language regarding their professional knowledge and skills. They allow and encourage patient participation, express scientific or medical information that ensures patient comprehension, and make note of the patient's responses and reactions. On the other hand, the aggressive communication style in the behavioral health realm imposes personal and professional views and does not seek to establish nor result in collaborative relationships. In fact, aggressive communication can actively work against collaborative relationship development. Richard et al. (2023) suggested that using assertive communication is well suited to healthcare due to it being conducive to patient trust-building. Patient trust is built when a provider shows confidence and professional credibility (i.e., therapeutic ethos), which are conveyed by the practitioners' actions. Trusting relationships may be weakened if these tenets of assertive communication are compromised. Such generalized links between assertiveness and relational trust are commonplace in the research literature (Rancer & Avtgis, 2014).

Conclusion

When providers learn how to communicate assertively as opposed to aggressively, they play an active role in eliciting therapeutic change and can then share opinions and treatment strategies in a safe, non-judgmental manner, allowing the patient to be interpersonally dominant. They can also use this trait to achieve goals and objectives while creating and reinforcing positive feelings in others. A provider's use of assertive communication can encourage patient responsibility, allowing the patient to take ownership of their thoughts, behaviors, and actions, resulting in greater personal responsibility and accountability, two critical components of long-term recovery.

Communication needs to be supportive and respectful, allowing healthcare providers to enhance the patient's experience by creating a safe space. Furthermore, such communication creates conditions that will help the patient move toward a healthier future. There is a need to identify the best communication practices for provider-patient communication, particularly for individuals who have a SUD. One can conclude the incontrovertible facts when it comes to aggressive communication and SUD: Aggressive communication is detrimental to the effective treatment of SUD; it may not be the cause of someone's failure in a recovery effort, but it certainly will be a contributing factor.

Recommended Readings/Resources

Avtgis, T. A., & Rancer, A. S. (Eds.). (2010). *Arguments aggression and conflict: New directions in theory and research.* Routledge.

Lederman, L. C. (2010). Health communication: The first twenty-five years. In J. W. Chesebro (Eds.), *A century of transformation: Studies in honor of the 100 anniversary of the eastern communication association* (pp. 236–254). Oxford.

McGinty, E., Pescosolido, B., Kennedy-Hendricks, A., & Barry, C. L. (2018). Communication strategies to counter stigma and improve mental illness and substance use disorder policy. *Psychiatric Services, 69,* 136–146. https://doi.org/10.1176/appi.ps.201700076

Rancer, A. S., & Avtgis, T. A. (2014). *Argumentative and aggressive communication: Theory research and application* (2nd ed.). Lang.

Wangensteen, T., & Hystad, J. (2022). Trust and collaboration between patients and staff in SUD treatment: A qualitative study of patients' reflections on inpatient SUD treatment four years after discharge. *Nordic Studies on Alcohol and Drugs, 39,* 418–436. http://doi.org/10.1177/14550725221082366

References

American Psychiatric Association. (2013). *Diagnostic and statistical manual of mental disorders* (5th ed.). https://doi.org/10.1176/appi.books.9780890425596

ASAM - *American Society of Addiction Medicine.* Default. (n.d.). https://www.asam.org/.

Avtgis, T. A. (2023). Training and development in argumentative and aggressive communication: Contributions of Dr. Andrew S. Rancer. *Journal of Business and Professional Communication Quarterly, 86,* 107–116. http://dx.doi.org.10.1177/23294906231

Avtgis, T. A., & Madlock, P. E. (2008). Diffusing the verbally aggressive patient: Creating a constructive environment. In E. P. Polack, V. P. Richmond, & J. C. McCroskey (Eds.), *Fundamentals of human communication in the health sciences: A core competency* (pp. 169–184). Kendall Hunt.

Avtgis, T. A., Polack, E. P., & Brefcznski-Lewis, J. B. (2010, May). *Charting a course: Meeting new horizons in mapping the verbally aggressive brain* [Presenter]. Eastern Communication Association, Baltimore, MD.

Avtgis, T. A., & Rancer, A. S. (2023). The theory of independent mindedness: Three decades of research. *Journal of business and professional communication quarterly, 87*(4), 670–683.

Avtgis, T. A., Wright, K. B., & Nuzzolo, V. (2024). *Medical communication: Physical and psychological wellness* (3rd ed.). Kendall Hunt.

Ball, S., Carroll, K., Canning-Ball, M., & Rounsaville, B. (2006). Reasons for dropout from drug abuse treatment: Symptoms, personality, and motivation. *Addictive Behaviors, 31*, 320–330. https://doi.org/10.1016/j.addbeh.2005.05.013

Beatty, M. J., & McCroskey, J. C. (2001). *The biology of communication: A communibiological perspective.* Hampton Press.

Beatty, M. J., Rudd, J. E., & Valencic, K. M. (1999). A re-examination of the verbal aggressiveness scale: One factor or two? *Communication Research Reports, 16*, 10–17. http://dx.doi.org/10.1080/08824099909388696

Cazalis, A., Lambert, L., & Auriacombe, M. (2023). Stigmatization of people with addiction by health professionals: Current knowledge. A scoping review. *Drug and Alcohol Dependence Reports, 9*, 100196. https://doi.org/10.1016/j.dadr.2023.100196

Centers for Disease Control. (2024a). *Drug overdose.* Retrieved on January 2, 2024 from www.cdc.gov/drugoverdose/featured-topics/substance-use-disorders/index.html

Centers for Disease Control (2024b). *Quick stats.* Retrieved on January 2, 2024 from www.cdc.gov/nchs/pressroom/quickstats.htm.

Chaudoir, S. R., Ernshaw, V. A., & Andel, S. (2013). "Discredited" versus "discreditable": Understanding how shared and unique stigma mechanisms affect psychological and physical health disparities. *Basic and Applied Social Psychology, 35*, 75–87. https://doi.org/10.1080/01973533.2012.746612

Conrad, P., & Barker, K. K. (2010). The social construction of illness: Key insights and policy implications. *Journal of Health and Social Behavior, 51*, S67–S79. https://doi.org/10.1177/0022146510383495

Davidson, C., Bansal, C., & Hartley, S. (2019). RIZE Massachusetts. Retrieved from https://rizema.org/wp-content/uploads/2019/07/GE-Rize-Shatterproof-White-Paper-Final.pdf

DeFlavio, J. R., Rolin, S. A., Nordstrom, B. R., & Kazal, L. A. (2015). Analysis of barriers to adoption of buprenorphine maintenance therapy by family physicians. *Rural and Remote Health, 15*, 93–103. http://dx.doi.org/10.22605/RRH3019

Eaton, L. (2004). *Reasons for dropout from drug abuse treatment: Symptoms, personality, and motivation.* Addictive behaviors. Retrieved on January 15, 2004 from https://pubmed.ncbi.nlm.nih.gov/15964152/

Eysenk, H. J., & Eysenk, M. W. (1985). *Personality and individual differences: A natural science approach.* Plenum.

Goffman, E. (1963). *Stigma: Notes on the management of spoiled identity.* John Wiley & Sons.

Heisel, A. D. (2010). Verbal aggression and prefrontal cortex asymmetry. In T. A. Avtgis & A. S. Rancer (Eds.), *Arguments, aggression, and conflict: New directions in theory and research* (pp. 26–43). Routledge.

Heisel, A. D., LaFrance, B. H., & Beatty, M. J. (2003). Self-reported extraversion, neuroticism, and psychoticism as predictors of peer rated verbal aggressiveness and affinity-seeking competence. *Communication Monographs, 70,* 1–15. https://dx.doi.org/10.1080/03637750302477

Helping you to help others. Home. (n.d.). https://www.naadac.org/

Infante, A. S., & Wigley, C. J. III. (1986). Verbal aggressiveness: An interpersonal model and measure. *Communication Monographs, 53*, 61–69. http://dx.doi.org/10.1080/03637758609376126

Infante, D. A. (1987). Aggressiveness. In J. C. McCroskey & J. A. Daly (Eds.), *Personality and interpersonal communication* (pp. 57–192). Sage.

Kelly, J. F., Dow, S. J., & Westerhoff, C. (2010). Does our choice of substance-related terms influence perceptions of treatment need? an empirical investigation with two commonly used terms. *Journal of Drug Issues, 40*, 805–818. https://doi.org/10.1177/002204261004000403

Kelly, J. F., Saitz, R., & Wakeman, S (2016). Language, substance use disorders, and policy: The need to reach consensus on an "addiction-ary". *Alcohol Treat Q*, 34, 116–123. https://doi.org/10.1080/07347324.2016.1113103

Kelly, J. F., Wakeman, S. E., & Saitz, R. (2015). Stop talking 'dirty': Clinicians, language, and quality of care for the leading cause of preventable death in the United States. *The American Journal of Medicine, 128*, 8–9. https://doi.org/10.1016/j.amjmed.2014.07.043.

Kelly, J. F., & Westerhoff, C. M. (2010). Does it matter how we refer to individuals with substance-related conditions? A randomized study of two commonly used terms. *International Journal of Drug Policy, 21*, 202–207. https://doi.org/10.1016/j.drugpo.2009.10.010

Kennedy-Hendricks, A., Busch, S. H., McGinty, E. E., Bachhuber, M. A., Niederdeppe, J., Gollust, S. E., Webster, D. W., Fiellin, D. A., & Barry, C. L. (2016). Primary care physicians' perspectives on the prescription opioid epidemic. *Drug and Alcohol Dependence, 165*, 61–70. https://doi.org/10.1016/j.drugalcdep.2016.05.010

Kinney, T. A., & Segrin, C. (1998). Cognitive moderators of negative reactions to verbal aggression. *Communication Studies, 49,* 49–72. http://dx.doi.org/10.1080/10510979809368518

Link, B. G. F. T., Cullen, E., Struening, P. E., Shrout, B. P., & Dohrenwerd, B. P. (1989). A modified labeling theory approach to mental disorders: An empirical assessment. *American Sociological Review, 54,* 400–423. https://doi.org/10.2307/2095613

Luoma, J. B., Twohig, M. P., Waltz, T., Hayes, S. C., Roget, N., Padilla, M., & Fisher, G. (2007). An investigation of stigma in individuals receiving treatment for substance abuse. *Addictive Behaviors, 32*, 1331–1346. https://doi.org/10.1016/j.addbeh.2006.09.008

Norton, R. W. (1978). Foundations of a communicator style construct. Human Communication Research, 4(2), 99–112. https://doi.org/10.1111/j.1468-2958.1978.tb00600.x

Opportunities to increase screening and treatment . . . – rize massachusetts. (n.d.). https://rizema.org/wp-content/uploads/2019/07/GE-Rize-Shatterproof-White-Paper- Final.pdf.

Paquette, C. E., Syvertsen, J. L., & Pollini, R. A. (2018, July). Stigma at every turn: Health services experiences among people who inject drugs. *The International Journal on Drug Policy, 57*, 104–110. https://www.ncbi.nlm.nih.gov/pmc/articles/PMC5994194/

Polcin, D. L., Galloway, G. P., Bond, J., Korcha, R., & Greenfield, T. K. (2010). How do residents of recovery houses experience confrontation between entry and 12-month follow-up? *Journal of Psychoactive Drugs, 42*, 49–62. https://doi.org/10.1080/02791072.2010.10399785

Polcin, D. L., Mulia, N., & Jones, L. (2012). Substance users' perspectives on helpful and unhelpful confrontation: Implications for recovery. *Journal of Psychoactive Drugs, 44*, 144–152. https://doi.org/10.1080/02791072.2012.684626

Rains, S. A. (2018). *Coping with illness digitally.* MIT Press.

Rancer, A. S., & Avtgis, T. A. (2006). *Argumentative and aggressive communication: Theory, research and application.* Sage.

Rancer, A. S., & Avtgis, T. A. (2014). *Argumentative and aggressive communication: Theory, research, and applications* (2nd ed.). Peter Lang.

Richard, C., Lussier, M.-T., Millette, B., & Tanoubi, I. (2023, December 1). *Healthcare providers and patients: An essay on the importance of professional assertiveness in healthcare today.* Medical education online. https://www.ncbi.nlm.nih.gov/pmc/articles/PMC10101662/

SAMHSA. (n.d.). *Tip 42: Substance abuse treatment for persons with co-occurring disorders.* https://www.samhsa.gov/resource/ebp/tip-42-substance-abuse-treatment-persons-co-occurring-disorders

Schomerus, G., Corrigan, P. W., Klauer, T., Kuwert, P., Freyberger, H. J., & Lucht, M. (2011). Self-stigma in alcohol dependence: Consequences for drinking-refusal self-efficacy. *Drug and Alcohol Dependence, 114*, 12–17. https://doi.org/10.1016/j.drugalcdep.2010.08.013

Spitzberg, B. H., & Cupach, W. R. (1984). *Interpersonal communication competence.* Sage.

Stone, E. M., Kennedy-Hendricks A., Barry C. L., Bachhuber M. A., & McGinty E. E. (2021). *The role of stigma in U.S. primary care physicians' treatment of opioid use disorder*. Drug and alcohol dependence. https://pubmed.ncbi.nlm.nih.gov/33621805/

U.S. Department of Health and Human Services. (n.d.). *Nida.nih.gov*. National Institutes of Health. https://nida.nih.gov/

Valencic, K. M., Beatty, M. J., Rudd, J. E., Dobos, J. A., & Heisel, A. D. (1998). An empirical test of a communibiological model. *Communication Quarterly*, *46*, 327–341. http://dx.doi.org/10.1080/01463379809370105

van Boekel, L. C., Brouwers, E. P. M., van Weeghel, J., & Garretsen, H. F. L. (2013). Stigma among health professionals towards patients with substance use disorders and its consequences for healthcare delivery: Systematic review. *Drug and Alcohol Dependence*, *131*(1–2), 23–35. https://doi.org/10.1016/j.drugalcdep.2013.02.018

van Boekel, L. C., Brouwers, E. P. M., van Weeghel, J., & Garretsen, H. F. L. (2014). Healthcare professionals' regard towards working with patients with substance use disorders: Comparison of primary care, general psychiatry and specialist addiction services. *Drug and Alcohol Dependence*, *134*, 92–98. https://doi.org/10.1016/j.drugalcdep.2013.09.012

Vik, P. W., Celucci, T., Jarchow, A., & Hedt, J. (2004). Cognitive impairment in substance abuse. *Psychiatric Clinics*, *27*, 97–109. https://doi.org/10.1016/S0193-953X(03)00110-2

Volkow, N. D. (2020) Stigma and the toll of addiction. *New England Journal of Medicine*, *382*, 1289–1290. doi:10.1056/nejmp1917360

Weiner, B., Perry, R. P., & Magnusson, J. (1988). An attributional analysis of reactions to stigmas. *Journal of Personality and Social Psychology*, *55*, 738. https://doi.org/10.1037/0022-3514.55.5.738

Werder, K., Curtis, A., Reynolds, S., & Satterfield, J. (2021). Addressing bias and stigma in the language we use with persons with opioid use disorder: A narrative review. *Journal of the American Psychiatric Nurses Association*, *28*, 9–22. https://doi.org/10.1177/10783903211050121

Wright, K. B., & Rains, S. A. (2013). Weak-tie support network preference, health-related stigma, and health outcomes in computer-mediated support groups. *Journal of Applied Communication Research*, *41*, 309–324. https://doi.org/10.1080/00909882.2013.792435

Yang, L. H., Wong, L. Y., Grivel, M. M., & Hasin, D. S. (2017). Stigma and substance use disorders: An international phenomenon. *Current Opinion in Psychiatry*, *30*, 378–388. https://doi.org/10.1097/YCO.0000000000000351

12

Rural Communities and Mental Health

Challenges and Recommendations from a Health Communication Perspective

Lindsey Jo Hand

When interviewed for a study on rural mental health (Hand, 2023), Randy (name changed for anonymity) discussed his experience living with mental illness in a rural Georgia community. He explained that he, along with many people in the community, faced several barriers to finding community support and specialized care for mental health. He discussed how the lack of access to care in the community and his financial situation hindered him from seeking care for his mental health. Randy explained, "But it's hard not to mention the fact you got no money, especially right now, right? I mean, my insurance is like, I got a $5,000 deductible. I mean, I can't go see anybody, even if I really wanted to." Randy went on to explain that when he sought care for his mental health in the past, he waited until he was experiencing suicidal ideation to seek treatment because he was so concerned about finances. He managed to find a counselor through telemedicine, which he credits with saving his life. Randy also talked about the cultural stigma of mental illness, which is common in rural communities, "They keep it quiet, uh, in the old Appalachian culture. And that's the culture that I grew up in. Uh, it's [mental illness] considered a weakness . . . 'just suck it up' is a common expression . . . that's a hand God dealt, you just live with." Randy went on to explain that he believed his experiences were not unique, and as a religious leader in his community, he personally knew many people in the community who would benefit from education on mental health as well as access to medical care for their mental health. The barriers described by Randy in this study (Hand, 2023) such as lack of education on mental health, stigma, poverty, and lack of access to care, are unfortunately common in many rural communities.

Rural Communities and Mental Health

Though roughly 60 million Americans live in rural areas and 98 percent of the United States' landmass is rural (America Counts Staff, 2021), rural health is an often overlooked and underfunded category of public health, especially initiatives targeting mental health. *Mental health* is defined by the World Health Organization (WHO) (2023) as "a state of well-being in which every individual realizes his or her own potential, can cope with the normal stresses of life, can work productively and fruitfully, and is able to contribute to her or his community" (para. 1). Approximately one in five adults in America experience mental illness (National Alliance on Mental Illness (NAMI), 2023), and though the prevalence of mental illness diagnoses in rural residents is similar to that of urban residents, rural residents experience significant disparities in mental health outcomes (Morales et al., 2020). For instance, rates of depression and suicide are higher in rural areas (NAMI, 2023; Rural Health Information Hub, 2023b). Suicide rates in rural areas are especially high among men, young people (20s and 30s), and older rural adults (CDC, 2015; Rural Health Information Hub, 2023a; Morales et al., 2020). Suicide rates of veterans in rural areas are also one of the highest in the country (Morales, 2020; CDC, 2023a).

Some common risk factors for mental health disparities in rural areas include socioeconomic status and higher rates of poverty, higher rates of uninsured residents or lack of coverage for mental health care, limited or no access to healthcare specialists, living long distances from clinics, ongoing shortages of mental health professionals in rural areas, lack of broadband access for telemedicine for mental health, the inability to recognize mental illness or lack of education on mental health, lack of culturally competent care, and the stigma of having mental illness or needing to seek mental healthcare services (CDC, 2023c; Rural Health Information Hub, 2022).

Addressing such risk factors for mental health needs in rural areas requires multiple approaches from an array of disciplines, as no single field or approach can address each unique challenge rural residents face. Communication research can contribute to addressing the complexities of mental health disparities in rural areas, specifically targeting mental health promotion and education, the use of telemedicine for mental health care, and culturally competent communication from healthcare providers.

How people in rural areas learn about and perceive mental health problems is essential to better understanding and addressing this public health issue. Researchers attempting to design communication campaigns that address rural mental health must consider additional cultural factors that might hinder seeking support for mental health issues. Communication research may aid in developing effective strategies that educate rural populations on mental health, change perceptions and stigma surrounding mental health, and improve care in clinical settings.

This book chapter explores the complexities of rural mental health problems, suggests health communication theories useful in the study of the implementation of intervention programs addressing rural mental health, and makes recommendations for future steps to improve mental health in rural America from a health communication perspective.

Problem Recognition: Understanding Mental Health Disparities in Rural America

The rise in rural suicide rates in recent years is potentially attributed to social isolation, lack of employment due to a decline in local economies, access to lethal means (firearms), the stigma of mental illness and/or suicidal ideation, cultural norms, and lack of access to adequate mental health services (Judd et al., 2006; Creighton et al., 2017; Kegler et al., 2017). To date, scholars of rural mental health have increasingly focused on the relationship between firearm ownership and accessibility to guns in rural areas, providing strong evidence that firearms in the home increase the likelihood of suicide (Branas et al., 2004; Kposowa, 2013; Mann & Michel, 2016). Death by firearms in rural areas is considered to be a public health crisis and is more likely to happen due to suicide than due to homicide or accidental firearm discharge (Branas et al., 2004). In rural areas, greater firearm ownership and availability of firearms are correlated with higher suicide rates and the likelihood that someone will take their own life using a gun (Judd et al., 2006; Nestadt et al., 2017; Mann & Michel, 2016; Morgan et al., 2018).

Scholars have also focused on geological isolation as a contributing factor to mental health disparities in rural areas. Geographical isolation encompasses isolation from one's community as well as physical distance from mental health clinics and services. People who live in rural areas are often isolated and have restricted access to specialized clinics or may have access to one clinic that provides basic, primary health care (Hollingsworth, 2018; Morgan et al., 2018). This geographic isolation contributes to a lack of access to care. Considered a result of geographical isolation, social isolation, loneliness, and lack of belonging are also well-established risk factors for suicide and are thought to be possible risk factors for elevated depression and suicide rates in rural areas (Judd et al., 2006; McPhedran & Diego, 2013; Monteith et al., 2021). Although not all rural communities are geographically isolated, the geographical isolation of rural communities is more likely to cause a lack of social connection and social capital.

Understanding risk factors of mental health disparities in rural areas is complex because they are not mutually exclusive, and one can affect another. For example, a lack of access to mental health services and isolation are often due to location and people residing in very remote areas with limited access to public transportation, but these factors can also be related to economic decline (Kegler et al., 2017). Social isolation also occurs in very specific types of rural communities as some rural communities may be far from an urban area, but the residents are not far from one another. Access to and attitudes regarding firearms and the stigma of mental health disorders are often considered cultural factors that contribute to this health disparity (Judd et al., 2006; Kegler et al., 2017).

Protective factors against mental health issues such as depression and suicidal ideation have not been studied as rigorously or as extensively as the aforementioned risk factors (CDC, 2023c), but they are worth recognizing as they play an important part in developing effective suicide and mental health stigma interventions in rural communities. One of the most commonly cited protective factors against suicide in rural communities is social connectedness/social capital, which decreases the likelihood of suicides in rural areas (McLean et al., 2008; Steelesmith et al., 2019). Social capital encompasses social relationships and social connectedness in which people have strong interpersonal and community connections that allow them to access various community resources that positively influence their health (McLean et al., 2008). Having strong social capital often results in having strong social support systems in which people experiencing depression or depressive symptoms can seek help and support from their social connections.

Communicative social capital consists of "an information and problem-solving resource that accrues to residents as they become more integrated into their local communication network of neighbors, community organizations, and local media" (Matsaganis & Wilkin, 2015, p. 377).

Using Health Communication to Address Rural Mental Health Disparities

Although communication research on rural mental health is somewhat sparse, there are multiple efforts underway to address mental health disparities in rural areas. In particular, health communication scholars are not only assets in the formation of mental health promotion programs but can also be extremely useful in providing evaluative and systematic approaches to developing and implementing health communication intervention programs.

Mental Health Promotion and Education

Mental health promotion and education programs often target groups that experience health disparities, and these types of programs may help reach rural populations. Mental health promotion and education programs are considered cost-effective ways to promote well-being and help people learn about mental health (Singh et al., 2022). Mental health promotion as a concept is broad and advocates for empowerment, collaboration, and participation from communities (Singh et al., 2022). Mental health education is intrinsic to mental health promotion as the promotion of improved mental health outcomes in a community is only possible when communities are empowered with knowledge. There is considerable evidence that mental health promotion and education programs are effective in targeting risk and protective factors for various mental illnesses, lowering the risk for the development of mental disorders (Singh et al., 2022). Educational approaches also tend to challenge stigma messages or inaccurate stereotypes about mental illness by replacing these messages with accurate information (Corrigan et al., 2012). Stigma is often considered a risk factor for poor mental health outcomes in rural areas as mental illness is often highly stigmatized and poorly understood, which can be a major barrier to seeking help (Winton, 2022).

Promotional and educational efforts often come in the form of public service announcements or media campaigns. Communication scholars should consider our potential roles in these types of campaigns as they require formative research, audience testing, communication strategies, and evaluative measures. Very little scholarship on the implementation and efficacy of mental health campaigns in rural areas is available. However, there are several health promotion and education programs available to study and evaluate. Three examples of such programs that communication scholars have assessed are the Real Men. Real Depression campaign, the Community Response to Eliminating Suicide (CORES) program, and the StigmaBeat program.

The *Real Men. Real Depression.* This campaign spearheaded by the National Institute of Mental Health in 2003 is one of the largest-scale health campaigns targeting men, depression, and suicide. Though this campaign did not solely focus on rural populations, rural populations were included in the target audience. The purpose of the campaign was to address suicide and depression among men, taking place on a national scale as a mass media campaign. The campaign was considered a success (Rochlen et al., 2005) because it reached an estimated 34 million people, including rural audiences, through television PSAs and another eight million through the website. However, the only measure of success was the reach of the campaign messages and not whether the messages educated or changed perceptions of depression.

Although this campaign did not use a theoretical framework, Rochlen et al. (2005) suggested that future campaigns of this nature should consider incorporating theory from a social marketing perspective and models that provide insight into social-psychological processes. While the campaign did not use an empirically based method to inform the design and implementation of the campaign, it was one of the first campaigns on this scale, and the reach was massive. It was a positive step toward addressing this public health issue (Rochlen et al., 2005).

The Community Response to Eliminating Suicide (CORES) program

As a community-based and gatekeeper education model developed in response to a high incidence rate of suicides over a short period in rural Australia (Jones et al., 2015). Elements of this program include education and starting a conversation about a taboo topic, promoting community engagement and support from the community, and providing training to community members. CORES has sought to do the following: (1) gather local people in the community to examine and understand their community, (2) foster an understanding of suicide, (3) develop the skills of local people to identify and respond to suicide at an early stage, (4) engage local people in the delivery of the program, (5) identify and link people to community and professional support services, and (6) empower the local community to own and manage the program (Jones et al., 2015, p. 2).

This intervention design promotes education and community involvement. It puts much of the responsibility of support on the community members. While CORES is lacking in evaluative measures, the design is informed by an ecological model and is empirically based. Since its implementation, suicide rates in rural Australia have declined, establishing a correlation between program implementation and reduced suicide rates. This program has shown that a community-based gatekeeper program can be effective and aid in the education and prevention of suicide (Jones et al., 2015).

StigmaBeat

StigmaBeat (Hine et al., 2023) is also a recent communication campaign effort aimed at reducing mental health stigma among young people (15–25 years) living in rural areas. This program uses a co-design approach to create short films on mental health stigma from the perspective of young people. This project resulted in the creation of audio-visual resources that reflected participants' lived experiences, which can potentially reduce the stigma of mental illness in young people (Hine et al., 2023). While StigmaBeat is a great example of participatory communication research, the program was not grounded in theory and did not have any formal evaluation of program efficacy.

Despite their shortcomings, these programs show where communication scholars can provide insight into what works, what does not, and what strategies to use going forward. One emerging lesson from the programs is that health communication scholars should work with rural communities as well as organizations that benefit these communities.

Telemedicine for Rural Mental Health

Telemedicine refers to any form of medical care provided through telecommunications devices such as phones and computers (Hand, 2021). Through telemedicine, rural residents may have access to care they wouldn't have otherwise, providing a means to meet with specialists virtually or a way for their primary care provider to consult with mental health professionals (Myers, 2018; Dwyer et al., 2021). Telemedicine also potentially addresses the stigmas surrounding mental illness and seeking medical help (Dwyer et al., 2021;

Hand, 2021). Residents can see a mental healthcare provider privately, without leaving their house or being seen by others in the community visiting a mental healthcare provider. As the lack of privacy is often a barrier to seeking care in rural communities (Hand, 2021; Bullard, 2020), telemedicine is likely the best way to reduce disparities in access to healthcare providers (Myers 2018; Dwyer et al., 2021).

Telemental health is also a component of several intervention programs aimed at addressing rural health disparities. Programs that may be of interest include the University of Vermont Medical Center's Nursing Home Telepsychiatry Service, Schools that Care, FirstLink Care and Support Program, the Rural Outreach Center, the Minnesota Integrative Behavioral Health Program, the Regional Behavioral Health Network, the SCDMH Emergency Department Telepsychiatry Consultation Program, and Indiana ASPIN Veteran's Services. Implementing programs such as these can benefit from the aid of trained social scientists who can guide evidence-based approaches to community intervention programs focused on telemedicine.

However, mental health care through telemedicine still needs to make progress. Bischoff et al. (2004) examined the implementation of a telemental health program in rural Nebraska, focusing on the efficacy of technology-mediated conversations compared to face-to-face conversations with mental healthcare providers. The study found that technology can affect the communication process, disrupting the therapeutic relationship between the patient and provider. The authors also focused on the lack of nonverbal communication and how to compensate for this loss during appointments (Bischoff et al., 2004).

Gibson et al. (2009) examined the attitudes of clinicians toward the use of telehealth technologies to provide mental health care in rural areas. This study focused on several barriers identified by healthcare workers, which illuminated apprehension in adopting the technology to deliver care. However, most clinicians recognize how useful telehealth can be in providing rural mental health services. This study is a good example of formative research on the adoption of technology in rural healthcare settings.

Regarding infrastructure, many rural areas have limited access to broadband and the technology necessary for telemental health appointments through teleconferencing software (Hand, 2021). Telemental health care can be administered simply through phone calls, and though this cannot completely replace in-person care with a provider, it is a step in a positive direction in providing access to mental health care in rural areas.

Cultural Competence Among Mental Healthcare Providers

Patient-clinician communication has been studied at length, but more studies are needed in the area of rural mental health. Cultural factors in rural communities shape mental health disparities in rural populations (Morales et al., 2020). The stigma of having mental illness and the stigma of seeking help for mental health are considered cultural factors that contribute to mental health disparities in rural areas (Morales et al., 2020). This stigma and reluctance to discuss mental health may impact mental health literacy as well (Morales et al., 2020). Cultural norms common in rural populations, such as individualism and rugged independence, are also considered risk factors for suicide, as these may impact seeking support from loved ones or medical professionals (Morales et al., 2020). Additionally, people living in rural areas, especially ethnic and racial minorities, tend to have very little trust in formal medical institutions (Deskins et al., 2006; Morales et al., 2020).

Providing culturally competent care can break down barriers to care and communication with the patient, even if the provider doesn't have the same cultural background as the patient (Bullard, 2020). The field of health communication is well positioned to aid in better understanding how clinicians may effectively communicate with rural patients by providing culturally competent care. For example, Taye et al. (2023) examined language barriers in healthcare communication in rural and urban hospitals in India. Their study highlighted how language, specifically the use of scientific terms used by medical professionals, can disrupt the communication process between the patient and clinician. To address this barrier, the authors tested the efficacy of infographics in clinics and found that well-designed infographics were impactful and more easily understood by patients than verbal explanations of complex medical concepts (Taye et al., 2023). This study is a great example of identifying a health communication problem and testing solutions that may improve clinical care for mental health patients living in rural areas.

Another exemplary study stresses the importance of shared language in rural behavioral health interventions (Staton, et al., 2019). This study found that the use of shared language and similar communication styles reflective of the patient's culture helped to shrink the perceived power gap between patient and provider (Staton et al., 2019). By sharing some of the same language patterns and communication styles, the clinician was able to build a sense of cultural congruence with participants (Staton et al., 2019). The authors also found that the use of humor, allowing for open discussion of religious beliefs, recognizing the importance of the homeplace, recognizing the importance of family, and providing empowerment and respect were all effective strategies in creating an open communication environment.

Recommended Theories for Rural Mental Health Communication

While the studies discussed in the previous section are great examples of how scholars may address rural mental health disparities using communication research, the studies that address the mental health of rural communities rarely use theoretical frameworks in the development and implementation of mental health promotion efforts. Recommended theories useful to the study of rural mental health communication are (a) the model of stigma communication and stigma management communication theory, (b) social cognitive theory, (c) the health belief model, (d) the theory of planned behavior, and (e) communication infrastructure theory. The following section will briefly describe these recommended theories.

Stigma—Model of Stigma Communication and Stigma Management Communication Theory

Social stigmas are defined as normalized, profoundly negative stereotypes or attributes of a group and its members (Goffman, 1963; Smith, 2007; Smith et al., 2019). Stigmas provide cues to distinguish and categorize people as a separate social entity (Smith, 2007). Two prominent frameworks in stigma communication research are the model of stigma communication and stigma management communication theory. Both frameworks presume that stigmatization is a social process in which communication plays a critical role in the creation and spread of social stigmas (Meisenbach, 2010; Smith et al., 2016; Smith & Bishop, 2019).

Smith's (2007) model of stigma communication identifies how stigmas are communicated and reacted to. The model aids in identifying the relationship between message choices, message reactions, and message effects (Smith, 2007). Message choices may include marks, group labeling, personal responsibility for having the condition, and peril/danger. These message choices can serve as social cues that categorize the stigmatized person(s) as separate from the group, indicating that they don't belong and should be avoided (Smith, 2007). Message reactions include any type of cognitive, affective, or behavioral reaction to the stigma message. Message effects involve the development of the stigma attitude, sharing the stigma message, and the isolation or removal of the stigmatized person(s) (Smith, 2007).

Stigma management communication theory complements the model of stigma communication and addresses how people manage messages of stigma. This theory categorizes the strategies people use to manage stigma, whereas the model of stigma communication identifies pathways in which people are exposed to stigmas and react to messages of stigmas. Key constructs of this theory are stigma communication, stigma type, potentially stigmatized individuals' attitudes toward the public's stigma beliefs and the applicability of the stigma to that individual, stigma management communication strategies, and outcomes/consequences (Meisenbach, 2010). Stigma management communication strategies involve using communication cues such as accepting, avoiding, evading responsibility, reducing offensiveness, denying, and displaying (Meisenbach, 2010). The outcomes/consequences can be anything from effects on self-esteem to achieving a health goal (Meisenbach, 2010).

Assuming that having mental health issues is one of the stigmatized problems, these two theories would be incredibly useful in assessing mental health communication in rural areas. Each theory gives insight into what stigma beliefs are prominent in a community and how these beliefs affect those in the stigmatized group regarding mental health issues. These theories would be useful in conducting formative research for a promotion and education intervention.

Health Belief Model

Rooted in psychosocial theories that examine cognition and behavioral intention, the Health Belief Model (HBM) was developed to enhance health education programs (Rosenstock, 1974). Concepts in this model aid in predicting health behaviors, specifically why people engage in preventive behaviors that screen for conditions or aid in illness management (Champion & Skinner, 2008).

Key constructs of HBM include perceived susceptibility, perceived severity, perceived benefits, perceived barriers, cues to action, and self-efficacy. Perceived susceptibility refers to the extent to which a person believes they are likely to be exposed to or get a disease. Perceived severity, sometimes referred to as seriousness, refers to the perceived risks and consequences of a particular disease or condition. Perceived benefits refer to how effective a person believes the advised action is in reducing risk or the seriousness of disease impact, whereas perceived barriers refer to the belief about the costs (tangible and intangible) of the advised action (Rosentock, 1974; Champion & Skinner, 2008). Cues to action refer to strategies used to get people to engage in a specific health behavior. Though previously defined in the previous section, self-efficacy refers to a person's confidence in their ability to complete a task or act (Champion & Skinner, 2008). HBM also considers other factors that influence health behaviors such as demographic variables (age, class, race, etc.) and psychological characteristics (personality, affect, peer groups, etc.) (Lin et al., 2005; Champion & Skinner, 2008).

Incorporating HBM in communication studies examining rural mental health may aid in assessing rural residents' susceptibility to depression and whether seeking treatment would be considered an option if experiencing depressive symptoms or suicidal ideation. The consideration of demographic and psychological variables can illuminate differences in perceptions and behavioral intentions among gender, socioeconomic status, race, etc., which makes this model useful in designing communicative interventions that examine mental health issues in rural populations.

Theory of Planned Behavior

The theory of planned behavior (TPB) considers the cognitive processes that go into making decisions and influencing behavioral outcomes, which allows for predicting behavior (Holden & Karsh, 2009). This theory assumes that decision-making is based on three types of beliefs: (1) behavioral, (2) normative, and (3) control (Ajzen, 1991), which are typically considered interdependent or related. Behavioral beliefs are salient attitudes one holds about the outcome of a certain behavior (Holden & Karsh, 2009). Normative beliefs involve how the individual perceives others' views or opinions regarding a particular behavior, and control beliefs essentially refer to self-efficacy or one's perception of their ability to behave effectively (Holden & Karsh, 2009).

The underlying assumption of TPB is that intention is one of the best predictors of behavior. An individual is more likely to adopt a specific health behavior if they believe the behavior will lead to outcomes that are personally valued, if the behavior is valued by others whose opinions matter to the individual, and if the person believes they can carry out the behavior (Ajzen, 1991). Using this theory to change health behaviors such as seeking help for mental health issues would be quite valuable in studying rural populations and implementing health communication intervention programs.

Communication Infrastructure Theory

Though not rooted in psychosocial constructs like the frameworks covered thus far, communication infrastructure theory (CIT) also provides a useful theoretical framework for communication scholars studying rural mental health. As a social-ecological theory, CIT conceptualizes communication infrastructure as a storytelling system set in its communication action context (CAC) (Ball-Rokeach et al., 2001). Storytelling systems include macro-, meso-, and micro-levels of storytelling agents, which are distinguished by their size, the main storytelling agents, and the imagined audience at each level (Ball-Rokeach et al., 2001; Wilkin, 2021). Macro-level agents include central institutions that have the resources to develop and disseminate information to a mass audience (Ball-Rokeach et al., 2001). Meso-level agents include smaller organizations that are locally based, such as community media or organizations that serve residents of a specific area (Ball-Rokeach et al., 2001). Micro-level agents are interpersonal networks such as family and friends (Ball-Rokeach et al., 2001). Storytelling in this context not only refers to the sharing of narratives but also to any form of generalized communication about topics. Storytelling may take place at any level, and "storytelling at one level affects storytelling at other levels" (Ball-Rokeach et al., 2001, p. 398). Recognizing this interdependence may be beneficial in understanding how messages about rural mental health are communicated and even reinforced at each level in the storytelling system.

According to CIT, the level to which information dissemination can occur depends on the communication action context (CAC). The CAC includes features of a geographical area that facilitates or hinders communicative action, and these features may include the physical, psychological, sociocultural, economic, and technological aspects of a community (Ball-Rokeach et al., 2001; Literat & Chen, 2013; Wilkin, 2021). Communication infrastructure theory can be useful in designing interventions that target health disparities, which can often occur in "hard-to-reach" populations such as rural populations. These populations often do not readily benefit from community-based providers, potentially due to a communication disconnect between individuals and community organizations (Matsaganis et al., 2014). CIT allows for developing interventions that take place on a community level, often providing connections to resources that are available on the local level (Matsaganis et al., 2014). Disadvantaged communities experiencing disparities often face unique community-level barriers that exacerbate negative health outcomes and disparities. CIT acknowledges these potential barriers as well as untapped community resources, presenting a theoretical approach to developing effective interventions in these disadvantaged communities (Harrington, 2013).

Conclusion

This book chapter has discussed various ways in which health communication research may be useful in addressing rural mental health disparities. Several studies were highlighted in the areas of mental health promotion and education, telemedicine, and culturally competent patient-provider communication. However, the most glaring omission from the studies highlighted in this chapter is the lack of theoretical frameworks to inform their work. In doing this, scholars and practitioners risk developing studies and implementing intervention programs that may not be as effective as they could be, which could often result in a waste of time and resources. Using theory as a guide allows for a better understanding of the target demographic, provides a roadmap for developing and implementing health communication intervention programs, and offers a clearer path to creating strategies that effectively address rural mental health. While there are many useful health communication theories, this chapter proposes the model of stigma communication, the theory of stigma management communication, the social cognitive theory, the health belief model, the theory of planned behavior, and the communication infrastructure theory. These theories offer valuable tools for addressing rural mental health through communication research.

Rural mental health disparities are complex, and there is no simple answer to addressing these disparities. However, health communication scholars can play a significant role in understanding and addressing these disparities by conducting evidence-based and theory-driven research.

Recommended Readings/Resources

Bryant, K., Haynes, T., Greer-Williams, N., & Hartwig, M. (2014). "Too blessed to be stressed": A rural faith community's views of African-American males and depression. *Journal of Religion & Health, 53*(3), 796–808. https://doi.org/10.1007/s10943-012-9672-z

Crumb, L., Mingo, T. M., & Crowe, A. (2019). "Get over it and move on": The impact of mental illness stigma in rural, low-income United States populations. *Mental Health & Prevention, 13*, 143–148. https://doi.org/10.1016/j.mhp.2019.01.010

Herbst, D. M., Griffith, N. R., & Slama, K. M. (2014). Rodeo cowboys: Conforming to masculine norms and help-seeking behaviors for depression. *Journal of Rural Mental Health, 38*(1), 20–35. https://doi.org/10.1037/rmh0000008

Morales, D. A., Barksdale, C. L., & Beckel-Mitchener, A. C. (2020). A call to action to address rural mental health disparities. *Journal of Clinical and Translational Science, 4*(5), 463–467. https://doi.org/10.1017/cts.2020.42

Smith, R. A., & Applegate, A. (2018). Mental health stigma and communication and their intersections with education. *Communication Education,67*(3), 382–393. https://doi.org/10.1080/03634523.2018.1465988

References

Ajzen, I., 1991. The theory of planned behavior. *Organizational Behavior and Human Decision Processes, 50*, 179–211. https://doi.org/10.1016/0749-5978(91)90020-T

America Counts Staff. (2021, October 8). *One in five Americans live in rural areas.* Census.gov. https://www.census.gov/library/stories/2017/08/rural-america.html

Ball-Rokeach, S. J., Kim, Y., & Matei, S. (2001). Storytelling neighborhood: Paths to belonging in diverse urban environments. *Communication Research, 28*(4), 392–428. https://doi.org/10.1177/009365001028004003

Bischoff, R., Hollist, C. S., Smith, C. W., & Flack, P. (2004). Addressing the mental health needs of the rural underserved: Findings from a multiple case study of a behavioral telehealth project. *Faculty Publications, Department of Child, Youth, and Family Studies, 44.* https://digitalcommons.unl.edu/famconfacpub/44

Bullard, J. (2020). *Using cultural humility to address rural mental health gaps.* RTI. https://healthcare.rti.org/insights/using-cultural-humility-address-rural-mental-health-gaps

Branas, C. C., Nance, M. L., Elliott, M. R., Richmond, T. S., & Schwab, C. W. (2004). Urban-rural shifts in intentional firearm death: Different causes, same results. *American Journal Of Public Health, 94*(10), 1750–1755. https://doi.org/10.2105/AJPH.94.10.1750

Centers for Disease Control and Prevention (CDC). (2015). *Understanding suicide.* https://www.cdc.gov/violenceprevention/pdf/suicide_factsheet-a.pdf

Center for Disease Control and Prevention (CDC). (2023a). *About rural health.* https://www.cdc.gov/ruralhealth/about.html

Centers for Disease Control and Prevention (CDC). (2023b). *Suicide in rural America.* https://www.cdc.gov/ruralhealth/Suicide.html

Centers for Disease Control and Prevention (CDC). (2023c). *Suicide policy brief: Preventing suicide in rural America*. https://www.cdc.gov/ruralhealth/suicide/policybrief.html

Champion, V. L., & Skinner, C. S. (2008). The health belief model. In K. Glanz, B. K. Rimer, & K. Visawanath (Eds.), *Health Behavior and Health Education* (4th ed., pp. 45–66). Jossey-Bass.

Corrigan, P. W., Morris, S. B., Michaels, P. J., Rafacz, J. D., & Rüsch, N. (2012). Challenging the public stigma of mental illness: A meta-analysis of outcome studies. *Psychiatric Services*, *63*, 963–973. https://doi.org/10.1176/appi.ps.201100529

Creighton, G., Oliffe, J., Ogrodniczuk, J., & Frank, B. (2017). "You've gotta be that tough crust exterior man": Depression and suicide in rural-based men. *Qualitative Health Research*, *27*(12), 1882–1891. https://doi.org/10.1177/1049732317718148

Deskins, S., Harris, C. V., Bradlyn, A. S., et al. (2006). Preventive care in Appalachia: Use of the theory of planned behavior to identify barriers to participation in cholesterol screenings among West Virginians. *Journal of Rural Health*, *22*(4), 367–374. https://doi.org/10.1111/j.1748-0361.2006.00060.x

Dwyer, A., de Almeida Neto, A., Estival, D., Li, W., Lam-Cassettari, C., & Antoniou, M. (2021). Suitability of text-based communications for the delivery of psychological therapeutic services to rural and remote communities: Scoping review. *Journal of Medical Internet Research*, *8*(2), e19478. https://mental.jmir.org/2021/2/e19478/

Gibson, K., Simms, D., O'Donnell, S., & Molyneaux, H. (2009). *Clinicians' attitudes toward the use of information and communication technologies for mental health services in remote and rural areas*. Canadian Society of Telehealth Conference, Canada. http://firstmile.ca/wp-content/uploads/2015/03/2009-Gibson_et_al_CST-final.pdf

Goffman, E. (1963). Stigma: *Notes on the management of spoiled identity*. Prentice Hall.

Hand, L. J. (2021). The role of telemedicine in rural mental health care around the globe. *Journal of Telemedicine and e-Health*, *23*(3), 285–294. https://doi.org/10.1089/tmj.2020.0536

Hand, L. J. (2023). *Addressing rural America's suicide disparity among men: How mental health stigma is communicated through storytelling networks* (Dissertation, Georgia State University). https://doi.org/10.57709/35397120

Harrington, N. G. (2013). Introduction to the special issue: Communication strategies to reduce health disparities. *Journal of Communication*, *63*, 1–7. https://doi.org/10.1111/jcom.12004

Hine, R., Gladstone, B., Reupert, A., O'Dea, L., Cuff, R., Yates, S., Hagström, A. S., McGaw, V, & Foster, K. (2023). StigmaBeat: Collaborating with rural young people to co-design films aimed at reducing mental health stigma. *Qualitative Health Research*, 34(6),491–506. doi: 10.1177/10497323231211454

Holden, R. J., & Karsh, B. T. (2009) A theoretical model of health information technology usage behaviour with implications for patient safety. *Behaviour & Information Technology, 28*(1), 21–38. https://doi.org/10.1080/01449290601138245

Hollingsworth, J. D. (2018). Is there a doctor in the house: How dismantling barriers to telemedicine practice can improve healthcare access for rural residents. *Howard Law Journal, 62*(2), 653–686. https://heinonline.org/HOL/LandingPage?handle=hein.journals/howlj62&div=27&id=&page=

Jones, S., Walker, C., Miles, A. J., De Silva, E., & Zimitat, C. (2015). A rural, community-based suicide awareness and intervention program. *Rural and Remote Health, 15*(1), 29–72. https://pubmed.ncbi.nlm.nih.gov/25832508/

Judd, F., Cooper, A., Fraser, C., & Davis, J. (2006). Rural suicide-people or place effects? *Australian & New Zealand Journal of Psychiatry, 40*(3), 208–216. https://doi.org/10.1111/j.1440 1614.2006.01776.x

Kegler S. R., Stone, D. M., & Holland, K. M. (2017). Trends in suicide by level of urbanization–United States, 1999–2015. *Morbidity and Mortality Weekly Report (MMWR), 66*(10), 270–273. doi: http://dx.doi.org/10.15585/mmwr.mm6610a2

Kposowa, A. (2013). Association of suicide rates, gun ownership, conservatism and individual suicide risk. *Social Psychiatry & Psychiatric Epidemiology, 48*(9), 1467–1479. https://doi.org/10.1007/s00127-013-0664-4

Lin, P., Simoni, J., & Zemon V. (2005). The health belief model, sexual behaviors, and HIV risk among Taiwanese immigrants. *AIDS Education and Prevention, 17*(5), 469–483. https://doi.org/10.1521/aeap.2005.17.5.469

Literat, I. & Chen, N. N. (2013). Communication infrastructure theory and entertainment-education: An integrative model for health communication. *Communication Theory, 24*(1), 83–103. https://doi.org/10.1111/comt.12011

Mann, J. J., & Michel, C. A. (2016). Prevention of firearm suicide in the United States: What works and what is possible. *American Journal of Psychiatry, 173*(10), 969–979. https://doi.org/10.1176/appi.ajp.2016.16010069

Matsaganis, M. D., Golden, A. G., & Scott, M. E. (2014). Communication infrastructure theory and reproductive health disparities: Enhancing storytelling network integration by developing interstitial actors. *International Journal of Communication, 8*, 1495–1515. https://ijoc.org/index.php/ijoc/article/view/2566/1145

Matsaganis, M. D., & Wilkin, H. A. (2015). Communicative social capital and collective efficacy as determinants of access to health-enhancing resources in residential communities. *Journal of Health Communication, 20*(4), 377–386. https://doi.org/10.1080/10810730.2014.927037

McLean, J., Maxwell, M., Platt, S., Harris, F., & Jepson, R. (2008). Risk and protective factors for suicide and suicidal behaviour: A literature review. Social Research, Scottish Government. https://www.pure.ed.ac.uk/ws/portalfiles/portal/15229108/0073687.pdf

McPhedran, S., & Diego, D. L. (2013). Risk factors for suicide among rural men: Are farmers more socially isolated? *International Journal of Sociology and Social Policy*, 33(11/12), 762–772.https://doi.org/10.1108/IJSSP-03-2013-0038

Meisenbach, R. J. (2010). Stigma management communication: A theory and agenda for applied research on how individuals manage moments of stigmatized identity. *Journal of Applied Communication Research, 38* (3), 268–292. https://doi.org/10.1080/00909882.2010.490841

Monteith, L. L., Holliday, R., Brown, T. L., Brenner, L. A., & Mohatt, N. V. (2021). Preventing suicide in rural communities during the COVID-19 pandemic. *The Journal of Rural Health, 37*(1), 179–184. https://doi.org/10.1111/jrh.12448

Morales, D. A., Barksdale, C. L., & Beckel-Mitchener, A. C. (2020). A call to action to address rural mental health disparities. *Journal of Clinical and Translational Science, 4*(5), 463–467. https://doi.org/10.1017/cts.2020.42

Morgan, E. R., Gomez, A., & Rowhani-Rahbar, A. (2018). Firearm ownership, storage practices, and suicide risk factors in Washington State, 2013–2016. *American Journal of Public Health, 108*(7), 882–888. https://doi.org/10.2105/AJPH.2018.304403

Myers, C. R. (2018). Using telehealth to remediate rural mental health and healthcare disparities. *Issues in Mental Health Nursing, 40*(3), 233–239. https://doi.org/10.1080/01612840.2018.1499157

National Alliance on Mental Health (NAMI). (2023). *Mental health by the numbers.* https://www.nami.org/mhstats

Nestadt, P. S., Triplett, P., Fowler, D. R., & Mojtabai, R. (2017). Urban-rural differences in suicide in the state of Maryland: The role of firearms. *American Journal of Public Health, 107*(10), 1548–1553. https://doi.org/10.2105/AJPH.2017.303865

Taye, R., Paswan, A., Singh, D. D., Kapil, M., Sharma, S., Choudhary, V., Prasad, J., & Pareek, G. (2023). Language as a barrier in health care communication: A comparative study on rural and urban hospitals. *Journal of Pharmaceutical Negative Results, 14*(3). https://www.pnrjournal.com/index.php/home/article/view/8118

Rochlen, A., Whilde, M., & Hoyer, W. (2005). The Real Men Real Depression campaign: Overview, theoretical implications, and research considerations. *Psychology of Men and Masculinity, 6*(3), 186–194. http://dx.doi.org/10.1037/1524 9220.6.3.186

Rosenstock, I. M. (1974). Historical origins of the Health Belief Model. *Health Education Monographs, 2*(4), 328–335.

Rural Health Information Hub. (2022). *Rural health disparities.* https://www.ruralhealthinfo.org/topics/rural-health-disparities

Rural Health Information Hub. (2023a). *Rural mental health: Models and innovations.* https://www.ruralhealthinfo.org/topics/mental-health/project-examples

Rural Health Information Hub. (2023b). *Rural mental health.* https://www.ruralhealthinfo.org/topics/mental-health

Singh, V., Kumar, A., & Gupta, S. (2022). Mental health prevention and promotion-A narrative review. *Frontiers in Psychiatry, 13*, 898009. https://doi.org/10.3389/fpsyt.2022.898009

Smith, R. A. (2007). Language of the lost: An explication of stigma communication. *Communication Theory*, *17*, 462–485. https://doi.org/10.1111/j.1468–2885.2007.00307.x

Smith, R. A., & Bishop, R. E. (2019). Insights into stigma management communication theory: Considering stigmatization as interpersonal influence. *Journal of Applied Communication Research: JACR*, *47*(5), 571–590. https://doi.org/10.1080/00909882.2019.1675894

Smith, R. A., Zhu, X., & Quesnell, M. (2016). Stigma and health/risk communication. In *Oxford Research Encyclopedia*. https://doi.org/10.1093/acrefore/9780190228613.013.96

Smith, R. A., Zhu, X., & Fink, E. L. (2019). Understanding the effects of stigma messages: Danger appraisal and message judgments. *Health Communication*, *34*(4), 424–436. https://doi.org/10.1080/10410236.2017.1405487

Staton, M., Cramer, J., Walker, R., Snell-Rood, C., & Kheibari, A. (2019). The importance of shared language in rural behavioral health interventions: An exploratory linguistic analysis. *Rural Mental Health*, *43*(4), 138–149. https://doi.org/10.1037/rmh0000117

Steelesmith, D. L., Fontanella, C.A., Campo, J. V., Bridge, J. A., Warren, K. L., & Root, E. D. (2019). Contextual factors associated with county-level suicide rates in the United States, 1999 to 2016. *JAMA Network Open, 2*(9), e1910936. https://doi.org/10.1001/jamanetworkopen.2019.10936

Wilkin, H. A. (2021). Communication infrastructure theory. In *International Encyclopedia of Health Communication*. Wiley.

Winton, J. (2022). Confronting mental health challenges in rural America. *National Alliance for Mental Illness*. https://www.nami.org/Blogs/NAMI-Blog/November-2022/Confronting-Mental-Health-Challenges-in-Rural-America#:~:text=Rural%20Americans%20experience%20higher%20rates,access%20mental%20health%20care%20services.

World Health Organization. (2023). Mental health. https://www.who.int/health-topics/mental-health#tab=tab_1

13

Mental Health Problems and Computer-Mediated Support

Focus on the Case of North Korean Defectors in South Korea

Surin Chung and Ma Angelica Mercado

Yujung Choi (a pseudonym used to protect her privacy) is a North Korean defector whom we interviewed for the present study. Currently, she is a senior at a college in Seoul. Her journey began during North Korea's Arduous March, which happened between 1995 and 2000. This severe famine and economic crisis killed her father when she was four years old. Her mother decided to defect the following year to escape starvation.

The mother and daughter escaped by crossing the dangerous Tumen River into China. While escaping from North Korea, Yujung's mother suffered a concussion from falling but could not receive proper medical treatment in China due to their illegal status. For three years in China, they lived in constant fear of the Chinese police and forced repatriation to North Korea.

Seeking legal status, Yujung and her mother eventually traveled to South Korea via Cambodia. They spent a year detained in a refugee camp and experienced multiple life-threatening situations in the country. Yujung finally arrived in South Korea with help from Korean missionaries, followed by her mother the next year.

It is challenging for Yujung and her mother to adapt to South Korea's different culture. Yujung's mother had to work despite her poor health condition. Also, Yujung struggled academically after missing nearly ten years of formal education and experienced identity issues, social prejudice, and discrimination against North Korean defectors. Ultimately, her childhood trauma, identity struggles, and ongoing fear of discrimination create persistent psychological stress and negatively impact her emotional well-being.

Following the armistice in 1953 that marked the end of the Korean War, North and South Korea implemented strict measures to maintain their separation (Millett, 2024). With rare exceptions approved by the respective governments, individuals have been barred from crossing the border, and any exchange of communications between the two nations has been prohibited (Chun, 2022; Park, 2022). Ongoing tensions between the two Koreas created limited opportunities for South Koreans to cultivate a mutual understanding of the lives of North Koreans, resulting in a lack of familiarity with this population. The only instance where this segregation is broken is when North Korean defectors choose South Korea as their new home (Chun, 2022; Lankov, 2006).

The term "North Korean defector" refers to individuals who have fled North Korea to South Korea due to political, ideological, religious, economic, moral, personal, or nutritional reasons (Poorman, 2019). According to the data provided by the Ministry of Unification of South Korea, North Korean defectors have been entering South Korea since the 1990s. The current estimated population of North Korean defectors is more than 33,000, with approximately 40 percent of them falling within the age range of ten to thirty years old (Ministry of Unification, 2023). Their numbers temporarily dropped during the COVID-19 pandemic, but a significant number (i.e., 196 defectors) entered South Korea afterward (Bae & Yeung, 2024). Accordingly, the adjustment of North Korean defectors to a new society has emerged as a significant social issue in South Korea.

Previous studies have reported that defectors from North Korea experience various types of physical and psychological stress before entering South Korea (George, 2010; Hollifield et al., 2002; Kim et al., 2023). For example, North Korean defectors tend to be exposed to life-or-death situations such as acts of violence (e.g., torture), threats, imprisonment, and a shortage of food while migrating to South Korea (George, 2010; Hollifield et al., 2002). Such extreme stressors may cause them to have mental health problems such as self-stigma, post-traumatic stress disorder (PTSD), and depression (Hollifield et al., 2002; George, 2010; Kim et al., 2023). On top of that, after entering South Korea, North Korean defectors face other stressful factors, such as cultural differences, social relations, loneliness, and unemployment, which make it difficult for them to adapt to South Korean society (Kim et al., 2023). Under these circumstances, defectors from North Korea must find a way of both relieving their mental stress and adjusting to a new society through available resources.

This chapter describes the various stressful factors that North Korean defectors experience during their migration and adjustment to South Korean society. Additionally, we provide various coping resources (e.g., tangible support, informational support, and emotional support) to alleviate their mental stress through a theoretical lens of social support. In particular, the present chapter explores how social support can facilitate the adaptation of North Korean defectors to South Korean society by applying the optimal matching model (OMM) to the context of North Korean defectors' mental stress (Cutrona & Suhr, 1992; Cutrona & Russell, 1990). Furthermore, the chapter discusses the available resources through computer-mediated communication that defectors from North Korea can utilize to seek social support. Digital communication technology (e.g., social media and smartphones) enables social support seekers to access various resources with fewer constraints (e.g., time and location). Therefore, the current chapter proposes potential social-seeking strategies through computer-mediated communication, drawing on the framework of the sensitive interaction systems theory (SIST; Barbee & Cunningham, 1995), which explains how North Korean defectors can effectively seek support to address their stress factors.

Problem Identification

Defectors from North Korea undergo challenging experiences during their migration and adjustment to South Korea (Kim & Yoo, 2018). As the number of North Korean defectors to South Korea has increased since the 1990s (Ministry of Unification, 2023), the cases of traumatic events and psychological distress that North Korean defectors experience have increased accordingly. Such factors and situations fall into three stages (i.e., before, during, and after defection), which can damage their mental health (see Table 13.1).

Before Defection

The hardships faced by North Korean defectors stem from the nature of political, economic, and social life in North Korea. North Korea is one of the poorest countries in the world, and approximately 60 percent of the total population was projected to live below the international poverty line in 2018 ($2.15 per day; Cuaresma, 2020). This severe economic situation leads to poor sanitation, an acute shortage of medication, and a lack of access to healthcare in many parts

Table 13.1 North Korean Defectors' Traumatic Experiences and Psychological Distress

Stage	Type of Stressor	Example
Before defection	Traumatic experiences	• Watching public executions, violent beatings, and torture due to political mistakes • Potential threats of torture, wrongful imprisonment, and forced labor in detention facilities • Watching their family die from starvation • Lack of access to health care, medicine • Lack of food and water, natural disasters (e.g., floods), and cold weather • Being raped
	Psychological distress	• Limiting the freedom of ideology, conscience, and expression • Controlling all forms of communication outside the world and surveillance
During defection	Traumatic experiences	• Starvation and lack of treatment • Death of family members • Torture, labor exploitation, human trafficking • Physical or sexual abuse
	Psychological distress	• Fear of being detected, arrested, and sent back to North Korea • Anxiety associated with being in a strange country • Separation from family • Feelings of guilt for having betrayed their homeland and leaving their family at risk of persecution
After defection	Psychological distress	• Language barrier • Cultural difference • Confusion of identity • Social isolation and social prejudice • Unemployment • Difficulties in family relationships • Difficulties in relationships with South Koreans

of the country (Lee et al., 2020). More importantly, North Korea has struggled to produce enough food for its population since the 1990s, and the situation has been exacerbated by the COVID-19 pandemic and natural disasters, including floods that have damaged harvests (Mackenzie, 2023; Yim, 2024). Additionally, food is not distributed equally in North Korea. Access to food varies by social class, engaged enterprise, and other factors, which forces North Koreans to carry out personal economic activities such as trading in markets and cultivating small plots of land to supplement the scarce food supply (Han et al., 2018).

A serious violation of human rights is another strain on people in North Korea. North Korea remains one of the most repressive countries in the world (Hassan, 2023). The country maintains the fearful obedience of the population through torture, public execution, wrongful imprisonment, enforced disappearances, and the widespread use of forced labor in detention facilities. Furthermore, the North Korean government deepened the isolation and repression during the COVID-19 pandemic (Hassan, 2023), exacerbating the threat to ordinary North Koreans' livelihoods and food security.

North Korea denies all fundamental liberties. People in North Korea lack freedom of ideology, conscience, and expression (Han et al., 2018). If North Koreans do not obey the government's policy, authorities send them to secretive political prison camps where they face torture, forced labor, and so on (Hassan, 2023). Additionally, the country maintains absolute and systematic control over all forms of communication with the outside world through extensive mass surveillance programs (Han et al., 2018). North Korea prohibits viewing "reactionary ideology and culture," which means that receiving information from abroad, especially from South Korea, may result in five to fifteen years in prison. Those who distribute such material face life imprisonment or even the death penalty (Seo & Lilieholm, 2024).

During Defection

Defectors from North Korea face more hardship after they flee the country. In many cases, defectors opt for overland routes to neighboring China because it is considered safer to defect to other countries via land routes (Hwang, 2023). However, since China has favorable diplomatic relations with North Korea, defectors to China are not recognized as refugees who can apply for asylum; they are considered economic migrants (Yeung & Seo, 2024). This puts defectors at risk of deportation back to North Korea (Poorman, 2019). Upon return to North Korea, defectors may face charges of treason and be punished with imprisonment, torture, or death (Hwang, 2023). Despite the danger, tens of thousands of North Koreans who are unable to travel to South Korea or other countries remain as undocumented immigrants in China (Poorman, 2019).

North Koreans experience a lot of traumatic events during defection. According to the findings from previous studies (Lee et al., 2022; Min, 2008; Noh & Lee, 2020), many North Korean defectors encounter life-or-death situations during their defection, such as starvation, sexual abuse, labor exploitation, torture, and human trafficking. Defectors also suffer from many emotional and psychological difficulties, such as fear of being found, anxiety associated with being an undocumented person in a new country (e.g., China), separation from their family, and feelings of guilt due to putting their family at risk of persecution (Kim et al., 2023; Lee et al., 2022). These tragic experiences may result in mental health problems for North Korean defectors, such as post-traumatic stress disorder (PTSD), anxiety, and depression (Lee et al., 2022), and thus make it more difficult for them to adjust to South Korean society later.

After Defection

The Constitution of South Korea allows North Koreans to apply for South Korean citizenship upon defection (Poorman, 2019). If North Korean defectors are determined to be non-suspicious by the National Intelligence Service (NIS), they can be admitted to Hanaone, the Settlement Support Center for North Korean defectors (Ji, 2022; Poorman, 2019) for three months. Hanaone, an organization under the Ministry of Unification, aims to provide North Korean defectors with social adjustment education programs that help them understand their new society, gain emotional stability, find employment, receive initial settlement support, and more (Ji, 2022). However, the vocational training that Hanaone offers mainly focuses on blue-collar work and thus tends not to meet the expectations of defectors with higher socio economic backgrounds (Yeung & Seo, 2023).

Although defectors from North Korea are no longer refugees after receiving South Korean citizenship, it is very challenging for them to adapt to a new society. A recent study found that around 19 percent of North Korean defectors regret moving to South Korea due to adaptation problems such as cultural/language differences, economic difficulties, and psychological isolation (Choi, 2022).

Defectors from North Korea have difficulty communicating with people in South Korea despite ostensibly speaking the same language. As the two countries have been divided for over seventy years, many words are used differently, or the exact words carry different meanings (Borowiec, 2014; Min, 2008). For example, South Koreans incorporate foreign languages in day-to-day conversations because South Korea has been culturally influenced by many other countries, such as the United States and Japan, for over seventy years. In contrast, North Koreans rarely incorporate foreign words into their conversations due to limited opportunities to communicate with the rest of the world (Borowiec, 2014; Min, 2008). As a result, North Korean defectors face many communication challenges in South Korea (Kwong, 2018).

Along with the language issue, many defectors from North Korea experience a confusion of identity. They expect to be accepted as fellow Koreans in South Korea, but the reality is that they are considered a "cultural other" (Chun, 2022). People in South Korea have a perception that North Korean defectors are refugees with different cultural traits and migrants with awkward social interactions (Poorman, 2019). This implies that although there is no reason to label North Korean defectors as less "Korean," their sociocultural identity is viewed as something unnatural even if they officially obtain South Korean citizenship (Chun, 2022). Furthermore, previous studies pointed out that since the socio cultural characteristics (e.g., a way of thinking and expressing emotions) that North Korean defectors possess do not fit into South Korean society's value system and codes of conduct, they can be portrayed as unequal or second-rate citizens (Chun, 2015, 2022; Lee, 2014). These prejudices make North Korean defectors unwilling to reveal their identity when interacting in South Korean society (Chun, 2022).

Economic difficulties are another issue that North Korean defectors have to cope with in South Korea. Although defectors from North Korea have the opportunity to be educated about how to engage in economic activity in South Korea at Hanaone, many of them still struggle with unemployment and the limited ability to survive in a competitive and industrialized society (Min, 2008). According to a 2023 survey conducted by the Center for North Korean Human Rights (Yim et al., 2023), defectors from North Korea earn an average of 2,128,200 KRW per month, which is 70.8 percent of the national average wage of 3,007,000 KRW. Another survey, conducted in 2022, revealed that around 69 percent of 300 North Korean respondents reported difficulties maintaining their livelihoods (Moon & Song, 2023). The survey also found that 48 percent of defectors struggled to establish financial security, and 45 percent faced discrimination and social prejudice in the workplace, which negatively impacted their economic status in South Korea (Moon & Song, 2023).

In addition, psychological isolation negatively affects North Korean defectors' mental health. Defectors' family situations are complicated and varied (Min,

2008). Some defectors left their families and came to South Korea alone. Other defectors married while they were in China or South Korea. In any case, many defectors miss their families who were left behind in North Korea (Choi, 2022; Min, 2008). North Korean defectors also have limited social networks due to their minority status, leading to increased levels of mental stress while adjusting to South Korean society (Korea Hana Foundation, 2020).

Lastly, if defectors are alone in South Korea, they tend to be frustrated and lonely in an unfamiliar society (Ko, 2022). According to a survey from the Korea Institute of Public Administration (Choi, 2023), the level of emotional temperature that South Koreans feel toward North Korean defectors is 40.3 points, which is lower than the level of emotional temperature they feel toward other foreigners living in South Korea (44.6 points). The same survey revealed that around 22 percent of South Koreans would not be able to accept any relationship (e.g., neighbors, coworkers, close friends, spouses) with North Korean defectors (Choi, 2023). These findings imply that defectors from North Korea are not as socially accepted as fellow South Koreans, which makes it hard for them to adapt to South Korean society.

In sum, North Korean defectors' lives are not smooth even if they successfully arrive in South Korea due to many economic, cultural, and psychological difficulties. These situations may cause or exacerbate North Korean defectors' mental health problems.

Communication Strategies Social Support and North Korean Defectors' Mental Well-Being

Over the last three decades, a considerable amount of literature consistently has shown a connection between traumatic and stressful events before and during the migration of refugees and adverse psychological outcomes (e.g., Johnson & Thompson, 2008; Mollica et al., 1998; Neuner et al., 2004; Steel et al., 2009). Moreover, previous studies have offered ample evidence that a higher accumulation of traumatic events is associated with the manifestation of more severe psychiatric symptoms among refugees (Knipscheer et al., 2015; Neuner et al., 2004; Steel et al., 2002).

After resettling in a new country, refugees may face numerous challenges, including delays in asylum, uncertainty about their status, rejected refugee claims, poor living conditions, concerns about family back home, social exclusion, and discrimination. These challenges can have a detrimental impact on refugees' mental health and well-being (Aragona et al., 2012; Hecker et al., 2018; Laban et al., 2005; Schick et al., 2016).

Several studies have revealed that mental health issues are prevalent among these refugees compared to the general population (Bogic et al., 2015; Fazel et al., 2005; Steel et al., 2009). However, studies have also identified various forms of social support that can play a crucial role in mitigating these adversities (Marinucci & Riva, 2021; Marinucci et al., 2022; Pouraghajan et al., 2023).

Social support is an integral resource intended to help individuals improve their ability to cope with stress (Cohen, 1985). According to Lynch et al. (1999), an individual can obtain social support through their connections with others, whether they be individuals, groups, or the broader community. Social support may offer health benefits for physically and psychologically vulnerable groups of people (e.g., cancer patients) through participation in social relationships (Goldsmith, 2004).

Scholars have defined concepts and measures of social support (Barrera, 1986; Goldsmith, 2004; House & Kahn, 1985) into three broad types: (1) social embeddedness, (2) perceived social support, and (3) enacted social support. First, social embeddedness is a sociological perspective that focuses on an individual's connections to a social group (Vangelisti, 2009). This type of social support explains the importance of the structure of social networks wherein each individual plays a specific role in offering social support; thus, how individuals are connected within their communities is a significant research topic (Albrecht & Adelman, 1987; Barrera, 1986; Stokes, 1983; Procidano & Heller, 1983).

Perceived social support is a psychological perspective that emphasizes how individuals' beliefs about the availability of social support help them adjust to stressful situations. This body of research mainly delves into individuals' subjective assessment of the availability and the quality of support they receive from their social networks (Albrecht & Adelman, 1987; Barrera, 1986; Stokes, 1983; Procidano & Heller, 1983). Perceived social support posits that the perceived availability of social support facilitates changing the appraisal of an adverse event and bolsters one's perceived ability to cope with a stressful situation accordingly (Lakey & Cohen, 2000).

Third, enacted social support mainly focuses on how individuals communicate with support recipients in need (Albrecht & Adelman, 1987). This body of research involves verbal and nonverbal communication behaviors when individuals render assistance (Barrera, 1986; Kim, 2014) and how interactions occur between support providers and recipients (Vangelisti, 2009).

While researchers have defined the characteristics of social support in various ways, they commonly emphasize that social support plays a crucial role in reducing the mental stress of individuals and thereby improving their psychological well-being (Topor et al., 2011; Wang et al. 2018; Vangelisti, 2009). The stress-buffering model, which follows the notion of perceived social support, posits that when individuals perceive that appropriate coping resources are available through the connections of a social network, these resources can serve as a stress buffer (Cohen & Wills, 1985). The stress-buffering model posits that the availability of social support helps individuals decrease the likelihood of interpreting adverse events as threats, which in turn reduces their stress levels and contributes to improved mental health (Cohen, 2004).

Following the stress-buffering perspective, when North Korean defectors perceive that appropriate social support is available, it may help them reduce negative emotional responses and thus adjust psychologically to a stressful situation (Wills & Cleary, 1996). This is because the perceived availability of social support can serve as a coping mechanism (Uchino, 2004). In other words, when North Korean defectors perceive that they have coping resources to manage the stressful events they experience in South Korea, they may appraise the event in a more positive way, which can result in less psychological distress (Lazarus & Folkman, 1984). Subsequently, they can better adjust to the stressful situation (Cohen & McKay, 1984; Uchino, 2009).

In summary, by applying the stress-buffering model's mechanism, we propose that the perceived availability of support can lead North Korean defectors to appraise their stressful situations in South Korea less negatively, which in turn may help improve their mental health issues through available coping resources.

Previous research has shown evidence supporting the assumption that North Korean defectors can benefit from social support as they adapt to life in South Korea. For example, a study found that North Korean defectors living in South Korea primarily addressed acculturative stress by seeking available social support (Park et al., 2023). This support involved engaging with members of culturally similar groups or peer groups (e.g., fellow North Korean defectors) and contacting supportive acquaintances within the South Korean community. Promoting social connections among North Korean defectors helps alleviate acculturative stress by reducing feelings of isolation and enhancing a sense of belonging (Park et al., 2023). Kim et al. (2023) conducted interviews with North Korean defectors residing in South Korea. They found that they appreciated those who provided them with practical information and education that helped them adapt to their new society. The interviewees noted various social support mechanisms, including practical information and supportive words, which helped them rebuild their lives in South Korea.

Similarly, Ekmen et al. (2021) found that social support from family contributes to reducing mental stress among Syrian refugees in Turkey. The study examined the relationships among perceived social support, stress, life satisfaction, COVID-19 anxiety, and social aid received by Syrian refugees. Another study involving Syrian refugees in Sweden found that a higher level of social support is significantly connected to lower instances of post-traumatic stress disorder (Gottvall et al., 2019).

For several decades, numerous studies have consistently demonstrated the positive impact of social support across various contexts, including reduced mortality rates, enhanced mental well-being, and improved interpersonal relationships (Miller & Ray, 1994; Pierce et al., 1992; Vangelisti, 2009). In examining the effects of social support on physical and psychological well-being, scholars have employed various theoretical frameworks to understand the different forms and dynamics (Cohen & Wills, 1985; Cutrona & Russell, 1990; Hirsch, 1980; House, 1981; Kahn, 1979; Weiss, 1974). The ideas tend to revolve around a shared set of five support dimensions: (1) emotional support, (2) network support, (3) esteem support, (4) tangible support, and (5) informational support (Cutrona & Suhr, 1992; Cutrona & Russell, 1990).

According to the optimal matching model (OMM; Cutrona & Russell, 1990; Cutrona & Suhr, 1992), emotional support can be understood as the provision of care, concern, empathy, love, and trust, and is delivered through the expressions of emotional words and body gestures. *Network support* indicates a sense of membership and belonging. It consists of a message that increases a sense of belonging to a group with similar interests or situations. *Esteem support* refers to a message that boosts one's skills, abilities, and intrinsic values, allowing social support recipients to feel reassured. *Tangible support* is perceived as providing practical goods and assistance to individuals, including physical or monetary aid. Lastly, *informational support* involves advice or guidance regarding potential solutions to a problem.

These five types of social support can be divided into two broad categories: action-facilitating support and nurturant support (Lazarus & Folkman, 1984). *Action-facilitating support* provides an individual with tangible and informational support (Cutrona & Russell, 1990), encompassing advice, factual information, and practical help and assistance. *Nurturant support* includes emotional, network, and esteem support, which involves expressing concern, showing empathy, and offering comfort (Cutrona & Russell, 1990).

The effects of each type of social support vary according to the condition. As Table 13.2 shows, the optimal matching model posits that the controllability of stress determines optimal matching between the needs of support seekers and the type of support offered by support providers (Cutrona & Suhr, 1992; Cutrona & Russell, 1990). For instance, in terms of refugees' mental health issues, action-facilitating support is effective in controlling refugees' mental stress by reducing or overcoming the cause of the stress (Cutrona & Suhr, 1992). On the other hand, when a stressful event is uncontrollable, nurturant support is appropriate because it allows refugees to diminish the adverse effects of aversive emotions (e.g., grief, loneliness) resulting from their mental health problems.

The optimal matching model offers valuable insights into how each type of social support works. The model serves as a compass for creating a support system that does not use a one-size-fits-all approach (Cutrona & Suhr, 1992; Cutrona & Russell, 1990). In other words, the model suggests that the effects of social support depend on matching a type of support with the specific needs of individuals. When appropriate support is offered in a specific context, there will be an improvement in the psychological quality of life compared to a scenario where there is a mismatch between the need for support and its provision (Cutrona, 1990; Merluzzi et al., 2015).

Table 13.2 Type of Social Support and Examples (Adapted from Cutrona & Russell, 1990)

Category	Type of Social Support	Description	Example
Action-facilitating support (Controllable situation)	Tangible Support	Providing goods and help	Giving concrete assistance, such as transportation or financial assistance, to those in need (Drageset, 2021)
	Informational Support	Giving advice and guidance	Providing factual or relevant information that can solve a problem (Wu et al., 2019)
Nurturant support (Uncontrollable situation)	Emotional Support	Giving care, empathy, love, and trust	Active listening and giving appropriate expression of empathy (Heo et al., 2014)
	Network Support	Sense of belonging to a group	Having a social relationship with others (e.g., family, peers, and community; Joyce & Liamputtong, 2017)
	Esteem Support	Boosting skills and values	Offering encouragement and reinforcement to someone (Holmstrom & Lim, 2023)

When applying the theoretical mechanism of OMM to the case of North Korean defectors in South Korean society, it is essential to understand the type of support that best matches the needs and circumstances of North Korean defectors. Presumably, by aligning support components with specific stressors that North Korean defectors experience, it is possible to develop more effective social support programs. For example, if defectors from North Korea have a foreign language issue in daily life that may be addressable, it would be better to provide action-facilitating support, including information about language education programs. On the other hand, if a defector from North Korea experiences difficulties due to social isolation, nurturant support may be an appropriate form of assistance (e.g., expressing empathy appropriately and facilitating social relationships within the community). Thus, it is necessary for health communicators to thoroughly examine the distinct needs and stressors of North Korean defectors to develop an effective social support intervention.

Social Support and Computer-Mediated Communication Benefits of Computer-Mediated Support

While the initial research areas of the optimal matching model (OMM) of social support were limited to face-to-face interactions, the proliferation of the internet and smartphones has facilitated social support seekers and providers finding each other with fewer constraints. The characteristics of computer-mediated communication have broadened and deepened the research domain of social support (Wright & Bell, 2003). Specifically, computer-mediated communication allows individuals to exchange social support with fewer geographical barriers (Wellman et al., 2001) and time constraints (Dimmick et al., 2007). Since content and contacts on social media are readily available, regardless of location and time, members of vulnerable groups can share opinions and concerns with those who have similar experiences via computer-mediated communication (Nesi et al., 2018).

The benefits that computer-mediated communication offers help vulnerable groups of people effectively address their difficulties, particularly when they cannot find the necessary resources in their physical environment (Wright & Bell, 2003). For example, Turner et al. (2001) found that cancer patients tended to seek alternative social support (e.g., emotional words) in online communities when they were dissatisfied with the support available in their daily lives. Ye

(2006) provided evidence that when individuals are unsure of how to address acculturation stress in unfamiliar circumstances (e.g., college students studying abroad), informational and emotional support via computer-mediated communication contributes to alleviating the feeling of uncertainty they may experience when coping with the stressful situation.

Another benefit of computer-mediated support is that it enables individuals to broadcast their support-seeking intention without disclosing their identity. According to Wright and Bell (2003), individuals can obtain diverse information from large groups of people simultaneously through computer-mediated communication, which can be defined as the public nature of communication (Nesi et al., 2018). At the same time, individuals can communicate comfortably with others without disclosing their identity or potentially embarrassing information, as computer-mediated communication allows for anonymity (Wright, 2000).

North Korean defectors can undoubtedly benefit from social support via computer-mediated communication. For example, when defectors need practical information to secure a job in South Korea, they may be able to obtain advice from other defectors who have settled into South Korean society through digital peer support groups. In that case, the defectors can obtain various suggestions from multiple people and preserve their anonymity without disclosing personal information (Wright & Bell, 2003). Although digital peer support groups have a weak-tie relationship with support recipients, sympathy and understanding from the peer groups can contribute to relieving the recipients' mental stress (Reinke & Solheim, 2015). In this regard, North Korean defectors can feel more socially connected to those who share similar experiences and feel less stigmatized in peer support groups in a digital environment (Ayobi et al., 2022).

Computer-Mediated Support and Support-Seeking Strategies

Previous research examining computer-mediated support focused mainly on two areas. The first body of research investigated why people rely on computer-mediated communication to give and receive social support (Tanis, 2008; Walther & Boyd, 2002; Wright, 2002). Another body of research aimed to identify what type of support individuals seek and receive via digital communication (Rains et al., 2015). These research patterns are observable in studies on refugees and computer-mediated support. For instance, Ahmed et al. (2020) examined why and how Syrian refugees in Canada utilized social media platforms (e.g.,

Facebook and Instagram) to seek necessary support resources. Their study found that Syrian refugees employed social media to obtain informational and tangible support, such as access to free services, practical help in obtaining essential goods, and advice on job opportunities. Another study revealed that Iraqi and Sudanese refugees in the United States sought emotional support from family and friends in their homelands by using social media platforms (Mikal & Woodfield, 2015). In line with the two bodies of research above, it is also necessary to inquire into how North Korean defectors in South Korean society may seek appropriate resources via computer-mediated communication to relieve their mental health problems. When individuals coping with stressors need encouragement, inspiration, or validation for positive events, they may seek support from others (Buehler et al., 2019).

According to MacGeorge et al. (2011), seeking support indicates "intentional communicative activity to elicit supportive actions from others" (p. 330). The concept of seeking support can be elaborated upon by sensitive interaction systems theory (SIST), one of the theoretical frameworks that describes how individuals seek social support within their social network (Barbee & Cunningham, 1995). SIST posits that support-seeking behaviors vary along two dimensions: (1) direct vs. indirect and (2) verbal vs. nonverbal (Barbee & Cunningham, 1995). Direct seeking means that individuals explicitly express their need for support verbally (e.g., asking for help) or nonverbally (e.g., crying). Additionally, indirect seeking suggests that support seekers convey their need for support through verbal (e.g., global complaining) or nonverbal (e.g., sighing) communication. Although SIST maintains that individuals can employ different types of support-seeking strategies depending on their needs, critics contend that the theory does not capture the dynamic nature of support-seeking communication via digital media. This is because SIST was developed to describe how to seek support in a face-to-face conversation (Buehler et al., 2019; Liu et al., 2021).

Using the theoretical mechanism of SIST, Buehler et al. (2019) suggested applicable support-seeking strategies using social media, with seven themes: (1) asking for support, (2) disclosing directly, (3) alluding to the stressor, (4) using humor, (5) celebrating achievements, (6) sharing stories and memories, and (7) shouting out (see Table 13.3). Asking for support indicates a post in which one directly asks friends for support (Buehler et al., 2019). This theme is similar to the direct verbal strategy in SIST. North Korean defectors can employ this strategy when seeking social support through computer-mediated

Table 13.3 Computer-Mediated Support-Seeking Strategies (Adapted from Buehler et al., 2019)

Strategy	Meaning	Sub-themes/Topics
Asking for support	Posting to ask for support directly to his/her friends	• Crowdsourcing helps • Requesting thoughts and prayers • Raising awareness
Disclosing directly	Posting to articulate a stressor without necessarily verbalizing a need for support	• Blunt disclosures (e.g., stating explicitly the topic that bothers a user on social media) • Laundry-list disclosures (e.g., venting about several sources of distress to signal one's need for support)
Alluding to the stressor	Posting to present indirectly one's need for support	• Vague venting • Rhetorical or abstract questions (e.g., alluding to stressors by obscuring the source of one's distress) • Quotations (e.g., using quotations to hint at the sources of stress)
Using humor	Posting to use comedy or wit to downplay one's need for support	• Salient state using humor • Self-deprecating humor
Sharing stories and memories	Posting to express emotions that indicate a need for support, sharing stories, and memories	• Tributes (e.g., seeking to pay respects to a lost loved one) • Throwbacks (e.g., remembering the good old days)
Celebrating achievements	Posting to acknowledge a positive accomplishment, milestone, or event in a person's life	• Milestones • Celebrations of holidays and special events
Shouting out	Posting shout-outs to the people who helped users through difficult times	• Praising the assistance that he/she received • Expressing appreciation to others for their assistance

communication. For example, the defectors can create a post on crowdfunding platforms or digital peer support groups to elicit tangible aid. It is also feasible that when North Korean defectors feel lonely, they can send a text via an instant messaging application to request thoughts and prayers.

Disclosing directly is a post articulating a stressor without necessarily verbalizing a need for support (Buehler et al., 2019). Typical examples of disclosing directly include stating explicitly the topic that bothers support seekers on social media and venting about the sources of distress to signal one's need for support. Alluding to the stressor refers to a post that presents one's need for support indirectly (Buehler et al., 2019). Support seekers can employ various techniques, including vague venting, rhetorical or abstract questions, and quotations, to indirectly request social support through computer-mediated communication. Notably, identifying a stressor can be effective because it helps people understand their stressors and formulate a plan to reduce stress (Deng, 2022; Seaward, 2021). Therefore, it will be helpful for North Korean defectors to directly and indirectly identify their stressors (i.e., disclosing directly, alluding to the stressor) through computer-mediated communication.

Many studies have revealed that when individuals are in a stressful situation, expressing emotions openly can be an adequate coping strategy to help relieve their depressive symptoms (Frazier et al., 2005; Pennebaker & Chung, 2011; Stanton & Low, 2012). Four newly added themes in SIST pertain to an emotional coping strategy (Buehler et al., 2019). To be specific, using humor is a tactic employing comedy or wit to downplay one's need for support. Buehler et al. (2019) found that self-deprecating humor is the most frequent form when individuals seek social support on social media. Additionally, individuals express emotions by sharing stories and memories to seek support. Paying tribute to a lost loved one and looking back at the past are key aspects of this strategy. Lastly, individuals can post a statement celebrating a positive accomplishment (i.e., celebrating achievements) and shout-outs to those who helped them through difficult times (i.e., shouting out). Indeed, North Korean defectors can utilize these four seeking strategies through computer-mediated communication, which will help them manage various stressors (e.g., identity confusion, social isolation, and social prejudice) that they experience in South Korean society.

Conclusion

North Korean defectors are a stigmatized group in South Korea. As noted earlier, North Korean defectors may become citizens of South Korea but are culturally not accepted as fellow South Koreans (Chun, 2022; Poorman, 2019). North Korean defectors' cultural identity is devalued or considered unnatural in South Korean society (Chun, 2022). This stigmatizing may disadvantage them in social interactions with other people, groups, and organizations (Yeshua-Katz et al., 2020). That exacerbates their mental health problems (Ahn et al., 2015).

The current chapter comprehensively presents the benefits of computer-mediated support and introduces seven support-seeking strategies online users have employed to obtain coping resources via computer-mediated communication. We believe that computer-mediated support will help North Korean defectors address their social stigma because they can obtain various coping resources (e.g., informational, emotional, and esteem support) without fearing social judgment (Yeshua-Katz et al., 2020). It is also worth noting that the seven support-seeking strategies have the potential to relieve North Korean defectors' mental health problems. The discussion in this chapter helps both communication scholars and health communicators by offering theoretical and practical insights into possible coping strategies to manage the mental health problems that North Korean defectors may have.

Recommended Readings/Resources

Buehler, E. M., Crowley, J. L., Peterson, A. M., & High, A. C. (2019). Broadcasting for help: A typology of support-seeking strategies on Facebook. *New Media & Society, 21*(11–12), 2566–2588. https://doi.org/10.1177/1461444819853821

Chun, K. H. (2022). North Korean defectors as cultural other in South Korea: Perception and construction of cultural differences. *Asian Journal of Peacebuilding, 10*(1), 185–213.

Cutrona, C. E. (1990). Stress and social support—in search of optimal matching. *Journal of Social and Clinical Psychology, 9*(1), 3–14. https://doi.org/10.1521/jscp.1990.9.1.3

Kim, H., Kim, Y., Yoon, J., Nam, J. K., & Kim, Y. (2023). A phenomenological study on the North Korean refugees' trauma experience and recovery process during the escape and resettlement in South Korea. *International Journal of Intercultural Relations, 92*, 101742. https://doi.org/10.1016/j.ijintrel.2022.101742

Wright, K. B., & Bell, S. B. (2003). Health-related support groups on the Internet: Linking empirical findings to social support and computer-mediated communication theory. *Journal of Health Psychology, 8*(1), 39–54.

References

Ahmed, R., Luisa, V., & Idris, A. (2020). Syrian refugee youths' use of social media as a space for communicating social support during resettlement. In L. K. Hamilton, V.

Luisa, & M. W. Robertson (Eds.), *A national project: Syrian refugee resettlement in Canada* (pp. 151–171). McGill-Queen's University Press.

Ahn, J. H., Kim, W. H., Choi, H. J., Jeon, J. Y., Song, I. G., & Bae, J. N. (2015). Stigma of mental illnesses as perceived by North Korean defectors living in South Korea. *Psychiatry Investigation, 12*(1), 9–15. https://doi.org/10.4306/pi.2015.12.1.9

Albrecht, T. L., & Adelman, M. B. (1987). *Communicating social support*. Sage Publications, Inc.

Aragona, M., Pucci, D., Mazzetti, M., & Geraci, S. (2012). Post-migration living difficulties as a significant risk factor for PTSD in immigrants: A primary care study. *Italian Journal of Public Health, 9*(3), 1–8. https://doi.org/10.2427/7525

Ayobi, A., Eardley, R., Soubutts, E., Gooberman-Hill, R., Craddock, I., & O'Kane, A. A. (2022). Digital mental health and social connectedness. *Proceedings of the ACM on Human-Computer Interaction, 6*(2), 1–27.

Bae, G., & Yeung, J. (2024). *Number of North Korean defectors nearly triples in 2023, including 'elite' diplomats, South Korea says*. CNN. https://edition.cnn.com/2024/01/19/asia/north-korea-defectors-elite-covid-intl- hnk/index.html#:~:text=The%20number%20of%20North%20Korean,of%20the%20North%2 0Korean%20elite

Barbee, A. P., & Cunningham, M. R. (1995). An experimental approach to social support communications: Interactive coping in close relationships. *Annals of the International Communication Association, 18*, 381–413. https://doi.org/10.1080/23808985.1995.11678921

Barrera, M. (1986). Distinctions between social support concepts, measures, and models. *American Journal of Community Psychology, 14*, 413–445. https://doi.org/10.1007/BF00922627

Bogic, M., Njoku, A., & Priebe, S. (2015). Long-term mental health of war-refugees: A systematic literature review. *BMC International Health and Human Rights, 15*(1), 1–41.

Borowiec, S. (July 11, 2014). Two Koreas make strides to talk the same language. *The Guardian*. https://www.theguardian.com/world/2014/jul/11/korean-peoples-comprehensive-dictionary

Buehler, E. M., Crowley, J. L., Peterson, A. M., & High, A. C. (2019). Broadcasting for help: A typology of support-seeking strategies on Facebook. *New Media & Society, 21*(11–12), 2566–2588. https://doi.org/10.1177/1461444819853821.

Choi, E. (2022). *Bukhan italjumin Namhan sahwe juckung silta* [North Korean defectors' adaptation to life in South Korean society]. The Seoul National University Institute for Peace and Unification Studies (IPUS). https://ipus.snu.ac.kr/wp-content/uploads/2022/05/6.-%EB%B6%81%ED%95%9C%EC%A3%BC%EB%AF%BC%E C%9D%98%EC%8B%9D%EC%A1%B0%EC%82%AC-%EB%B6%81%ED%95%9C%EC%9D%B4%ED%83%88%EC%A3%BC%EB%AF%BC%EC%A0%81%EC%9D%91%EC%8B%A4%ED%83%9C-20220425–1.pdf

Choi, S. (2023). *Sahwe tonghwap siltae* [Korea social integration survey]. Korea Institute of Public Administration. https://www.kipa.re.kr/site/kipa/research/selectBaseView.do;jsessionid=B9ABB0F6949054AFA9F59F03710AEA76seSubCode=BIZ017A001&seqNo=BASE_000000000000732

Chun, K. H. (2015). Perspectives on North Korea between same-nation-ness and multiculturalism: Otherization in South Korea. *Social Science Review, 23*(1): 274–299.

Chun, K. H. (2022). North Korean defectors as cultural other in South Korea: Perception and construction of cultural differences. *Asian Journal of Peacebuilding, 10*(1), 185–213. https://doi.org/10.18588/202203.00a227

Cohen, S. (2004). Social relationships and health. *American Psychologist, 59*(8), 676–684. doi:10.1037/0003-066X.59.8.676

Cohen, S., & McKay, G. (1984). Social support, stress and the buffering hypothesis: A theoretical analysis. In A. Baum, S. E. Taylor, & J. E. Singer (Eds.), *Handbook of psychology and health* (pp. 253-267). Hillsdale, NJ: Erlbaum.

Cohen, S., & Wills, T. A. (1985). Stress, social support, and the buffering hypothesis. *Psychological Bulletin, 98*(2), 310–357.

Cuaresma, C. J., Danylo, O., Fritz, S., Hofer, M., Kjaras, H., & Baya, J. C. (2020). What do we know about poverty in North Korea?. *Palgrave Communications, 6*(40). https://doi.org/10.1057/s41599-020-0417-4

Cutrona, C. E. (1990). Stress and social support—in search of optimal matching. *Journal of Social and Clinical Psychology, 9*(1), 3–14. https://doi.org/10.1521/jscp.1990.9.1.3

Cutrona, C. E., & Russell, D. W. (1990). Type of social support and specific stress: Toward a theory of optimal matching. In B. R. Sarason, I. G. Sarason, & G. R. Pierce (Eds.), *Social support: An interactional view* (pp. 319–366). John Wiley & sons.

Cutrona, C. E., & Suhr, J. A. (1992). Controllability of stressful events and satisfaction with spouse support behaviors. *Communication Research, 19*(2), 154–174. https://doi.org/10.1177/009365092019002002

Deng, Y., Cherian, J., Khan, N. U. N., Kumari, K., Sial, M. S., Comite, U., Gavurova, B., & Popp, J. (2022). Family and academic stress and their impact on students' depression level and academic performance. *Front Psychiatry, 13*, 869337. https://doi.org/10.3389/fpsyt.2022.869337

Dimmick, J., Ramirez Jr, A., Wang, T., & Lin, S. F. (2007). Extending society: The role of personal networks and gratification-utilities in the use of interactive communication media. *New Media & Society, 9*(5), 795–810. https://doi.org/10.1177/1461444807081225

Drageset J. (2021). Social support. In G. Haugan & M. Eriksson (Eds.), *Health promotion in health care – Vital theories and research.* Springer. Available from: https://www.ncbi.nlm.nih.gov/books/NBK585650/; https://doi.org/10.1007/978-3-030-63135- 2_11

Ekmen, E., Kocak, O., Solmaz, U., Kopuz, K., Younis, M. Z., & Orman, D. (2021). How does the social support affect refugees' life satisfaction in Turkey? Stress as a mediator, social aids and coronavirus anxiety as moderators. *Sustainability, 13*(22), 12727.

Fazel, M., Wheeler, J., & Danesh, J. (2005). Prevalence of serious mental disorder in 7000 refugees resettled in Western countries: A systematic review. *The Lancet, 365*(9467), 1309–1314.

Frazier, P. A., Mortensen, H., & Steward, J. (2005). Coping strategies as mediators of the relations among perceived control and distress in sexual assault survivors. *Journal of Counseling Psychology, 52*, 267–278.

George, M. (2010). A theoretical understanding of refugee trauma. *Clinical Social Work Journal, 38*(4), 379–387. https://doi.org/10.1007/s10615-009-0252-y

Goldsmith, D. J. (2004). *Communicating social support.* Cambridge University Press. https://doi.org/10.1017/CBO9780511606984

Gottvall, M., Vaez, M., & Saboonchi, F. (2019). Social support attenuates the link between torture exposure and post-traumatic stress disorder among male and female Syrian refugees in Sweden. *BMC International Health and Human Rights, 19*, 1–11.

Han, D., Lee, K., Do, K., Hong, J., & Kim, S (2018). *Bukhan ingwon baeseo* [White paper on human rights in North Korea]. Korea Institute for National Unification. https://repo.kinu.or.kr/handle/2015.oak/9003

Hassan, T. (2023). North Korea. *Events of 2022.* https://www.hrw.org/world-report/2023/country-chapters/north-korea

Hecker, T., Huber, S., Maier, T., & Maercker, A. (2018). Differential associations among PTSD and complex PTSD symptoms and traumatic experiences and postmigration difficulties in a culturally diverse refugee sample. *Journal of Trauma Stress, 31*(6), 795–804.

Heo, S., Lennie, T. A., Moser, D. K., & Kennedy, R. L. (2014). Types of social support and their relationships to physical and depressive symptoms and health-related quality of life in patients with heart failure. *Heart & Lung, 43*(4), 299–305.

Hirsch, B. J. (1980). Natural support systems and coping with major life changes. *American Journal of Community Psychology, 8*(2), 159–172. https://doi.org/10.1007/BF00912658.

Hollifield, M., Warner, T. D., Lian, N., Krakow, B., Jenkins, J. H., Kesler, J., Stevenson, J., & Westermeyer, J. (2002). Measuring trauma and health status in refugees: A critical review. *JAMA, 288*(5), 611–621. : https://doi.org/10.1001/jama.288.5.611

Holmstrom, A. J., & Lim, J. I. (2023). Responsiveness and esteem support. *Current Opinion in Psychology*, 52, 101591. doi.org/10.1016/j.copsyc.2023.101591

House, J. S., & Kahn, R. (1985). Measures and concepts of social support. In S. Cohen & S. L. Syme (Eds.), *Social support and health.* Academic Press.

Hwang, S. (2023). North Korean defector plans new life after high-risk escape by sea. *The Japan Times*. https://www.japantimes.co.jp/news/2023/12/06/asia-pacific/social-issues/north-korean-defector-escape-by-sea/
Hwang, S. (2023). North Korean defector plans new life after high-risk escape by sea. *The Japan Times*. https://www.japantimes.co.jp/news/2023/12/06/asia-pacific/social-issues/north-korean-defector-escape-by-sea/
Ji, D. G. (2022). Inside Hanawon: How N. Korean defectors build a new life in S. Korea. *The Korea Herald*. https://www.koreaherald.com/view.php?ud=20220710000202

Johnson, H., & Thompson, A. (2008). The development and maintenance of post-traumatic stress disorder (PTSD) in civilian adult survivors of war trauma and torture: A review. *Clinical Psychology Review*, *28*(1), 36–47. https://doi.org/10.1016/j.cpr.2007.01.017

Joyce, L., & Liamputtong, P. (2017). Acculturation stress and social support for young refugees in regional areas. *Children and Youth Services Review*, *77*, 18–26.

Kahn, R. L. (1979). Aging and social support. In M. W. Riley (Ed.), *Aging from birth to death: Interdisciplinary perspectives* (pp. 77–91). Westview.

Kim, H. (2014). Enacted social support on social media and subjective well-being. *International Journal of Communication*, *8*, 2201–2221.

Kim, H., Kim, Y., Yoon, J., Nam, J. K., & Kim, Y. (2023). A phenomenological study on the North Korean refugees' trauma experience and recovery process during the escape and resettlement in South Korea. *International Journal of Intercultural Relations*, 92. https://doi.org/10.1016/j.ijintrel.2022.101742

Kim, J. A., & Yoo, S. S. (2018). The concerns and potential of North Korean defector students' education: Teachers' perceptions at "A alternative school." *North Korean Review*, *14*(2), 5–25. https://www.jstor.org/stable/26632403

Knipscheer, J. W., Sleijpen, M., Mooren, T., ter Heide, F. J. J., & van der Aa, N. (2015). Trauma exposure and refugee status as predictors of mental health outcomes in treatment-seeking refugees. *BJPsych Bulletin*, 39(4), 178–182. https://doi.org/10.1192/pb.bp.114.047951

Ko, B. (2022). Nearly 1 in 5 N. Korean defectors say they regret coming to S. Korea. *Hankyoreh*. https://english.hani.co.kr/arti/english_edition/e_national/1040480

Korea Hana Foundation (2020). *2019 Bukhan Italjumin Sahoetonghap Josa* [2019 social integration survey of North Korean refugees in South Korea] https://www.koreahana.or.kr/data_room/pro_data.jsp

Kwong, M. (March 2, 2018). *A North Korean's unexpected challenges in the South: Learning the language, ditching the accent*. CBC. https://www.cbc.ca/news/world/north- korean-language-accent-1.4554545

Laban, C. J., Gernaat, H. B., Komproe, I. H., van der Tweel, I., & De Jong, J. T. (2005). Postmigration living problems and common psychiatric disorders in Iraqi asylum seekers in the Netherlands. *Journal of Nervous and Mental Disease, 193*(12), 825–832. DOI: 10.1097/01.nmd.0000188977.44657.1d. PMID: 16319706.

Lakey, B., & Cohen, S. (2000). Support theory and measurement. In S. Cohen, L. Underwood, & B. H. Gottlieb (Eds.), *Social support measurement and interventions: A guide for health and social scientists* (pp. 29–52). Oxford University Press.

Lankov, A. (2006). Bitter taste of paradise: North Korean refugees in South Korea. *Journal of East Asian Studies, 6*, 105–37.

Lazarus, R. S., & Folkman, S. (1984). *Stress, appraisal, and coping*. Springer.

Lee, S.-M. (2014). T'albukyŏsŏngŭn ŏttŏk'e marhal su innŭn'ga? t'ellebijŏn t'ok'ŭsyo "ijemannarŏ kamnida" (Ch'aenŏlA)e taehan pip'anjŏng punsŏkŭl chungshimŭro [How can North Korean women defectors speak? A critical analysis of television talk show "Now, Going to Meet" (Channel A)]. *Media, Gender and Culture, 29*(2), 75–115.

Lee, H., Robinson, C., Kim, J., McKee, M., & Cha, J. (2020). Health and healthcare in North Korea: A retrospective study among defectors. *Conflict Health. 14*(41). DOI: 10.1186/s13031-020-00284-y.

Lee, M. K., Kim, O., Kim, K-A., & Chu, S. H. (2022). Factors associated with posttraumatic growth among North Korean defectors in South Korea. *Scientific reports, 12*, 3989. https://doi.org/10.1038/s41598-022-07945-3

Liu, Y., Zhu, Y., & Xia, Y. (2021). Support-seeking strategies and social support provided in Chinese online health communities related to COVID-19. *Front Psychology*, 12:783135. DOI: 10.3389/fpsyg.2021.783135

Lynch, T. R., Mendelson, T., Robins, C. J., Krishnan, K. R. R., George, L. K., Johnson, C. S., & Blazer, D. G. (1999). Perceived social support among depressed elderly, middle-aged, and young-adult samples. *Journal of Affective Disorders, 55*(2–3), 159–170. https://doi.org/10.1016/S0165-0327(99)00017-8

MacGeorge, E. L., Feng, B., & Burleson, B. R. (2011). Supportive communication. In M. L. Knapp & J. A. Daly (Eds.), *Handbook of Interpersonal Communication* (4th ed., pp. 317–354). Thousand Oaks, CA: Sage.

Mackenzie, J. (2023). North Korea: *Residents tell BBC of neighbours starving to death. BBC.* https://www.bbc.com/news/world-asia-65881803

Marinucci, M., & Riva, P. (2021). How intergroup social connections shape immigrants' responses to social exclusion. *Group Processes & Intergroup Relations, 24*(3), 411-435.

Marinucci, M., Mazzoni, D., Pancani, L., & Riva, P. (2022). To whom should I turn? Intergroup social connections moderate social exclusion's short-and long-term psychological impact on immigrants. *Journal of Experimental Social Psychology, 99*, 104275.

Merluzzi, T. V., Philip, E. J., Yang, M., & Heitzmann, C. A. (2015). Matching of received social support with need for support in adjusting to cancer and cancer survivorship. *Psycho-Oncology, 25*(6), 684–690. https://doi.org/10.1002/pon.3896

Mikal, J. P., & Woodfield, B. (2015). Refugees, post-migration stress, and internet use: A qualitative analysis of intercultural adjustment and internet use among Iraqi and Sudanese refugees to the United States. *Qualitative health research*, *25*(10), 1319–1333. https://doi.org/10.1177/1049732315601089

Millett, A. R. (2024, February 6). Korean War. *Encyclopedia Britannica*. https://www.britannica.com/event/Korean-War

Miller, K., & Ray, E. B. (1994). Beyond the ties that bind: Exploring the "meaning" of supportive messages and relationships. In B. R. Burleson, T. L. Albrecht, & I. G. Sarason (Eds.), *Communication of social support: Messages, interactions, relationships, and community* (pp. 215–228). Sage.

Min, S. K. (2008). Divided countries, divided mind 1: Psycho-social issues in adaptation problems of North Korean defectors. *Psychiatry Investigation*, *5*(1):1–13. doi: 10.4306/pi.2008.5.1.1.

Ministry of Unification. (2023). *Policy on North Korean Defectors*. Ministry of Unification. https://www.unikorea.go.kr/eng_unikorea/relations/statistics/defectors/

Mollica, R. F., McInnes, K., Pool, C., & Tor, S. (1998). Dose-effect relationships of trauma to symptoms of depression and post-traumatic stress disorder among Cambodian survivors of mass violence. *British Journal of Psychiatry*, *173*(6), 482–488. https://doi.org/10.1192/bjp.173.6.482

Moon, I., & Song, M. (2023). *Seoulsi BukhanitalJumin Kyungjehwaldong Sameuijil Siltaejosawha Jungchaeckbanghyung* [Policy and assessment on economic activity and quality of life of North Korea defectors in Seoul], The Seoul Institute. https://www.si.re.kr/node/67740

Neuner, F., Schauer, M., Karunakara, U., Klaschik, C., Robert, C., & Elbert, T. (2004). Psychological trauma and evidence for enhanced vulnerability for posttraumatic stress disorder through previous trauma among West Nile refugees. *BMC Psychiatry*, *4*(1). https://doi.org/10.1186/1471-244x-4-34

Nesi, J., Choukas-Bradley, S., & Prinstein, M. J. (2018). Transformation of adolescent peer relations in the social media context: Part 1—A theoretical framework and application to dyadic peer relationships. *Clinical Child and Family Psychology Review*, *21*(3), 267–294. https://doi.org/10.1007/s10567-018-0261-x

Noh, J. W., & Lee, S. H. (2020). Trauma history and mental health of North Korean defectors. *Current Behavioral Neuroscience Reports*, *7*, 250–257. https://doi.org/10.1007/s40473-020-00219-0

Park, S. (2022). From an alienated to an active English learner: The case of a North Korean refugee in South Korea. *System*, *107*, 102812. https://doi.org/10.1016/j.system.2022.102812

Park, S., Wenzel, J. A., & Surkan, P. J. (2023). How do North Korean refugees in South Korea utilize social support to cope with acculturative stress?. *SSM-Mental Health*, 4, 100272. https://doi.org/10.1016/j.ssmmh.2023.100272

Pennebaker, J. W., & Chung, C. K. (2011). Expressive writing, emotional upheavals, and health. In H. S. Friedman (Ed.), *The Oxford handbook of health psychology* (pp. 417–437). Oxford University Press.

Pierce, G. R., Sarason, B. R., & Sarson, I. G. (1992). General and specific support expectations and stress as predictors of perceived supportiveness: An experimental study. *Journal of Personality and Social PsychologyI 63*, 297–307.

Poorman, E. (2019). North Korean defectors in South Korea and asylum seekers in the United States: A comparison. *Northwestern Journal of Human Rights, 17*(1). https://scholarlycommons.law.northwestern.edu/njihr/vol17/iss1/4.

Pouraghajan, S., Ullrich, J., & Morina, N. (2023). Mental health of asylum seekers and refugees: The role of trauma and postmigration living difficulties and the moderating effect of intergroup contact. *Current Research in Ecological and Social Psychology, 4*, 100118. https://doi.org/10.1016/j.cresp.2023.100118

Procidano, M. E., & Heller, K. (1983). Measures of perceived social support from friends and from family: Three validation studies. *American Journal of Community Psychology*, 11(1), 1–24. https://doi.org/10.1007/BF00898416

Rains, S. A., Peterson, E., & Wright, K. B. (2015). Communicating social support in computer-mediated contexts: A meta-analytic review of content analyses examining support messages shared online among individuals coping with illness. *Communication Monographs, 82*, 403–430. doi:10.1080/03637751.2015.1019530

Reinke, J. S., & Solheim, C.A. (2015). Online social support experiences of mothers of children with autism spectrum disorder. *Journal of Child and Family Studies, 24*, 2364–2373. https://doi.org/10.1007/s10826-014-0039-9

Schick, M., Zumwald, A., Knöpfli, B., Nickerson, A., Bryant, R. A., Schnyder, U., Müller, J., & Morina, N. (2016). Challenging future, challenging past: The relationship of social integration and psychological impairment in traumatized refugees. *European Journal of Psychotraumatology, 7*, Article 28057. https://doi.org/10.3402/ejpt.v7.28057

Seaward, B. L. (2021). *Essentials of managing stress* (5th Edition). Jones & Bartlett Learning.

Seo, Y., & Lilieholm, L. (2024). Rare footage shows North Korean teens punished for watching South Korean dramas, research group claims. *CNN*. https://edition.cnn.com/2024/01/24/asia/north-korea-teens-punished-kdrama-intl- hnk/index.html

Stanton, A. L., & Low, C. A. (2012). Expressing emotions in stressful contexts: Benefits, moderators, and mechanisms. *Current Directions in Psychological Science, 21*(2), 124–128. https://doi.org/10.1177/0963721411434978

Steel, Z., Silove, D., Phan, T., & Bauman, A. (2002). Long-term effect of psychological trauma on the mental health of Vietnamese refugees resettled in Australia: A population-based study. *The Lancet, 360*(9339), 1056–1062.

Steel, Z., Chey, T., Silove, D., Marnane, C., Bryant, R. A., & van Ommeren, M. (2009). Association of torture and other potentially traumatic events with mental health outcomes among populations exposed to mass conflict and displacement. *JAMA, 302*(5), 537. https://doi.org/10.1001/jama.2009.1132

Stokes, J. P. (1983). Predicting satisfaction with social support from social network structure. *American Journal of Community Psychology, 11*(2), 141–152. https://doi.org/10.1007/BF00894363

Tanis, M. (2008). What makes the Internet a place to seek social support. In E. A. Konijin, S. Utz, M. Tanis, & S. B. Barnes (Eds.), *Mediated interpersonal communication* (pp. 290–308). Routledge.

Topor, A., Borg, M., Girolamo, S. D., & Davidson, L. (2011). Not just an individual journey: Social aspects of recovery. *International Journal of Social Psychiatry, 57* (1): 90–99. doi:10.1177/0020764009345062.

Turner, J. W., Grube, J. A., & Meyers, J. (2001). Developing an optimal match within online communities: An exploration of CMC support communities and traditional support. *Journal of Communication, 51*(2), 231–251. https://doi.org/10.1111/j.1460-2466.2001.tb02879.x

Uchino, B. N. (2004). *Social support and physical health: Understanding the health consequences of our relationships.* Yale University Press.

Uchino, B. N. (2009). Understanding the links between social support and physical health: A life-span perspective with emphasis on the separability of perceived and received support. *Perspectives on Psychological Science, 4*(3), 236–255. doi:10.1111/j.1745-6924.2009.01122.x

Vangelisti, A. L. (2009). Challenges in conceptualizing social support. *Journal of Social and Personal Relationships, 26*(1), 39–51. https://doi.org/10.1177/0265407509105520

Walther, J. B., & Boyd, S. (2002). Attraction to computer-mediated social support. In C. A. Lin & D. Atkin (Eds.), *Communication technology and society: Audience adoption and uses* (pp. 153–188). Hampton Press.

Wang, J., Mann, F., Lloyd-Evans, B., Ma, R., & Johnson, S. (2018). Associations between loneliness and perceived social support and outcomes of mental health problems: A systematic review. *BMC Psychiatry, 18*(1): 156. https://doi.org/10.1186/s12888-018-1736-5

Wills, T. A., & Cleary, S. D. (1996). How are social support effects mediated? A test with parental support and adolescent substance use. *Journal Personality and Social Psychology, 71*(5), 937–952. DOI:10.1037//0022-3514.71.5.937

Wu, J. J., Khan, H. A., Chien, S. H., & Lee, Y. P. (2019). Impact of emotional support, informational support, and norms of reciprocity on trust toward the medical aesthetic community: The moderating effect of core self-evaluations. *Interactive Journal of Medical Research, 8*(1), e11750.

Weiss, R. (1974). The provisions of social relationships. In: Rubin, Z., Ed., *Doing unto others*, Prentice Hall, Englewood Cliffs, 17–26.

Wellman, B., Haase, A. Q., Witte, J., & Hampton, K. (2001). Does the Internet increase, decrease, or supplement social capital? Social networks, participation, and community commitment. *American Behavioral Scientist*, *45*(3), 436–455. https://doi.org/10.1177/00027640121957286.

Wright, K. B. (2000). Computer-mediated social support, older adults, and coping. *Journal of Communication*, *50*(3), 100–118.

Wright, K. B. (2002). Social support within an on-line cancer community: An assessment of emotional support, perceptions of advantages and disadvantages, and motives for using the community. *Journal of Applied Communication Research*, *30*, 195–209. doi:10.1080/00909880216586.

Wright, K. B., & Bell, S. B. (2003). Health-related support groups on the Internet: Linking empirical findings to social support and computer-mediated communication theory. *Journal of Health Psychology*, *8*(1), 39–54.

Ye, J. (2006). An examination of acculturative stress, interpersonal social support, and use of online ethnic social groups among Chinese international students. *The Howard Journal of Communications*, *17*(1), 1–20. https://doi.org/10.1080/10646170500487764

Yeung, J. & Seo, Y. (2023). *Inside the school teaching North Korean defectors how to live in the outside world. CNN.* https://edition.cnn.com/2023/07/15/asia/south-north-korea-defectors-school-intl-hnk-dst/index.html.

Yeung, J. & Seo, Y. (2024). She fled North Korea but was sold to a man in China. Her second escape came nearly 20 years later. *CNN.* https://edition.cnn.com/2024/03/08/asia/north-korean-refugees-trafficked-china-intl-hnk-dst/index.html

Yeshua-Katz, D., Rains, S. A., Peterson, E. B. & Wright, K. B. (2020). Digital stigma coping strategies: A meta-analytic review of the association between health-related stigma dimensions and social support messages shared online, *The Information Society*, *36*(1), 19–29.

Yim, H. (2024). *North Korea's Kim warns failure to provide food a 'serious political issue'.* Reuters. https://www.reuters.com/world/asia-pacific/north-koreas-kim-warns-failure-provide-food-serious-political-issue-2024-01-25/#:~:text=North%20Korea%20has%20over%20recent,such%20as%20floods%20da maging%20harvests.

Yim, S., Sung, M., & Lee, S. (2023). *Bukhanitaljumin Sahwetonghwah Siltae* [Social and economic cohesion of North Korea defectors in South Korea]. The Center for North Korean Human Rights. https://nkdb.org/publication/?idx=17155488&bmode=view

14

Cross-Cultural Dialogues

Unraveling and Addressing Mental Health Challenges in International Students through Innovative Health Communication Strategies

Anne Amegbeha Amissah, Sarah A. Geegan, and Kimberly A. Parker

In recent years, the global landscape of higher education has witnessed unprecedented mobility of students across borders, with millions embarking on journeys to pursue academic qualifications abroad (Abdullah et al., 2017; Bista et al., 2018; Islam, 2019; Kirloskar & Inamdar, 2021). A report from the Organization for Economic Cooperation and Development (OECD, 2023) shows that more than 6 million students globally have crossed international borders for their education. This number reflects both the growing accessibility of global education and the increasing desire among students to study abroad. In the United States alone, during the 2018–19 academic year, there were over 1 million international students, highlighting the country's role as a prominent destination for educational advancement (Institute of International Education, 2023). This trend underscores the importance of understanding the unique experiences, challenges, and contributions of international students within the academic communities they join.

The movement of students across borders for educational pursuits has become a commonplace phenomenon (Abdullah et al., 2017; Bista et al., 2018; Islam, 2019; Kirloskar & Inamdar, 2021). However, this transnational journey, while offering numerous opportunities, also brings forth a plethora of challenges, especially in the realm of mental health (Brown, 2018; Forbes-Mewett & Sawyer, 2019; Kirloskar & Inamdar, 2021). International students, navigating the complexities of cultural dislocation, linguistic barriers, and unique academic pressures, find themselves at the intersection of diverse and often conflicting crossroads. This chapter seeks to cast a wide lens on international students' mental health. We will (a) analyze case studies, (b) unearth underlying problems, and (c) offer perspectives grounded in theoretical frameworks and empirical evidence.

Mental health for international students is paramount, yet it is an area that has not been sufficiently explored within the realm of health communication. As highlighted in the Mental Health Tips column by US News and World Report, Durrani (2023) emphasized that being far from home in a new academic and social environment can affect international students differently. Hence, students need to know what support is available. This statement underscores the critical need for enhanced awareness and accessibility of support services for international students navigating the complexities of adapting to a new cultural and academic landscape.

Current literature, rich in its exploration of general health concerns, often overlooks the nuanced mental health intricacies international students face. Therefore, this chapter aims to fill this gap while offering insights that move beyond the surface of the observable and delve into what lies beneath. Central to this exploration is the role of communication. We will explore how international students perceive, interpret, and navigate the mental health support available. We also will examine the impact of cultural and linguistic differences on students' help-seeking behaviors.

The chapter begins by presenting two cases that illustrate the multifaceted nature of mental health challenges faced by international students. These cases serve as a springboard for identifying critical communication problems and set the stage for a theoretical assessment.

Case 1: Esi's Odyssey: Navigating Uncharted Waters of Academia and Motherhood

Alone in the heart of London, far from the warm, bustling streets of Accra, Ghana, Esi's story unfolds—a tale of resilience, struggle, and the undying spirit of a mother who is also a student. At thirty, Esi found herself in a world vastly different from the one she knew, grappling with challenges that stretched her to her limits. Esi's journey began with a dream: to advance her education and provide a better future for her family. With her husband's supportive words echoing in her mind and her children's hopeful faces in her heart, she embarked on a path to obtain her master's degree in public health in the United Kingdom.

However, this dream quickly collided with reality, as Esi faced the daunting task of balancing her rigorous academic responsibilities with caring for her two young children, aged 1 and 6, alone, like so many others like her.

The cultural tapestry of London was a stark contrast to the communal life of Ghana. Esi struggled to adjust to the new educational system, where practices and expectations differed vastly. She often felt like an *outsider*, navigating through a labyrinth of academic jargon and unfamiliar customs. The university's classrooms and libraries, filled with her peers' chatter, only deepened her sense of isolation. They were worlds apart from her reality—a reality marked by sleepless nights, endless assignments, and the cries of her children needing their mother. Time became her most scarce resource as Esi walked the tightrope of her dual roles. Every minute spent in the library was a minute away from her children, and every moment with her children was a moment away from her studies. The balance was overwhelming, often leaving her drained, both emotionally and physically.

The challenge of affordable childcare loomed large, casting a shadow on her academic journey. Esi's schedule was a complex puzzle, with classes and study sessions that did not align with traditional childcare hours. Financial constraints tightened their grip on her, as the costs of living and childcare in London were steep, far beyond what she had anticipated.

Amid these tumultuous waves, Esi contemplated seeking support from the university's counseling services. Yet, another hurdle stood in her way. The faces that greeted her at the counseling center were friendly, but none reflected hers. The lack of representatives of color, individuals who might understand the depths of her cultural struggles, and the unique challenges of being an African single mother in a foreign land made her hesitate. Would they understand her story, her sacrifices, her fears? Or would her words fall on ears that, despite their best intentions, could not fully grasp the weight of her journey?

Debrief

Esi's odyssey (A. A. Amissah, personal communication, February 14, 2024) is more than a narrative of hardship; it is a testament to the resilience of the human spirit. Her story sheds light on the intricate and often overlooked struggles of international students, particularly those who juggle parenthood, academia, and the nuances of cultural dissonance. Esi's journey is a clarion call for a deeper understanding, empathy, and tailored support in the academic landscape—to ensure that the dreams and aspirations of students like her are not lost in the uncharted waters of international education.

Esi's story, rich with challenges and triumphs, serves not only as a testament to her resilience but also as a mirror reflecting the broader experiences of international students navigating the complexities of academia abroad. As we transition from her compelling narrative to a deeper analysis, let us delve into the intricacies of the mental health challenges highlighted by her journey. This debrief aims to dissect the multifaceted issues Esi encountered.

International students who embark on their academic journey while navigating parenthood face challenges beyond those their peers encounter. Balancing the demands of rigorous academic pursuits with parenting responsibilities is a formidable task that requires meticulous time management and emotional resilience. As students, they are expected to immerse themselves in their studies, engage in research, and produce high-quality work to meet the academic standards set forth by their institutions. Concurrently, as parents, they bear the critical responsibility of guiding their children through their educational journeys and supporting their involvement in extracurricular activities. This dual role significantly amplifies their workload and stress levels, distinguishing them from colleagues who may not share the same familial obligations. The complexities of managing these dual identities often lead to increased pressures, impacting their academic performance and ability to provide a nurturing environment for their children (Pantha, 2023; Kim, E. 2009; Sawir et al., 2008).

Esi's experience sheds light on the broader struggles shared by immigrant student parents, who must navigate not only the academic and cultural transitions inherent in moving to a new country but also the added pressures of parenting and managing family survival in an unfamiliar context. As highlighted by insights from Chaze (2013) in University Affairs, immigrant student parents like Esi require multifaceted support that extends beyond traditional academic and mental health services. They need comprehensive guidance on adapting to life in their new country, including information on the local education system, advice on balancing school with parenting duties, and assistance in accessing services to ease their transition and provide relevant support (Migration Data Portal, 2021; National Association of Foreign Student Advisers (NAFSA): Association of International Educators, n.d.). This context underscores the importance of developing targeted support mechanisms that address the unique needs of this vulnerable group, ensuring they have the necessary resources to thrive academically, personally, and as families in their host countries.

The cultural and educational divergence that Esi experienced highlights a common challenge for international students: the struggle to adapt to different academic practices and expectations (Bethel et al., 2020; Byrne et al., 2019; Russell et al., 2010). This adjustment difficulty can exacerbate feelings of isolation and alienation, significantly impacting students' mental health (Smith & Khawaja, 2011; Rhoden & Kinchington, 2021). Esi's sense of being an outsider, compounded by her responsibilities as a single mother, underscores the intense isolation that can arise from the disconnect between one's home culture and the culture of the host country (Bethel et al., 2020; Byrne et al., 2019).

Moreover, Esi's challenge of finding affordable childcare elucidates the financial stressors that international students face, which are further magnified for those with dependents (Forbes-Mewett, 2019). The high cost of living and childcare in many host countries places an additional burden on students, contributing to their overall stress and impacting their mental well-being and academic performance (Myers-Walls et al., 2011; Mbous et al., 2022).

Esi's hesitation to seek help from the university's counseling services due to a lack of cultural representation points to a broader issue of accessibility and inclusivity in mental health support for international students (Forbes-Mewett & Sawyer, 2019). The importance of culturally competent mental health services cannot be overstated, as students from diverse backgrounds may require different approaches to therapy and support that acknowledge and respect their cultural identities (Bethel et al., 2020; Byrne et al., 2019; Russell et al., 2010; Sue et al., 2012).

Case 2: Lee's Quiet Storm: The Unseen Struggle Behind Academic Excellence

In the bustling heart of Toronto, Lee embarked on a journey that was supposed to be the pinnacle of his young life—pursuing a business degree in Canada, a dream nurtured not just by him but also by his family in China. However, a tumultuous sea of expectations and unspoken pressures lay beneath the surface of this academic endeavor. Raised in a culture where academic success was not just a personal achievement but a family triumph, Lee felt an immense burden to excel. The high expectations, deeply ingrained in him since childhood, became a constant companion in his solitary dorm room, in lecture halls, and amid the pages of his textbooks.

As the academic year unfolded, the initial excitement waned, and the reality of his situation began to take its toll. Lee found himself in an unrelenting grip of stress and insomnia, the result of ceaseless pressure to maintain high grades. Nights were spent staring at the ceiling, grappling with a mind that refused to rest, haunted by the fear of failure and its repercussions. What compounded Lee's struggle was the cultural stigma attached to mental health in his community. Back home, discussions about mental health were often cloaked in silence, viewed as a sign of weakness or a blemish on the family's reputation. This cultural backdrop left Lee feeling trapped in his mind, unable to voice his struggles to his family for fear of being a disappointment.

The prospect of seeking help seemed like a distant thought. Though available, campus counseling services felt like an alien concept to Lee. Would they understand his cultural context? Could they grasp the intricate dynamics of his familial expectations? These questions swirled in Lee's mind, creating a barrier as real as any physical wall.

Debrief

These cases serve as a poignant gateway to a broader exploration of the challenges ahead. They not only illuminate the personal battles waged in silence but also pave the way for an in-depth examination of the systemic issues that exacerbate the struggles of international students. Moving forward, we will unravel the complexity surrounding these problems, seeking recommendations and strategies that foster a more inclusive and supportive academic environment for all.

Lee's story (A. A. Amissah, personal communication, February 14, 2024) provides a stark illustration of the mental health challenges that arise from the confluence of high familial expectations, the cultural stigma surrounding mental health, and the alienation felt in seeking support in a foreign educational system. Lee's experiences shed light on the intense pressure to succeed academically (Zheng et al., 2020), a pressure that is magnified by the cultural emphasis on academic achievement as a marker of personal and familial honor (Cao et al., 2021; Lian & Wallace, 2020; Ma et al., 2020). This pressure is not merely an internal drive but a deeply rooted expectation that can lead to significant mental health issues, such as stress and insomnia, as seen in Lee's case (Segú-Odriozola, 2025). The silence surrounding mental health discussions in his home culture further exacerbates these challenges, leaving Lee to struggle in isolation without the support he desperately needs (Segú-Odriozola, 2025).

Mental Health Stigma: The cultural stigma attached to mental health, prevalent in many societies, acts as a formidable barrier to seeking help (Forbes-Mewett & Sawyer, 2019). This stigma, coupled with the fear of disappointing one's family, can create a sense of entrapment within one's mind, as highlighted by Lee's reluctance to communicate his struggles to his family or seek assistance from campus counseling services (Adu et al., 2024). The perception of counseling services as an *alien concept* underscores the need for educational institutions to offer culturally sensitive mental health support that acknowledges and respects the diverse backgrounds of international students (Smith & Khawaja, 2011).

The systemic barriers to accessing support, such as unfamiliarity with the healthcare system in the host country and concerns about confidentiality, further compound the mental health challenges faced by international students (Carbonell et al., 2020).

Lost in Transition: Unraveling the Cultural and Linguistic Problems in International Student Mental Health

International students bring a rich tapestry of cultural perspectives and experiences to their host countries, significantly enriching the educational environment for all students. They contribute to the diversity of thoughts, foster cross-cultural understanding and dialogue, and enhance the global outlook of their institutions. However, the journey of an international student is fraught with challenges beyond academic adjustments. The narratives of students, as explored in our case studies, shine a light on these multifaceted challenges, particularly the issues of social isolation, financial stress, cultural dissonance, the stigma associated with mental health, and seeking mental health support.

Although the growing number of international students studying abroad reflects the interconnectedness and globalization of higher education, it also calls for a deeper understanding (Myers-Walls et al., 2011; Forbes-Mewett & Sawyer, 2019; Mbous et al., 2022) and responsiveness to the unique needs of these students, as expounded in the following sections.

Cultural Dissonance in Academic and Social Integration: Cultural dissonance represents a significant barrier to the academic success and well-being of international students, as vividly illustrated by the experiences of Esi and Lee. This dissonance, a clash between the familiar cultural norms of home countries and the new customs and expectations of host countries, poses unique challenges to students navigating this transitional space (Migration Data Portal, 2021; National Association of Foreign Student Advisers (NAFSA): Association of International Educators, n.d.). Esi and Lee embody the complexities of adapting to not only a new educational environment but also a foreign social landscape.

Cultural Shifts in Learning: Esi's journey into the heart of London's academic world, like many other international students, was marked by a transition from the communal and collaborative educational practices of Ghana to the more individualistic and competitive environment of the UK (Myers-Walls et al., 2011; Mbous et al., 2022). This shift is emblematic of the broader challenges of academic integration faced by international students, who often encounter pedagogical styles vastly different from those in their home countries (Smith & Khawaja, 2011). The emphasis on critical thinking and participatory learning in most Western educational institutions can be disorienting for students accustomed to more *rote-based* learning and hierarchical teacher-student relationships, leading to increased stress and a sense of academic inadequacy (Lee & Rice, 2007). *Rote-based* learning, often referred to as rote memorization, is a learning technique that focuses on memorizing information through repetition (Mayer, 2004). This method does not necessarily require understanding the meaning or context of the material being learned but relies on the repeated exposure or rehearsal of data until it is committed to memory (Mayer, 2004).

Stigma and Silence: The problem of stigma and silence, as highlighted in Lee's case, presents a profound barrier to mental health support for international students, especially Asian students (Sue et al., 2012). Lee's internalization of the stigma surrounding mental health discussions, ingrained through cultural upbringing, exemplifies a widespread issue that transcends individual cases, affecting a significant portion of the international student population. This internalized stigma not only inhibits students from seeking help but also perpetuates a cycle of silence and suffering, underscoring the urgent need for targeted interventions (Sue et al., 2012).

Research indicates that stigma associated with mental health can lead to decreased help-seeking behavior among students, particularly those from cultures where discussing mental health issues is considered taboo (Cogan et al., 2023). The silence that stems from this stigma is not merely a personal choice but a reflection of broader societal norms and attitudes that devalue and misunderstand mental health struggles (Cogan et al., 2023). This silence can be particularly detrimental in academic settings, where the pressure to succeed exacerbates mental health challenges, and the need for support is critical (Juma et al., 2022). Furthermore, in many cultures, there is a pervasive belief that poor mental health equates to a weak mentality (Sakiz & Jencius, 2024; Yeager & Dweck, 2020), compounding the challenges for international students. This cultural perception can severely impede students from acknowledging their mental health issues, let alone seeking necessary help (Juma et al., 2022). The stigma often intensifies in foreign academic environments (Mbous et al., 2022), where students feel additional pressure to demonstrate resilience and independence (Rudra, 2025). Such environments can create a paradox where students are simultaneously more in need of mental health support due to the stresses of adapting to a new culture and less likely to seek it, fearing that it may confirm stereotypes of inadequacy or weakness (Takeuchi & Sakagami, 2018).

Systemic Barriers to Accessing Support: Esi's reluctance to approach university counseling services due to the absence of culturally representative staff and Lee's perception of these services as foreign and unapproachable exemplifies the broader issue of accessibility and inclusivity within campus mental health systems (Segú-Odriozola, 2025). Students from diverse backgrounds often have unique cultural and contextual factors that influence their mental health and help-seeking behaviors (Zhou et al., 2022). For instance, the lack of culturally representative counselors can deter students from seeking help due to fears of being misunderstood or facing cultural insensitivity (Cheng et al., 2013). This highlights the critical need for educational institutions to prioritize the recruitment and training of counseling staff from a variety of cultural backgrounds, ensuring that the services offered are reflective of and sensitive to the diverse student population ((Doyle et al., 2016; Sawir et al., 2008; Cheng et al., 2013).

In the meantime, navigating the healthcare system in a foreign country presents a formidable challenge for international students, who often encounter a labyrinth of healthcare services, insurance policies, and procedural intricacies that differ markedly from those in their home countries (Andrade, 2006; Sawir et al., 2008; Wawera & McCamley, 2020). This complexity can significantly hinder their ability to access mental health services due to uncertainties about where to seek help, the availability of services, and how to engage with the healthcare administration (Nguyen et al., 2021; Salimi et al., 2023). A lack of transparent, easily accessible information on mental health resources further compounds these difficulties (Sawir et al., 2008).

Financial Stress and Childcare Challenges: As illustrated by Esi's narrative, the dual challenges of financial stress and childcare logistics underscore a critical and often overlooked aspect of the international student experience. The intersection of financial burdens with the necessity of securing affordable childcare creates a multifaceted stressor that directly impacts the mental health and academic performance of student parents. Esi's struggle to balance her academic aspirations with her role as a mother, all while navigating the financial constraints of living and studying in London, highlights the broader issue faced by many international students with families.

Financial stress, a prevalent concern among international students (Coffey et al., 2021; Morris et al., 2023; Wilson et al., 2023), is exacerbated for those with dependents due to the added costs of childcare, which can consume a significant portion of their budget. Studies have shown that financial stress is linked to adverse mental health outcomes, including anxiety and depression, which can, in turn, affect academic performance (Wilson et al., 2023). The challenge of accessing affordable childcare compounds this issue, as the availability of such services often does not align with the needs of student parents who may have irregular schedules and limited financial resources (Lutz et al., 2023).

Familial Expectations and Academic Pressure: The narratives of Esi and Lee, representing international students, illuminate the pervasive issue of academic pressure, underscored by heightened familial expectations. This pressure, while intended to motivate, often manifests as an undoubted source of stress, precipitating a range of mental health issues from anxiety to depression (Page, 2021; Smith & Khawaja, 2011; Szabo et al., 2016). The intricacies of this challenge demand a nuanced understanding and a comprehensive approach to mitigating its impact on students' well-being and academic performance. Academic pressure, particularly among international students, is compounded by the additional challenges of cultural adjustment and the quest for personal identity in a foreign milieu. The expectations set forth by families often reflect broader cultural values surrounding education and success, placing the student at the intersection of personal aspirations and collective family honor (Sue et al., 2012). This intersection can create an intense psychological burden, as failure is perceived not only as a personal setback but also as a familial disappointment, amplifying the stress experienced by students (Sue et al., 2012).

Social Isolation and Lack of Support Networks: The phenomenon of social isolation and the challenges associated with the lack of support networks are critical concerns for international students, impacting their mental health and overall well-being significantly (Girmay & Singh, 2019; Lukács, 2021; Maeda, 2017). Transitioning to a new country for education often means leaving behind the familiar support structures of family and community, leading to a sense of profound disconnection (Smith & Khawaja, 2011). This disconnection is not just a matter of geographical distance but represents a deeper emotional and social gap that can manifest as loneliness, homesickness, and alienation (Sawir et al., 2008). These feelings, if not adequately addressed, have the potential to develop into more severe mental health issues, such as depression and anxiety (Liu, 2020).

Re-establishing a support network in a new country is fraught with challenges. International students must navigate cultural, linguistic, and social barriers, complicating the formation of new connections (Zhou et al., 2008). The difficulty in establishing these connections can exacerbate the sense of isolation, potentially leading to a decline in mental health (Rosenthal et al., 2007).

Beyond the Surface: Unveiling the Complex Tapestry of Challenges in International Student Mental Health

In addition to the problems identified through the case studies of Esi and Lee, there are several other critical issues that international students face in the context of mental health and communication.

The temporary residency status of international students can also influence their engagement with mental health services. Confidentiality concerns, the impermanent nature of their stay, and a perception of mental health issues as transient barriers to be overcome may discourage them from seeking necessary support (Brooks & Waters, 2021; Brown, 2009; Gu et al., 2010). These obstacles, coupled with the financial pressures of overseas education and living expenses, exacerbate the mental health challenges these students face. Economic constraints are particularly acute for those in countries where mental health services are not readily accessible or affordable to international students (Myers-Walls et al., 2011).

Socio political factors further complicate the mental health landscape for international students. Visa uncertainties, potential experiences of discrimination, and the political climate of the host country can all contribute to heightened stress and anxiety levels (Brooks & Waters, 2021; Narea, 2020; Treisman, 2020). The fear of jeopardizing their student status or encountering discrimination creates an environment that may adversely affect their mental health (Lee & Rice, 2007).

In 2020, during the Trump administration, the ICE policy not only heightened concerns about student visa statuses but also instilled a profound fear of deportation during a global health crisis, highlighting how governmental actions can directly impact the well-being of international students (Narea, 2020). The abrupt announcement and subsequent retraction of this policy underscored the vulnerability of these students to sudden legal changes that could dramatically alter their ability to remain in the United States legally and pursue their education (Treisman, 2020). This incident exemplifies broader systemic challenges international students face, where policies not directly related to education can profoundly affect their mental health and academic stability. The resultant fear and uncertainty can exacerbate existing mental health conditions, leading to increased anxiety, isolation, and stress among this demographic (Treisman, 2020).

In summary, the spectrum of challenges impacting the mental health and well-being of international students is extensive, encompassing systemic hurdles such as navigating unfamiliar healthcare systems, cultural incongruities in treatment modalities, financial limitations, and socio political concerns, alongside personal obstacles like language barriers, cultural stigma, and social isolation. To ensure the delivery of adequate mental health support for this vulnerable population, we must develop a comprehensive understanding of these issues and proactively address them (Poyrazli & Grahame, 2007).

Intersecting Lenses: Theoretical Foundations for Culturally Informed Health Communication Strategies

It is essential to anchor strategies in robust theoretical frameworks to navigate the intricate landscape of mental health communication within diverse international student populations. Such a foundation would not only illuminate the multifaceted challenges these students face but also guide the development of culturally informed approaches to support students' mental well-being.

Intercultural communication theory. The foundation of culturally informed health communication strategies is intricately tied to understanding the intercultural communication theory (Logan et al., 2014). This theory is instrumental in deciphering the complex dynamics of mental health communication across diverse student populations, maintaining that cultural variances profoundly shape the essence of communication. These differences significantly affect how messages are crafted, conveyed, and interpreted (Kreuter et al., 2003; Okamoto et al., 2014; Rüsch et al., 2005). This framework is particularly relevant in mental health services for international students. The theory elucidates the critical role cultural norms, values, and communicative practices play in shaping students' perceptions and interactions with mental health support systems.

Hofstede's (1984) conceptualization of cultural dimensions is central to the discourse on intercultural communication theory. These dimensions—individualism versus collectivism, power distance, uncertainty avoidance, masculinity versus femininity, and long-term versus short-term orientation—offer a scaffold for appreciating the heterogeneous cultural backdrops of international students. For example, the preference for a communal approach to mental health support in collectivist cultures underscores the importance of integrating family and community in the therapeutic process, contrasting sharply with the individualistic ethos emphasizing autonomy in decision-making (Hofstede, 1984).

Health Belief Model. Complementing this is the health belief model (HBM), which delineates the motivational factors behind health-seeking behaviors. This model posits that an individual's health-related actions are motivated by their perceived vulnerability to a health issue, the potential severity of the condition, the benefits of taking preventive action, and the perceived barriers to such action (Rosenstock, 1974). In the milieu of international students, the HBM offers insights into the myriad obstacles—ranging from stigma and linguistic challenges to a lack of awareness about available services—that deter engagement with mental health services and the motivators that could drive their utilization.

Social Support. The social support theory (Cohen & Wills, 1985) further highlights the significance of social networks in the mental health continuum of international students. This framework accentuates the value of emotional, informational, and instrumental support in navigating stressors and mental health challenges. Since international students often find themselves distanced from their ingrained support systems, establishing new support networks within their host countries becomes crucial for their mental health (Cohen & Wills, 1985).

Self-determination theory. Moreover, self-determination theory (SDT) sheds light on the pivotal roles of autonomy, competence, and relatedness in fostering mental health and well-being. SDT argues that satisfying these fundamental psychological needs is crucial for maintaining psychological health (Ryan & Deci, 2000). For international students, this translates into interventions designed to empower autonomy, enhance competence in new academic and social environments, and cultivate a sense of belonging and connection (Yue & Lu, 2022; Cho et al., 2023; Zheng et al., 2020).

In synthesizing these theoretical perspectives, a comprehensive framework emerges for addressing the mental health challenges of international students. This approach underscores the importance of culturally sensitive, socially supportive, and individual-centric strategies in health communication and mental health service provision.

Strategic Communication Recommendations

Strategic communication efforts can be essential in raising awareness about mental health issues, addressing stigma, and promoting help-seeking behaviors among international students (Clough et al., 2020; McGinty et al., 2018). The following section will discuss recommendations for how strategic communication may improve these efforts. Note that the theories discussed above could be used to frame message design for the various strategies outlined below.

To begin, universities should develop broad strategies for promoting mental health resources in culturally appropriate ways. Providing culturally sensitive information about available resources may encourage help-seeking behaviors and reduce the number of students who discontinue services (Kim & Zane, 2016). Such efforts should consider a campus's international student population's cultural background to develop messages that resonate with students' values and beliefs. Wide-ranging evidence demonstrates that messages tailored to a particular culture are more persuasive, particularly in health (e.g., Dobson et al., 2017; Uskul & Oyserman, 2010). Of course, universities enroll international students from a variety of cultures. As such, campus communication strategists should consider the best channels for delivering segmented and tailored messaging to the different audiences in terms of campus partners (e.g., through an international office, advising units, etc.) and communication platforms (e.g., social media, email, campus newsletters, outdoor advertising, and flyers). For instance, Hofstede's cultural dimensions, which emphasize cultural variances in communication, can guide the creation of tailored messages that are more persuasive and relatable, encouraging help-seeking behaviors among students from different cultural backgrounds (Kim & Zane, 2016; Uskul & Oyserman, 2010).

Furthermore, there is a need to consider health literacy and a diverse understanding of mental health help-seeking across cultures when developing these strategies (Cogan et al., 2023). In mental health literacy, or *knowledge and beliefs about mental disorders that aid their recognition, management, or prevention* (Jorm et al., 1997, p. 182), international students perineally have been shown to lag behind their domestic peers (e.g., Clough et al., 2019; Cogan et al., 2023; Gorczynski et al., 2017). As such, strategic communication objectives should be reflective of an audience with low health literacy. Subsequent strategies should revolve around providing basic information about available mental health resources and services, including counseling services, support groups, and crisis hotlines, with clear instructions regarding how to access this support. If possible, university messaging should also emphasize where international students may access services tailored to their cultural and language needs.

Along these lines, concerted efforts should be expended to encourage help-seeking, focusing on culturally specific barriers. For example, some cultures may see mental health issues as a sign of weakness; others may value the health and well-being of the collective over the individual (Sakiz & Jencius, 2024). As such, university communication officials should target these barriers and dispel negative perceptions by tailoring messages to distinct groups of international students for whom specific barriers appear more intransigent. This can be achieved by promoting a culture of open communication, especially between students and the campus international office. Additionally, advisors should be trained in cultural competency, equipping them to communicate one-on-one with students about specific barriers (Han et al., 2013).

The Health Belief Model will be instrumental in shaping our understanding of the barriers to and motivators for seeking mental health services. Strategic communication should therefore focus on increasing health literacy, clearly outlining the benefits of engaging with mental health resources while addressing perceived barriers such as stigma and linguistic challenges. Campaigns should include basic information about available services and emphasize how these services cater to the unique cultural and language needs of international students (Cogan et al., 2023).

As universities continue to attract international students from diverse linguistic and cultural backgrounds, the importance of translating health messages into multiple languages cannot be understated. Scholars have called for an intentional focus on language, conceptualized as a social determinant of health (Federici, 2022). Moreover, in a study by Sue et al., (1991), matching help-seekers and therapists in language was associated with lower dropout rates and better mental health outcomes. This can likely be attributed to participants' comfort in using their native language to discuss sensitive topics or to express particular emotions. For example, Santiago-Rivera et al. (2009) demonstrated that bilingual individuals receiving mental health care from a bilingual provider switched to their native language when describing experiences that evoked anger. Given the importance of language in this context, promotional messages written in various languages would signal to the students the availability (if applicable) of resources responsive to their distinct needs (Geegan et al., 2023).

Reflecting on the importance of language as highlighted by Social Determinants of Health Theory, universities should ensure that health messages are available in multiple languages. This approach acknowledges the comfort and clarity that come from receiving information in one's native language, which can be critical when discussing sensitive topics like mental health (Federici, 2022; Sue et al., 1991).

Next, collaborating with student organizations can play a critical role in promoting mental health among international students. Often, international students seek organizations that allow them to gather with individuals from their home countries or with other international students similarly adapting to the host culture (Poyrazli & Grahame, 2007). Campaign and outreach efforts should involve partnering with student organizations to develop culturally appropriate messages and disseminate information about mental health resources and services.

According to Social Support Theory, creating robust support networks is essential for the mental well-being of international students. Strategic initiatives should therefore involve collaborations with student organizations that share cultural ties with the students. These partnerships can help develop and disseminate culturally appropriate messages and foster a sense of community and support among the students (Poyrazli & Grahame, 2007). Also, with Self-Determination Theory in mind, communication strategies should aim to empower students by supporting their autonomy, competence, and relatedness. This might include programs and workshops that help students develop skills to navigate their new environment, promote their academic and social integration, and build meaningful connections within the university community (Ryan & Deci, 2000).

For example, Harvard University has implemented a comprehensive mental health strategy in response to the findings of the Task Force on Student Mental Health (Milkowski, 2022), which revealed significant issues like anxiety, depression, and loneliness among students. The strategy addresses these challenges by focusing on access, awareness, prevention, and support. Key initiatives include the formation of an Access Team at Counseling and Mental Health Services (CAMHS), a partnership with TimelyMD for telehealth counseling, and the development of learning modules tailored for undergraduate and graduate students. Additionally, the *We're All Human* campaign aims to change the campus culture around mental health by promoting well-being and making mental health resources more accessible. This holistic approach signifies Harvard's commitment to improving student mental health and fostering a supportive academic environment.

While Harvard University's comprehensive approach to addressing mental health challenges through access, awareness, prevention, and support represents a significant advancement in fostering a supportive academic environment (Milkowski, 2022), it highlights an area in need of further development: the absence of mental health programs specifically tailored to the unique needs of international students. This oversight is noteworthy considering the distinct challenges faced by this demographic, including cultural adjustment, language barriers, social isolation, and the complexities of navigating mental health care in an unfamiliar healthcare system.

Lastly, providing supportive facilities for student parents is crucial to creating an inclusive academic environment, particularly for international students who face the added challenge of navigating a new cultural and educational landscape far from their support networks. An example of this support can be seen at the University of Sussex (Kistnasamy, November 2018), which has taken significant steps to accommodate the needs of student parents on campus. The university offers sixty family units within its accommodation, providing much-needed housing options for students with families. Despite the competitive nature of securing these units, their availability is a testament to the university's commitment to supporting student parents.

Furthermore, recognizing the importance of recreational and study spaces that cater to families, Sussex has established a family room on the library's first floor. This room, equipped with children's toys and books, allows children to be entertained in a designated area while their parents study or use the available computers and desks. Such facilities are invaluable, particularly during colder months when outdoor activities are limited, offering a practical solution for student parents seeking to balance their academic responsibilities with childcare. However, the popularity of this space, especially during school breaks, highlights the growing demand for such family-oriented facilities on campus.

The University of Sussex's approach exemplifies how institutions can effectively support student parents' well-being and academic success through thoughtful campus planning and resources. This model is a corroborative example of the positive impact of dedicated support services and facilities on student parents' mental health and academic experiences, encouraging a balance between study commitments and family life.

In conclusion, improving strategic communication efforts can be crucial in promoting mental health among international students. By developing culturally appropriate messages, using multiple channels of communication, collaborating with student organizations, addressing stigma, providing information about available resources, and encouraging help-seeking behaviors, we can work toward creating a more supportive and inclusive campus culture around mental health.

Conclusion

The mental health of international students encompasses a complex array of challenges that necessitate a nuanced and comprehensive approach from academic institutions. Through examining case studies, such as those of Esi and Lee, alongside the implementation of broad-scale initiatives like those at Harvard University, it becomes evident that significant gaps remain while strides are being made. Remarkably, the absence of programs specifically tailored to international students' cultural, social, and emotional needs highlights an area ripe for development. Addressing this gap requires a concerted effort to integrate culturally sensitive practices, targeted support mechanisms, and an inclusive dialogue that respects and acknowledges the diverse backgrounds of the international student body. As universities continue to evolve and adapt their mental health strategies, the ultimate goal should be to foster an environment where every student, regardless of their origin, feels supported, understood, and empowered to achieve academic success and personal well-being.

Recommended Readings/Resources

Bradley, G. (2000). Responding effectively to the mental health needs of international students. *Higher Education*, *39,* 417–433.

Federici, F. M. (2022). Translating health risks: Language as a social determinant of health. In F. M. Federici (Eds.), *Language as a social determinant of health: Palgrave studies in translating and interpreting.* Palgrave Macmillan. https://doi.org/10.1007/978-3-030-87817-7_1

King, N., Rivera, D., Cunningham, S., Pickett, W., Harkness, K., McNevin, S. H., . . . & Duffy, A. (2023). Mental health and academic outcomes over the first year at university in international compared to domestic Canadian students. *Journal of American College Health, 71*(9), 2663–2672.

Minutillo, S., Cleary, M., P. Hills, A., & Visentin, D. (2020). Mental health considerations for international students. *Issues in Mental Health Nursing, 41*(6), 494–499.

Yeung, T. S., Hyun, S., Zhang, E., Wong, F., Stevens, C., Liu, C. H., & Chen, J. A. (2022). Prevalence and correlates of mental health symptoms and disorders among US international college students. *Journal of American College Health, 70*(8), 2470–2475.

References

Abdullah, D., Abd Aziz, M. I., & Mohd Ibrahim, A. L. (2017). The stories they tell: Understanding international student mobility through higher education policy. *Journal of Studies in International Education*, *21*(5), 450–466. https://doi.org/10.1177/1028315317720766

Abrams, Z. (2022, October 1). Mental health on campus: Student mental health is in crisis. Campuses are rethinking their approach. *Monitor on Psychology, 53*(7), 60. Retrieved from https://www.apa.org/monitor/2022/10/mental-health-campus-care

Adu, J., Oudshoorn, A., Anderson, K., Marshall, C. A., & Stuart, H. (2024). Negotiating familial mental illness stigma: The role of family members of persons living with mental illnesses. *PloS one*, *19*(9), e0311170. https://doi.org/10.1371/journal.pone.0311170

Ajzen, I., & Fishbein, M. (1980). *Understanding attitudes and predicting social behavior.* Prentice-Hall.

Andrade, M. S. (2006). International students in English-speaking universities: Adjustment factors. *Journal of Research in International Education, 5*(2), 131–154. https://doi.org/10.1177/1475240906065589

Berry, J. W. (1997). Immigration, acculturation, and adaptation. *Applied Psychology, 46*(1), 5–34.

Bethel, A., Ward, C., & Fetvadjiev, V. H. (2020). Cross-cultural transition and psychological adaptation of international students: The mediating role of host national connectedness. *Frontiers in Education, 5*, 539950. Frontiers Media SA. https://doi.org/10.3389/feduc.2020.539950

Bista, K., Sharma, G., & Gaulee, U. (2018). International student mobility: Examining trends and tensions. In *International student mobility and opportunities for growth in the global marketplace* (pp. 1–14). IGI Global. https://doi.org/10.4018/978-1-5225-3451-8.ch001

Brooks, R., & Waters, J. (2021). International students and alternative visions of diaspora. *British Journal of Educational Studies, 69*(5), 557–577. https://doi.org/10.1080/00071005.2021.1948501

Brown, J. S. (2018). Student mental health: some answers and more questions. *Journal of Mental Health, 27*(3), 193–196.

Brown, L. (2009). The transformative power of the international sojourn: An ethnographic study of the international student experience. *Annals of Tourism Research, 36*(3), 502–521. https://doi.org/10.1016/j.annals.2009.03.002

Byrne, E., Brugha, R., & McGarvey, A. (2019). 'A melting pot of cultures'–challenges in social adaptation and interactions amongst international medical students. *BMC Medical Education, 19*(1), 1–14. https://doi.org/10.1186/s12909-019-1514–1

Cao, C., Zhu, C., & Meng, Q. (2021). Chinese international students' coping strategies, social support resources in response to academic stressors: Does heritage culture or host context matter? *Current Psychology, 40*, 242–252. https://doi.org/10.1007/s12144-018-9929-0

Carbonell, A., Navarro-Pérez, J. J., & Mestre, M. V. (2020). Challenges and barriers in mental healthcare systems and their impact on the family: A systematic integrative review. *Health & social care in the community, 28*(5), 1366–1379.

Chaze, F. (2013, January 23). *Immigrant student parents are a group apart.* University Affairs. Retrieved from https://universityaffairs.ca/opinion/in-my-opinion/immigrant-student- parents-are-a-group-apart/

Cheng, H. L., Kwan, K. L. K., & Sevig, T. (2013). Racial and ethnic minority college students' stigma associated with seeking psychological help: Examining psychocultural correlates. Journal of Counseling Psychology, 60(1), 98. https://doi.org/10.1037/a0031169

Cho, H. J., Levesque-Bristol, C., & Yough, M. (2023). How autonomy-supportive learning environments promote Asian international students' academic adjustment: A self-determination theory perspective. *Learning Environments Research, 26*(1), 51–76. https://doi.org/10.1007/s10984-021-09401-x

Clough, B. A., Nazareth, S. M., & Casey, L. M. (2020). Making the grade: A pilot investigation of an e-intervention to increase mental health literacy and help-seeking intentions among international university students. *British Journal of Guidance & Counselling, 48*(3), 347–359.

Clough, B. A., Nazareth, S. M., Day, J. J., & Casey, L. M. (2019). A comparison of mental health literacy, attitudes, and help-seeking intentions among domestic and international tertiary students. *British Journal of Guidance & Counselling, 47*(1), 123–135. https://doi.org/10.1080/03069885.2018.1459473

Coffey, J., Cook, J., Farrugia, D., Threadgold, S., & Burke, P. J. (2021). Intersecting marginalities: International students' struggles for "survival" in COVID-19. *Gender, Work & Organization, 28*(4), 1337–1351. https://doi.org/10.1111/gwao.12610

Cogan, N. A., Liu, X., Chin-Van Chau, Y., Kelly, S. W., Anderson, T., Flynn, C., ... & Corrigan, P. (2023). The taboo of mental health problems, stigma and fear of disclosure among Asian international students: Implications for help-seeking, guidance and support. *British Journal of Guidance & Counselling*, 52(4), 697–715. https://doi.org/10.1080/03069885.2023.2214307

Cohen, S., & Wills, T. A. (1985). Stress, social support, and the buffering hypothesis. *Psychological Bulletin, 98*(2), 310.

Dobson, R., Whittaker, R., Bartley, H., Connor, A., Chen, R., Ross, M., & McCool, J. (2017). Development of a culturally tailored text message maternal health program: TextMATCH. *JMIR mHealth and uHealth*, 5(4), e7205. https://doi.org/10.2196/mhealth.7205

Doyle, S., Loveridge, J., & Faamanatu-Eteuati, N. (2016). Counting family: Making the family of international students visible in higher education policy and practice. *Higher Education Policy, 29*, 184–198. https://doi.org/10.1057/hep.2015.20

Durrani, A. (2023, December). *Mental health tips for international students.* U.S. News & World Report. Retrieved from https://www.usnews.com/education/best-global-universities/articles/mental-health-tips-for-international-students

Forbes-Mewett, H., & Sawyer, A. M. (2019). International students and mental health. *Journal of International Students, 6*(3), 661–677.

Gee, C. B., Khera, G. S., Poblete, A. T., Kim, B., & Buchwach, S. Y. (2020). Barriers to mental health service use in Asian American and European American college students. *Asian American Journal of Psychology, 11*(2), 98. https://doi.org/10.1037/aap0000178

Geegan, S. A., Parker, K. A., Pfeiffer, S. N., Rodriguez, D., & Tristan, A. (2023). The complexities of mental health help seeking among latinx college students:

Qualitative inquiry using the theory of planned behavior. *Hispanic Journal of Behavioral Sciences*, *45*(2), 91–120. https://doi.org/10.1177/07399863231214

Girmay, M., & Singh, G. K. (2019). Social isolation, loneliness, and mental and emotional well- being among international students in the United States. *International Journal of Translational Medical Research and Public Health*, *3*(2), 75–82. https://doi.org/10.21106/ijtmrph.82

Gorczynski, P., Sims-Schouten, W., Hill, D., & Wilson, J. C. (2017). Examining mental health literacy, help seeking behaviours, and mental health outcomes in UK university students. *The Journal of Mental Health Training, Education and Practice*, *12*(2), 111–120. https://doi.org/10.1108/JMHTEP-05-20160027

Gu, Q., Schweisfurth, M., & Day, C. (2010). Learning and growing in a 'foreign' context: Intercultural experiences of international students. *Compare*, *40*(1), 7–23. https://doi.org/10.1080/03057920903115983

Han, X., Han, X., Luo, Q., Jacobs, S., & Jean-Baptiste, M. (2013). Report of a mental health survey among Chinese international students at Yale University. *Journal of American College Health*, *61*(1), 1–8. https://doi.org/10.1080/07448481.2012.738267

Hofstede, G. (1984). *Culture's consequences: International differences in work-related values* (Vol. 5). Sage.

Islam, M. T. (2019). (Re) Searching for the development of a conceptual model of education for citizenship in the context of young people's globalised mobility in higher education. *Globalisation, Societies and Education*, *17*(2), 194–207. https://doi.org/10.1080/14767724.2019.1583093

Institute of International Education (IIE). (2023). *Open doors report on international educational exchange*. Retrieved from: https://www.iie.org/Research-and-Insights/Open-Doors

Jorm, A. F., Korten, A. E., Jacomb, P. A., Christensen, H., Rodgers, B., & Pollitt, P. (1997). "Mental health literacy": a survey of the public's ability to recognise mental disorders and their beliefs about the effectiveness of treatment. Medical Journal of Australia, 166(4), 182–186. https://doi.org/10.5694/j.1326-5377.1997.tb140071.x

Juma, O., Husiyin, M., Akhat, A., & Habibulla, I. (2022). Students' classroom silence and hopelessness: The impact of teachers' immediacy on mainstream education. Frontiers in Psychology, 12, 819821. https://doi.org/10.3389/fpsyg.2021.819821

Kim, E. (2009). Navigating college life: The role of peer networks in first-year college adaptation experience of minority immigrant students. Journal of the First-Year Experience & Students in Transition, 21(2), 9–34.

Kim, J. E., & Zane, N. (2016). Help-seeking intentions among Asian American and White American students in psychological distress: Application of the health belief model. *Cultural Diversity and Ethnic Minority Psychology*, *22*(3), 311.

Kirloskar, P., & Inamdar, N. (2021). Shifting international student mobility directions and factors influencing students' higher education destination choices. *Journal of*

Higher Education Policy and Leadership Studies, 2(3), 160–178. https://doi.org/10.52547/johepal.2.3.160

Kistnasamy, J. (2018, November 14). My experience as an international student parent. *Sussex Business School Blog.* Retrieved from https://blogs.sussex.ac.uk/business-school/2018/11/14/my-experience-as-an-international-student-parent/

Kramer E. J., Kwong K., Lee E., Chung H. (2002) Cultural factors influencing the mental health of Asian Americans. *Western Journal of Medicine, 176*(4), 227–31.

Kreuter, M. W., Lukwago, S. N., Bucholtz, D. C., Clark, E. M., & Sanders-Thompson, V. (2003). Achieving cultural appropriateness in health promotion programs: Targeted and tailored approaches. *Health Education & Behavior, 30*(2), 133–146. https://doi.org/10.1177/1090198102251021

Lee, J. J., & Rice, C. (2007). Welcome to America? International student perceptions of discrimination. *Higher Education, 53*(3), 381–409. https://doi.org/10.1007/s10734-005-4508-3

Lian, Z., & Wallace, B. C. (2020). Prevalence of past-year mental disorders and its correlates among Chinese international students in US higher education. *Journal of American College Health, 68*(2), 176–184. https://doi.org/10.1080/07448481.2018.1538147

Liu, H., Wong, Y. J., Mitts, N. G., Li, P. J., & Cheng, J. (2020). A phenomenological study of East Asian international students' experience of counseling. *International Journal for the Advancement of Counselling, 42*, 269–291. https://doi.org/10.1007/s10447-020-09399-6

Logan, S., Steel, Z., & Hunt, C. (2014). A systematic review of effective intercultural communication in mental health. Cross-Cultural Communication, 10(5), 1–11. http://dx.doi.org/10.3968/5407

Lukács, A. (2021). Mental well-being of university students in social isolation. *European Journal of Health Psychology, 28*(1), 22–29. https://doi.org/10.1027/2512-8442/a000065

Lutz, A., Lee, S., & Bokayev, B. (2023). Intensive mothering in the time of Coronavirus. *Journal of Social Issues, 79*(3), 997–1021. https://doi.org/10.1111/josi.12515

Ma, K., Pitner, R., Sakamoto, I., & Park, H. Y. (2020). Challenges in acculturation among international students from Asian Collectivist Cultures. *Higher Education Studies, 10*(3), 34–43. https://doi.org/10.5539/hes.v10n3p34

Maeda, J. (2017). Self-efficacy reduces impediments to classroom discussion for international students: Fear, embarrassment, social isolation, judgment, and discrimination. *IAFOR Journal of Education, 5*(2), 141–159.

Mayer, R. E. (2004). Should there be a three-strikes rule against pure discovery learning? *American Psychologist, 59*(1), 14. https://doi.org/10.1037/0003-066X.59.1.14

Mbous, Y. P. V., Mohamed, R., & Rudisill, T. M. (2022). International students challenges during the COVID-19 pandemic in a university in the United States: A focus group study. *Current Psychology*, 1–13. https://doi.org/10.1007/s12144-022-02776-x

McGinty E., Pescosolido B., Kennedy-Hendricks A., & Barry C. L. (2018). Communication strategies to counter stigma and improve mental illness and substance use disorder policy. *Psychiatric Services*, *69*(2), 136–146. https://doi.org/10.1176/appi.ps.201700076

Migration Data Portal. (2021). *International students*. Retrieved from https://www.migrationdataportal.org/themes/international-students

Milkowski, G. (2022, October). 'Access, awareness, prevention, and support': Harvard moves to implement Student Mental Health task force recommendations. *The Harvard Gazette*. Retrieved from: https://news.harvard.edu/gazette/story/2022/10/harvard-moves-to- implement-recommendations-for-student-mental-health/

Morris, A., Wilson, S., Mitchell, E., Ramia, G., & Hastings, C. (2023). International students struggling in the private rental sector in Australia prior to and during the pandemic. *Housing Studies*, *38*(8), 1589–1610. https://doi.org/10.1080/02673037.2021.1961695

Myers-Walls, J. A., Frias, L. V., Kwon, K. A., Ko, M. J. M., & Lu, T. (2011). Living life in two worlds: Acculturative stress among Asian international graduate student parents and spouses. Journal of Comparative Family Studies, 42(4), 455–478.

NAFSA: Association of International Educators. (n.d.). *Trends in U.S. study abroad*. Retrieved from https://www.nafsa.org/policy-and-advocacy/policy-resources/trends-us-study-abroad

Narea, N. (2020, July 8). Trump is trying to kick out foreign students amid the pandemic. *Vox*. Retrieved from: https://www.vox.com/2020/7/8/21317059/trump-foreign-students-ice

Nguyen, M. H., Le, T. T., Nguyen, H. K. T., Ho, M. T., Nguyen, H. T. T., & Vuong, Q. H. (2021). Alice in suicideland: Exploring the suicidal ideation mechanism through the sense of connectedness and help-seeking behaviors. *International Journal of Environmental Research and Public Health*, *18*(7), 3681. https://doi.org/10.3390/ijerph18073681

OECD. (2023). *Education at a glance 2023: OECD indicators*. OECD Publishing. https://doi.org/10.1787/e13bef63-en.

Okamoto, S. K., Kulis, S., Marsiglia, F. F., Holleran Steiker, L. K., & Dustman, P. (2014). A continuum of approaches toward developing culturally focused prevention interventions: From adaptation to grounding. *The Journal of Primary Prevention*, *35*, 103–112. https://doi.org/10.1007/s10935-013-0334-z

Page, A. G. (2021). From familial pressure to seeking one's fortune: Chinese international students' search for geographical and social mobility as a response to societal and familial pressures. In *migration to and from welfare states: Lived experiences of the welfare–migration nexus in a globalised world*, 49–65. https://doi.org/10.1007/978-3-030- 67615-5_4

Pantha, S. (2023, July 19). Life with kids as an international student in Melbourne. *Study Melbourne*. Retrieved from https://www.studymelbourne.vic.gov.au/living-here/welcome/student-stories-welcome/life-with-kids-as-an-international-student-in-melbourne

Poyrazli, S., & Grahame, K. M. (2007). Barriers to adjustment: Needs of international students within a semi-urban campus community. *Journal of Instructional Psychology*, *34*(1), 28.

Rhoden, M., & Kinchington, F. (2021). Examining the challenges faced by international women with preschool children studying for a postgraduate built environment degree in the UK. *Journal of International Students*, *11*(4), 970–987. https://doi.org/10.32674/jis.v11i4.2398

Rosenstock, I. M. (1974). The health belief model and preventive health behavior. *Health Education Monographs*, *2*(4), 354–386. https://journals.sagepub.com/doi/10.1177/109019817400200405

Rosenthal, D. A., Russell, J., & Thomson, G. (2007). Social connectedness among international students at an Australian university. *Social Indicators Research*, *84*(1), 71–82. https://link.springer.com/article/10.1007/s11205-006-9075-1

Rudra, P. K. (2025). Examining the relationship between acculturation levels, help-seeking attitudes, and self-stigma perspectives among international students. Journal of International Students, 15(8), 121.

Rüsch, N., Angermeyer, M. C., & Corrigan, P. W. (2005). Mental illness stigma: Concepts, consequences, and initiatives to reduce stigma. *European Psychiatry*, *20*(8), 529–539. https://doi.org/10.1016/j.eurpsy.2005.04.004

Russell, J., Rosenthal, D., & Thomson, G. (2010). The international student experience: Three styles of adaptation. *Higher Education*, *60*, 235–249. https://doi.org/10.1007/s10734-009-9297-7

Ryan, R. M., & Deci, E. L. (2000). Self-determination theory and the facilitation of intrinsic motivation, social development, and well-being. *American psychologist*, *55*(1), 68.

Sakiz H, & Jencius M. (2024). Inclusive mental health support for international students: Unveiling delivery components in higher education. *Cambridge Prisms: Global Mental Health*, *11*, e8. https://doi.org/10.1017/gmh.2024.1

Salimi, N., Gere, B., Talley, W., & Irioogbe, B. (2023). College students mental health challenges: Concerns and considerations in the COVID-19 pandemic. *Journal of College Student Psychotherapy*, *37*(1), 39–51. https://doi.org/10.1080/87568225.2021.1890298

Santiago-Rivera, A. L., Altarriba, J., Poll, N., Gonzalez-Miller, N., & Cragun, C. (2009). Therapists' views on working with bilingual Spanish–English speaking clients: A qualitative investigation. Professional Psychology: Research and Practice, 40(5), 436–443. https://doi.org/10.1037/a001593

Sawir, E., Marginson, S., Deumert, A., Nyland, C., & Ramia, G. (2008). Loneliness and international students: An Australian study. *Journal of studies in International Education*, *12*(2), 148–180. https://doi.org/10.1177/1028315307299699

Segú-Odriozola, M. (2025). The Mental Health of University Students: A Social Ecology Perspective. Societies, 15(4), 110. https://doi.org/10.3390/soc15040110

Smith, R. A., & Khawaja, N. G. (2011). A review of the acculturation experiences of international students. *International Journal of Intercultural Relations*, *35*(6), 699–713. https://doi.org/10.1016/j.ijintrel.2011.08.004

Sue, S., Cheng, J. K. Y., Saad, C. S., & Chu, J. P. (2012). Asian American mental health: A call to action. *American Psychologist*, *67*(7), 532. https://doi.org/10.1037/a0028900

Sue, S., Fujino, D. C., Hu, L.-t., Takeuchi, D. T., & Zane, N. W. S. (1991). Community mental health services for ethnic minority groups: A test of the cultural responsiveness hypothesis. Journal of Consulting and Clinical Psychology, *59*(4), 533–540. https://doi.org/10.1037/0022-006X.59.4.533

Szabo, A., Ward, C., & Jose, P. E. (2016). Uprooting stress, coping, and anxiety: A longitudinal study of international students. *International Journal of Stress Management*, *23*(2), 190. https://doi.org/10.1037/a0039771

Takeuchi, J., & Sakagami, Y. (2018). Stigma among international students is associated with knowledge of mental illness. Nagoya Journal Of Medical Science, 80(3), 367–378. https://doi.org/10.18999/nagjms.80.3.367

Treisman, R. (2020, July 14). ICE agrees to rescind policy barring foreign students from online study in the U.S. *NPR*. Retrieved from https://www.gpb.org/news/coronavirus-live-updates/2020/07/14/ice-agrees-rescind-policy-barring-foreign-students-online

United States Census Bureau. (2022, February). *Over a quarter of children lived with at least one foreign-born parent*. Retrieved from https://www.census.gov/library/stories/2022/02/over-quarter-of-children-lived-with-at- least-one-foreign-born-parent.html

Uskul, A. K., & Oyserman, D. (2010). When message-frame fits salient cultural-frame, messages feel more persuasive. *Psychology and Health*, *25*(3), 321–337. https://doi.org/10.1080/08870440902759156

Wawera, A. S., & McCamley, A. (2020). Loneliness among international students in the UK. *Journal of Further and Higher Education*, *44*(9), 1262–1274. https://doi.org/10.1080/0309877X.2019.1673326

Wilson, S., Hastings, C., Morris, A., Ramia, G., & Mitchell, E. (2023). International students on the edge: The precarious impacts of financial stress. *Journal of Sociology*, *59*(4), 952–974. https://doi.org/10.1177/14407833221084756

Yeager, D. S. & Dweck, C. S. (2020). What can be learned from growth mindset controversies?. *American Psychologist*, *75*(9), 1269–1284. https://doi.org/10.1037/amp0000794.

Yue, Y., & Lu, J. (2022). International students' motivation to study abroad: An empirical study based on expectancy-value theory and self-determination theory. *Frontiers in Psychology*, *13*, 841122. https://doi.org/10.3389/fpsyg.2022.841122

Zheng, F., Hu, P., Lian, Z., Wang, Y. L., Wu, S., & Li, H. (2020). Contributing factors to the improvement of international students' health literacy in China: A self-determination theory perspective. *Frontiers in Public Health*, *8*, 390. https://doi.org/10.3389/fpubh.2020.00390

Zheng, X., Wang, C., Shen, Z., & Fang, X. (2020). Associations of private tutoring with Chinese students' academic achievement, emotional well-being, and parent-child relationship. *Children and Youth Services Review*, 112, 104934. https://www.sciencedirect.com/science/article/abs/pii/S0190740919313891?via%3Dihub

Zhou, E., Kyeong, Y., Cheung, C. S., & Michalska, K. J. (2022). Shared cultural values influence mental health help-seeking behaviors in Asian and Latinx college students. Journal of Racial and Ethnic Health Disparities, 9(4), 1325–1334.

Zhou, Y., Jindal-Snape, D., Topping, K., & Todman, J. (2008). Theoretical models of culture shock and adaptation in international students in higher education. *Studies in Higher Education*, *33*(1), 63–75. https://doi.org/10.1080/03075070701794833

Index

www.ingramcontent.com/pod-product-compliance
Ingram Content Group UK Ltd.
Pitfield, Milton Keynes, MK11 3LW, UK
UKHW020221290926
15470UKWH00001B/317